MAGIC MINERAL

MAGIC MINERAL
TO KILLER DUST

Turner & Newall and the Asbestos Hazard

GEOFFREY TWEEDALE

with additional research by Philip Hansen

OXFORD

UNIVERSITY PRESS

*This book has been printed digitally and produced in a standard specification
in order to ensure its continuing availability*

OXFORD
UNIVERSITY PRESS

Great Clarendon Street, Oxford OX2 6DP

Oxford University Press is a department of the University of Oxford.
It furthers the University's objective of excellence in research, scholarship,
and education by publishing worldwide in

Oxford New York

Auckland Bangkok Buenos Aires Cape Town Chennai
Dar es Salaam Delhi Hong Kong Istanbul Karachi Kolkata
Kuala Lumpur Madrid Melbourne Mexico City Mumbai Nairobi
São Paulo Shanghai Singapore Taipei Tokyo Toronto

with an associated company in Berlin

Oxford is a registered trade mark of Oxford University Press
in the UK and in certain other countries

Published in the United States
by Oxford University Press Inc., New York

ISBN 0-19-829690-8

Jacket illustration shows amosite fibres under an electron microscope.

To

David J. Jeremy

friend, colleague, and prime mover in this book

PREFACE

> Looking back in the light of present knowledge, it is impossible not
> to feel that opportunities for discovery and prevention [of asbestos
> disease] were badly missed.
>
> Thomas Legge, *Industrial Maladies* (Oxford, 1934), 191

This book is well timed for an anniversary, though not one of the traditional kind that commemorates the life of a captain of industry or a
hundred years of 'progress' of an important firm. The year 2000 is the centenary of an event that is rarely remembered—the death of a worker from
an industrial disease.

The 33-year-old worker in question was admitted in 1899 to Charing
Cross Hospital in London, suffering from breathlessness caused by his
job. He told his physician, Montague Murray, that he had worked for fourteen years in the asbestos industry and that he was the only survivor from
amongst ten others in his workroom. Within a year, the worker (who has
never been identified) was dead. When Murray examined his lungs at the
subsequent post-mortem, he found that they were stiff and black with the
fibrosis caused by inhaling asbestos dust.

The death of Montague Murray's patient aroused almost no interest at
the time. Such occupational deaths were a commonplace among British
workers at the turn of the century. Yet this death has returned to haunt
us. Since 1900, the rise in the mortality from asbestos-related diseases has
been frightening. In the 1990s, such illnesses constitute the most serious
category of occupational disease in the UK. Three diseases are involved:

- asbestosis, a chronic lung fibrosis of the type that killed Murray's
  patient;
- lung cancer (often combined with asbestosis);
- and mesothelioma, a relatively rare but virulent malignancy of the
  lining of the lungs or abdomen.

These diseases now account for over 3,000 deaths each year, a number
that is still rising. According to one estimate, annual male mesothelioma
deaths alone could hit 3,300 by 2020. Assuming that for every one
mesothelioma death, there is at least another from asbestos-induced lung
cancer, then the death toll could reach between 5,000 and 10,000 annually.
By any standards, asbestos is one of the leading causes of occupationally-
related deaths in the twentieth century.

Most of us regard the asbestos hazard as a 'scare' and 'epidemic' of
fairly recent times—say from the 1970s and early 1980s, when the dangers

of asbestos and its lethal effects regularly featured in the media. It was then that most of us learned about asbestos disease. Newspaper headlines about the 'the dust of death', the 'asbestos time-bomb', and the 'hidden killer' forever implanted in the public mind the idea that one of the most widely used of all industrial materials was a hazard to public health.

However, as the Montague Murray case demonstrates, harbingers of the lethal nature of asbestos have a long lineage. That death in 1900 was not an isolated incident. In the same year, the government's Factory Inspectors warned of the dangers of asbestos manufacture and were soon reporting further deaths among the workforce. By the time Factory Inspector Sir Thomas Legge registered his regrets, asbestosis had been recognized by some doctors for at least ten years. Indeed, in 1930 the government decided that asbestos manufacture was so dangerous that health regulations were needed. Henceforth, asbestos became one of the few British industries that were subject to specific factory regulations and health checks. This meant that the Factory Inspectorate visited asbestos premises, seeking to apply government dust control requirements. Insurers were drawn into the industry's problems. Various medical groups—local practitioners, company physicians, government inspectors, pathologists, and medical researchers—became involved with asbestos. Trade unions, too, began taking an interest in health and safety measures in the asbestos industry and joined negotiations with the government.

During the 1940s and 1950s, asbestos began to show an even more sinister hand. As asbestosis deaths began to rise, industrialists and doctors realized that inhaling asbestos could cause lung cancer and mesothelioma. Yet against this backdrop of growing knowledge and rising mortality, asbestos production continued to expand. Indeed, it became a major industry, with asbestos percolating into almost every sphere of our lives. Asbestos (some of it still in place) insulated steam pipes and power stations; it fireproofed offices and ships; it lined car brakes; distributed and filtered our beer and water; sheathed electrical cables; acoustically damped our cinemas; roofed our factories; and lined our oven mitts, toasters, and ironing boards. In whatever capacity it was used, asbestos was universally recognized as the ideal fire-retardant and lifesaver, whose key selling point was *safety*. Ironically, the industry was at its most expansive and profitable precisely during those decades—the 1950s and the 1960s—when the full health implications of asbestos had become apparent.

This book sets out to explain this paradox and show why the asbestos health problem has become so intractable. It takes us into an area that has hardly featured in most historical accounts of British industrialization or medicine—occupational health and safety. Medical and social historians have shown little interest in this subject, preferring instead to chronicle the triumphs over infectious diseases and the heroic exploits of great physicians. Business historians have generally found the study of man-agement more congenial than labour, reflecting the conservative nature of the discipline. The writing of business history is mostly management oriented (and sometimes management funded), heavily influenced by the American business school approach, which focuses on businessmen and corporate strategies. At best, workers' deaths and injuries, if they are mentioned at all, are seen as the unintentional results of industrialization—regrettable perhaps, but not really a factor in the onward and upward march of the economy. It follows that corporations are invariably seen as eminently respectable organizations, which are mainly concerned with innovation, progressive management, and dynamic entrepreneurship. The darker aspects of industrialization—the abuse of power, media manipulation, cutthroat rivalry, short-term expediency, and corporate misconduct—are rarely depicted by academics.

To be sure, historians in these areas face the problem of finding archive material, as in the so-called 'dangerous trades' the records are rarely available. In Britain there is no freedom of information law and no public right-to-know. Thus, historians face exactly the same difficulty as plaintiffs—access to documentation. Nowhere are these problems better illustrated than in the history of asbestos manufacture. However, a stream of American legal actions in the 1980s and early 1990s has brought into the public domain a vast archive on the asbestos industry. The fair settlement of US civil damage suits is encouraged by the process of 'discovery', which gives each party wide powers in searching for relevant documents. As a result, the records of the leading British asbestos firm, Turner & Newall, have been 'discovered', for the benefit of plaintiffs and historians alike. In 1995 Chase Manhattan Bank sued T & N for the costs of removing asbestos from its New York skyscraper. Before the trial, the Bank's lawyers microfilmed a million T & N records at its Manchester repository.

Widely dispersed by Chase, this windfall of documents is now being utilized by historians, journalists, and medico-legal experts. A start has been made in unravelling the complex story of how the asbestos industry, the government, and the medical fraternity coped with the insidious health consequences of the mineral. Predictably, the asbestos industry itself has been seen as the chief culprit. Paul Brodeur's exposé, *Outrageous Misconduct* (1985), began the job of digging up the industry's controversial past. Asbestos manufacture was seen an example of capitalism at its worst, where dominant market forces militated against the full protection of workers and the effective control of pollution. David Jeremy's article-length study of Turner & Newall, based on the Chase material, has reinforced this critical picture. Meanwhile, surveys by Morris Greenberg have explored the growth of early knowledge about asbestos disease, tracing the earliest references to the late nineteenth century. Generally, these works have reiterated Legge's regrets that warnings went unheeded and that opportunities for averting a social disaster were not taken.

What does this book add to the growing list of publications? At the risk of generalization, the medical aspects have been covered in encyclopaedic detail by Irving Selikoff and Douglas Lee in their book, *Asbestos and Disease* (1978). The legal and historical aspects are treated in Barry Castleman's equally magisterial, *Asbestos* (1996), another American study which deserves to be much more widely known in Britain. In the UK, Nick Wikeley's book, *Compensation for Industrial Disease* (1993), has explored the legal aspects of asbestos disability. As yet, however, no book has been written on the history of the asbestos hazard from the viewpoint of a single company. In fact, no detailed historical study has been written of *any* British company or industry from an occupational and environmental health perspective.

Turner & Newall is the ideal subject for such a work. Even by the 1920s, its dominance made it synonymous with the country's asbestos industry. By the early 1950s under its sobriquet the 'Asbestos Giant', it accounted for about 60 per cent of Britain's asbestos industry, and its factory in Rochdale was the largest asbestos textile factory in the world. Not only was Turner & Newall an industry leader, but its involvement in occupational health (or as it was then known, industrial hygiene) also made it prominent in safety legislation both nationally and internationally. It was at the centre of all the key issues—dust control; medical surveillance; workman's compensation; the cancer threat; and corporate responsibility for environmental safety.

The vast Turner & Newall archive—certainly the most extraordinary collection of business documents I have ever read—gives an unprecedented insider's view of these areas. It also offers far more. The micro-environment of Turner & Newall provides an understanding of the wider social and economic context in which the asbestos business operated. Trade unions and labour organizations, the medical community, the Factory Inspectorate, the courts, the media, victims' pressure groups, and public opinion—these are also illuminated in detail.

This book is therefore not simply a muckraking tale of corporate misconduct (though some may choose to read it that way). Asbestos-related disease is not an obscure workplace hazard, linked to a fading industrial past, that has no contemporary relevance. If that were so, then the story of asbestos, no matter how tragic or sensational, would be of merely antiquarian interest. What remains deeply interesting about the metamorphosis of asbestos from magic mineral to killer dust, is the light it sheds on current attitudes to occupational diseases and society's mechanisms for dealing with them. These mechanisms are shown to be woefully inadequate. This is disturbing, because asbestos is only one of a number of potential hazards—radioactivity, pesticides, lead, and air pollution, to name only a few—that may result in insidious, long-term damage to our health. Therefore, the failure by management, capital, the state, and labour to provide effective safeguards against asbestos inevitably has considerable contemporary relevance for debates about every aspect of occupational health—a subject we neglect at our peril.

ACKNOWLEDGEMENTS

The historian A. J. P. Taylor once remarked that all his books were suggested by others. I can certainly claim no originality for the present study. It developed from the work of my friend and colleague David Jeremy, who in the 1980s began a wide-ranging historical study of business in north-west England. In the early 1990s, his interest in the region's declining textile firms and in business ethics led him to look at the asbestos industry. However, having completed a detailed preliminary examination of the subject, his interests changed and in 1995 he generously asked me if I would like to pick up the baton.

If this study of occupational and environmental health owes most to David Jeremy's initiative and path-breaking research, it needed three other things to make it possible. First, it required substantial funding. In the medical community and among medical historians, one grant body stands out in reputation and size—the Wellcome Trust. In 1995, David Jeremy and I made a joint application to the Wellcome Trustees for a three-year grant to examine the subject of asbestos-disease in industry. The generosity of the Wellcome Trust in awarding this funding has provided the financial bedrock for this book.

Second, we needed support within Manchester Metropolitan University for office space, computer and copying facilities, research staff and legal advice. These were provided within the International Business Unit under the Dean of the Faculty of Management & Business, Andrew Lock. In a difficult university financial climate, he ensured that the Wellcome project had adequate accommodation and backing. The head of department, Frank MacDonald, also made an important contribution by providing essential office support. Tim Hendley kindly co-ordinated legal advice between the university, its solicitors (Robert Stoker and Addleshaw Booth), and the publisher.

Last, but by no means least, we also needed access to the relevant company archives—in this case, the business records of the leading UK asbestos producer, Turner & Newall. These documents were brought into the public domain by Chase Manhattan Bank, when it took T & N to court in New York in 1995 in a property-damage suit. In the months before the trial, T & N's huge archive was given worldwide publicity by Chase's vice-president and senior associate counsel, Michael O'Connor. At the start of this study, we were fortunate to gain the help of Mr O'Connor (and his assistant, Eric Rytter), who provided us with the relevant papers, alongside the necessary finding aids, trial transcripts, and depositions.

Without their help and without the freedom of information enjoyed by Americans, this book could never have been written.

Reading and interpreting this material has been an enormous task. Fortunately, I have not worked alone. Although writing this book has been my responsibility, the fact that I have been able to get so far and so fast has been due to the assistance of Philip Hansen. Before his departure for a post in Japan, he willingly undertook some of the more thankless tasks, such as locating and photocopying obscure journals and newspapers, and also helping me sift through thousands of records on the Chase microfilms. Together, we cannot claim to have read every word in the T & N archive; however, we have examined the bulk of the documents.

After the research had been completed, I was delighted to have the book accepted by my first-choice publisher—Oxford University Press. Research on controversial subjects cannot be disseminated widely unless it is published, and so OUP assumed another key role in this project. Once again, it has been a pleasure to work with my editor, David Musson, and others at the Press, including legal adviser Carol Leighton-Davis and Sarah Dobson; Roy Porter and several referees also helped to smooth the path.

I have benefited from the help of many other individuals, who are far more experienced in matters of asbestos and health than myself. They have provided advice, references and often read through drafts of my work. They include Lorna Arblaster, Barry Castleman, Richard Doll, Morris Greenberg, Laurie Kazan-Allen (British Asbestos Newsletter), Jock McCulloch, John Pickering, William Kerns, Iain McKechnie (Clydeside Action on Asbestos), William Nicholson, David Ozonoff, Nancy Tait (OEDA), and Nick Wikeley. Others who contributed were David Allen, Adrian Budgen, Pauline Chandler, Gillian Cookson, Douglas Farnie, Laurie Flynn, David Gee, the Health & Safety Executive (Sheffield), Claire Hodgson, Manchester Metropolitan University Library, John Malin, George Peters, Margaret Potton, Robert Proctor, David Reid, Rochdale Cemetery Records Office, Rochdale Local Studies Library, John Rylands University Library, Stephen Suttle, Paul Titchmarsh, John Todd, Steve Tombs, Paul Tweedale, Owen Wade, Richard Warren, and Dave Whyte. As ever, Mary Titchmarsh's cheerfulness and unstinting support provided an essential antidote to the dismal realities of Rochdale's magic mineral/killer dust.

Geoffrey Tweedale

CONTENTS

LIST OF FIGURES

LIST OF MAPS

LIST OF GRAPHS

LIST OF TABLES

LIST OF ABBREVIATIONS

ACA	Advisory Committee on Asbestos
AIA/NA	Asbestos Information Association/North America
AIC	Asbestos Information Committee
APEX	Association of Professional, Executive, Clerical, and Computer Staff
ARC	Asbestosis Research Council
BBA	British Belting & Asbestos
BIP	British Industrial Plastics
BMA	British Medical Association
BMJ	*British Medical Journal*
BOHS	British Occupational Hygiene Society
BSSRS	British Society for Social Responsibility in Science
ca.	carcinoma
CCR	Center for Claims Resolution
CEGB	Central Electricity Generating Board
CJD	Creutzfeld–Jacob Disease
CMO	Chief Medical Officer
CU	Commercial Union
DHHS	Department of Health & Social Security
EMAS	Employment Medical Advisory Service
f/cc	fibres per cubic centimetre
f/ml	fibres per cubic millilitre
GMWU	General & Municipal Workers' Union
HCL	Hilton C. Lewinsohn
HSC	Health & Safety Commission
HSE	Health & Safety Executive
IOIH	Institute of Occupational & Industrial Health
JWR	J. W. Roberts
MRC	Medical Research Council
NI	Newalls Insulations
PLA	Port of London Authority
PMP	Pneumoconiosis Medical Panel
PRU	Pneumoconiosis Research Unit
QAMA	Quebec Asbestos Mining Association
SPAID	Society for the Prevention of Asbestosis and Industrial Diseases
TAC	Turners Asbestos Cement
TAF	Turners Asbestos Fibres

TAP	Turners Asbestos Products
TBA	Turner Brothers Asbestos
TGWU	Transport & General Workers' Union
TLV	Threshold Limit Value
T & N	Turner & Newall
TNO	Turner & Newall Overseas
TUC	Trades Union Congress
UCATT	Union of Construction, Allied Trades & Technicians
WCC	Washington Chemical Company

Note: Citation of archive sources: In this book, T & N documents copied on the Chase Manhattan Bank microfilm are identified by using the Bank's reel and frame numbers. For example, a document found on frame 200 of reel 12 of the Bank's film is referenced as 12/200. Unreferenced documents are on microfiche.

1

A Physical Paradox

Asbestos . . . the world's most wonderful mineral.

A. L. Summers, *Asbestos and the Asbestos Industry* (1919).

ASBESTOS WORKER'S DEATH: MINERAL PARTICLES
IN LUNGS THE FIRST CAUSE

Headline in the *Rochdale Times*, 2 Apr. 1924.

THE ASBESTOS GIANT

On a blustery and showery morning in August 1924, a funeral procession
gathered in Rochdale, a town some 8 miles north of Manchester. After a
service at a house in one of the better-class districts in the town, the
mourners began the slow journey towards the town cemetery. It was a
funeral cortège in the grand Victorian manner. Several hundred people
had gathered in the town centre to pay their respects, and as the hearse
headed past the Town Hall and out towards the cemetery it was followed
by nearly sixty carriages and motor cars. At the graveside, fulsome tribute
was paid to one of Rochdale's most famous sons.

The dead man was Sir Samuel Turner, an 84-year-old industrialist, who
had died from a stroke the previous week at a hotel in Harrogate. The
Turners were one of the town's leading families: worthy Victorian 'men
of mark', who could be said to have risen from humble origins by dint of
their own 'enterprise' and practical skill. An honorary freeman and
former mayor of Rochdale, Samuel Turner had been knighted in 1914,
when he already had the wealth and trappings of a latter-day multi-
millionaire. As a Methodist and Liberal, Turner had naturally balanced
his wealth with paternalism and a commitment to the local community.
His residence, Chaseley, from where his funeral cortège set out, was
opposite the park he had donated to the town.

To one obituarist, Turner's career was an uplifting tale of 'commercial
romance'.[1] Its origins lay, appropriately, in that seedbed of the Industrial
Revolution—the Lancashire textile industry—in a town famous for its
production of flannel. Among Rochdale's fertile textile and engineering

---

[1] *Rochdale Observer*, 13, 23 Aug. 1924.

base was the calico-weaving business of Samuel Turner & Company. It had been founded by Sir Samuel Turner's father—confusingly also named Samuel Turner (1807–80)—who in 1856 had occupied the Clod Mill in Spotland, a district only a mile or so west of the town centre. Samuel Turner I had three sons—John, Robert, and Samuel—who in 1871 launched Turner Brothers, a separate operation within Clod Mill. The new venture was established to manufacture cotton seals (packings) for keeping the pistons of engines steam-tight. The inspiration for this business was the second Samuel Turner (1840–1924), the owner's son and the man later buried with such ceremony in Rochdale Cemetery. In 1879, hindered by the deficiencies of cotton as a packing material, Turner had seized on the availability of what was then a relatively little-known industrial raw material—asbestos.

A naturally occurring mineral, asbestos had been known since ancient times, though originally more as an object of wonder and curiosity than as a useful item of commerce. A folklore had grown up around the material. The Greeks were believed to have used asbestos wicks in lamps for their temples; while another story has Charlemagne astonishing guests by cleaning an asbestos tablecloth by fire. Royal bodies were said to have been wrapped in asbestos cloth to prevent their ashes mingling with those from the funeral pyre: hence, asbestos became known as the funeral dress of kings. Certainly the indestructible and fireproof qualities of asbestos were well appreciated before the modern commercial era began in the late nineteenth century.[2] A key event occurred in the 1870s in Canada, where a forest fire in the Thetford area near Quebec revealed large deposits of the material.

By the time Samuel Turner II saw his first asbestos, geologists had already described its main characteristics and had divided the fibrous mineral into two geological classifications—serpentine and amphibole (Table 1.1 and Figure 1.1). Chrysotile (or white asbestos) was the material that Turner would have seen first. This type of asbestos, which was to be mined in substantial quantities in Canada, was to dominate the industry and eventually accounted for some 95 per cent of asbestos mined worldwide. Crocidolite (blue asbestos) was also known in the nineteenth century, but it never became as significant commercially: it did, however, have exceptional acid resistance. The other important form, known as amosite (brown asbestos)—a name derived from the Asbestos Mines of South Africa—was to become available after 1917 and was prized for its fire-resistance.

Like the ancients, nineteenth-century industrialists were fascinated by a mineral that, when crushed, released a multitude of soft filaments.

---

[2] The ancient history is documented in I. J. Selikoff and D. H. K. Lee, *Asbestos and Disease* (1978), 3–8.

Table 1.1. *Asbestos types and their characteristics*

	Chrysotile	Crocidolite	Amosite
Main sources	Canada, South Africa, Russia	South Africa	South Africa
Fibre colour	White	Blue	Grey-yellow
Characteristics	Silky, soft, excellent flexibility and tough	Harsh, reasonably flexible and tough	Coarse, usually brittle
Attributes	Very good spinning potential, excellent resistance to heat and all liquids except strong acids.	Resistant to heat and to very strong acids	Heat resistant
Main uses	Asbestos textiles; asbestos cement	Asbestos textiles; spray	Preformed slab-type thermal insulation; spray

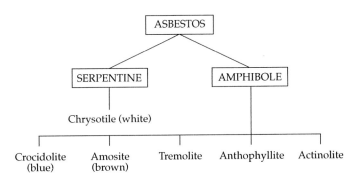

Fig. 1.1. *Asbestos groups*

Asbestos was described as one of the most 'marvellous productions' of inorganic nature—'a physical paradox'—that combined the properties of rock and silk and could be spun into strands that weighed less than an ounce to a hundred yards.[3] It now had more than curiosity value. As Europe and America industrialized, asbestos became inextricably linked

[3] R. H. Jones, *Asbestos and Asbestic* (1897), 1–2.

with the new steam age. Steam was synonymous with heat; and where there was heat, fireproofing and insulation materials were essential. Asbestos was the logical choice, because it resisted decay and destruction by superheated steam or grease. Contemporaries noted admiringly that it was impervious to the pounding meted out by marine, hydraulic, or other engines: 'So little influence of a chemical nature does [asbestos] exert over any metal, with which it is brought into contact, that, if a joint be broken, the surfaces will be found entirely free from corrosion. Moreover, its incombustible nature and slow conduction of heat render it a complete protection from flames.'[4]

Turner had realized that asbestos would be ideal in the packings for steam engines and also for insulation. He saw at once 'the commercial value of the article, providing it could be spun and manufactured'.[5] Turner's breakthrough was to spin and weave asbestos by power-driven machinery. The tough and slippery asbestos fibres made this difficult, but the problem was solved by adding a small amount of cotton or other organic fibre to the mineral.[6] Turner recalled: 'No sooner was it discovered that I could produce packing indestructible by heat than the demand became out of all proportions to supply.' Later he would utilize other innovations from America and Austria. These included adding asbestos fibre to magnesia for use in pre-formed insulation products; and mixing asbestos with cement to produce sheets for roofing and walls.[7] All these products made use of asbestos's indestructibility, high tensile strength, and fireproofing and insulating properties.

Turner Brothers (which in 1880 employed only about five hands) was not the first British company to market asbestos, but it led the way in its large-scale production.[8] Alongside the original and successful cotton business, Turner Brothers began growing steadily. By 1900, about fifty were employed in the asbestos side of the business, which occupied the southern end of the Spotland site. A decade later, employment was over 300. By 1914, asbestos production at the factory embraced a wide variety of asbestos cloths, including rubber-proofed varieties, besides compressed asbestos fibre (CAF) jointing, and brake linings. In 1913, the company had also opened an asbestos cement plant on the fast-growing industrial estate in Trafford Park, Manchester, which would later tap the huge twentieth-century market for asbestos-cement building materials.

[4] Jones, *Asbestos*, 2–3.
[5] *Rochdale Observer*, 13 Aug. 1924, quoting *Family Circle*, 27 Aug. 1895.
[6] On the technical problems, see W. J. Ellison, 'Early Years in the Life of Turner Brothers Asbestos Company Ltd', *Firefly* (Winter Supp., 1966), 13–20.
[7] Magnesia insulation contained up to 15 per cent asbestos; for asbestos cement, the figure was between 15 and 30 per cent asbestos (usually chrysotile).
[8] W. J. Ellison, *Some Notes on the Earlier History and Development to 1939 of Turner Brothers Asbestos Company Ltd* (1939), 8.

During the First World War, the firm—renamed Turner Brothers Asbestos (TBA)—continued to expand and not only in Rochdale. The company took its first steps towards multinational status, with the registration in 1907 of a Canadian selling agency (later known as Atlas Asbestos). All the fibre used in Britain had to be imported: that, and the fact that the quality from different suppliers was often variable, led Turner to integrate backwards into asbestos mining.[9] In 1917, TBA directors were appointed to the board of the Rhodesia & General Asbestos Corporation, as the company began buying up mines in the Mashaba district in southern Rhodesia.

By the early twentieth century, sales of asbestos were booming. TBA had single-handedly repeated the trick of the Lancashire textile industry by taking a common, relatively cheap imported raw material, and then transforming it with local expertise into a profitable product. In 1918, TBA's trade advertisements depicted asbestos in allegorical fashion as 'Lady Asbestos'—a Greek goddess armed with a shield, defending 'civilization' (shipbuilding, engineering, building, and electricity) from the fiery elements. A big selling point was the ability of asbestos to save lives, both on land and at sea. Asbestos in skyscrapers, offices, theatres, houses, brakes, and ships was already gaining a reputation of saving thousands of lives a year.[10]

After the First World War, TBA not only rapidly swallowed its cotton parent, but it also became a fully integrated business. In 1920, Turner & Newall was founded as a private company by the merger of four older businesses, with Sir Samuel Turner II as the first chairman. After his death, in 1924, another firm was added to Turner & Newall's operations and it became a public company, with an issued capital of £2.5 million and a workforce of 5,000. The five main businesses (shown in the map) included:

- *Turner Brothers Asbestos.* This was the Rochdale headquarters of the group and included the asbestos textile business at Spotland, the asbestos cement works at Trafford Park, and the overseas operations in Canada and Africa.
- *Washington Chemical Company.* Located in Wearside, County Durham, this company dated from 1842 and had become the largest producer of magnesia chemicals in the world by the First World War. From 1893,

---

[9] T & N's main 20th-century competitor—Cape Asbestos—followed the opposite route. Starting with asbestos mines in South Africa, it later began manufacturing in the UK in 1893. See Cape Asbestos Ltd, *The Story of the Cape Asbestos Company Ltd* (1953).

[10] A. L. Summers, *Asbestos and the Asbestos Industry* (1919), 49, reproduces details of fatalities from the world's theatre fires in the 1870s and 1880s, showing an 'appalling total' of 2,216 deaths. He argued that 95 per cent of those lives could have been saved by asbestos.

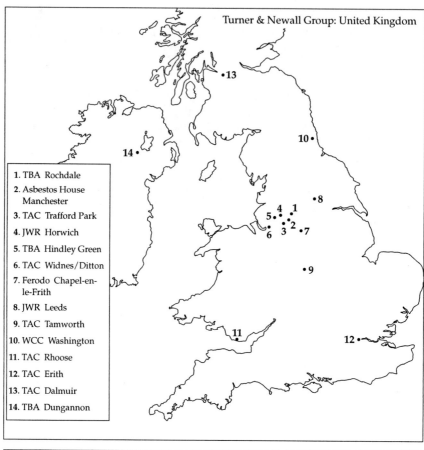

Turner & Newall Group: United Kingdom

1. TBA Rochdale
2. Asbestos House Manchester
3. TAC Trafford Park
4. JWR Horwich
5. TBA Hindley Green
6. TAC Widnes/Ditton
7. Ferodo Chapel-en-le-Frith
8. JWR Leeds
9. TAC Tamworth
10. WCC Washington
11. TAC Rhoose
12. TAC Erith
13. TAC Dalmuir
14. TBA Dungannon

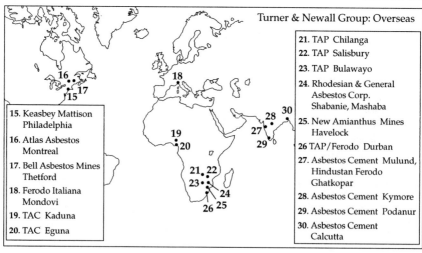

Turner & Newall Group: Overseas

15. Keasbey Mattison Philadelphia
16. Atlas Asbestos Montreal
17. Bell Asbestos Mines Thetford
18. Ferodo Italiana Mondovi
19. TAC Kaduna
20. TAC Eguna

21. TAP Chilanga
22. TAP Salisbury
23. TAP Bulawayo
24. Rhodesian & General Asbestos Corp. Shabanie, Mashaba
25. New Amianthus Mines Havelock
26 TAP/Ferodo Durban
27. Asbestos Cement Mulund, Hindustan Ferodo Ghatkopar
28. Asbestos Cement Kymore
29. Asbestos Cement Podanur
30. Asbestos Cement Calcutta

Turner & Newall Group

the company had pioneered in the UK the production of magnesia insulation, helped by the proximity to the main shipbuilding centres.

- *Newalls Insulation.* This was the contracting wing of Washington Chemical Company and had been founded in 1903 as Magnesia Coverings Ltd. Its name had been changed in 1908 and it had soon become the largest insulation contracting business in Britain.
- *J. W. Roberts.* Situated in Armley, a suburb of Leeds, this small factory had been founded in 1874 and, like TBA, originally made steam and pump packings. By 1906, when it was known as the Midland Works, it had begun specializing in asbestos mattresses for locomotives and was said to have been one of only two factories in the world processing blue asbestos.
- *Ferodo.* Established in about 1899, Ferodo (an anagram of Herbert Frood, its founder) was a leading producer of friction materials (such as asbestos brake linings) and was the only company in the world devoted to their manufacture. Based at Chapel-en-le-Frith in Derbyshire, Turner & Newall acquired most of its shares in 1925.

The Turner family was large enough to provide new recruits to the business, the most important of whom was another (Sir) Samuel Turner (1878–1955), a son of Robert. This third Samuel, who was chairman from 1929 to 1944, provided continuity as the firm returned to peacetime production. In this period, the family abandoned its Liberalism in favour of Conservatism, but its philanthropic and Methodist activities continued. Samuel Turner III endowed a department of industrial administration at Manchester College of Technology, a dental school at Manchester University, and he had a reputation as an advocate of workers' safety. A frequent overseas traveller, he was much troubled by Britain's declining competitiveness and wrote books and pamphlets with titles such as *What is Wrong with Britain and Why?* (1930).

Under Samuel Turner III, the company's development was spectacular. In 1929, Turner & Newall purchased Bell's United Asbestos Company with its string of asbestos cement factories; and it also acquired seven asbestos insulation companies around the country. In 1931, Turner & Newall rationalized these companies, with the main groupings in asbestos fibre, textiles, cement, insulation, brake products, and chemicals. The result was a multidivisional structure—then a relatively new phenomenon in British industry. Major policy decisions were taken at the centre in Rochdale (where TBA was the group headquarters and the largest asbestos textile factory in the world), with each subsidiary or unit company acting as 'managers or agents'. Expansion also took place abroad, continuing the trail blazed by Samuel Turner II. North America not only offered an important source of chrysotile, but also a huge potential market. For a time, Ferodo operated a small factory in New Jersey, but Turner & Newall's major involvement in the USA began with the purchase in 1934 of Keasbey & Mattison. This Philadelphia-based company had been one of the first asbestos firms in America and had pioneered the manufacture of magnesia/asbestos insulation. Its plant at Ambler had a similar product range to TBA, concentrating on asbestos textiles, magnesia insulations, and asbestos-cement. Keasbey & Mattison also controlled the Bell Asbestos Mines in Quebec, which Turner & Newall soon split from the American parent as a separate entity.

Besides using Canada as a source of supply, Turner & Newall expanded its chrysotile mining operations in southern Rhodesia, centred on Mashaba (Gath's and King mines) and Shabani (the Nil Desperandum and Birthday mines). Another focus of Turner & Newall mining activity was in Swaziland in the eastern Transvaal. In the 1920s and 1930s, the company worked the Amianthus Mine in the Barberton district, and when this was exhausted opened up the Havelock Mine in the same region.

India was the other overseas market in which Turner & Newall was especially interested. In the 1930s, the company opened a string of asbestos-cement factories in Kymore (central India), in Mulund (near Bombay), and in Calcutta. In expanding into these territories, the directors saw themselves not as 'as parasites, but as one of the primary constructive forces upon which depend the evolution of civilisation . . . adventuring into wild unopened country, building railroads, homes, hospitals, clubs, in fact entire townships, with their usual social services'.[11] The Rochdale company's ambitions had become global and it was soon at the centre of a number of cartels and other secret (and restrictive) arrangements, which aimed at the world control of asbestos fibre and the fixing of prices in North America and Europe. In the inter-war period, these organizations were regarded with pride. In its annual report in 1929, the Turner & Newall directors reported candidly that they were involved with ten European countries in an international asbestos cartel—'a miniature League of Nations . . . based upon the principle of mutual help', which had now displaced the 'previous atmosphere of mistrust and suspicion'. The arrangement was intended to smooth any inconvenient fluctuations in supply and prices for the major producers, while 'even the smallest manufacturer anywhere' would not want for asbestos fibre.

One of the architects of this international strategy was (Sir) Walker Shepherd (1895–1959), who had joined the group as company secretary in 1927 and succeeded Sir Samuel Turner III in 1944. Shepherd cut his teeth in the American market, from where he relayed detailed reports on the company's subsidiaries and the state of the American market. Shepherd

---

[11] T & N, *Report and Balance Sheet* (1929), 8–9.

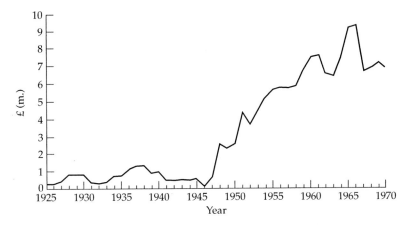

Graph 1.1. Turner & Newall: profits after tax, 1925–70

became the John D. Rockefeller of the asbestos world. A shadowy, secretive figure—reputed at his death to be among the highest-paid British businessmen of his day—he awed his fellow directors with his 'power of thinking on the largest scale'.[12] He conceived the industry as a vast, inter-related mechanism, and thought in terms of long-term plans and strategic alliances, at the centre of which was Turner & Newall.

By the end of the inter-war period—when it was among the top 100 UK firms—the company's profits had reached about £1 million a year and its issued capital had tripled (see Graph 1.1). So prominent had the firm become that in 1939 it was obliged to issue a report denying that it was a monopoly, as it only had 20 per cent of the world asbestos market! This success was all the more remarkable, in view of the slump and depression. While many companies—especially those in the Lancashire textile trade—struggled to pay any dividends, Turner & Newall's shareholders enjoyed consistently good returns. Launched on the back of a textile industry that was doomed to contract, the company had hit upon a product that was almost recession proof. Asbestos became so fundamental to the country's engineering and construction industries, that even if one sector of the economy fell on hard times, other business could be found elsewhere. Thus, when the insulation trade was hit by the decline in shipbuilding orders, other products made by Turner & Newall—such as brake-linings and asbestos cement—took up the slack. As the country emerged from the depression in the late 1930s and as the country began to rearm, asbestos hit its stride.

During the Second World War and the 1950s, the asbestos industry and

---

[12] 40/297–8. Directors' meeting, T & N (Overseas) Ltd, 19 Mar. 1959.

Turner & Newall especially enjoyed its greatest era of growth. The firm's profits climbed steadily: moreover, its rates of profit were substantially above the average for UK manufacturing industry.[13] The company's share of the UK trade in asbestos products was about 60 per cent in the mid-1950s and though this fell to about 43 per cent in the early 1970s, it remained the largest importer of asbestos fibre in the country with a similar percentage share (by weight) of the market. The company easily outranked its closest rivals, Cape Asbestos and British Belting & Asbestos. Overseas the company was increasingly active in America, where it operated Keasbey & Mattison. Factories at St Louis and New Orleans extended that company's presence in the American asbestos-cement market during the 1950s. In Canada, Atlas Asbestos continued to market Turner & Newall's products, helped by the establishment of a factory in Montreal in 1946 which produced brake-linings, asbestos textiles and cement, and also contracted for insulation work.[14] As the African economy developed, Turner & Newall expanded its activities from mining into asbestos products. In the 1950s and early 1960s, asbestos-cement factories were opened in Salisbury, Bulawayo, and Chilanga in Rhodesia; in Enugu and Kaduna in Nigeria; and in Durban (where there was also a Ferodo plant). In the 1950s, Turner & Newall extended its operations in India, where another building materials factory was established in the south at Podanur. Ferodo meanwhile had pursued its strategy, begun in the inter-war period, of opening overseas agencies and licensing foreign manufacturers. It also founded its own factories. In 1956, a friction materials company (later named Hindustan Ferodo) was established in Ghatkopar, Bombay, which by the 1960s produced a whole range of asbestos textiles, jointings, and millboard. In 1964, Ferodo built a factory at Mondovi, near Turin, to exploit the demand for brakes from Italian car manufacturers.

By 1970, the firm that had been virtually a one-man business a century or so before, now had an issued capital of £65 million, a workforce of 36,775 (25,500 in the UK), and profits of over £7 million a year. Turner & Newall was now the 'Asbestos Giant'. When the company celebrated its golden jubilee in 1970 with the obligatory house history, the chairman Ralph Bateman dwelt with satisfaction on its success. He told his readers that this was not the end of the story, but the beginning of another, that would be 'more exciting and more challenging still'. Bateman spoke truly: the period after 1970 would certainly be challenging for the company, though not in the way he envisaged. Within a decade, Turner & Newall

---

[13] In the 1950s, T & N's rate of profit (as percentages of capital employed) was about 30 per cent; the rate for UK manufacturing industry was about 18 per cent. See Monopolies Commission, *Asbestos and Certain Asbestos Products* (1973), 141.

[14] The Ferodo operations in New Jersey had been closed in 1946, with the equipment transferred to Montreal.

would be vilified, its main source of profit a scare word, and the company close to bankruptcy. Why? The reasons are scarcely hinted at in the firm's house history, except for one brief comment:

After it was realised in 1930 that asbestos dust could be injurious to health if inhaled in substantial amounts over a long period of time, [Turner & Newall] took prompt measures for dust suppression and personal protection wherever the risk called for them in its plants. Indeed, the unceasing efforts of Turner & Newall and of other asbestos companies in this country to eliminate such risks, however small, have made Britain the world's leader in the field of industrial hygiene.[15]

These debatable assertions gave no idea of the real situation. They failed to mention that 1970 was also the year when new government regulations—the first since the 1930s—came into force to protect society against the adverse health effects of asbestos. They gave no hint that the health problem was causing a major crisis at the company. Asbestos—that physical paradox—had other paradoxical qualities. 'Lady Asbestos', as well as saving so many lives, was also responsible for taking them.

ASBESTOS POISONING

The name Nellie Kershaw would have meant little to most of the mourners at Sir Samuel Turner's funeral in 1924. Yet this 33-year-old Rochdale mother had been buried only a few months previously in the same cemetery. The contrast between her demise and that of the town's 'Asbestos King' could not have been greater. While Turner died full of years, with a personal fortune of £½ million, and with his last resting place topped by a marble monument, Mrs Kershaw died in poverty and was buried in an unmarked grave.

Yet the two deaths were connected. Nellie Kershaw, too, had been featured extensively in the local press in 1924, though for far different reasons. In March, the *Rochdale Observer* reported that an inquest had been opened into her death and provided details of the dead woman's life.[16] She had been born in 1891 and had begun work in a cotton mill when she was 12, leaving after only five months to start another job at a local asbestos company. After fourteen years in this factory, she moved to TBA in 1917, where she became a rover in the spinning room, working on machines that twisted strands of asbestos. Meanwhile, she had married and had one child.

It was during this period that Nellie Kershaw came into contact with

---

[15] *Turner & Newall Ltd: The First Fifty Years 1920–1970* (1970), 28. Unaccredited, but written by L. T. C. Rolt.
[16] See the *Rochdale Observer*, 15, 19 Mar., 2 Apr. 1924.

the asbestos dust that would eventually kill her. Turner & Newall had from the first manufactured a material that was wonderfully utilitarian and profitable, but the fibres retained their elemental character once released from their rocky prison. A mineral that could resist fire and acid and wear down the steel parts of machines was unlikely to be very forgiving for those who worked with it. Labourers in the asbestos mills soon noticed that the fibres (especially amosite and crocidolite) could penetrate the skin and raise permanent scars, which they named asbestos corns. These were harmless. However, workers such as Nellie Kershaw soon found that severe health effects could follow if, as invariably happened, asbestos fibres were inhaled.

Dust was easily released during almost every process in asbestos manufacture, especially in textiles, where fibres were whipped, pulled, and twisted at high speed over rough guides, bobbins, and rollers. The dusty trail began in the mines of Africa or Canada with the preliminary breaking down or *opening* of large clusters of fibres from the rock. The crude asbestos then arrived at the factory in hessian sacks, where it was carried to a rotary mill, which continued the opening process by *disintegrating* (beating). Once the rock was fully separated, the fibre then passed to an enclosed machine for *fiberizing*, which finally delivered a flocculent, soft, and fibrous material. Blending was done by emptying a number of bags on the floor and raking the material over with shovels. Cotton was then incorporated so that the asbestos could be sent for *carding*. In this process, the material was fed between rotating cylinders which used innumerable hooks to comb the fibres into the required fleece. From the end of this machine, the material was delivered by *condensing* into a sliver. By giving the sliver a slight twist, *rovings* were produced for rope. However, most of the output of the carding machines was transferred to *spinning* frames, which twisted the slivers into a yarn. Brass wire or pure cotton yarn could be added at this stage. *Doubling* twisted two or more yarns together; and *weaving* interlaced the yarns on a loom to form a cloth. For non-textiles, fiberized asbestos was mixed with clay, cement, and water and then run through a series of sedimentation tanks to form a pulp. The doughy mass was then delivered to a forming cylinder from which sheets of asbestos could be cut as required.

Dust, of course, was nothing new in the Lancashire textile mills (or indeed in many other industries, such as coal mining and cutlery grinding). Ever since workers had been crammed for long hours into textile factories, some had suffered from 'mill fever', or byssinosis, an occupational asthma caused by breathing cotton dusts. Asbestos, however, proved far more dangerous than cotton for three main reasons: the fibres are extraordinarily fine; asbestos is virtually indestructible; and the mineral induces cancer.

Lady Inspectors of Factories, who were among the first to note the injurious effects of asbestos, commented in 1898 on its less attractive features. One of them observed 'the sharp, glass-like, jagged nature of the particles'.[17] Others noted the way in which asbestos, by fracturing longitudinally, seemed able to produce fibres endlessly—a process known as 'silking out'. Twentieth-century science has confirmed these characteristics, but it has required the most sophisticated technology available to explore fully the nature of asbestos. Individual asbestos fibres are the finest natural fibres known. The average fibre-length for spinning is about 1½ inches (3.75 cm), but an ordinary 'fibre' is not broken down to anything like its ultimate extent. An asbestos fibre about the diameter of a human hair (say 0.0015 inches thick, or 40 microns) is actually a bundle of nearly 2 million fibres.[18] Asbestos as fine as this is invisible even under the most powerful optical microscope: indeed, since the 1960s transmission electron microscopy has been used to view specimens for experimental and medical purposes. Fibres of this size (or more correctly, fibrils) defeat our comprehension unless some kind of analogy is used. Thus, it is said that 2 million fibres can fit on a pinhead; or an inch cube of asbestos contains 15 million miles of fibre. Not surprisingly such fine dust, which has only mild powers as a reflex irritant, is readily inhaled into the lungs if it becomes airborne.

Not all inhaled asbestos dust is harmful: many particles are caught by the body's natural defence mechanisms—the lining of the nose or the mucociliary 'escalator' in the lungs, which regularly sweeps unwanted particles into the throat, where they can be coughed out or swallowed. As a final line of defence, the body's scavenger cells—phagocytes—engulf the particles and transport them to the areas of ciliary action, or into the lung lymphatics. However, the body's defences are largely ineffective with the finest asbestos fibres and once inhaled they can penetrate deep into the most sensitive areas of the lungs—the respiratory bronchioles, alveolar ducts, and alveoli—where they can trigger pathological reactions. This is not the worst. While the body attempts to sequester asbestos, the fibres can continue to divide in the lungs and also migrate through tissue. Thus asbestos fibres can penetrate into the lymph system, the bloodstream, and, more ominously, can also work their way through to the sensitive lining of the lungs (the pleurae) or the membrane surrounding the abdomen (peritoneum). The thin, needle-like fibres of crocidolite seem to be especially dangerous in this respect. Such insidious effects of inhaling

---

[17] Chief Inspector of Factories and Workshops, *Annual Report . . . for the Year 1898* (1899), ii, 172.

[18] Selikoff and Lee, *Asbestos and Disease*, 42–4; and H. C. W. Skinner *et al.*, *Asbestos and Other Fibrous Materials* (1988). Selikoff and Lee note that chrysotile fibres can have a diameter of 0.0007 'thous' inch (0.02 microns).

asbestos can place an individual at risk from several diseases—all unpleasant, all highly painful, and, even now, all virtually impossible to treat.

Much of this was either unknown or imperfectly understood when Nellie Kershaw joined TBA; however, there was no mistaking the health effects of breathing asbestos dust. Soon after starting at TBA, Mrs Kershaw consulted her local physician, Dr Walter Joss, about her deteriorating health. She was suffering from breathlessness, weight loss, and night sweats. We now know that Mrs Kershaw had tuberculosis: but she was also showing the first symptoms of the chronic lung disease later known as asbestosis—the first disease to be associated with asbestos. It is caused by the trauma inflicted on lung tissue by the mineral. The particles of asbestos cause inflammation and then scarring (fibrosis), which gradually renders the lung stiff and inelastic. In the worst cases, the delicate, spongy mass of pink lung tissue is gradually obliterated by areas of greyish, blue-black fibrosis. In the beginning, this fibrosis can be seen on X-rays as hazy 'ground-glass' opacities, usually in the lower lobes of the lungs—though as the disease advances the heart and pulmonary vessels can also gradually be obscured radiographically. The whole process has been likened to the work of a spider, criss-crossing the lungs with a web of scar tissue, until the victim is slowly strangled.

As the fibrosis progresses (it continues even after the original trauma is over), the worker begins to suffer from the first physical signs of asbestosis—usually a dry cough and then breathlessness (dyspnoea). As the months or years go by, the cough and breathlessness worsen, so that even talking may require a great effort. Some individuals develop a characteristic clubbing of the fingers. As one physician noted: 'This is at the stage at which old hands in the industry recognise that asbestosis is present . . . Some of these [workers] cough up large volumes of foul-smelling, infected, green sputum, occasionally blood-stained, which may explain a curious remark I once heard from a retired supervisor, that he could diagnose asbestosis by smell.'[19] Sometimes asbestos 'bodies' are coughed up in the sputum: these are microscopic asbestos fibres coated with an iron protein, which give such bodies a characteristic kebab appearance. These are the debris of the lungs' battle to digest the fibres and thus are especially prevalent in asbestotics.

Although asbestosis was not an official medical disease when Nellie Kershaw consulted Dr Joss, his previous experience in Rochdale meant that he had little difficulty in identifying the cause of his patient's illness. In 1922, he told her she was suffering from 'asbestos poisoning'.

It usually takes years of exposure to produce asbestosis, though in the

[19] G. L. Leathart, 'Asbestos: A Medical Hazard of the 20th Century', *Journal for Industrial Nurses* (1964), 119–31, 122.

inter-war period (when workers were heavily exposed) the disease could occur after only months. In those days, the complete course of the disease from first symptom to death was usually five to ten years, though it could progress more rapidly. Alternatively, asbestosis can occur through exposure many years previously with a long period of non-exposure intervening. The disease is incurable and, though not always fatal, can greatly compromise longevity. This is particularly so, as asbestosis sufferers—and indeed anyone, who has had a significant exposure to asbestos—have an increased risk of cancer.

Asbestosis eventually suffocates its victim if the disease runs its course, though often complications intervene. Cor pulmonale (literally meaning, heart of the lung) hastened the deaths of many workers with classical asbestosis: this was right-sided heart failure, caused by the constant effort of that organ to pump blood through the obstructed lungs. Naturally, workers with diseased lungs and weakened hearts were easy prey to pneumonia and other infections. Nellie Kershaw herself did not long survive. Her health declined steadily and in the summer of 1922 she gave up work. She died two years later in March 1924.

Nellie Kershaw's death has been recognized as a landmark by medical historians, who have accorded her short life a significance she never enjoyed in her lifetime. The subsequent inquest was the first on an asbestos worker. The coroner ordered a post-mortem and microscopic examination of the lungs confirmed that she had died through breathing asbestos. When the pathologist involved, Dr William Cooke, wrote up the case in 1927, he coined the term by which the disease has since been known—'pulmonary asbestosis' (or more simply, asbestosis).[20]

The Kershaw case struck a chord that has continued to reverberate through the subsequent decades, highlighting attitudes and policies that were to underlie much of Turner & Newall's approach to the asbestos problem. Its directors wrote to Dr Joss, extolling the virtues of the company's dust prevention system ('we have been repeatedly congratulated by the Home Office'), inviting him to visit the works, but also demanding to know what he had told his patient about 'asbestos poisoning' (thereby inviting him to break his oath of confidentiality). They then aggressively denied liability, writing to Mrs Kershaw's Friendly Society:

We repudiate the term 'Asbestos Poisoning'. Asbestos is not poisonous and no definition or knowledge of such a disease exists. Such a description is not to be

---

[20] W. E. Cooke, 'Fibrosis of the Lungs Due to the Inhalation of Asbestos Dust', *BMJ* (26 July 1924), ii, 147; Cooke, 'Pulmonary Asbestosis', *BMJ* (3 Dec. 1927), ii, 1024–5. See also I. Selikoff and Morris Greenberg, 'A Landmark Case in Asbestosis', *Journal of the American Medical Association* 265 (20 Feb. 1991), 898–901. Cooke also identified the 'curious bodies', which were later termed asbestos bodies.

found amongst the list of industrial diseases in the schedule published with the Workmen's Compensation Act. This case was not due to an accident.[21]

It might be wondered how this apparent ignorance of the hazards of asbestos squares with Dr Joss's remark that he saw nearly a dozen cases a year of lung conditions in asbestos workers; and also with the problems with respiratory disease that the company was experiencing at its Leeds factory (see below).

Certainly Turner & Newall were correct in stating that asbestos disease was not compensatable. Nellie Kershaw applied for benefits to her local Friendly Society (registered under the National Health Insurance Act), but as her certificate diagnosed 'asbestos poisoning', the Society naturally assumed that her employer would pay compensation. When TBA refused and took refuge behind the fact that asbestos was not scheduled under the Act, Nellie Kershaw fell between two stools. In the last months of her life, obviously destitute, she made pathetic overtures to her employer: 'I have been at home nine weeks now and not received a penny . . . I am needing nourishments.'[22] Eventually, she received 7s [35p] a week National Health Insurance for about seven months in the last year of her life, but TBA never paid her anything. When she died, the company contested the pathologist's findings and blamed her previous asbestos employer. In contrast to the dead woman's reported statement that she worked in a room 'full of dust', the TBA works manager testified at the inquest that asbestos roving created little dust; and, anyway, TBA had 'given just consideration to the dust arising from the work and in the last few years they have spent large sums of money to make the works as perfect as possible'.[23] Finally, the company rebuffed her widower's claim for compensation and even a request for help with the funeral costs. One of the firm's managers advised that to do so 'would create a precedent, and admit responsibility which has hitherto been repudiated, and furthermore if a payment be made there would no doubt be further applications by Kershaw later'.[24]

GOVERNMENT REGULATION

Even before Nellie Kershaw's death, the government knew that asbestos was a health hazard. In the *Annual Report* of the Chief Inspector of Factories and Workshops for 1898, Lady Inspectors drew attention to the 'evil effects' of asbestos manufacture, because of its 'easily demonstrated

---

[21] 68/1709. TBA to Newbold Approved Society, 15 Dec. 1922.
[22] 68/1710. Kershaw to TBA, 29 Sept. 1922.
[23] 68/1764. P. G. Kenyon inquest deposition.
[24] 68/1766. Memo made at Mr Rupert's request, 25 July 1928.

danger to the health of the worker'.[25] These problems were underlined
again by the Lady Inspectors in the *Annual Report* for 1906, which stated
that of all the dusty trades none surpassed asbestos 'in injuriousness to
the workers'.[26]

The *Report* for 1906 carried the first indications that the dust was
causing premature deaths among workers. Similar findings at this time
from a French Inspector of Factories underlined high workers' mortality
from asbestos textile production.[27] Meanwhile, the medical profession
began taking an interest in asbestos. In 1899, Montague Murray's patient
(mentioned in the Preface) was diagnosed at Charing Cross Hospital as
suffering from asbestosis (a disease then known as fibroid phthisis).[28] Yet
although Murray later reported the case to a government enquiry in 1907,
neither this nor subsequent Factory Inspectorate reporting on workers'
mortality were enough to persuade the government to introduce dust-
control legislation or a system of compensation. The small size of the
industry and the long latency of asbestosis were no doubt responsible; so
too the sparsity of the medical literature.[29]

However, following Cooke's published report of the Kershaw case in
the *British Medical Journal* in 1927, the pace of medical writing on asbestosis suddenly quickened. Between 1928 and 1929, a dozen separate medical
publications carried discussions and reports about the disease. This
reflected a rising death toll from asbestosis. Between Nellie Kershaw's
death and 1931, post-mortems and inquests were held on five more TBA
workers, each of whom suffered from asbestosis to a greater or lesser
degree (see Table 1.2). The asbestosis problem was also emerging at J. W.
Roberts in Armley, where two local doctors, Archibald Haddow and Ian
Grieve, and the professor of pathology at Leeds University, Matthew
Stewart, noted the rising incidence of the disease. While Haddow and
Stewart wrote up their findings for the medical press and discussed them
at British Medical Association meetings,[30] Grieve completed a remarkable

---

[25] Chief Inspector of Factories and Workshops, *Annual Report . . . for the Year 1898* (1899),
Pt. ii, 171. See also Selikoff and Lee, *Asbestos and Disease*, 20–5.

[26] Chief Inspector of Factories and Workshops, *Annual Report . . . for the Year 1906: Report
and Statistics* (1907), 219.

[27] M. Auribault, 'Note sur l'Hygiène et la Sécurité des Ouvriers dans les Filatures et
Tissages d'Amiante', *Bulletin de l'Inspection du Travail* (1906), 120–32.

[28] M. Greenberg, 'Classical Syndromes in Occupational Medicine: The Montague Murray
Case', *American Journal of Industrial Medicine* 3 (1982), 351–6; Greenberg, 'Knowledge of the
Health Hazard of Asbestos Prior to the Merewether and Price Report of 1930', *Social History
of Medicine* 7 (Dec. 1994), 493–516.

[29] There was also no legislation in America at this time, though by 1918 the Prudential
Insurance Co. had already identified asbestos as a hazardous trade and was refusing to
insure workers. See B. I. Castleman, *Asbestos: Medical and Legal Aspects* (1996), 5–6.

[30] A. C. Haddow, 'Clinical Aspects of Pulmonary Fibrosis', *BMJ* (28 Sept. 1929), ii, 580–1;
T. Oliver, 'Pulmonary Asbestosis in Clinical Aspects', *Journal of Industrial Hygiene* 9 (1927),
483–5.

Table 1.2. *Asbestosis deaths at TBA and J. W. Roberts, 1924–31*

Name	Years employed	Job	Cause of death	Post-mortem	Inquest
Nellie Kershaw* (1891–1924)	c.10	Roving	TB/asbestosis	Yes	Yes
Harriet Slater (c.1879–1927)	c.24	Mattresses	Asbestosis	No	No
May Speke (c.1893–1927)	c.20	Mattresses	Asbestosis	Yes	No
Walter Leadbeater (c.1894–1928)	14	Mattresses	Pneumonia/asbestosis	Yes	Yes
Margaret Marsden (c.1895–1928)	16	Mattresses	Asbestosis	Yes	Yes
Lily Hemsley (c.1888–1929)	19	Mattresses	Asbestosis	Yes	Yes ('misadventure')
Abraham Jowett (c.1891–1929)	6	Rope making	Heart failure/pneumonia/asbestosis	Yes	Yes ('natural causes')
Albert E. Witham (c.1894–1930)	c.14	Mattresses	TB/asbestosis	Yes	Yes ('misadventure')
John Torkington* (c.1855–1930)	c.15	Weaving	Asbestosis/TB	Yes	Yes
Richard Hardman* (c.1870–1930)	c.10	Waste sorting	TB/arteriosclerosis/asbestosis	Yes	Yes
John J. Butterworth* (c.1893–1930)	14	Weaving	Pneumonia/heart failure/asbestosis	Yes	Yes
Thomas Stott* (1867–1930)	c.27	Carding	Asbestosis	Yes	Yes
Doris Leadbeater (c.1900–31)	c.12	Mattresses	Asbestosis	Yes	Yes ('misadventure')
Herbert Wright* (c.1878–1931)	c.22	Weaving	Heart failure/cirrhosis/asbestosis	Yes	Yes

*TBA.

Sources: T & N compensation claims files and death certificates; and I. M. D. Grieve, 'Asbestosis' (Edinburgh University MD thesis, 1927), which provides information on Hemsley, the Leadbeaters, Slater, and Speke. Some of these cases are also listed anonymously in E. R. A. Merewether, 'The Occurrence of Pulmonary Fibrosis and Other Pulmonary Affections in Asbestos Workers', *Journal of Industrial Hygiene* 12 (June 1930), 239–57, 52. Merewether also lists another worker, 'JC', who died in 1928 and may have been employed at Roberts. Unfortunately, this individual died on a farm in the country and is therefore impossible to trace. I have identified Harriet Slater from Merewether and Grieve, but have not been able to trace a death certificate.

unpublished study on asbestosis. In 1927 he reported that workers at Roberts regarded the disease as inevitable and that the owners were so 'wide awake to the risks' that they needed 'factory measures on a scale beyond the requirements of the Factory and Work Shops Act'.[31] He presented more than a dozen case studies of the disease. His graphic details of emaciated and hollow-eyed young men and women, few of whom survived more than five years in the factory without developing symptoms of the disease, make sombre reading. One of Grieve's patients, insulation mattress-maker May Speke, had died from asbestosis by 1927. When he attended the post-mortem, he noted that when the lung was cut open, the knife almost appeared to grate. Mattress-making was clearly a death trap, as other workers from the same department also soon succumbed. Altogether at least eight workers had died at Roberts by the summer of 1931—facts that were duly reported to the Rochdale board.

Turner & Newall's attitude towards these sick Roberts' workers can be shown by focusing on a single case. In March 1928, Walter Leadbeater, a 34-year-old labourer at the Midland Works, died from pneumonia and asbestosis. The verdict seemed straightforward, but Turner & Newall briefed a barrister to question the witnesses thoroughly. However, this did little to shake the post-mortem findings. The company also engaged its own pathologist to examine the lungs, but again this merely confirmed the original diagnosis made by the Leeds pathologist. Company secretary, Walker Shepherd, noted that the company did not submit its own pathology evidence, but in cross-examination used 'the small differences' between the two pathologists in an attempt to influence the coroner.[32] Like Nellie Kershaw's widower, Leadbeater's dependants (a wife and a 4-year-old boy) got little sympathy from the firm. First, asbestosis was still not compensatable under the law and so the family had no legal claim. Second, the Roberts' management felt that the family's income was sufficient: the widow, Doris, was also a mattress-maker at the factory and Leadbeater himself had once worked 'in the evenings as a bar waiter at some local public house'.[33] Despite pleas from the family's solicitor that a voluntary payment would be a 'gracious act', Doris Leadbeater received nothing. Even more tragically, she was already suffering from asbestosis herself and died from the disease in 1931.

At Walter Leadbeater's inquest, Shepherd had comforted himself with the belief that the government was far from convinced that asbestosis existed, and although an enquiry might be in the offing, the issue would not be prejudged. Such complacency, however, could not hide the growing number of asbestosis deaths around the country. Another disease

---

[31] See I. A. D. Grieve, 'Asbestosis' (Edinburgh University MD thesis, 1927), 1.
[32] 61/445. Shepherd to S. Turner, 2 Apr. 1928.
[33] 61/460. Roberts to Shepherd, 16 Apr. 1928.

cluster was emerging in Barking, near London, where Cape Asbestos seem to have had an even worse asbestosis record than Roberts'. A medical examination of eighty workers in 1928 showed that nearly all had 'definite evidences' of asbestosis.[34] Barking medical officers began noting the first deaths by 1929 and one doctor—an unusually critical physician, Dr Leonard Williams—warned that such deaths would occur for at least the next fifteen years.[35]

By now, the Factory Inspectors were watching the situation closely. Most of the Rochdale and Leeds inquests had been attended by Dr Edward Merewether, a Medical Inspector of Factories, who was to become a leading authority on asbestos disease.[36] Alerted to the growing number of asbestos deaths, in 1928 the government had commissioned Merewether and Charles Price, an Engineering Inspector, to prepare a study of workers' health in the asbestos textile industry. The findings of their report—which was published in 1930 and has been recognized as a classic work in occupational health—were unequivocal.[37] Choosing workers with as 'pure' an exposure to asbestos dust as possible (so as to exclude workers who worked with mixed dusts), Merewether and Price selected 363 asbestos factory workers from an estimated UK workforce of 2,200. The sample was deliberately weighted with employees who had long employment histories and many workers from TBA were included. Around one-quarter (95) of the sample had asbestosis, and 21 more had early signs of the disease. The incidence of the disease increased markedly with duration of employment: excluding those employed under five years, the incidence of asbestosis was about 35 per cent. After twenty years, four out of five workers still in the industry had asbestosis.

These were not dramatically high rates of disease when compared with silicosis in steel grinding and refractories, even though Merewether had almost certainly undercounted. Not all workers were X-rayed and only current employees were examined, thus ignoring workers who had left the industry through ill-health. Only the asbestos textile industry was considered and no workers in the asbestos cement or lagging trades were examined.[38] Nevertheless, the prevalence of asbestosis clearly called for

---

[34] W. Burton Wood, 'Pulmonary Asbestosis', *British Journal of Radiology* 7 (1934), 277–80.

[35] Barking Town Urban District Council, *Reports of the Medical Officer of Health* (1928, 1929, 1930, 1945).

[36] E. R. A. Merewether (1892–1970) had joined the medical branch of the Home Office's factory department in 1927, soon after Dr John Bridge had taken over from Sir Thomas Legge as senior medical inspector. Merewether became senior medical inspector between 1943 and 1947.

[37] E. R. A. Merewether and C. W. Price, *Report on Effects of Asbestos Dust on the Lungs and Dust Suppression in the Asbestos Industry* (1930).

[38] Merewether's estimate of 2,200 workers in asbestos textiles in 1929 appears to have been a gross underestimate. According to the Census of Production, the total employment in asbestos textiles in 1930 was 8,500. See Business Statistics Office, *Historical Records of the Census of Production, 1907–1970* (1978).

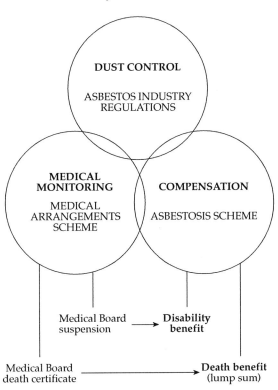

Fig. 1.2. *Government asbestosis regulation, 1931*

action by the government and in 1930 discussions began with the leading manufacturers. Legislation followed within a year with three linked measures (Figure 1.2):

- The Asbestos Industry Regulations (1931) were introduced to control the dust.
- A Medical Arrangements Scheme was to screen new employees and monitor them annually by means of a government Medical Board, which could certify and suspend the sick. Necropsies were to be performed on suspected cases and asbestosis was to be confirmed by a special death certificate.
- The asbestos industry was to be brought within the Workmen's Compensation Act by an Asbestosis Scheme. Workers disabled by asbestosis were to be compensated by the industry; and the dependants of those who died were to be awarded a lump sum death benefit.

Two points should be emphasized about the Asbestosis Scheme and its attendant regulations. First, it was a pioneering piece of legislation. Thanks to Merewether and Price, Britain was the first country officially to recognize asbestosis. Second, the legislation was to remain largely unaltered until 1969. To be sure, the compensation aspects were revised in 1943 (when compensation was extended to cover 'pneumoconiosis' more generally, not simply asbestosis and silicosis); and in 1948, when National Insurance relieved individual employers of their liability to pay compensation—replacing it with a system of state benefits from an Industrial Injuries Fund to which every employer and employee contributed weekly.[39] A number of other relatively narrow government statutes provided theoretical protection for some asbestos employees.[40] However, the 1931 Regulations and the Medical and Asbestosis Schemes were to be the basis for asbestos workers' safety from the 1930s until 1970.

The following chapters examine in detail how these government measures worked in practice and why they remained unchanged for so long, despite a rising toll of asbestos-related deaths.

[39] The Pneumoconiosis and Byssinosis Benefit Scheme (1952) covered a few workers, who were excluded for administrative reasons from the Workmen's Compensation Act and the National Insurance Act 1946. This scheme has been extended gradually to include, beside asbestosis, mesothelioma and lung cancer (in association with asbestosis or bilateral pleural thickening). See N. Wikeley, *Compensation for Industrial Disease* (1993), 65–6.

[40] For example, the 1937 Factories Act required precautions to protect workers from dust (irrespective of type); the 1948 Building (Safety, Health & Welfare) Regulations required reasonable precautions to prevent the inhalation of any dust, including asbestos, in certain operations; and the 1960 Shipbuilding and Ship-repairing Regulations required adequate ventilation and extraction of asbestos dust, and the use of respirators for specific operations.

2

Dust Control and Mortality: 1931 to the 1940s

provision of efficient exhaust ventilation plant in asbestos textile works is a very important matter, and . . . in a large measure the health—indeed the lives—of the workers are dependent upon it.

C. W. Price, 'Exhaust Ventilation in Asbestos Textile Works', Institution of Heating & Ventilation Engineers reprint (6 Oct. 1931).

All asbestos fibre dust, whether it arises in a factory or elsewhere, is a danger to lungs . . . [however], if we can produce evidence from this country that the [asbestos cement] industry is not responsible for any asbestosis claims, we may be able to avoid tiresome regulations and the introduction of dangerous occupation talk.

62/1434-7. R. H. Turner to W. H. Rooksby, T&N Mulund Works, Bombay, 1 June 1937, 14 May 1938.

The dust problem in the asbestos industry is difficult to write about in retrospect. We have no way of knowing exactly how dusty were the manufacturing processes in the early twentieth century. In fact, not until the 1960s was the technology available to measure, except experimentally, fibre concentration in asbestos factories. Moreover, it is easy to apply retrospective judgements regarding dust levels. Dust was an accepted fact of life in many industries, besides asbestos. Sandstone wheels in the Sheffield cutlery trades had been killing grinders for generations before asbestos production even began. Late nineteenth-century bosses and their workers had no reason to believe that asbestos was any more dangerous than many other industrial killers. However, one thing is certain: dust control was crucial. If dust could be abolished then much of the medical and compensation legislation of 1931 would become redundant. It was to be ironic, then, that much of the government's activity should be directed at the medical monitoring of workers rather than the basic cause of the problem.

The need to ventilate workshops was recognized both by the manufacturers themselves and the Factory Inspectors in the first decade of the twentieth century. Some progress had been made. In 1906, the Inspectors reported that there was now far less complaint of injury to health. In what may have been a reference to Turner & Newall, they remarked: 'In one very large asbestos works in the textile district of Lancashire an excellent system of exhaust ventilation has been applied to every machine, and it is reported that the health record is good.'[1] Generally, however, poor ventilation and respiratory disease remained rife in the industry.[2] Unfortunately, we have little information on how much manufacturers did in this sphere. TBA's works manager at the Nellie Kershaw inquest stated that the company had spent £4,000 between 1917 and 1920 on exhaust ventilation for the carding and spinning rooms.[3] The company also used respirators (face masks) for some jobs. TBA claimed that conditions compared favourably with other cotton textile mills.

However, accounts of Turner & Newall workshops before the Merewether–Price report (and later) make grisly reading. In the 1950s and 1960s, TBA directors and technologists were told by old hands at the company about working conditions of thirty or forty years ago. Fibre was blended on the floor by hand and most machines were fed manually. Looms were only partially ventilated and workers recalled that asbestos fibre was literally knee-deep under them. Each week some 14 lbs of fibre per loom were shed onto the floor, all of which had to be cleaned up by hand. Stripping (or cleaning) of carding engines and looms was also done by hand—an operation so dusty that a man was unrecognizable at six feet. However, this was not the worst job:

The ventilation system exhausted into settling chambers which were cleaned out by a gang of men every Saturday morning. The men, wearing respirators, went into the settling chamber, shovelled the dust into wheelbarrows which were then wheeled along and their contents tipped down a chute where it was mixed with water to form a sludge for disposal. The dust clouds formed during this tipping operation can be imagined.[4]

TBA workers recalled that as conditions slowly improved over the years, first they could see across the carding room, then they could see the foreman's cabin, and finally the clock at the end of the room emerged from the dust clouds.[5]

Mattress-making for locomotive boilers at Roberts' Leeds factory was also a very dusty job. As local doctor Ian Grieve observed in 1927: 'The mattresses emerge from the weaving process somewhat shapeless and lumpy and it is necessary to beat them into shape before completing the quilting process. This beating can only be done by hand. A male worker, invariably wearing a mask, rapidly performs this task and immediately

[1] Chief Inspector of Workshops and Factories, *Annual Report . . . for the Year 1906; Report and Statistics* (1907), 220.

[2] Chief Inspector of Workshops and Factories, *Annual Report . . . for the Year 1911* (1912), 149.

[3] 68/1737. Percy Kenyon statement, 20 Mar. 1924.

[4] D. W. Hills, 'Economics of Dust Control', *Annals of the New York Academy of Sciences* 132 (1965), 322–34, 323.

[5] W. P. Bamblin, 'Dust Control in the Asbestos Textile Industry', *Annals of Occupational Hygiene* 2 (1959), 54–74, 55.

leaves the room to allow the volumes of dust to settle. No one is supposed to enter the room until half an hour has elapsed.'[6] The sudden rise in asbestosis deaths among mattress-makers in the late 1920s had concentrated the minds of the Roberts family, who were concerned that workers were getting 'windy' about their job. Dust extraction and a water spray were installed and workers were urged to wear masks more often. The results were good enough to impress pathologist Matthew Stewart,[7] who thought that the Roberts' directors had taken 'enormous pains . . . to overcome the dangers of asbestos dust'.[8] Whether these measures were as efficient in practice as they appeared to Stewart on an organized visit may perhaps be questioned. The extractor fans blew asbestos dust into the surrounding streets, which accounted for the fact that Stewart had already found asbestos bodies in a man who had lived close to the Roberts' factory but had never worked there.[9] As Grieve noted, other safety measures were confounded by workers on piece rates who re-entered the room before the dust had cleared and also neglected to wear respirators.

When Merewether and Price prepared their well-known report, it naturally included a consideration of the dust problem. This was even more problematic than diagnosing asbestosis, as dust-counting technology was then very crude. The dust sampler available to the two men was known as an Owens jet counter, which trapped dust by sucking it into a tube through a narrow slit and then depositing the particles on a glass plate. The sample was then placed under an optical microscope for counting. The Owens counter was useful only for taking 'snap' samples in very dusty environments, as subsequent strokes of the pump tended to disturb the previous samples. Its lack of refinement meant that counts were given in terms of the number of *particles*—in other words, there was no attempt to differentiate asbestos *fibres* from other types of dust. Another problem was that in asbestos factories a variety of processes would be conducted under the same roof, making it impossible to isolate readings for individual jobs. Unsurprisingly, Merewether and Price provided no precise details of the dust levels found and simply took some fifty readings to give a 'rough idea' of the dustiness of various processes.[10] However, they

[6] I. A. D Grieve, 'Asbestosis' (Edinburgh University MD thesis, 1927), 11.

[7] M. J. Stewart (1885–1956) was professor of pathology at Leeds University between 1918 and 1950. He specialized in industrial diseases of the lung and developed an interest in asbestosis in the late 1920s.

[8] Brotherton Library, Leeds University, M. J. Stewart Diary, 22 Apr. 1929. I am grateful to Lorna Arblaster for relevant photocopies from Stewart's diaries.

[9] Brotherton Library, Stewart Diary, 15 Mar. 1929. Stewart wrote: 'Haddow has sent me lung puncture smears from a man who has never been an asbestos worker but who has lived close to Roberts' mill all his life. *I found asbestosis bodies present!* in small numbers.'

[10] However, Merewether did later publish some dust counts. See 'The Occurrence of Pulmonary Fibrosis and Other Pulmonary Affections in Asbestos Workers', *Journal of Industrial Hygiene* 12 (June 1930), 239–57, 246–7.

did postulate the existence of a threshold below which they believed the incidence of fibrosis would be relatively low. That threshold—which Merewether and Price labelled the 'dust datum'—was set by the average level of dust experienced by the spinners, since these workers appeared to have a lower incidence of fibrosis and their disease also took longer to develop.

The 'dust datum' was an entirely rule-of-thumb measure. It was criticized at the time by the TUC, which told the government: 'the discrepancy between the figures for carding and other dusty processes was not so striking in our opinion as to justify taking spinning, winding, doubling, braiding and plaiting as a dust datum below which application of exhaust ventilation should be regarded as unnecessary from a health point of view'.[11] As if to underline the point, Merewether and Price had found a dozen cases of asbestosis in their sample from the spinning section of the industry. Yet the dust datum was approved by the government as an acceptable level of risk, when it came to framing the government's dust suppression measures.

These regulations were introduced after discussions between the government, the trade unions, and the manufacturers. The TUC's interest in the asbestosis problem was limited (as was its influence) and so the key negotiations were between the government and the industry. In July 1930, the Home Office invited the leading manufacturers—notably TBA, Cape, and British Belting & Asbestos—for informal discussions about introducing the necessary controls. Ministers wished to establish a committee to examine the problem, but the asbestos manufacturers were not enthusiastic.[12] Some doubted whether a committee was actually necessary.[13] After convening their own sub-committee to consider the problem, the industrialists eventually acquiesced, but were prepared to agree to only a minimum level of improvement in the factories and argued that the dust produced in some of the processes was too small to warrant suppression.

Privately, however, the companies appreciated that they had a problem. Prompted by the government and with the help of local doctors, Turner & Newall launched a detailed investigation of the health risks in its various factories. Since 1928, TBA had been advised by local doctor Hirst

---

[11] Quoted in N. J. Wikeley, 'Measurement of Asbestos Dust Levels in British Asbestos Factories in the 1930s', *American Journal of Industrial Medicine* 24 (1993), 509–20. See also S. Holmes, 'Developments in Dust Sampling and Counting Techniques in the Asbestos Industry', *Annals of the New York Academy of Sciences* 132 (1965), 288–97.

[12] N. Wikeley, *Compensation for Industrial Disease* (1993), 102–11. See also Wikeley, 'The Asbestos Regulations 1931: A Licence to Kill?', *Journal of Law and Society* 19 (Autumn 1992), 365–78.

[13] 351/923–5. 'Notes on Conferences with Asbestos Textile Manufacturers at Home Office', 8 July 1930.

Bateman; while Roberts had retained Professor Matthew Stewart as its pathologist. The asbestosis problem was discussed at meetings between the Rochdale and Armley directors, and sometimes Bateman, Stewart, and Merewether were invited. Stewart wanted to research Roberts's problems more fully with a modest epidemiological study, having in 1929 been awarded a Medical Research Council grant for the purpose. However, by 1931 Stewart had told the MRC that the work had been postponed 'owing to some uneasiness in industry regarding health conditions'.[14] Turner & Newall, however, did allow Stewart to conduct experiments at Rochdale and elsewhere in which guinea pigs were exposed to asbestos. The work was later published in a specialist medical journal.[15] Meanwhile, in October 1930, Bateman was also asked to prepare some general notes on the Merewether–Price findings. He commented: 'Exposure in some degree to asbestos dust is common throughout all the factories, but steps have been taken extending over many years to deal with dust produced at many points, *though the necessary degree of efficiency has generally speaking, not been reached.*' [Bateman's emphasis.][16]

Turner & Newall and the other firms could hardly deny the need for better dust control, so an accommodation with the government had to be reached.[17] The manufacturers agreed that the dust level in spinning was as good a benchmark as any for a safe environment; while the government emphasized that the dust datum was 'clearly provisional' and would be subject to alteration in the light of further medical knowledge (in fact, it would stay in place for nearly forty years). However, the manufacturers had signalled their hostility to government interference and this was reflected in the final legislation.

The Asbestos Industry Regulations—framed in 1931 and effective from March 1933—covered the main manufacturing processes listed under the Asbestosis Scheme (see Chapter 4).[18] These were crushing, spinning and weaving, and the manufacture of leading asbestos products. Exhaust ventilation was to be applied for these jobs, in order to prevent 'the escape of asbestos dust into the air of any room in which persons work'. Some processes, such as hand-weaving or blending and mattress-making, were singled out for special attention. Workshops were to be kept clean and adequately lit, and impermeable sacks were to be introduced. Overalls

[14] M. Greenberg, 'Professor Matthew Stewart: Asbestosis Research 1929–1934', *American Journal of Industrial Medicine* 32 (1997), 562–9, 567.

[15] M. J. Stewart, 'Asbestosis Bodies in the Lungs of Guinea Pigs after Three to Five Months' Exposure in the Asbestos Factory', *Journal of Pathology and Bacteriology* 33 (1930), 848.

[16] 9/693. Bateman report, 3 Oct. 1930.

[17] Home Office, *Report on Conferences between Employees and Inspectors concerning Methods for Suppressing Dust in Textile Factories* (1931).

[18] Home Office, *The Asbestos Industry Regulations, 1931 (Statutory Rules and Orders, 1931, No. 1140)* (1931).

and masks were to be used for the dustiest operations and some attempt was made to protect bystanders and young workers (the latter, for example, were banned from mattress-making and cleaning).

These dust Regulations looked comprehensive, yet they had some crucial limitations. Cleaning up the workshops and issuing new sacks, overalls, and face masks certainly helped, but the rules looked better on paper than in practice. The problems of using respirators were well known. The masks available then were rudimentary (merely gauze and cotton filter pads held by an elastic headband): they were almost useless for fine asbestos dust, uncomfortable to wear, and soon became clogged. Workers had to remove them to talk or smoke—or often never used them anyway, despite management admonishments. When the asbestos Regulations were devised, no specific respirator for asbestos had been tried and tested by the Home Office.[19] The masks often gave a false sense of security to both management and workers. Sometimes they had the unhappy effect (from the manufacturers' viewpoint) of alerting workers to the dangers, making their universal use in the industry a vexed issue. Workers later found that if masks were seen to have failed— in other words, if workers developed asbestosis—non-compliance of the workforce could be used, at least initially, as a defence by the manufacturers.

However, the main problem was that—as we shall see—the whole legislative framework of dust control, medical examination, and compensation applied only to a restricted number of asbestos jobs. These were in the so-called 'scheduled areas' of the factories where the main manufacturing processes—crushing, carding, spinning, weaving, and mattress-making—were conducted. The government had acquiesced in the industry's wish to confine regulation to asbestos fibre alone in its dry and raw state and to certain dusty manufacturing processes. Many workers outside the scheduled areas were excluded from dust protection, medical surveillance, and often from compensation. The key rules did not apply to processes where asbestos was mixed with water; and though ventilation was supposed to apply to the mixing and blending of asbestos by hand, the exhaust only needed to suppress dust 'as far as practicable'. One clause effectively excluded those laggers and factory workers (such as machinery cleaners) whose work in mixing asbestos materials was only 'occasional'—defined as no more than eight hours in any week. The government could also relax the regulations at its discretion, thus allowing the industry to lobby for exemptions in certain asbestos processes.

---

[19] Apparently, the first Home Office approval for a specific respirator was not issued until 1938, when the Mark IV, manufactured by Siebe–Gorman, was recommended. A similar respirator, made by J. E. Baxter, was also approved in 1939. Though these masks could filter out some respirable dusts, they were impossible to wear for long periods.

Table 2.1. *Turner & Newall employees in the scheduled processes, 1933*

	Males	Females	Total
Textile & Allied			
Turner Brothers Asbestos	263	267	530
Ferodo	27	9	36
J. W. Roberts	37	43	80
Quasi-Arc	–	15	15
Total	327	334	661
Insulation			
Washington Chemical Company	81	100	181
Total	81	100	181
Asbestos Cement			
TAC Trafford Park	67	6	73
TAC Widnes	25	1	26
TAC Erith	6	–	6
Total	98	7	105
Grand Total	506	441	947

Source: 10/2107.

The concept of scheduled areas merely reflected a mixture of political expediency and fairly crude science, but from the industry's viewpoint it did have the merit of keeping large numbers of workers outside the scheme. Tables 2.1 and 2.2 can be compared to show the situation at Turner & Newall, where less than a quarter of the workforce was covered. At TBA the whole of the asbestos textile division came within the legislation—over 500 workers. These included all the Harridge Mill employees and a large section of the Clod Mill, where carding, spinning, and weaving were conducted. However, about half the thousand-strong workforce was exempt. Departments outside the scheme included the stockrooms, sample room, receipt and dispatch, maintenance, most of the rubber shed, the garage, and the canteen. About eighty Roberts' workers at Leeds (most of the workforce) were within the Scheme, signifying that it was potentially the most dangerous unit company. However, in the outposts of the Turner & Newall empire the coverage of the new legislation grew weaker and the situation was more mixed. Only 10 per cent or fewer of the workers at Washington Chemical Company or TAC were within the various schemes.

Turner & Newall began acting on these regulations during 1932, when Commercial Union was asked to investigate conditions at Rochdale. The

Table 2.2. *Turner & Newall employees in asbestos manufacture, 1932–66*

	1932	1937	1942	1947	1952	1957	1962	1966
Turner Brothers Asbestos	987 21%	1,804 18%	1,987 20%	2,381 22%	3,002 26%	3,153 27%	2,879 25%	3,299 27%
Turners Asbestos Cement	1,847 40%	5,158 51%	4,499 46%	4,497 41%	4,372 37%	3,798 32%	3,799 33%	3,722 31%
Washington Chemical/ Newalls	1,173 ·25%	2,142 21%	2,384 24%	2,462 22%	2,531 22%	2,864 24%	2,304 20%	2,579 21%
Ferodo	550 12%	839 8%	781 8%	1,408 13%	1,624 14%	1,854 16%	2,455 21%	2,185 18%
J. W. Roberts	76 2%	161 2%	227 2%	224 2%	236 2%	169 1%	69 1%	290 2%
Totals	4,633 100%	10,104 100%	9,878 100%	10,972 100%	11,765 100%	11,838 100%	11,506 100%	12,075 100%

Source: 9/214. T & N Board Papers: J. M. Atkinson to J. Waddell, board meeting, 25 May 1967.

insurers revealed a disquieting situation. The Harridge Mill, which was to provide many of the first asbestosis cases, was particularly criticized. This was the building where many of the preparatory processes took place. Bag emptying was a very dusty operation, and the Commercial Union man saw workers who 'exist in a cloud of dust' without overalls and respirators. Fan doors were left open in one room, shrouding one end in dust. In the weaving section, conditions were not much better:

machines for the most part are too close together and the roof is low . . . loose dust is removed by a suction plant, but the worker is always standing immediately over his work and quantities of dust, which are not removed by the exhaust fans cloud the air and saturate the clothing of operatives. Practically all the operatives, both male and female, do not wear a head cover . . . [and] . . . it is obvious that with the clothing saturated with asbestos every time, both in and out of the works, [when] any movement is made by the individual small clouds of this pernicious dust must enter the lungs of the worker.[20]

These comments make nonsense of Turner & Newall's previous statements, repeated at various inquests, that its factories were dustless and that large sums had been spent on eliminating dust.

On the other hand, a dust suppression programme was launched at the

---

[20] 8/1461–3. W. Davies's report, 21 Mar. 1932.

company, which—superficially—looked impressive. Processes were relocated and enclosed; new dust extraction plant was installed; new sacks were ordered; respirators and overalls were issued; and warning notices pinned up around the works. Samuel Turner III pressed home the safety policy when he asked the firm's directors 'to redouble their efforts to safeguard the workers'. He also suggested that Robert H. Turner should pressurize other manufacturers 'to do everything possible whatever the cost, to bring about the desired result, the issue involved being a moral issue, the health of the workers'.[21] In the event, the cost was very modest. The estimated expenditure for the whole group was £9,825, with two-thirds earmarked for the Rochdale site—this at a time, when the company's annual profits (after tax) were over £360,000.[22]

In August 1932, Bateman and Robert H. Turner made their own inspection of health and safety in the group. Their report presented a generally favourable picture, with several factories given an almost clean bill of health.[23] The plants at Chapel-en-le-Frith, Trafford Park, Erith, and London (Quasi-Arc, the electrode company) were all described as basically 'clean and healthy'. Roberts was 'fairly clean and . . . healthy', despite the fact that discarded rubbish and fibre littered the workshops. At the main Rochdale factory, however, the situation was more complex. Here new exhaust arrangements were well in hand and in some areas won the praise of Charles Price, the co-author of the government report.[24] However, it was evident from Price's remarks that much remained to be done, and Bateman and Robert H. Turner admitted that there were problems. Bateman added some extra remarks in a separate letter to the latter. The main difficulty was that the buildings were old and unsuitable, with the Harridge Mill actually due for closure. In particular, blending, disintegrating, and opening needed rehousing to reduce the dust. The waste recovery section was 'unsatisfactory and should have the attention of the management as soon as possible'. Bateman warned that overall 'the basic problems of dust prevention in some of the processes have not yet been solved', and 'constant attention to detail is necessary to render them free from danger'.[25]

If Turner & Newall's directors showed some intention to control dust in the 'scheduled areas' in Rochdale, they adopted a different attitude to its workforce elsewhere. The Rochdale board and the unit companies did

---

[21] 9/528. Directors' meeting, 30 June 1932. Robert H. Turner was the son of Charles Turner (who was the brother of Samuel Turner III). He was a T & N director between 1928 and 1965.
[22] 43/290–6. Directors' meeting, 8 Apr. 1932.   [23] 9/496–509. Aug. 1932.
[24] 113/1809. C. W. Price, 'Exhaust Ventilation in Asbestos Textile Works', reprint from Institution of Heating & Ventilation Engineers (6 Oct. 1931), 16. Price found that the dust extraction system in some of the weaving sheds, devised by works manager Percy Kenyon, was 'very satisfactory'. See also 113/1799–1801. Typescript memo by Price, 22 Mar. 1933.
[25] 9/515/6. Letter 19 Sept. 1932.

what they could to limit the scope and cost of the Regulations. A manager at the company's asbestos cement works in Widnes regarded the Home Office booklet of regulations as 'a definite handicap to our industry', and spoke of 'limiting its issue to the smallest possible number of operatives'.[26] The Erith plant hoped that the Rochdale headquarters would be able to pressurize the government into exempting all its processes except crushing and disintegrating. Robert H. Turner did not recommend that unloaders of fibre should be brought within the Scheme, despite the fact that he admitted that there was an asbestosis risk. The continued danger was due to the fact that the Home Office, despite the legislation, still allowed manufacturers to ship fibre in permeable hessian bags and also turned a blind eye to their continued use *inside* the factories.[27] To counter the problems with jobs such as unloading, Turner merely advised a change of operative every two or three years. As he explained to one manager: 'It is in our interest to see that we do not have any claims from operations outside those already scheduled, otherwise these operators will also be included and we shall have to spend a lot of money in overcoming the problem in handling crude.'[28] This strategy of switching workers was to become company policy for many years, yet it had the effect of spreading the risk.

Eventually, the group's asbestos-cement factories were mostly exempt from the Regulations. Raybestos–Belaco (brake linings) was outside the government scheme; so was most of the Ferodo factory. A Home Office representative met one Ferodo director, who wanted exemption for its woven asbestos materials and also for its brake-shoes. Concerning the latter, the Ferodo man was heard with some sympathy and the Home Office apparently agreed that 'it would be simply absurd to bring users of asbestos goods into the Scheme'.[29]

In Robert H. Turner's words, such exclusions offered the possibility of 'stretching the regulations to suit our own ends'.[30] There were other ways of circumventing the guidelines. One idea was to turn dry-mixing processes into wet ones and then use casual labour to do the mixing. Wilfred Roberts wrote from Leeds: 'Each new job gets fresh labourers'.[31] Thus the ruling over 'occasional' work could be confounded. Robert H. Turner felt that the definition of 'occasional' was, anyway, far too strict. The company had hoped that workers who did a job once a week could be exempted as 'occasional', but the Home Office was not impressed with

---

[26] 10/1736. J. Paravicini to B. E. Williams, Trafford Park, 28 Sept. 1931.
[27] Impermeable (though not indestructible) paper-lined bags were sometimes used for 'compo' and asbestos spray mixtures, but this was dictated by the possibility of water spoiling the product, not by health considerations.
[28] 37/575. R. H. Turner to Mr Whittaker, 27 Feb. 1932.
[29] 10/1774–6. Report of A. Blackham's interview with E. Field, Home Office, 15 July 1931.
[30] 10/1625. R. H. Turner to G. S. Newall, 30 Dec. 1932.
[31] 10/2096. W. N. Roberts to R. H. Turner, 15 July 1931.

the argument. A Factory Inspector warned Robert H. Turner: 'The medical opinion is, I understand, that there might be considerable risk if there was exposure to a high concentration of dust for eight hours per week.'[32] Nevertheless, Turner gave the go-ahead for Newalls to continue repairing ships' boiler-mattresses at local depots and warehouses (such as at Cardiff) without using dust extractors—in direct contravention of the regulations. By limiting such work to emergency repairs and by ensuring that respirators were worn, Turner felt he could take a 'small risk', rather than lose this business to other competitors.[33]

The country's growing army of laggers and other insulation workers did not come within the Regulations (or the Medical Scheme)—a particularly tragic omission that was to cost many workers their lives. Over sixty firms were involved with this business by 1931 in London, the Midlands, and Cardiff alone. The insulation wing of Turner & Newall—Washington Chemical Company and Newalls—had a few workers in the Washington factory and in the shipyards (mattress-making) who came within the legislation. However, most did not, the company noting that this would mean that any claims for danger money could be swiftly rejected. Turner & Newall were instrumental in ensuring that its insulation workers—whose numbers in the 1930s doubled from 400 to over 800—were not medically monitored (though they were within the compensation scheme, if they could prove their unfitness). Yet the company knew that these 'unscheduled' workers were exposed to substantial quantities of dust.

When Turner and Bateman had visited Washington in September 1932, they were troubled by the dust problem at the company. The section where 'plastic' (the magnesia/asbestos mixture) was bagged, weighed, and loaded was 'very far short of being satisfactory'. Leaky hoppers made bag-sewing a 'dangerous operation'. In the cutting and trimming of insulation slabs—despite considerable improvement—there was still a 'tremendous amount to do'. The same was true of band-sawing asbestos felt sheets. The impermeable bags (sack lined with paper) were also unsatisfactory; and evidently floors and surfaces were not being damped before sweeping.[34] Improvements were underway, but even when complete the Washington Works had deficiencies. An undated report in about 1932, describing dust-suppression measures under the Scheme, believed that most of the dust requirements had been met. However, disintegrators were still hand-fed (albeit that workers were supplied with respirators) and other comments—such as that mattress-beating was 'not violent and with the damped mattress very little dust is liberated'—are not very

---

[32] 10/1645. S. Hird, HM Inspector of Factories to R. H. Turner, 7 Oct. 1932.
[33] 10/1625. R. H. Turner to G. S. Newall, 30 Dec. 1932.
[34] 9/493–5. Turner–Bateman Report, WCC, 5 Sept. 1932.

convincing.[35] Factory Inspectors, who visited Washington at this time, were unhappy with the mattress department, which took several years to modernize and isolate.[36] Between 1935 and 1937, Inspectors made several complaints about dusty machines, defective exhaust machinery, and inadequate dust suppression by water-spray or vacuum.[37]

Bateman and Turner did not tour outside sites where Newalls' laggers were at work and so did not describe their working conditions. This work was especially dusty: indeed, it was often dustier and more hazardous than asbestos manufacture. Paper or hessian bags of asbestos-based powder ('compo' or 'maggi') would arrive on site and be manhandled to the job. Split bags were not uncommon, generating dust. The bags were cut open and emptied into a tub—usually an old oil drum—and then water was added, before the mixture was turned over with a shovel or paddle. Sometimes workers used their hands. These procedures, which were unskilled and often given to young apprentices, created a dust cloud and there was no exhaust ventilation. Paste would be applied wet, but would soon dry out leaving fibres on the floors and the workmen's clothing. Preformed pipe- and boiler-sections of pure asbestos bonded with magnesia or calcium silicate had to be cut and shaped by handsaw and 'gouging out' with other tools, and then fitted by 'knocking on'—all tasks that raised local dust. Asbestos-based rope was sometimes used and this also shed fibre. Insulation mattresses were sometimes made on site, with workers creating clouds of dust as they manually stuffed asbestos quilts with loose fibre. Asbestos cloth was another popular lagging material and the dusty practice of tearing the cloth by hand was almost universal, especially in the shipyards. Dust was also generated during the final stages, when wire netting was wound round insulation, following by trowelling over with a hard-setting composition and a lick of paint. The dust problem was exacerbated by the nature of the work, which was usually hot and strenuous and made the wearing of masks an impossibility.

Conditions were at their worst in the shipbuilding industry—one of the best customers for asbestos. Both the merchant and naval marine required a wide range of asbestos materials for insulating engine rooms, lagging pipes, covering electric wires, and soundproofing. Between 1900 and 1950 the bulk of the heat insulation was in the form of asbestos mattresses (85 per cent magnesia/15 per cent amosite) and asbestos cloth. Sprayed asbestos (described below) was used increasingly, especially during the 1940s, and in this process the fibre mostly used was crocidolite. Even in the 1930s, workers recognized amosite and crocidolite as the unhealthiest types of asbestos—a view confirmed scientifically after 1960.

[35] 10/1520. Suppression of Dust at Washington Works, n.d., c.1931–2.
[36] 3/83–4, 197–8, 235–6. Local Board Meetings, 17 Oct. 1933; 21 Nov. 1934; 20 Feb. 1935.
[37] 53/326–7, 389–90, 477. WCC Local Board Meetings, 19 Nov. 1935; 21 Apr. 1936; 27 Jan. 1937.

Besides fibre type, several other features of the shipbuilding industry were to make the use of asbestos highly hazardous. There was its ubiquity on board ship, where, as one expert commented, 'it is difficult to find a compartment where there is no asbestos'.[38] Controlling dust was impossible in the maze of pipes and machinery below decks, where there was no exhaust ventilation and often no fresh air. These dust problems were exacerbated by refits, especially in Royal Navy dockyards, where lagging material was ripped out and hacked off—a process that often generated more dust than installation. Sometimes workers would trample and break up asbestos underfoot and then re-bag it for recycling. Old asbestos had to be manhandled out of the ship, making heavy wetting beforehand difficult as it increased the weight. Even worse, a host of trades and ancillary staff became involved (albeit indirectly) with the material. On the 'front line' were the asbestos mattress workers, laggers and sprayers, who were contracted out by firms such as Newalls Insulation. However, sailmakers, strippers, and storemen handled asbestos; and plumbers, riveters, and boilermakers were also exposed. The workforce in the dockyards was also a large one, providing employment for thousands.

Originally, it seemed as if the laws would apply to insulators because they often mixed asbestos compositions. However, Turner & Newall did not accept that there was a dust problem, where water was used. As one director put it: 'Plastic and compo is never applied in its powder form but it is always mixed with water, which prevents anything in the form of dust . . .'.[39] They also argued that lagging was not a manufacturing (scheduled) process. A director observed:

Compo is mixed in various factories where this operation is already covered by the Medical Scheme, the bags of mixed compo being emptied out on the job, where water is added. I contend that this is only wetting the previously prepared mixture, and not mixing. If this point is agreed, I feel that these outside men should only come under the Compensation Scheme because of the cutting of sections which contain asbestos fibre in the dry state.[40]

The Home Office concurred with this assessment and agreed that the Regulations (which had specified exhaust ventilation for mixing and blending by hand as far as practicable) and the medical scheme would not apply to laggers.[41] One Factory Inspector informed Turner & Newall's Belfast

---

[38] P. G. Harries, 'Asbestos Hazards in Naval Dockyards', *Annals of Occupational Hygiene* 11 (1968), 135–42, 136.

[39] 10/1971. George Carter to W. W. F. Shepherd, 2 July 1931.

[40] 10/1518. Asbestosis memo, n.d.

[41] In the lagging trades, where there was no medical monitoring by asbestos companies, workers had to apply to the Medical Board independently. This involved paying a fee, not all of which was returned, even if a worker was suspended. Very few workers, it appears, ever applied for an independent medical assessment; some professed to be completely ignorant of their rights in this matter.

insulating subsidiary that the amount of work that would come under the
regulations in Northern Ireland was so small that he believed that they
should not be adopted there either.[42]

Ironically, the year that the government legislated for asbestos dust protection, Turner & Newall devised a new technique of applying asbestos
that was to prove highly profitable (and controversial). This was the brain-
child of Norman Dolbey (*c.*1898–1965), a chemical engineer who had
joined Roberts in 1927. The increasing use of all-steel coaches on the railways had led to a demand for a superior form of asbestos insulation and
sound-proofing, which avoided the problems of asbestos board (corrosion
and condensation behind the panels) and was quicker to apply than hand-
trowelled asbestos paste. It seemed logical to *spray* the material onto the
walls and ceilings. As devised by Dolbey, the technique involved loading
a dry asbestos–cement mixture into a portable machine, which separated
and fluffed the fibres with a spiked belt and then blew them through a
compressed-air gun with atomized water. It was quickly discovered that
asbestos spray (usually 60 per cent asbestos and the rest cement) would
stick to almost any surface. With thermal insulation, fireproofing, noise
reduction, acoustical correction, and condensation control as its selling
points, sprayed 'Limpet' asbestos became Roberts's main product and a
major money-spinner for the whole Turner & Newall group. Roberts did
not spray Limpet itself—though it established a Spray School in 1945 at
the Armley factory—but it processed and bagged the spray materials.
(The mixture was mostly crocidolite and cement, though amosite was
increasingly used after the 1950s.) It also licensed the technique to Newalls
and TAC and to users worldwide.

Spraying was a very dusty job. Asbestos cement would arrive on the
site in large ¾-cwt bags, which were ripped open by labourers and
apprentices, who then fed fibre by hand into the spraying machine.
Besides the hopper filler and the sprayer, an assistant used a roller
to 'matt' the asbestos coating and so provide a final finish. Both the
hopper-filler and sprayer were exposed to very high dust concentrations.
One Newalls' shipyard sprayer (who later died of mesothelioma) recalled
that:

the dust was everywhere. It covered my clothing, it covered all machinery
and covered everything within the vicinity of where I worked. I was given a
rubber face mask for protection only. However this soon became uncomfortable
because of the heat from the boilers . . . and I normally discarded it. I was
never told or warned against working without a face mask. I was not issued
with overalls or special footwear or any other form of protection by my employers. We were never provided with ventilation or exhaust equipment to

---

[42] 10/1675. Reid, McFarlane to Shepherd, 23 Oct. 1931.

remove the dust from the environment. Water was never used to damp down the dust in any way.[43]

The lethal nature of this work was recognized immediately. An editorial in *The Lancet* in 1932 commented on spraying in the London tube railway, where asbestos was being tried for its acoustic properties. It noted that workmen were covered in dust and predicted a 'large increase' in asbestosis in years to come.[44] However, Turner & Newall insisted that spraying was outside the Regulations, as the process was 'wet'—a point upon which the government agreed. Masks would eventually be provided for sprayers by the 1940s, but not until the 1960s would the use of such protection for the spray team be enforced.

It could be argued that the exclusion of laggers and ancillary workers from the 1931 Asbestos Regulations and the medical scheme was hardly surprising. The Depression had made implementing any occupational health scheme a great struggle; and monitoring the insulating trade, scattered as it was around the country, would have been a difficult and relatively costly undertaking. Similarly, the casual attitude to safety was, it might be argued, no more than a reflection of an era when the dangers of dust were accepted as part of the job. Moreover, with conditions so poor in the factories themselves, was it any surprise that the possible dangers of environmental exposure outside the works were ignored?

These arguments, however, can be pushed only so far. Even at the time, there were doubts about the creation of 'scheduled areas' and some discussion as to whether the exclusion clauses were wise. The TUC were given informal advice by a self-appointed but knowledgeable 'Asbestos Research Worker', Reginald Tage. The personal history of this shadowy and eccentric individual has been unearthed by Nick Wikeley.[45] Tage had no official position, but seems to have had links with the trade unions and a brother who worked at Cape's London factory. In 1931, he informed Sir Thomas Legge (the TUC's medical adviser) not only that asbestos caused cancer, but also that asbestosis affected those outside the government scheme. He cited by name five packers, two storekeepers, one carpenter, one labourer, one outworker, and one assistant works manager, all of

[43] Quoted in J. M. Parsons, 'Asbestos Related Disease Claims—A Continuing Cause for Concern in the 1990s and Beyond', *Journal of Personal Injury Litigation* (1997), i, 5–29, 30. See also G. Tweedale, 'Sprayed "Limpet" Asbestos: Technical, Commercial, and Regulatory Aspects', in G. A. Peters and B. J. Peters (eds.), *Sourcebook on Asbestos Diseases*, 18 (1999).

[44] 'Asbestos in the London Tube Railways', *Lancet* 222 (20 Feb. 1932), i, 410. Cited in B. I. Castleman, *Asbestos: Medical and Legal Aspects* (1996), 426. The company replied to this criticism with the argument that the dust was blown away by the 'natural current of air' in the tunnel. See letter to *Lancet* 222 (5 Mar. 1932), i, 542–3.

[45] N. Wikeley, 'Asbestos and Cancer: An Early Warning to the British TUC', *American Journal of Industrial Medicine* 22 (1992), 449–54. See also M. Greenberg, 'Reginald Tage: A UK Asbestos Prophet—A Postscript', *American Journal of Industrial Medicine* 24 (1993), 521–4.

whom had been certified with asbestosis.[46] Legge chose to ignore this presumptuous advice and patronizingly wrote: '[Tage] is inclined to develop the wrong ideas about the possible effects of asbestos.'[47]

However, Merewether was also concerned about the ancillary asbestos trades. With the help of E. L. Middleton, a Medical Inspector of Factories, he had extended his first study to investigate the health of asbestos packers.[48] Again, the findings were unequivocal. Although packing was a small industry and it was difficult to find workers who did packing alone (as some did other jobs in the asbestos factories), Merewether and Middleton selected seventeen men. Two had diffuse fibrosis of the lungs. As regards other workers: of eight warehousemen and storekeepers, one showed the early clinical signs of asbestosis, and of fifteen packers, who also worked in the main manufacturing areas, five definite cases of asbestosis were found. The message was clear: packers, warehousemen, and storekeepers were at risk and the report recommended that they should be included in the Scheme.

In June 1932, Home Office officials called a meeting in London with the asbestos manufacturers, including Turner & Newall, to discuss these proposals. The manufacturers were opposed to any extension of the Scheme and met beforehand—at Turner & Newall's suggestion—'to arrange an organised line of resistance'.[49] They took the opportunity to draw up a long list of complaints against the Home Office, especially about the charges for medical examinations. Robert H. Turner intimated to one fellow manufacturer: 'I am in complete agreement with your suggestion that we should endeavour to have the asbestos industry removed from the schedule of dangerous occupations.'[50] At the subsequent meeting with the government, the industry representatives successfully deflected any new proposals. The Home Office meekly agreed that 'almost all cases so far investigated could be regarded as covered by the Scheme', thus ignoring Merewether and Middleton. However, the manufacturers did give a 'definite assurance' that the Scheme would be 'interpreted broadly, so as to cover all genuine cases of asbestosis occurring in the works'.[51] On the whole they were well pleased at the outcome. Noted Robert H. Turner, in a letter to the Glasgow MP, Douglas Jamieson: 'the Home Office have not yet had sufficient experience of the Scheme to make any modifications, and until more experience has been gained they feel that matters should be left as they are.'[52]

[46] Tage's younger brother was also to die from asbestosis.
[47] Wikeley, 'Asbestos and Cancer', 453.
[48] 12/20. E. R. A. Merewether, 'Asbestosis: Report of Inquiry into the Existence of the Disease in Packers of Manufactured Articles' (1932).
[49] 12/59. R. H. Turner to BBA Ltd, 7 June 1932.
[50] 10/1617. Turner to K. MacLellan, Glasgow Asbestos Co., 3. Nov. 1932.
[51] 12/100. J. M. Duckland, Home Office, to British Fibro-Cement Co., 20 July 1932.
[52] 10/1620. R. H. Turner to D. Jamieson, 10 Nov. 1932.

If asbestosis was a risk for packers, then logically it was a greater risk for laggers, who were exposed to higher dust levels. Merewether and Middleton had emphasized that the dust produced by insulating materials and sections was considerable, and the work was comparable with scheduled jobs. Medical reports soon confirmed the dangers. In 1934, a study based on a hundred cases of asbestosis among London workers (mostly from Cape Asbestos) showed the following: an 18-year-old van boy, who had spent his spare time over 30 months in mixing asbestos powders in an open yard; a middle-aged boiler riveter, who had been exposed to dust from asbestos pipe-lagging; and a man who had worked with asbestos mattresses in the open air at an aerodrome.[53] No comparative study was published at this time of Turner & Newall workers, but there is some evidence from the firm's incomplete records that it experienced similar cases of asbestosis. The company had already had an asbestosis claim from a lagger by 1934, which prodded the Rochdale board to make an 'experiment' at Washington by medically examining contract workers.[54] The results of the survey, if it took place, are not recorded, but evidently no action followed.

Turner & Newall, like the government, let things lie during the 1930s. The dust problem does not appear to have been a major concern for the company in that decade. No dust-count surveys were taken at TBA (or elsewhere), except for a government-inspired attempt to discover dust levels at Roberts in 1938. Dust-counting technology was still primitive, but the results indicated that dust levels at both the 'dust datum' and during spraying were very high.[55] Evidently, with rearmament underway there was little interest in undertaking further surveys. In 1931, TBA first had the idea of damping yarn to suppress the dust, but this was not very successful and was not implemented until 1939. According to TBA itself, damping was the only significant advance made in controlling dust until the mid-1950s. Dr Bateman's duties were to be wound down in 1932, especially after he had given the directors a shock by billing them £110 for his services. Meanwhile, the company kept alert for the visits of the Factory Inspectors and continued to oppose any extension of the Regulations.

Despite the fact that the company had watered down some of the Regulations, there seems to have been a genuine belief that the asbestosis problem would wither away and that any new cases would simply be a legacy of the bad old days before 1931. Robert H. Turner wrote to the leading American asbestos company, Johns–Manville, in 1932: 'employees are not likely to contract asbestosis under three years' exposure to bad conditions, but I think it is very probable that in the course of the next few years we shall entirely eliminate any difficulty from this source. We

[53] W. B. Wood and S. R. Gloyne, 'Pulmonary Asbestosis', *Lancet* 227 (22 Dec. 1934), 1383–5.
[54] 37/681. T & N Secretary to W. H. Bateman, 2 June 1934.
[55] Wikeley, 'Measurement of Dust'.

are now suffering from cases contracted during the last thirty years or so, when many dusty jobs prevailed in our factories.'[56] That remained the company's position in 1937, when chairman Samuel Turner felt confident enough to tell shareholders that dust control had been 'so completely successful that I can with confidence state that new cases of asbestosis in your companies' factories are extremely unlikely, the cases with which we have to deal at present being simply the inheritance of the days when unfortunately this danger was not realised'.[57] That was Turner's only public statement on asbestosis: the subject would never be mentioned again in a Turner & Newall annual report until 1968.

Merewether had the same view. When he visited Washington in 1937, he complimented the company on the mattress department and stated that soon the risk of asbestosis in such factories would be entirely eliminated.[58] The annual reports of the Chief Inspector of Factories (Dr J. C. Bridge) in the early 1930s also presented a reassuring picture of 'a high standard of ventilation in the industry', and manufacturers using the 'utmost expedition' in complying with the Regulations.

This false dawn had probably been fostered by the relatively low number of suspensions and deaths in the industry in the early 1930s (discussed more fully in Chapter 3). It is noticeable, however, that Turner & Newall had already adopted the attitude of interpreting statistics to present a slightly more optimistic view than was warranted. When a member of the Medical Board wrote to TBA in 1936 enquiring about workers' mortality, the employment manager responded with the appropriate data. Twenty-eight workers from the scheduled areas were shown to have died between 1930 and 1935. Several had died from asbestosis; however, their number was lessened by the fact that in four cases where asbestosis was a factor in the death, the company did not mention it.[59]

Favourable views were impressed more directly on other doctors. In 1938, Dr William Brockbank, a physician at Manchester Royal Infirmary wrote to TBA asking for photographs of dusty processes and details of the firm's health precautions for his lectures on lung diseases. John Collins, the company secretary, told TBA director Frank Bussy that the physician perhaps ought to visit Rochdale, where he could be informed that 'the risk of asbestosis in the future will be negligible as a result of the precautions which we take, and also . . . that all our asbestosis cases are employees who have been in our service for a long time'. Added Collins: 'If Dr Brockbank obtains a correct view of the position from us this ought

[56] 8/1402. Turner to S. E. Josi, 18 Aug. 1932.
[57] T & N, *Annual Reports and Accounts* (1937), 15.
[58] 53/529–30. WCC Local Board Meeting, 26 May 1937.
[59] 301/670. Ellison, 'Return of Mortality Rates . . . 1930–1935'.

to be helpful as large numbers of students will no doubt be passing through his hands in future years.'[60]

Underlying this need to influence the medical community, was a nagging disquiet that asbestosis was not withering away. At the end of the 1930s, when wartime demands began compromising workers' safety, the problem began raising its head again. A TAC manager at Trafford Park made the prophetic warning to Walker Shepherd in 1939 that 'people are apt to get slack in regard to treating [asbestosis] with the interest it deserves, and if any such slackness creeps into our organisation, we shall only be creating trouble for the future'.[61] At the start of the war itself, the workforce was also becoming anxious. Many workers applied to leave TBA and there were also a number of appeals against directives to work at the company. The reason was a sudden flurry of asbestosis deaths among TBA workers—at least fifteen between 1940 and 1942—and in the same period there had also been eighteen suspensions. At some of the inquests, cancer had been mentioned alongside asbestosis. This triggered an 'asbestosis scare' in Rochdale, which according to the company, 'appears to be greater outside the factory than it is among our own workpeople'.[62] The directors reacted by launching a series of initiatives: they began organizing TBA's first scientific research into asbestosis; they reviewed the incidence of disease at the factory; and launched a public relations drive by inviting local doctors, magistrates, and employment officers to see the latest dust improvements.

By 1942, as part of Turner & Newall's wartime commitment to industrial research, an Asbestosis Research Committee had been established at TBA. At its first meeting, in May 1942, Sir Samuel Turner and his fellow TBA directors met to discuss dust-counting technology and the launch of a research programme. Both Merewether and the Senior Medical Inspector of Factories, Dr John Bridge, attended the discussions. Merewether had suggested that the asbestosis research might best be conducted at the British Postgraduate Medical School at Hammersmith by two Canadian-born pathologists, Dr Earl King and Thomas Belt. With TBA funding, a series of animal and tissue-culture experiments began in 1943 into the pathology of asbestosis. The company was interested in pursuing a number of lines of enquiry. Was asbestos readily dissolved in the lungs, as TBA's research director, Dr W. Francis, believed? Were longer particles above 5 microns the most dangerous? Samuel Turner thought so and American research funded by the asbestos industry seemed to agree. Another North American idea was that aluminium powder could reduce silicosis in miners. If this was so, then TBA directors reasoned, aluminium

[60] 8/1392. Collins to Bussy, 1 July 1938.
[61] 8/1253. B. Williams to Shepherd, 29 Sept. 1939.
[62] 161/266. TBA Directors' meeting, 4 Feb. 1943.

dust introduced into the work's atmosphere might act as an antidote to asbestosis.

The Hammersmith work seemed to begin promisingly and TBA quickly utilized it for publicity. In May 1943, a symposium, 'Medical Research and the Asbestos Industry', was organized in Rochdale with a film and slide-show.[63] The audience was shown slides of phagocytes gobbling up asbestos particles and told that asbestos was not toxic and did not damage cells. Broadly, long-fibre asbestos was held mainly responsible for fibrosis. This was particularly reassuring as the longer fibres could obviously be more easily removed by factory ventilation. However, the research underlying these conclusions was decidedly shaky. Work at Hammersmith had been disrupted by air raids, staff sickness, and army conscription. Many of the rats died prematurely, escaped, or ate each other (and this aside from the complex problem of applying animal data to humans). Eventually, TBA gave cautious approval to the publication of two papers from the work,[64] while believing that it had yielded 'practically nothing of value'.[65] This was a reflection of its modest funding: the total cost was only £2,350. The idea of scattering aluminium dust in the works was fortunately soon abandoned. A dust-counting programme began in 1942, using the Owens jet counter, and by 1944 a factory survey was planned with 'dust settlement discs'.[66] However, the programme was not actively pursued until the 1950s.

Between 1942 and 1945 the TBA directors did launch an internal review of the whole asbestosis question. The appointment of a chief medical officer was planned, better compensation payments were considered, and a more open discussion of the dangers was felt by some to be necessary. Remarked one manager: 'Silence by the management on the subject of asbestosis, while due to the best of motives, is bound to give credit to the gossipers and horror-mongers.'[67] Others called for an 'accurate knowledge of the facts'. In 1942, therefore, TBA director Frank Bussy prepared a memorandum on asbestosis for the workers' committee. Another of the company's Methodist directors and a respected member of the local community (he was soon to become a Rochdale town councillor, with seats on various hospital boards), Bussy must have seemed the ideal man to

[63] 8/1211–14. 'Medical Research and the Asbestos Industry', 26 May 1943. See also 302/1323–4. 'Experimental Asbestosis. Report of Work Done in Dept. of Pathology, British Postgraduate Medical School, Nov. 1941–May 1943.'

[64] See also E. J. King *et al.*, 'The Effects of Asbestos, and of Asbestos and Aluminium, on the Lungs of Rabbits', *Thorax* 1 (Sept. 1946), 188–97; T. H. Belt *et al.*, 'The Effect of Asbestos on Tissue Cultures: A Comparative Study of Quartz and Coal Dust', *Journal of Pathology and Bacteriology* 59 (Jan.–Apr. 1947), 159–64.

[65] 117/677. R. G. Soothill to E. L. Dawson, 31 Dec. 1947.

[66] 161/289. TBA Directors' Meeting, 2 Mar. 1944.

[67] 301/914–19. Memo on Asbestosis by M. E. Oliver.

present an accurate picture. His chief interest, it was said, was in 'the sphere of health'.[68] Bussy believed that the danger of the disease was 'very often exaggerated', yet told the workers that 'the truth should be known'.[69]

According to Bussy, the truth was as follows: prior to 1931 no one knew that asbestos was harmful. Henceforth, the company had implemented a costly dust prevention programme, which the directors believed would eliminate the health risk. He painted a picture of a factory in which 'large volumes of fresh air' swept through the mill, where working conditions were better than other cotton factories, and where scientific research was moving ahead on the asbestosis problem. Asbestosis cases had occurred, but in Bussy's words, 'these must have been caused before it was known that the dust was harmful and proper precautions taken'. He admitted that fifty-three workers had been suspended and that there had been twenty-four deaths. However, Bussy quickly added that in many of these cases:

there have been all sorts of complications, consequently it might or might not be correct to say that asbestosis was a contributory cause. Some of the cases were heart disease, cancer and the usual other diseases which occur whatever the occupation or sphere of life may be, and which risks everyone has to face. We do not doubt the *bona fides* of the opinions expressed by doctors after a post-mortem, but when a man has cancer, or heart disease and his lungs are also affected in greater or lesser degree by asbestosis, it is an almost impossible scientific task for anyone to say exactly what has been the actual cause of death.

Thus, explained Bussy, asbestos was only involved in six deaths. Not that the company viewed even this small percentage complacently. The directors felt 'the greatest sympathy for the workers suspended'; compensation had not been limited to the statutory amounts. Payments had been increased where necessary 'to enable the individual to live in comfort'; or alternative work had been found in the factory. The remaining suspended workers were either retired under the Asbestosis Scheme or were following some other occupation.

Unfortunately, Bussy's picture did not square with the reality. TBA's extant compensation files shows a much more alarming situation at Rochdale. Twenty-two suspended workers had died by 1941 with asbestosis as a significant factor. However, even this understated the true picture, because—as Bussy must have known—workers did not need to be suspended to die of asbestosis. Eighteen more workers had died of asbestosis-related disease at TBA by 1941, and asbestos may have been

[68] *Rochdale Observer*, 2 Oct. 1957.
[69] 8/1848–9 Memo 4 Feb. 1942. Bussy's figures were based on a review of asbestosis cases sent to Sir S. Turner, 31 Dec. 1941. See 301/901.

involved in the deaths of about ten others. The true figure was forty or more asbestos deaths, not six as Bussy suggested—though even this would have missed some workers who had left and others whose asbestosis (or other diseases) had not been recognized. Bussy's data was therefore highly selective. It was, however, characteristic of the way the company minimized asbestos mortality by using very narrow medical criteria and by considering only official suspensions.

The company could also claim that any asbestosis cases were simply a legacy of the past. Certainly, if 1932 was taken as the benchmark when a new order of dust control was introduced, then for a number of years there were no reported suspensions or deaths among workers who had joined the industry after the Regulations began operating. However, this argument, which had been advanced by Samuel Turner, was unsound, given the known extended latency of asbestosis. Five or six years or even a decade was simply too short a period in which to evaluate fully whether the Regulations had eradicated asbestosis. By the end of the Second World War, although the incidence of disease was certainly cut, it was not disappearing—in other words, workers were still developing asbestosis, even if they had joined the company after 1932. Edward Roberts, a mixer at an insulation subsidiary, was suspended with tuberculosis and asbestosis in 1938 (he had started work in 1933). George Fryer, a cement room attendant at Rhoose since 1935, was suspended with asbestosis in 1941. Joseph Cowlam, a Roberts' mattress-maker since 1934, was suspended with asbestosis in 1944.

This shows that working conditions were far from benign or pleasant. Predictably, much-needed capital expenditure and reorganization had been delayed at Rochdale—as it had in many other UK industries—while old plant was flogged to death day and night to supply the war effort. During wartime, with its blackout requirements and need for higher output, the asbestos Regulations had been relaxed. At the beginning of 1945, the company earmarked over £2 million for all its plants, though it believed that it might not be until 1950 before modernization was complete. At TBA, the old Harridge Mill still needed urgent replacement, partly because it was a health hazard. Storage facilities were recognized as being especially 'dangerous' to the handlers. Much of the dust-collecting plant at factories such as Ferodo was also obsolete and overloaded.[70]

More serious for Turner & Newall was the evidence from the insulating trades and the shipyards, where the company had claimed that there was no risk. At Washington, the trade unions were starting to take an interest in asbestosis. One local trade unionist had attended a talk on the

[70] T & N Board Meeting, 25 Jan. 1945. 'Post-war Capital Expenditure Programme'.

subject at Manchester and the board were concerned that the man might 'easily have obtained a wrong impression'. However, the directors agreed that in some places the dust conditions could be improved.[71] The question as to whether the Asbestosis and Medical Arrangements Schemes should be extended to the works was discussed by the local board in 1944. However, no action followed, as the company maintained that 'no cases of asbestosis have occurred among the employees at Washington'.[72] This was inaccurate: Washington workers Florence Watts, Charles Jenkins, James Kay, and Mary Keegan had all been suspended or had died from asbestosis by the summer of 1944 (see Table 6.2). No doubt the company had found ways of convincing themselves that these individuals were not truly asbestotics. Jenkins and Keegan, for example, had tuberculosis besides asbestosis; and James Kay had left the company within days of the 1931 Scheme coming into operation, so the company was able to state: 'we are not treating this case as an Asbestosis case for purposes of record at all.'[73] However, at a board meeting in 1944 a truer picture of the health risks at Washington was provided by Sir Samuel Turner's directive that employees in certain jobs should be rotated every few years. This was just as well: some of the processes at Washington were very dusty and not well controlled. In November 1944, a Factory Inspector warned the company about the excessive dust in bag-opening in the Compo department.[74] In April 1946, the company agreed with trade union complaints about conditions in the fibre-treatment area, which was proving unsuitable for expanding demand.[75] By now, the spate of asbestosis cases—Job Bordess, John Scorer, the Watkins (father and son), and John Benson—was beginning to focus the minds of the local directors, who felt that the Regulations would soon be revised.

In the shipyards, too, more evidence was accumulating about asbestos disease. In the war, Limpet was used extensively under licence by the Admiralty for the insulation of warships. By the summer of 1944, Newalls (licensed by Roberts) was swamped with orders: jobs worth £¼ million were on hand with a three-year order book.[76] Washington Chemical Company now employed nearly a thousand workers, with a further 1,500 at Newalls—and there was still enough work for another 500. Despite operating over seventy spray machines (with another fifteen promised

---

[71] 54/2203. WCC/Newalls Directors' Minutes, 28 Sept. 1943.

[72] 55/170. WCC/Newall's Directors' Minutes, 4 July 1944.

[73] 61/1588. J. L. Collins to WCC, 26 Nov. 1938.

[74] 55/314. WCC/Newalls Directors' Minutes, 28 Nov. 1944. Sir Samuel Turner suggested that workers be transferred from the Fibre and Compo departments after six months (a tacit admission that the processes were hazardous), though they would be allowed to return at a later date if they wished.

[75] 55/838. WCC/Newalls Directors' Minutes, 24 Apr. 1946.

[76] Between 1932 and 1945, T & N's net profits from spray were £286,488 (£112,065 of which had been accrued during the war). Board Papers, Dec. 1947.

from Leeds), the company was considering turning orders away. With demand soaring, the ill-effects of asbestos exposure were becoming more apparent. As Table 6.2 shows, several Newall's workers had contracted asbestosis by the 1930s. The first unscheduled Newall's marine lagger with asbestosis was Bernard Stevenson, who was suspended in 1939 and died in 1942.[77] In May 1944, Andersons Insulation, a subsidiary linked with the Washington firm, had written to the latter informing them that one of its laggers had been suspended with asbestosis. The man had been employed for about twenty-two years, mostly working on vessels in Vickers' Barrow shipyards. Andersons initially did not accept liability, but privately admitted that it would probably lose the case in court: 'Further, the publicity might lead to new regulations etc. and we feel that it is advisable to settle the claim as quietly as possible, if we can.'[78] John Collins, who monitored the situation from Rochdale, concurred with Andersons' assessment.

Naturally, the Factory Inspectorate and Merewether were also aware of asbestosis in the shipyards in the 1930s and 1940s. In 1942, an Inspector had watched mattress production at a Newalls' site in Belfast (where the Asbestos Regulations did not yet apply) and had recommended the damping of the bench and floor surfaces and advised the use of respirators. The company complied.[79] The spray process, in particular, gave cause for concern. In 1943, Turner & Newall were told by the Inspector in the Newcastle area that masks should be provided for sprayers and their assistants. Washington Chemical Company and Newalls implemented the request, though they felt that the amount of dust created was 'quite slight' and reported that John Brown's felt that the 'fuss made about dust is largely unjustified'. However, one firm, Fairfields, objected to spray and demanded asbestos sheets instead—a request with which Turner & Newall had to comply if they wished to keep competitors like Cape out of the shipyards.[80]

Merewether also noted some of the problems in spraying after visiting London's docklands in 1943. He saw six Newalls' sprayers at work, all aged under 18, and one of them was not using a respirator. He wrote to Norman Dolbey:

You will agree, I have no doubt, from your great experience and from consideration of the tenor of the Asbestos Industry Regulations, not only that young persons should not be exposed to the risk, but also that the full precautions originally devised for your own sprayers should be carried out. I am not clear as to why the

---

[77] T & N also settled in 1943 the claim of William Presland, a Newalls' worker suspended in 1931. However, he was a scheduled worker.
[78] 8/1379. R. W. Anderson to Newalls Insulation, 11 May 1944.
[79] 54/1478. WCC/Newalls Directors' Minutes, 31 Mar. 1942.
[80] 54/2021. WCC/Newalls Directors' Minutes, 4 May 1943.

positive pressure air line respirators were not used for this work, but in any case there was evidently lack of adequate supervision which is particularly regrettable in view of the under age of these sprayers. The Factory Department will have to consider the problems raised by the extension of this process aboard ships . . .[81]

In his reply, Dolbey admitted that there was 'no excuse for slackness' in applying the Regulations, but then provided one. The success of the spray process had meant that demand had outstripped the supply of available labour. 'The spraying of asbestos', he told Merewether, 'is being carried out wherever ships are being built or refitted in this country'.[82] As regards compressed air respirators, this idea had been abandoned as the air supply in the dockyards was foul and the operators found rubber hoses a hindrance below decks and on scaffolding.

Merewether's prodding evidently forced the Rochdale board to review briefly its spraying policy. In February 1944, Collins, Shepherd, and Ronald Soothill exchanged letters on the subject.[83] They admitted that had spraying been developed a few years earlier it would have been included in the Regulations. They were also well aware that some spray jobs, such as hopper-filling, could be construed as falling within the Regulations. Nevertheless, they took refuge in the legalities of the situation as it stood, only agreeing to provide masks and to avoid employing juveniles. Collins himself, however, was clearly unsure as to whether these recommendations were followed by Turner & Newall subsidiaries.[84] The company declined to include any spray operatives within the main part of the company's private compensation scheme.

A month later there was another reminder about the problem. A terse letter headed 'Spraying of Asbestos: Your Workers' from J. MacColl, a Factory Inspector in Hull, landed on Collins's desk.[85] The letter warned that Newalls' shipyard sprayers in Hull were endangering nearby plasterers, who did not have respirators. What to the Factory Inspector was a simple suggestion that plasterers should wear masks was to Collins a question of 'major importance'.[86] If such men were supplied with masks, where would the line be drawn? As Newalls pointed out, 'joiners, electricians, etc., working in the same spaces, would more than likely make a claim for respirators or "danger money" on our shipbuilding clients themselves'.[87] The problem had already reared its head in the previous year

[81] 30/321–2. Merewether to Dolbey, 16 Oct. 1943.
[82] 30–322–3. Dolbey to Merewether, 20 Oct. 1943.
[83] R. G. Soothill (1898–1980) was a T & N director, who became chairman between 1959 and 1967. The son of a Methodist minister, Soothill was a Cadbury Brothers management trainee before joining the Rochdale company in 1928.
[84] 160/582–95. Collins, Shepherd, Soothill letters, 28 Jan.–10 Feb. 1944.
[85] 12/157. J. MacColl to Newalls, 21 Mar. 1944.
[86] 57/1264–5. Collins to A. Grieve, 31 Mar. 1944.
[87] 57/1276. A. Grieve to Collins, 25 Apr. 1944.

when John Brown's workers on the Clyde had demanded bonuses for operating in the same space as Turner & Newall spray machines.[88] The company directors were especially sensitive to these matters, as they invariably had to sign potentially costly indemnity contracts with the shipyards as a condition for operating there. These indemnities were very wide-ranging and a constant source of irritation to contract firms such as Turner & Newall.

Collins's legalistic mind was employed to good effect in this situation. He replied by pointing out that spraying was not within the Asbestosis Scheme or Dust Regulations and that by supplying its own workers with masks the company was already exceeding its statutory requirements.[89] As to the plasterers working alongside sprayers, Collins described this as 'purely a War-time problem, i.e. on account of the urgency of the work, and I expect that even under present War-time conditions this only happens occasionally. Therefore, if there is any risk, which I rather doubt, the plasterers are only involved occasionally, and I understand that this simultaneous work by Spray operatives and plasterers only takes place when the necessity of completing the job speedily makes this unavoidable.' Anyway, concluded Collins, despite the spray process's widespread use 'there have been no cases of asbestosis among any of the [sprayers] concerned'.[90] The Factory Inspector was clearly not impressed by Collins's response and his return letter brought a simple instruction: 'Respirators should be supplied to the Plasterers.'[91] Collins, not to be so easily admonished, asked by what statutory authority the request was made. MacColl replied that the instruction was made on behalf of the Divisional Medical Inspector and added: 'I should have thought that the provision of the few respirators considered necessary would not have presented any difficulty to a firm of your standing and repute.'[92] Finally, Collins did agree to supply the respirators, 'provided that our action not be construed as admitting that there is any obligation to do so, as there is no Statutory authority for the request'.[93]

The company took the same line, when another Factory Inspector in Belfast requested that Newalls' sprayers should be examined medically every six months. The Belfast manager was ready to comply and also thought that the examinations should be extended to all the boiler and steam-pipe coverers to avoid causing controversy.[94] Collins was made of sterner stuff: he thought that medical examinations would create 'a dan-

[88] 54/1958. WCC/Newalls Directors' Minutes, 2 Mar. 1943.
[89] According to T & N, masks had been supplied for spray work since the 1930s.
[90] 12/158. Collins to HM Inspector of Factories, 31 Mar. 1944.
[91] 12/162. MacColl to Collins, 17 Apr. 1944.
[92] 12/165. MacColl to Collins, 22 Apr. 1944.
[93] 12/167. Collins's draft letter to HM District Inspector of Factories, n.d.
[94] 30/175–6. George C. Hutton to A. Grieve, Head Office, 24 Nov. 1944.

gerous precedent'.[95] He warned the manager not to be drawn into any arguments and then wrote to the Inspector, W. McCaughey, directly. He pointed out that the government had agreed that the Asbestosis Scheme and Regulations did not 'in general' apply to the spray process, so that:

a question of principle is involved, as in our view the Medical Arrangements Scheme does not apply to the Spray process (the sprayed material being a mixture and the fibre damp) and therefore there is in our opinion no statutory obligation . . . for medical examinations . . .

It may be of interest to mention that, although the Spray process was patented some 13 years ago and has been used for several years to a very considerable extent indeed, there have been no cases of asbestosis among any of the employers concerned.[96]

McCaughey replied that it was a colleague who had suggested the medical examinations—though he himself agreed, as during spraying the material 'gets on the man's clothing, floors, etc., where it dries quickly and may give rise to dust likely to be drawn into the respiratory system'.[97] However, he recognized that Merewether and the company were looking at the problem and deferred any final decision. Collins did not deign even to acknowledge his letter, 'as it appears preferable to adopt delaying tactics, it being felt that eventually the Regulations will be made to apply to the Spray process'.[98]

For Turner & Newall, these were minor skirmishes with relatively low-ranking civil servants. More difficult to rebuff was a circular in August 1945 from the Chief Inspector of Factories, Sir Wilfred Garrett. This letter, which was sent to the asbestos companies and contractors (such as J. W. Roberts), was headed 'Asbestos Insulation Aboard Ships' and expressed concern at the growth in asbestos usage during the war and the increased risk of asbestosis. Garrett emphasized that 'while asbestos dust may not have any apparent effects at first, experience shows that, particularly if the workers are exposed to the dust in substantial concentrations, serious results are apt to develop'.[99] The letter made a number of suggestions. Some involved a slight tightening of the 1931 Regulations. Thus, Garrett urged that mattress-making be conducted in separate sheds; and that every effort should be made on the ships to minimize dust. Other suggestions were more novel and involved a modest extension of the Regulations. Garrett wanted respirators for those working with dry insulation

---

[95] 55/320. WCC/Newalls Directors' Minutes, 28 Nov. 1944.
[96] 30/185–8. Collins to McCaughey, 11 Dec. 1944.
[97] 30/191–2. McCaughey to T & N, 28 Dec. 1944.
[98] 55/352. WCC/Newalls Directors' Minutes, 9 Jan. 1945.
[99] 12/194. HM Chief Inspector of Factories, August 1945. This letter was to be cited frequently when workers and their solicitors began making claims against the asbestos companies after the 1960s.

materials. He also urged that no one under 18 should be employed on dusty jobs on the ships; and that respirators should be properly monitored and maintained. An important suggestion was that respirators were to be used by all spray operators. Moreover, during spraying *'no other person should work in the same compartment unless also provided with a respirator'* (author's italics).

The government circular had not mentioned any significant revision of the 1931 Regulations—such as extending the medical and compensation schemes into asbestos insulation. Nevertheless, Newalls were far from happy with the government's suggestions. They argued that an order to wear respirators would cause immediate trouble with other shipyard employees: 'tradesmen would absolutely decline to wear a respirator, in which event trouble would at once arise and the completion of the vessel be delayed . . .'.[100] On the other hand, Collins could see that a blanket refusal to co-operate with the Inspectorate would be impossible. He told a Newalls' director: 'I have the feeling that if we give the Chief Inspector the impression that we are being obstructive and do not want to co-operate, this may accelerate the widening of the Asbestosis Regulations, which might very well be done in a way which would not suit us.'[101] One complication was that Turner & Newall had already agreed in one or two cases that people working in the same confined space where spray was being used (such as plasterers in Hull) should have a respirator. As Collins admitted, 'if it is necessary for the Spray operatives themselves it is equally necessary for those working close to them'.

In his eventual reply, Collins argued that most of Garrett's suggestions were needless. According to Collins, his company was already complying with them and it had an impeccable health record. Several times Collins repeated his assertion that shipyard asbestos work was virtually risk-free. As regards supplying respirators to workmen involved in removing dry asbestos, Collins told the Inspector:

such action is quite unnecessary, and of course if any such action were taken it would mean in effect a very wide extension to the present Asbestosis Regulations. As you know, the Regulations apply in general to manufacturing processes only and do not in any way apply to the finished goods, and in this connection it is very significant that our experience in the past has shown that no cases have arisen amongst employees handling and applying finished products . . .

Your letter indicates that the question of strengthening the Regulations will arise if, as regards workers engaged on heat and sound insulation work on board ship, 'the risk is found to continue', but in our view no such risk at present exists or, if at all, only to completely negligible extent. That this is so is borne out by the fact

---

[100] 57/1273–4. G. Wilson to Collins, 21 Sept. 1945.
[101] 57/1279–80. Collins to Wilson, 24 Sept. 1945.

that (according to our records here) all our asbestosis cases have been among actual factory employees, engaged for many years in the scheduled processes themselves. The fact that Newalls Insulation Co. Ltd and their predecessors have carried out insulation work on board ship continuously and on a very large scale for 35 years, and that no asbestosis cases have occurred amongst the large number (no doubt several thousands of men during that period) engaged on this work is we feel most significant.[102]

Aware that the government's circular could damage Turner & Newall's lucrative shipyard work, Collins was quick to provide shipbuilders with exactly the same reassurances when they asked the company if the new measures were to be applied. One shipbuilder was told that the government's suggestions were already in operation and that Turner & Newall 'were quite satisfied therefore that there is no real risk in actual fact'.[103]

Collins's assertion about workers' mortality was, of course, not warranted. He himself admitted to the board at the end of 1946 that several asbestosis cases had occurred in the insulation division.[104] Table 6.2 shows that nearly a dozen workers at Newalls and Washington Chemical Company (both scheduled and non-scheduled) had been suspended with asbestosis or had died from it by 1945. The trend would continue.

Meanwhile, the government did nothing. It did not follow up the Garrett circular for several years and allowed the matter to rest.[105] Plans to regulate spraying also did not have much priority. In 1948, Merewether was still examining the process and assuring Dolbey that he had no intention of drawing up any regulations until he knew all about the matter.[106] Perhaps Merewether was displaying some of the procrastination for which he was noted later in his career. When he visited Leeds in 1948, the company unveiled its new 'virtually dustless' spray-machine, which had an additional pre-damping drum for wetting the fibre before it went into the hopper. This was assisted by a continuous damping device inside the hopper, which trickled water onto the fibre from a bar. A board meeting in December 1947 stated that pre-damping would help delay the 'scheduling' of spray under the Medical Arrangements Scheme. This proved accurate, as apparently Merewether was 'quite satisfied' by the new technique when he saw it demonstrated. The company did not expect any further complications.

Dolbey soon sent reassuring letters to the Health Department in Quebec

---

[102] 12/355 Collins to HM Chief Inspector of Factories, 4 Oct. 1945.

[103] 12/204. Draft letter to be written by Mr Grieve to Fairfield Shipbuilding & Engineering Co. Ltd and D. & W. Henderson, Jan. 1946.

[104] Board Papers. Asbestosis Fund Report, Dec. 1946.

[105] Similar problems and inaction occurred in American shipyards. See J. K. Corn, 'Historical Perspectives on Asbestos: Policies and Protective Measures in World War II Shipbuilding', *American Journal of Industrial Medicine* 11 (1987), 359–73.

[106] 30/150–1. Dolbey to Collins, 21 July 1948. See 160/581. Collins to Dolbey, 8 Sept. 1948.

and to the group's Canadian subsidiary, the Atlas Asbestos Company, with the (slightly contradictory) messages that asbestosis never occurred among sprayers and that the new 'dustless' damping process would largely discount the risk. Dolbey wrote to Atlas:

I think you should know that we have never had a single case of asbestosis amongst our spray workers, and that every one of our original spray operators still with us is in good health after some 20 years regular work in the process. Whilst I attribute this largely to the care that these men have taken, in addition to the presence of considerable quantities of water vapour when the application is carried out in the proper manner, this is not to say that the old system is entirely safe, as a careless operator can cause a great deal of real dust, and whilst the authorities are of the opinion that the operator himself can be protected, they are much more concerned with the health of other workers in the vicinity, so that unless you do take prompt measures to advise the authorities of the steps that are being taken to overcome the objection, they may think fit to issue regulations, which once established may cause you very serious and quite unnecessary inconvenience.[107]

It would be some time before Turner & Newall would experience any such inconvenience from government regulators. Meanwhile, the industry would need to rely on medical monitoring and compensation to deal with the health consequences of producing asbestos.

[107] 9/1622–3. Dolbey to H. A. Williamson, 6 July 1949.

3

Medical Provision, Diagnosis, and Prescription

it seems evident that our workers generally are a contented lot. Their greatest worry is no doubt the fear of contracting asbestosis. This feeling is intensified by the frequent examinations of the Medical Board.

305/1670. William M. Ellison, 'Observations', 12 Feb. 1938.

For most workers who joined or were employed in the asbestos industry, there was no indication that they were working with a hazardous material. However, for the minority employed in the 'scheduled areas'—in other words, workers engaged in jobs such as crushing, carding, spinning, and mattress-making—the situation was different. They came within the Medical Arrangements Scheme of 1931.[1] They were handed a small booklet, a 'Worker's Register', which explained the basics of the medical and compensation scheme and gave them space to enter their job and medical examination details. The text contained no warnings about asbestosis or descriptions of the symptoms of the disease, though it did explain that workers would have to present themselves regularly before a Medical Board.

The Medical Board system had originally been established to deal with silicosis and so the location of its offices reflected the distribution of the country's dusty trades. The centres were in Sheffield (cutlery grinding and refractories), Stoke-on-Trent (pottery), Cardiff and Swansea (coal), and Manchester (asbestos). Sheffield was the headquarters and Dr Charles Sutherland was appointed there as chief medical officer.[2] Each office was staffed by two 'specially qualified medical practitioners' appointed by the government, who monitored scheduled workers and occasionally examined those outside the scheme. The employer funded this monitoring through the fees for medical examinations and certificates. In addition, the firms had to arrange for the examination of new workers, for as one

[1] *The Silicosis and Asbestosis (Medical Arrangements) Scheme 1931 (Statutory Rules and Orders 1931, No 341)* (1931).

[2] A. Meiklejohn, 'The Development of Compensation for Occupational Diseases of the Lungs in Great Britain', *British Journal of Industrial Medicine* 11 (July 1954), 198–212. See also G. Tweedale and P. Hansen, 'Protecting the Workers: The Medical Board and the Asbestos Industry, 1930s–1960s', *Medical History* 42 (1998), 439–57.

company physician remarked: 'only those with healthy lungs and hearts should be exposed to the risk.'[3] The company also had to furnish a room at the works and other facilities for the periodic medical examinations. Any workers suspended as unfit by the Medical Board (or who died from asbestosis) were to be brought within the scope of the Workmen's Compensation Act, which awarded workers (or their dependants) compensation or death benefit. Coroners and registrars were instructed to enquire into the deaths of retired asbestos workers or whenever death from asbestosis was suspected. In all certified cases, necropsies were to be performed and tissue examined histologically. If the Medical Board was satisfied that death was due to asbestosis, it issued (on payment of a fee) a special death certificate, so that a worker's dependants could claim death benefit. Decisions regarding suspension and causes of death were final and could not be reversed.

At TBA, workers might also be examined by a company physician. The employment of such doctors was not compulsory and in the inter-war period only a few firms—Pilkington, ICI, Boots, and Lyons—had any significant medical service.[4] However, in 1928, Turner & Newall hired the Rochdale doctor Hirst Bateman (1874–1958), as a consultant. A Lancastrian, Bateman had been trained at Manchester University, served in various north-west hospitals, and then had taken over 'Daisy Bank', a practice within walking distance of TBA. The company found it convenient to consult him on a fee basis whenever workers needed an examination, or the company required specific medical advice. Bateman was able to continue his other work as a consultant orthopaedic surgeon at Rochdale Infirmary. His relationship with the Turners became increasingly close. One of his sons, (Sir) Ralph Bateman, was to become chairman of Turner & Newall; another, (Sir) Geoffrey Bateman, became a surgeon and later married the daughter of Sir Samuel Turner III.

In 1949, Bateman was succeeded by John Knox (1898–1972), a Belfast-trained physician who had worked as a ship's medical officer. After 1926, Knox too had specialized in orthopaedics at Rochdale Infirmary and friendship with Bateman no doubt provided the entrée to TBA. On his appointment, the company made his job permanent—probably the first such position in any asbestos factory[5]—though Knox continued to run the Daisy Bank practice. This launched an overhaul of the company's private medical arrangements. An X-ray machine was purchased for the Rochdale factory, a clerk was appointed, and medical records were gradually com-

[3] H. Wyers, 'That Legislative Measures Have Proved Generally Effective in the Control of Asbestosis' (Glasgow University MD thesis, 1946), 4.

[4] R. E. Lane, 'My Fifty Years in Industrial Medicine', *Journal of the Society of Occupational Medicine* 28 (1978), 115–24.

[5] Cape had a physician after 1946, though it is not known whether the post was full-time. BBA had a medical adviser by 1941, though the position did not become full-time until 1968.

piled on all scheduled workers. By 1950, regular radiological filming of the workers began and within a year nearly a thousand films had been taken. Knox's main responsibility was at TBA, where he submitted an annual report on the medical arrangements scheme: however, he advised on all medical matters concerning Turner & Newall and occasionally visited group factories (which could only draw on infrequent calls by local doctors). Knox became chief medical officer at TBA in 1958, when he gave up his general practice. Until his retirement in the 1960s, he was the dominant medical voice at Turner & Newall. A humane man, deeply loyal to the company, he influenced both the company's strategies towards the asbestos health problem and also had a significant national impact on asbestos health standards.

Such was the medical protection offered to *some* asbestos workers after 1931. How did the Medical Board system operate in practice? Turner & Newall's internal documentation sheds considerable light on this question.

The Scheme seems to have been launched smoothly at Turner & Newall, though the firm evidently found certain features extremely irksome. The main complaint was over what the company described as the 'exorbitant fees' charged by the Medical Board for its examinations.[6] Turner & Newall felt that these were a burden on the whole industry and said so when it met the Home Office in 1932 to plead for a reduction in charges.[7] The industry also lobbied sympathetic MPs, such as Douglas Jamieson in Glasgow. His parliamentary question highlighted the 'large expenses incurred' in medical examinations for such a small group of unfit men.[8] Turner & Newall (and others in the industry) complained also about the fact that suspension by the Medical Board could not be reversed and that the Board did not need to justify its decision or supply any further information, even to the worker.[9] In the 1930s, Turner & Newall pressured the government about the frequency of annual examinations, which they said raised needless fears about asbestosis and caused workers to lose pay. (X-rays were done initially in Manchester, entailing a loss of a half-day's pay, which the company billed to the worker.) The Medical Board was unsympathetic to most of these complaints. In particular, Turner & Newall

[6] Home Office, *The Silicosis and Asbestosis (Medical Fees) Regulations 1931 (Statutory Rules and Orders 1931, No. 412)* (1931).

[7] 43/318. Asbestosis Committee Minute Book, re. Home Office deputation, 27 Sept. 1932, 1–5.

[8] According to Sir John Gilmour, in answer to Jamieson's question in 1932, the total amount paid into the Medical Expenses Fund by the employers was £2,300. See 10/1619. *Hansard* clipping.

[9] The Medical Board suspended a TBA worker, Jessica Kershaw, in 1933. They refused to give a reason and when Ellison explained that her mother intended to visit the works, he was told: 'if girl's mother is worrying about the reasons for the suspension, you may assure her that there is nothing seriously wrong.' 37/1253. Medical Board to W. M. Ellison, 9 Dec. 1933.

were unsuccessful in their request that the workers' medical records should be open for consultation by the company.[10] Not surprisingly, the relationship between Turner & Newall and the Medical Board—though superficially cordial—was occasionally marked by distrust and thinly veiled contempt.

The Medical Board stood as the ultimate medical arbiter, but its assessments were evidently not always dictated by purely clinical considerations. This becomes apparent when we reflect for a moment on the situation that Merewether and Price had uncovered. They had found 95 definite cases of asbestosis and 21 workers with 'precursive signs of the disease'—this in only a sample of 363 workers from an industry that, according to Merewether, employed about 2,200 (but actually probably employed four times that number). Yet remarkably, in the first year of the Scheme's operation the Medical Board found only 32 cases of total disablement from 1,516 examinations. This had risen to 60 cases of disablement and three deaths by 1934.[11] At Turner & Newall itself, less than 30 workers were suspended between 1931 and 1933 for the whole group. Even by 1940, the Medical Board had suspended only 142 workers with asbestosis in the *entire* asbestos industry (see Tables 3.1 and 3.2).[12] What reasons can be advanced for such a low suspension rate?

Possibly asbestosis was such a newly prescribed disease that the Medical Board was conservative in its diagnoses. Asbestosis was not always easy to identify, even with annual examinations.[13] This was especially so in the 1930s and 1940s, when lung function tests were not yet widely used and radiographic reading techniques were still improving. It was simple enough to diagnose advanced asbestosis, especially with a clear history, but far less straightforward to identify the disease in its early stages. The transition from health to disease was not clear cut. Asbestosis was treacherous: it could progress for many years, with scarcely any ill-effects on the lungs, then suddenly the worker would start to deteriorate. Merewether described it as a 'deceitful' disease that even in its advanced phase could masquerade as chronic bronchitis, pulmonary tuberculosis, or broncho-pneumonia. This was a particular problem in Rochdale, where

---

[10] 43/279. Asbestosis Committee Minute Book, 20 Jan. 1932, 2.

[11] 37/617–24. C. L. Sutherland, 'Report on the First Periodic Examinations in the Asbestos Industry' (1933); Home Office, *Memorandum on the Industrial Diseases of Silicosis and Asbestosis* (1935), 3.

[12] However, as will be apparent from the discussion below, a worker did not need to be certified to suffer or die from asbestosis (or cancer).

[13] Most T & N workers were examined regularly, though sometimes it could be eighteen months to two years between appointments. The Medical Board certainly developed a severe backlog during the war at all the group's factories. Eventually, by the 1970s the check-ups were made every other year, with T & N medical officers examining the worker in the intervening period—in other words, a *de facto* annual examination.

Table 3.1. Turner & Newall asbestosis cases, 1931–66

	1931	1932	1933	1934	1935	1936	1937	1938	1939	1940	1941	1942	1943	1944	1945	1946	1947	1948	Total
TAC	2													1		2			5
TBA		14	4		8	1	5	6	7	1	13	4	4	3	5	4	2		81
WCC/Newalls	1	2			1			2	1		2			2			6	3	20
JWR	1	4	1	3	10	1	1		1			2	2	1	3	4	1	1	36
Total	4	20	5	3	19	2	6	8	9	1	15	6	6	7	8	10	9	4	142

	1949	1950	1951	1952	1953	1954	1955	1956	1957	1958	1959	1960	1961	1962	1963	1964	1965	1966	Total
TAC		2	1								1	2	2				1	2	11
TBA	5	3	6		1	3	5	7	2	3	4	5	2	2	4	5	5		62
Ferodo													1	1		1	1	1	5
WCC/Newalls	5	3	3	4	5	7	2	6	10	7	4	5	6	13	19	11	19	8	137
JWR	3		2	2	4	4	3	9	6	2	1	2		1	3	1	1	1	45
Total	13	8	12	6	10	14	10	22	18	12	10	14	11	17	26	18	27	12	260

Source: 64/343. List of asbestosis cases.

Note: This is a company listing, probably based on the number of suspensions. It tallies mostly (though not always) with the individual compensation files in the T & N archive (which are unfortunately not complete enough for the author to provide a definitive list). It should be noted that this table only provides a rough guide to the extent of asbestos disease at the company. Non-suspended workers dying from asbestosis and cancer are evidently not recorded and their number is significant (for example, at least fifty such workers died between 1931 and 1948).

Table 3.2. *Medical Board (and TBA) asbestosis statistics, 1931–40*

Year	Periodic examinations				Examinations after application	
	Clinical exams	X-Rays	Suspensions: asbestosis	Suspensions: tuberculosis	Workmen examined	Suspended: asbestosis
1931	**782**	**127**	**2**	**1**	**1**	**1**
	?	*?*	*?*	*?*	*?*	*?*
1932	**665**	**95**	**26**	**2**	**6**	**4**
	16	*2*	*14*	*–*	*–*	*–*
1933	**1,157**	**123**	**7**	**3**	**16**	**6**
	541	*18*	*2*	*3*	*2*	*1*
1934	**530**	**86**	**9**	**1**	**10**	**7**
	–	*–*	*–*	*–*	*2*	*1*
1935	**1,099**	**150**	**32**	**–**	**9**	**4**
	509	*59*	*11*	*–*	*1*	*1*
1936	**1,223**	**126**	**12**	**–**	**3**	**–**
	543	*28*	*–*	*–*	*–*	*–*
1937	**863**	**73**	**4**	**–**	**7**	**3**
	22	*1*	*6*	*–*	*2*	*1*
1938	**1,463**	**185**	**10**	**2**	**10**	**3**
	564	*84*	*6*	*–*	*1*	*–*
1939	**1,547**	**105**	**4**	**2**	**6**	**5**
	716	*41*	*5*	*–*	*4*	*4*
1940	**1,595**	**104**	**–**	**–**	**4**	**3**
	535	*44*	*1*	*–*	*1*	*1*
Total	**10,924**	**1,174**	**106**	**11**	**72**	**36**
	3,446	*277*	*45*	*3*	*13*	*9*

Medical Board figures in bold; TBA in italics.
Source: Home Office, *Workmen's Compensation Statistics* (London, 1933); 113/1668. F. Bussy memorandum, 16 Feb. 1942.

bronchial troubles, especially tuberculosis, were common before the Second World War.

Another reason for the low suspension rate could have been the limited nature of Medical Board examinations. Merewether believed that, even in the 1930s, diagnoses could be made with *fair certainty* if asbestosis was present in some degree and if both physical and radiological examinations were made. However, X-rays were evidently used sparingly by the Medical Board in the 1930s and 1940s and were utilized only when symptoms became very pronounced or if a worker needed to be suspended (when an X-ray was mandatory). Table 3.2 shows that in the 1930s only about one in ten workers was X-rayed at their annual examinations.

Yet these factors should have been counterbalanced by the medical knowledge that was accumulating on the unique dangers of asbestos. The disease was already known to be much worse than that old enemy silicosis. In 1931, asbestosis was killing workers at the average age of 40 (thirteen years before the typical silicosis sufferer). Moreover, the average duration of employment needed to produce asbestosis was only fifteen years, while for silicosis it was over forty.[14] In 1933, Merewether had warned that even a moderate degree of asbestosis was 'a serious and ever-present potential risk to life', because of the ability of the disease to destroy the body's reserve capacity.[15] Other physicians had realized that once asbestosis was established it was a 'progressive disease with a bad prognosis'.[16]

However, a more vigorous programme of Medical Board suspensions was hindered by the economic and political context of asbestosis. The interests and reputation of the employer were at stake. So, too, was the worker's livelihood—the loss of which could be catastrophic in the early 1930s. Consequently, the Medical Board often gave workers the 'benefit' of any doubt about the diagnosis. As one official explained in 1933, regarding a worker whom the Board had not suspended (yet died from asbestosis soon after):

the Board were naturally cautious in certifying as a result of the first examination that a workman was suffering from asbestosis to such a degree as to render it dangerous for him to continue in the industry, and ... there were a considerable

---

[14] P. Ellman, 'Pulmonary Asbestosis', *British Journal of Radiology* 7 (1934), 281–95. Ellman, an east London physician, recorded that even a ratting dog at an asbestos factory (probably Cape) developed asbestosis after ten years.

[15] E. R. A. Merewether, 'A Memorandum on Asbestosis', *Tubercle* 15 (Dec. 1933), 114.

[16] P. Ellman, 'Pulmonary Asbestosis: Its Clinical, Radiological and Pathological Features, and Associated Risk of Tuberculous Infection', *Journal of Industrial Medicine* 15 (July 1933), 165–83, 183.

number of cases which were classified as distinct fibrosis which were not considered sufficiently definite to justify suspension.[17]

One might ask how something could be 'distinct', but not 'definite'—a
subtlety that did not greatly trouble the Board doctors. They had
found seventy-nine cases of 'distinct fibrosis' by 1933, but did nothing.
Ultimately, all that mattered was whether it was 'dangerous for [the
worker] to continue in the industry'—a phrase from the Workmen's Compensation Act itself. Providing that nebulous condition was met, the
worker was usually free to return to the factory with a 'no action' certificate. Clinically diffuse fibrosis was quite compatible with continued work
in the industry, especially since most asbestos jobs did not demand great
exertion.

Moreover, the Medical Board could exempt workers if it believed their
general physical capacity was not impaired or if there was some other
reason. Roberts' carder Arthur Greensmith was issued with a certificate
of suspension in 1939, when the Medical Board told him that he had
asbestosis in its 'early stage'. With the worker's approval, however, an
appeal was made for him to continue carding and the Medical Board
waived the suspension. He was never properly suspended from work,
though he left his job in August 1943—three months before his death from
asbestosis.[18] One TBA spinner was told by the Board in 1940 that she had
asbestosis 'to some degree' and Turner & Newall were also 'unofficially'
informed. Yet she was issued with a 'no action' certificate and was not
suspended until 1942—eight years before her death from lung cancer and
asbestosis.[19]

The war led the Medical Board to relax its suspension policy, especially
if workers were involved with 'wet weaving', where fibre was damped
with water in a vain attempt to reduce the dust. John Mitchell, a TBA
weaver in his forties, was certified 'no action' eight times; but in 1941 he
was informed by letter (an insensitive way of delivering the news) that
he had asbestosis, though the Board proposed to take 'no action in the
meantime'. Mitchell died from asbestosis in the same year. The Board also
took no action over TBA weaver Harvey Hollows, who was told he had
asbestosis in 1941. He was allowed to continue wet weaving until 1952—
two years before his death from asbestosis. James Isherwood, a TBA
weaver suspended with medium impairment in 1935, was allowed to
undertake wet weaving in 1942. He died from lung cancer and asbestosis
in 1948. Joseph Dorber, another TBA weaver, was suspended as partially
disabled in 1935, but as he had no pronounced disability due to asbesto-

[17] 67/351–3. E. Field (Silicosis & Asbestos Medical Expenses Fund), to W. M. Ellison, TBA,
5 Aug. 1933. Grindrod file.
[18] 37/2239. 'Arthur Greensmith, Deceased'.
[19] 122/1167. Memo 6 Dec. 1942. Louisa F. Roney file.

sis he was allowed to stay on as a wet weaver. By 1948, a re-examination found him still fit for light work, but he died from asbestosis in the same year.

Even after 1943, when compensation for coal miners' pneumoconiosis was introduced and the Medical Boards were reorganized as Pneumoconiosis Medical Panels (PMPs),[20] the latter still gave workers with asbestosis considerable leeway. The Panels did not notify the employer when skilled or long-serving workers (those over 45 years of age and with twenty or more years' service) had asbestosis, without the latter's consent. This was a legacy of the old silicosis compensation legislation and Turner & Newall were among those who requested its retention as a 'valuable safeguard', so that old workers might be retained.[21] Mostly workers did allow the Panels to inform the company, but there were occasions when they kept the diagnosis to themselves, an action that meant that some cases of asbestosis were not notified to the company. Even in the early 1970s, TBA's chief medical officer discovered two such workers, who had been diagnosed with asbestosis and had received disablement benefit without the company's knowledge. When he complained to a senior government medical officer, he was told: 'Suspension . . . cannot be enforced. If it *could* be enforced suspensions would put a claimant completely out of the industry and put him more or less on the scrapheap at an age when he would be very unlikely to get another job.'[22]

The Panel told skilled and long-serving employees that it had no power to suspend them unless they applied in writing for a certificate and also that they could continue in their old job, providing that their working conditions did not get any dustier. In 1956, for example, a TBA beamer, Harry Maden, was told that he had pneumoconiosis (i.e. asbestosis) in its early stage, but that he could 'continue in his present occupation provided he work[ed] in dust conditions no worse than at present'.[23] Some workers decided that they would continue working. In the summer of 1935, Ellen Hinchcliffe, a TBA rover in her fifties with over thirty years' service with the firm, was certified as unfit by the Medical Board. Her age and experience meant that she could not be compulsorily suspended and she chose to continue. Dogged by ill-health, she struggled on with her work until the following year when she died from asbestosis. At the inquest, some

[20] After 1943, asbestos workers were suspended with *pneumoconiosis*, and the term asbestosis was no longer used for suspensions.

[21] 43/301. Asbestosis Committee meeting, 26 June 1932. In 1935, T & N pressed the Home Office to allow all workers diagnosed with asbestosis the option of continuing with their jobs. See 301/1590–1. E. Field to T & N, 27 Aug. 1935.

[22] 9/1920. R. M. McGowan, 8 May 1972. See also 9/113–14. John Collins's memo, Dec. 1954. Of course, the company's complaints are ironic, given that T & N had themselves argued against compulsory suspension in 1932.

[23] 123/2688. PMP to TBA, Mar. 1956. TBA moved him to the maintenance department in the same year, but he died from asbestosis in 1965.

confusion and bitterness ensued when a relative claimed that she only continued working because the company had told her she would get no compensation.[24] A Roberts' asbestos crusher, William Birch, was told he had early-stage asbestosis in 1951, but the Panel gave him the chance to stay on if he worked in conditions no worse than crushing. The company found him a less strenuous job at a fibre-opening machine, but only four years later he died after a gastric ulcer operation. An inquest recorded that his death was partly caused by asbestosis. A chief clerk at the Armley works testified at the inquest that fibre opening was 'not so dusty' [as Birch's previous job], adding for good measure: 'It was by his own choice that he continued working.'[25] TBA fiberizer, Thomas Hayde, also decided to continue working after he was certified with 20 per cent disability due to asbestosis in 1969. Both the PMP and TBA deferred to the worker's decision. Hayde did not retire until 1971—six years before his death from cor pulmonale due to asbestosis.[26]

Exactly why workers continued working is difficult to say. Some may have been sensitive to their disability becoming known; others may have tried to ignore their physical problems. Probably economic security was uppermost in their minds. Rates of pay in the asbestos industry were usually better than elsewhere and there was little public safety net for those unemployed. The Medical Board may also have given workers the impression that their health was being carefully observed and protected. According to one Turner & Newall chief medical officer: 'the annual medical examinations acted as a reassurance for the employee, giving a false sense of security . . . [and] . . . by allowing them to remain in their dusty occupation if they so wished . . . the Panel diminished the seriousness of the condition in the minds of the workers'.[27]

Whatever the reasons—the war, reluctance to put workers on the dole, or simply a fear of upsetting the bosses—it is striking how often Turner & Newall 'scheduled' workers were demonstrated at post-mortem to have had asbestosis, yet were passed as apparently free from the disease (or to have suffered from some other disease) by the Medical Board. For example, Lily Fowler, a Roberts' mattress-maker, was suspended with tuberculosis (not asbestosis) in 1938, thus denying her a claim for compensation. Her solicitors fought to have this reversed, since further tests

---

[24] 305/1065. *Rochdale Observer*, 1 Apr. 1936. No Medical Board death certificate was issued after Hinchcliffe's death and no compensation was paid.

[25] 116/773. R. E. Nutt, 14 Nov. 1955. With impeccable Rochdale logic, TBA directors had once argued that in old workers with severe asbestosis, 'the least personal harm would be done to the employee . . . by permitting him to remain at his present work . . . [as] . . . further exposure to a dusty atmosphere cannot produce additional harm'. 161/49. TBA directors' meeting, 12 Nov. 1930.

[26] 46/1006–28. Thomas Hayde (1913–77) file.

[27] Dr W. Kerns, letter to author, 8 Apr. 1997.

had detected asbestosis. However, the Medical Board do not appear to have issued another certificate, which was unfortunate: she died from tuberculosis and asbestosis in 1943. No death benefits appear to have been paid. Florence Fairbourn, a Roberts' weaver, received no less than a dozen 'no action' certificates between 1932 and 1945, and also had an X-ray in 1943. She was last examined by the Medical Board in October 1946 and sent for another radiographic examination, but before the results were known she died in December 1946 (aged 36). The coroner returned a verdict in accordance with the medical evidence: heart disease and asbestosis.[28] Joseph Buckley, in TBA's carding and spinning department, had five 'no action' certificates, before his work as a hoist operator took him out of the scheduled areas and beyond the reach of the Medical Board examiners. He retired at 65 in 1941 and died in the same year from asbestosis accelerated by tuberculosis.

The Grindrod case in 1933 is even more striking. James Grindrod was a 40-year-old Rochdale weaver, who was told by his local doctor in 1931 to give up his asbestos job because of dyspnoea. However, the Medical Board examined him at the factory in 1933, when a 'no action' certificate was issued. He died the same year from pneumonia and asbestosis. At the inquest, the coroner remarked on the 'somewhat curious case of a man having been examined by the Medical Board specially set up to deal with cases in the industry, and they came to the conclusion that his condition was satisfactory'.[29] Coroners were making the same comments some twenty years later. At the inquest of Roberts' carder Harold Kaye, who died from asbestosis and cancer of the peritoneum in 1952, the coroner was clearly puzzled that the Medical Board had allowed him to continue working in the industry after they had found in 1932 that he had a 'slight degree of fibrosis of the lungs'. Kaye was only suspended in 1943, after nine further 'no action' certificates.[30]

These problems in diagnosis evidently continued into the 1950s and beyond. Rebecca James, in TBA's spinning and weaving section, had eleven 'no actions' up to 1947, yet died from tuberculosis accelerated by asbestosis in 1951. Mark Tweedale had worked for thirty-five years in the scheduled areas, having joined TBA in 1920 as a labourer in the carding division. The Medical Board had reached no decision on him, yet by 1955 he was virtually incapacitated with asbestosis. The company found him a job sweeping up in the warehouse, but a departmental memo refers to him finding it 'difficult even to walk about. It is pitiful to see him in his present condition, but he cannot be allowed to come into work and not

---

[28] However, the Medical Board refused to confirm this. See below.
[29] *Rochdale Observer*, 10 June 1933.
[30] A Roberts's manager argued that slight fibrosis of the lungs was not necessarily an indication of asbestosis. 113/1880. Bain to J. Waddell, 7 Aug. 1952.

do a little work.'[31] Company physician Bateman examined him and found him breathless even in a chair. He died in August 1955, aged 57, from pneumonia and asbestosis, having never been suspended by the Medical Board.

Lily Taylor, a TBA carder and spinner, who had worked in the scheduled areas for thirty years, was a similar case. She was given no less than eleven Medical Board examinations and one X-ray between 1931 and 1947, each with a 'no action' decision. She retired ill in 1949 and died in 1957 from congestive heart failure and asbestosis. After the inquest, personnel manager George Chadwick wrote to one of his colleagues: 'There is no doubt that this verdict caused some surprise as Miss Taylor had been regularly examined by the Medical Board during her employment with us and on each occasion a "no action" report was issued.'[32] As this discussion has shown, however, it should have been no surprise as the situation had happened several times at the company. The trend would continue into the 1960s. Sarah Holt, in carding and spinning, was never suspended by the Board, though a medical examination in 1961 showed she had asbestosis, which killed her in the same year. William Clegg, a TBA weaver, was never suspended by the PMP, though bizarrely they advised him to leave the industry due to a long history of bronchitis. He died within a year of his retirement in 1970, with a fatal combination of pneumonia, asbestosis, and lung cancer. Clearly, it does not appear to have been either government or company policy to follow up workers.

These are only a few examples: in the company files are at least a score of other workers (from about 200 cases under the Asbestosis Scheme) whose state of health was misdiagnosed by the government's medical officers. Records for other asbestos companies apparently have not survived, though isolated press reports suggest that the experience of their workers was similar.[33] Such cases not only had serious implications for the victims, but also for their relatives as it tended to weaken their hand when claiming compensation. The lack of a prior diagnosis of asbestosis gave Turner & Newall a lever in negotiations, as such workers were evidently not considered normal asbestotics in the company's eyes. It is significant that apart from Grindrod, none of the above-named cases appears to have elicited any lump sum compensation payment. In cases where the Board had not suspended a worker, but then issued an asbestosis death

[31] 65/0817. Memo by F. Shears, n.d.
[32] 122/1336. Chadwick to J. Kemp, 4 Nov. 1957.
[33] Miss Lily Harris, a 25-year-old worker at Cape Asbestos in Barking, died from asbestosis in April 1934. She had been medically examined by the Board in 1931 and in March 1933 was passed as fit. The post-mortem found advanced asbestosis and tuberculosis. 8/1270. 'Girl's Death Due to Asbestosis: Eight Years with Barking Firm', *Ilford Recorder*, 3 May 1934.

certificate, Turner & Newall were furious. In the Grindrod case, Bateman privately ridiculed the Medical Board's 'claim to pontifical infallibility', while the company formally protested at the Board's decision, declined initially to pay the certificate fee, and clearly implied that the process favoured the dependants. The Medical Board's response to Turner & Newall was brusque. Certainly the Medical Board did occasionally suspend a worker with fibrosis, whose lungs at post-mortem were found to be free of the disease. However, among the hundreds of Turner & Newall compensation files, this only happened about three times[34]— underlining a very conservative policy of diagnosis, which favoured the industry.

If the workers (or employers) were depending on the Medical Boards to provide protection and advanced warning, then many would be disappointed. Charles Jenkins, a magnesia composition worker at the Washington Chemical Company, was suspended in June 1938, but died in November from asbestosis and tuberculosis. John Jesson, a TBA beamer and creeler, was given a clean bill of health six times before his suspension in 1940; he died a year later, a thin and emaciated wreck of a man, from asbestosis accelerated by tuberculosis. Mary Keegan, who had worked with magnesia insulation slabs at the Washington Chemical Company since 1912, was suddenly suspended as totally disabled by asbestosis (and tuberculosis) in 1938: diseases that had killed her by the following year. The experience of Rochdale asbestos weaver William Kershaw was almost identical: same diseases, same date of suspension and death in 1939. Weaver Fred Greenwood was diagnosed as having 'slight fibrosis' in 1935 and was dead two years later from heart failure and asbestosis. George Humphries, another TBA weaver, had six 'no action' certificates, before suddenly being classed as totally disabled by asbestosis in 1941 (two years before he died from the disease). Doris Sanderson, a Roberts' carder and spinner, was suspended in 1935 and died a year later from asbestosis. In 1937, it was stated that the Medical Board was beginning to suspend workers sooner.[35] However, it was often not soon enough. A TBA carder and spinner, Frank Bolton, was classed as partially disabled in 1960 and died from asbestosis four years later.

One might have expected that Turner & Newall's company doctor and medical advisers would have strengthened medical protection for

[34] The deceased workers all died in the early 1960s. They were Joseph Irving, Edith Shears, and Winston Bamford, who all died from pneumonia and other complications (such as heart disease), but no fibrosis (though in the case of Irving and Shears, and possibly Bamford, there was no inquest). T & N grumbled about the Irving case, but admitted such an occasion was rare.

[35] 36/1558. Collins wrote to a manager at Trafford Park, 26 Jan. 1937: 'the Medical Board are now being very much more particular and are suspending cases in the very early stages of the disease.'

workers, perhaps by questioning the findings of the Medical Board, pressing for re-assessments or transferring workers themselves. However,
this never seems to have been done. Turner & Newall only complained
to the Medical Board when decisions went against their interests; they
never appear to have protested on behalf of their workers. Not until
the 1970s did TBA utilize fully its power to transfer workers out of the
scheduled areas at the earliest signs of disease. Meanwhile, the diagnoses
of Turner & Newall's medical staff and their private doctors were often
as conservative or erroneous as those of the Medical Board. John Lynch,
a carding engine cleaner, died from tuberculosis and asbestosis in 1941;
yet only three years before, Bateman had examined him and diagnosed
him as almost purely a tuberculosis case: 'There may be a slight degree
of asbestosis present, but this is doubtful.'[36] The casual approach to
workers' health was typified by the experience of Sydney Hall, a Roberts'
carder. Hall had suffered a severe bout of pneumonia in 1949, necessitat-
ing the removal of two ribs to relieve a pleural effusion. He returned
to his job, but by early 1955 a doctor advising the company diagnosed
bronchitis, dyspnoea, and heart failure. Picking up on the diagnosis
of bronchitis, a director wrote to the doctor: 'I think you consider that
there is no point in referring him to the Medical Board since they would
be unlikely to certify him as suffering from any degree of asbestosis.'
In reply the doctor did not mention asbestosis and was indeed in no hurry
to refer him to the PMP, instead suggesting that Hall could stay at work.[37]
Yet, in the summer of 1955 the PMP suspended Hall with 50 per cent
disablement due to asbestosis. He died in 1964, when an inquest established that he had died from peritoneal mesothelioma due to asbestosis
('misadventure').

   Turner & Newall refused to accept any diagnoses from doctors outside
the company's sphere of influence. Despite the mistakes of its own
medical men, they regarded general practitioners with disdain when it
came to diagnosing asbestosis. In the case of TAC worker Samuel Pennill,
Salford Royal Hospital diagnosed the man with asbestosis in 1945, but the
Medical Board declined to issue a certificate. A TAC manager wrote to
Collins that it confirmed 'how little the ordinary medical practitioner may
know about asbestosis'.[38] This view was echoed by TBA's employment
manager, when trying to rebuff a compensation claim in 1938:

the general practitioner's knowledge of the disease is not sufficiently specialised.
We have had confirmation of this in several cases which have come to our notice
where panel doctors have stated that chest trouble is due to asbestos dust and the
people concerned have not been engaged in asbestos processes ... [Thus] we

   [36] 38/1029. Bateman to TBA, 13 Apr. 1939.
   [37] 114/204–6. Letters between Waddell and G. W. S. Hawbrook, 28 Feb., 2 Mar. 1955.
   [38] 36/1675. TAC to Collins, 29 Mar. 1945.

should not be disposed to accept the verdict of any doctor who has not a special knowledge of the disease.[39]

Yet, when it suited them, Turner & Newall were quite happy to rely on the independence of such men, as in 1935 when it had a suspended Roberts' worker re-examined by a local doctor. The doctor's verdict, which favoured the company, was used to lodge a complaint against the Medical Board about the fact that the asbestos firms (or their workers) had no right of appeal against suspensions.[40]

Turner & Newall workers outside TBA seem to have been particularly disadvantaged with respect to health monitoring. Certainly, some cases were not picked up, though they were diagnosed outside the factory. In the case of Alec Franks, a Trafford Park mixerman, a local doctor in 1966 diagnosed asbestosis—though TAC's medical adviser disagreed. The differing viewpoints were never reconciled and Franks was never referred to the PMP. He was allowed to continue working until his death from heart failure and asbestosis in 1966. He was 37 and had spent only six years at the firm.[41]

Some occupational health physicians have argued that the Medical Board scheme 'worked well and without substantial complaint'.[42] However, the evidence presented here does not endorse that view. Rather, the Turner & Newall experience supports critics of the Medical Boards, who have emphasized (with evidence since the 1960s) regional variations in decision-making and the conservatism of diagnoses. Admittedly government doctors were in an invidious position: the medical arrangements scheme was based upon an assumption, later proved to be false, that by monitoring asbestosis the disease and mortality could be controlled. However, by the time the Medical Board could diagnose and suspend workers the damage had already been done. Even a more interventionist policy would probably not have had a major impact on mortality, as the underlying problem could only be solved by better dust control and more rigorous government inspection. By the 1960s, the obvious conclusion had finally dawned on some PMP physicians, one of whom wrote: 'What evidence is there that periodic examinations have prevented the development of asbestosis and its sequelae? As regards initial examinations the Pneumoconiosis Medical Panels have to decide whether new entrants are suitable for the industry. The question that should be asked is, whether the employment is suitable for the worker.'[43]

[39] Ellison to CU, 1 June 1938. Elsie Shears's file.
[40] 65/1828–9. Draft letter by Bussy to Home Office, 30 Mar. 1935.
[41] 27/1714–18, 1786–8, 1790–1802. Alec Franks (c.1929–66) file.
[42] Meiklejohn, 'Compensation', 207.
[43] J. C. McVittie, 'Asbestosis in Great Britain', *Annals of the New York Academy of Sciences* 132 (1965), i, 128–38, 137–8.

However, physicians did not help themselves or their patients by operating a suspension policy that was far too conservative and limited ever to provide what its supporters hoped—an early warning sign of asbestosis. To be sure, they faced diagnostic problems stemming from a newly prescribed disease. However, this chapter has highlighted other factors, which were economic and social, not medical. Among them was the evident reluctance of the Medical Board to make workers redundant and unemployable, especially during the depression and wartime. The opposition of the asbestos industry, which was a growing economic force in this period, was also crucial. Merewether believed that if the Medical Board had used a wider definition of asbestosis—one that included slight as well as distinct fibrosis—it would have 'raised a panic in the industry'.[44] The medical community also sometimes had its own reasons for not upsetting industry: as we shall see, after the 1950s the asbestos companies not only provided employment for factory workers, they also provided jobs, research funding, access to data, and university endowments for doctors.

[44] Merewether letter to J. C. Bridge, HM Senior Medical Inspector of Factories, 1934. Quoted in I. J. Selikoff and M. Greenberg, 'A Landmark Case in Asbestosis', *Journal of the American Medical Association* 265 (20 Feb. 1991), 898–901, 901.

4

Compensation for Asbestos Workers

Adequacy of compensation has never been a guiding principle of British Workmen's Compensation Law. Payments thereunder have always been regarded, with some justification, as contributions wrung from employers, who collectively and individually insisted upon the 'principle' that the injured workman should shoulder a part of the loss arising from circumstances, which, in most cases, were wholly beyond their control.

> A. Wilson and H. Levy, *Workmen's Compensation* (1941), ii, 113.

For a number of years we have adopted the principle here of treating generously all cases of asbestosis definitely established as such by the Medical Board, and in fact in a number of cases we make *ex-gratia* payments as additions to the statutory compensation. Also in certain instances where an employee (though he may be actually suffering from asbestosis) has no standing (i.e. no legal claim under the Scheme) for some technicality, we pay compensation as it appears desirable to deal with the problem on broad lines, and not to rely on some legal point in our favour . . .

> 8/1375–6. J. L. Collins (Turner & Newall) to R. W. Anderson, 16 May 1944.

Workmen's compensation is a complex and forbidding subject for the historian, as it was for the workers who were unlucky enough to have to claim it. Not only are the numerous statutes and rules difficult to understand, but also most people do not find this area of much interest. Therefore, at the risk of simplifying a complex subject, perhaps we can begin with a simple statement: compensation paid to sick workers either by industries or by the state has never fully compensated victims of industrial disease. Indeed, one might say that the whole idea of 'compensation' is misconceived: for how can anyone be properly compensated for the loss of their health, breath, or life?

The idea of paying workers anything for injuries and diseases was a relatively late industrial phenomenon. Not until 1897 was a Workmen's Compensation Act enacted that promised to pay compensation for work-related injuries irrespective of fault. The Act was not inspired solely by altruism: it was a Conservative government that introduced it and the measure allowed employers to avoid costly compulsory insurance and diluted the threat of common law claims from workers. In any case, the law referred initially to accidents, not occupational diseases. Even when the compensation scheme was extended to industrial disease in 1906, it was limited to specific diseases caused by a few toxic substances, such as phosphorus, arsenic, mercury, and lead. Silicosis, which was prevalent among cutlery grinders, potters, and ganister miners since at least the nineteenth century was only included under the Workmen's Compensation Act in 1918. However, this formed a precedent and laid the groundwork for the government's later scheme for compensating asbestosis.

The Asbestosis Scheme was introduced in 1931.[1] Like the dust and medical regulations, the legislation applied only to 'scheduled areas'—in other words, the main preparatory and textile processes; the making of insulation slabs and mattresses; the dry sawing and grinding of asbestos articles; and the cleaning of machinery.[2] Workers such as laggers could theoretically claim compensation, but only if they could prove to the Medical Board that they were unfit—a difficult task when the medical scheme excluded them from periodic examination. The Asbestosis Scheme contained other serious weaknesses from the viewpoint of the workers. For example, the Scheme came into force on 1 June 1931 and applied to scheduled workers employed on or after 1 May 1931. Workers who had left the industry before then and who later developed asbestosis were not covered. Even those within the scheme had to claim within three years of leaving the industry—a ridiculous demand, given the already known extended latency of asbestos disease.[3] Compensation payments were also, as we shall see, hardly princely.

Despite the limited nature of the Scheme, the official recognition of asbestos manufacture as a 'dangerous trade' was clearly very worrying for the Turner & Newall directors. It seemed that they would no longer be able to deny all liability for asbestosis deaths and shift the financial burdens onto the workers. As the leading firm in the asbestos industry, Turner & Newall were affected by the legislation more than most. Since the employer was expected to pay for medical surveillance, compensation, and death benefit (to say nothing of the capital cost for dust suppression), the company was now apparently facing a major new item of expenditure.

---

[1] *The Asbestos Industry (Asbestosis) Scheme 1931 (Statutory Rules and Orders 1931, No. 344)* (1931).

[2] The compensation clauses within the Asbestosis Scheme covered a slightly wider number of manufacturing processes than the Medical Scheme. This led to a number of anomalies, with some workers eligible for compensation (provided they could prove that they were unfit), but denied regular medical examinations.

[3] In 1939, the time-limit was extended to five years, and then abolished completely in 1958.

As regards compensation, Turner & Newall and the other asbestos firms had a simple choice: they could either insure against the risk or carry the costs themselves. Turner & Newall first approached the Midland Employers' Mutual Assurance Company, which covered the firm's liabilities under the ordinary workmen's compensation scheme (which excluded asbestosis), but did not find their quotation acceptable. It proved much more attractive for Turner & Newall (and nearly all the other firms) to pay worker's compensation themselves. The company set up its own Asbestosis Fund and so made compensation 'a purely internal question' for the board.[4]

The Asbestosis Fund placed the compensation costs on the subsidiary companies that generated them. In other words, the company's multidivisional structure was extended to its compensation system. The Fund itself had two parts. Into Fund A, subsidiaries subscribed $7\frac{1}{2}$ per cent of the total wages paid by the company to employees who came within the Medical Arrangements Scheme. This covered scheduled employees who were subject to periodic Medical Board examinations. Fund B was established to meet the claims of workers who came within the Compensation Act, but were not covered by the Medical Arrangements Scheme. These workers might develop asbestosis and then make a successful claim against a Turner & Newall company. Subscriptions to this second fund were originally at the rate of $2\frac{1}{2}$ per cent of the total wage bill paid to such employees.[5] Table 4.1 shows the number of workers covered by the two Funds in 1948.

All medical and compensation claims were to be cleared at TBA in Rochdale, where a number of individuals organized asbestosis compensation. These were William M. Ellison (1883–1975), the employment manager at TBA in the 1930s;[6] Frank Bussy (1885–1957), who became a TBA director in 1927; and John L. Collins (1892–1963). The latter was the company secretary at Turner & Newall in the early 1930s and remained in that post until 1953, when he became a legal adviser to the company. The son of a successful Rochdale solicitor, Collins's own legal training made him an influential figure at Turner & Newall.[7] An unobtrusive individual (he seems to have taken no part in public life and the Rochdale newspapers carried no obituary for him), his surviving correspondence nevertheless gives many insights into the company's strategy on asbestos disease. He set the tone of the company's response to asbestosis, though

[4] 8/1368. J. L. Collins to Refractories Industries Compensation Fund, 20 Feb. 1944.
[5] 43/271–2. Asbestosis Minute Book, 6 Oct. 1931, 1–2.
[6] W. M. Ellison, who left TBA in about 1943, was the son of a Bolton print finisher. His brother Wilfred J. Ellison (1889–1977) also joined the firm in 1912 and became a TBA director between 1942 and 1949.
[7] John Lissant Collins's brother, Geoffrey Collins, was a partner in a solicitor's firm in Rochdale and was also sometimes consulted by the company.

Table 4.1. *Employees in the Asbestosis Fund, 1948*

Company	Asbestosis Fund A	Asbestosis Fund B	Total
Turner Brothers Asbestos	1,406	–	1,406
J. W. Roberts	200	–	200
Ferodo	7	–	7
Washington Chemical	74	236	310
Newalls	–	1,131	1,131
Turners Asbestos Cement	196	285	481
Total	1,883	1,652	3,535

Source: Board Papers: Asbestosis Scheme to 30 Sept. 1948.

the fact that so many of his letters have survived should not blind us to the fact that he was often merely voicing opinions and policies that had been decided at board level.

Yet although asbestosis compensation was 'in-house', Turner & Newall took an unusual step. They engaged an insurance company to administer the new Asbestosis Fund. In April 1932, it was agreed that any claims would be passed to the Manchester branch of Commercial Union Assurance Company, with Turner & Newall providing information and advice only when necessary. Structurally, this externalized the compensation process at Turner & Newall and distanced the company from the painful business of corresponding with claimants and distraught relatives, whose letters were simply passed to Commercial Union. Workers and their families now had the disconcerting experience of dealing not with the company where some had spent most of their working lives but with the strictly formal procedures of a major insurance company.

For Turner & Newall, the link with Commercial Union proved a bargain. For a small annual fee of 100 guineas (plus travelling costs), Turner & Newall could sideline the problem and place it in the hands of a company well versed in compensation law, 'loss adjusting' (the insurance industry's polite euphemism for limiting claims), and collecting personal information on claimants. The benefits of Commercial Union's approach were soon apparent. In the first claim on the compensation fund, when a Roberts' worker died from asbestosis in 1932, director Walker Shepherd noted the 'satisfactory' final settlement of £254—about £50 below the statutory lump sum payment. He 'pointed out the advantages of such being negotiated by the insurance company, it being noted that the saving effected in this particular case alone represented approximately one half of the fee which is payable to the insurance company for a year'.[8] Commercial Union proved so zealous that in 1932 Turner & Newall had to rein them in, as their penchant for pushing through settlements on the basis of 75 per cent of liability was not only unlawful but was also causing hardship.[9]

It was often a shattering blow for a worker to find himself classed as permanently or partially disabled after a Medical Board examination. In some workers, the shock caused a nervous breakdown.[10] Even those who did not immediately realize the full implications of the diagnosis now had to confront—often well before the age of retirement—a range of social, economic, and psychological problems. Instead of being able to earn their living, such workers had become old before their time. They could face medical bills, a low-fixed income, and social isolation; whilst their families and spouses faced hardship and an increased burden of caring.[11] The main pillar of support for such workers was the compensation that the company was obliged to pay them.

Compensation payments depended on the worker's level of disability, as defined by the Medical Board. Partial incapacity brought a payment of half the difference between a worker's present wage (or assessed earning capacity) and his pre-suspension earnings; total compensation for complete incapacity could not exceed 50 per cent of the worker's average weekly earnings.[12] No compensation payment could exceed 30s [£1.50] a week.[13] Setting compensation could be complicated as Turner & Newall had to calculate pre-suspension earnings and sometimes assess the future earning capacity of the worker. Varying levels of disability, individual circumstances, early retirement, and transfers to other departments in the factory could all influence levels of compensation and income. The attitude of Turner & Newall was another factor. They had little enthusiasm for full compensation and regarded such payments as an 'expensive proposition'. On one occasion the statement was made: 'If full compensation is paid there is no effort made to obtain other work.'[14]

---

[8] 43/284. Asbestosis Minute Book, 8 Apr. 1932, 7. Leeds County Court later spoiled Shepherd's satisfaction by forcing the company to raise slightly its compensation, but T & N still made a saving and it was a sign of things to come.

[9] 43/302–3. Asbestosis Minute Book, 28 June 1932, 25–6. See 10/1924. Bussy to R. H. Turner, 29 Apr. 1932.

[10] For example, TBA carder and spinner Elizabeth Johnson suffered a severe mental breakdown in 1963 after a diagnosis of asbestosis.

[11] See generally P. Bartrip, *Workmen's Compensation in Twentieth Century Britain* (1987).

[12] If a worker's average wages or assessed earnings were so low that the weekly compensation payment fell below 25s [£1.25], then an additional sum could be paid setting compensation at three-quarters of the average wages.

[13] By 1952, under the National Insurance (Industrial Injuries Act), disablement benefit was on a scale of from 5s 6d [28p] per week (for 5–10 per cent disability) to 55s [£2.75] per week (for total disability). See *Pneumoconiosis (Silicosis, Asbestosis. etc.) and Byssinosis* (London, 1952).

[14] 66/893. Memo in Margaret Griffin file, re. a worker who was suspended in 1933.

Whatever compensation the worker received, it did not raise wages to the pre-suspension level. Even the maximum payment of 30s [£1.50] was well below most worker's wages and penalized the better paid, as all workers were treated by the Act as alike, whether skilled/unskilled or married/single. There was no extra allowance for dependants. Turner & Newall's compensation files in the 1930s show this reduction in wages quite clearly. For example, Fred Greenwood, a TBA weaver, was suspended as partially disabled in 1935. His average weekly pre-suspension average wage was £3 6s 10d [£3.34], while his future earnings were assessed at £2 a week. He was therefore entitled to 13s 5d compensation, which raised his theoretical earnings to £2 13s 5d [£2.67]—well below his old wage (and he still had to find a job). James Isherwood, another TBA weaver, was awarded full compensation of 30s a week in 1936: his assessed earning capacity was 30s a week, bringing his total (and hypothetical) income up to £3 a week. However, his pre-suspension average was £3 4s 1d [£3.20]. Thus the cost of industrial compensation did not fall entirely on the employer: it was fully intended that the worker, besides experiencing the physical disability, should also share the financial cost of his injury.

Almost uniquely among the industrial nations, British compensation law provided no income for medical costs or rehabilitation; and it did not compensate for less tangible aspects of illness, such as reduced mobility and loss of status. Sick workers also found that their income now had an element of uncertainty about it: often constant adjustments had to be made to allow for dependants, sickness, and changing employment circumstances. The file of Ellis Taylor, a Roberts' carder, who left in 1943 with moderate asbestosis and then became a bus conductor, shows the endless correspondence and adjustments in compensation payments when a worker moved elsewhere. Crucially, compensation was based on earning power—a highly discriminatory yardstick. For the low paid, half pay could entail a catastrophic drop in living standards. Earnings were also dependent on the vagaries of pre-suspension earnings. The latter were particularly influenced by the lean years of the depression, which coincided with the introduction of the Asbestosis Scheme. One 'sufferer' wrote to the *Daily Worker* in 1932 complaining of injustices in the system caused by short-time working, which in some cases affected pre-suspension earnings and thus the level of compensation. He cited several instances where long-serving disabled workers found that their income had fallen drastically.[15] As Table 4.2 shows, such cases can be found in Turner & Newall's own compensation files. The nine individuals were all totally disabled with asbestosis, their pre-suspension wages had usually

---

[15] 8/1300. *Daily Worker*, 9 June 1932.

Table 4.2. *Asbestosis Scheme: Turner Brothers Asbestos weekly compensation payments, 1932*

Name	Average wages	Calculation of amount due		
		Half wages	Supplement	Full compensation
Peter Flood Snr	25. 0*d*	12. 6*d*	6. 3*d*	18. 9*d*
Joseph Hartley	20. 0*d*	10. 0*d*	5. 0*d*	15. 0*d*
Joseph Lowe Snr	38. 2*d*	19. 1*d*	2. 11*d*	22. 0*d*
Edmund Ashworth	26. 5*d*	13. 3*d*	5. 10*d*	19. 1*d*
Mary A. Wall	29. 3*d*	14. 8*d*	5. 2*d*	19. 10*d*
Barker Greenwood	30. 2*d*	10. 7*d*	5. 4*d*	15. 11*d*
Edward T. Butterworth	30. 2*d*	15. 0*d*	5. 0*d*	20. 0*d*
Tom Slater	30. 8*d*	15. 4*d*	4. 10*d*	20. 2*d*
Stephen Rossi	25. 0*d*	12. 6*d*	6. 3*d*	18. 9*d*

Source: 305/1,500. Asbestosis claims.

been below 25*s* a week, and even full compensation involved a substantial fall in income.

Moreover, the worker's medical condition could obviously change rapidly from 'partial' to 'total' disablement, yet compensation could not be adjusted without more doctor's reports and fresh claims. Workers (who, one must remember, were often desperately ill and living in reduced circumstances) frequently found that being paid became a complicated business, with all the paraphernalia of form-filling, arguments over rights, and problems caused by delays in payment, especially if they had moved out of the area.[16]

Even when the Asbestosis Scheme was replaced by National Insurance in 1946, problems with compensation payments remained. The old baseline using pre-suspension earnings was replaced by one in which benefits for a manager or a foreman were the same as for a labourer. In the early 1950s, total disablement brought compensation of £2 15*s* 0*d* [£2.75], a figure reduced in line with lesser disability. However, there was still a loss of earnings for almost every worker.

Reducing compensation saved money for the company, but the policy had drawbacks: labour would be difficult to recruit in Rochdale's closely knit community if sick workers were penalized too heavily for their

---

[16] For the problems of one suspended worker, who moved to London after TBA were unable to find him a job, see 38/1231: file of William Lewis (*c.*1890–1941). When he died from TB and asbestosis, he was receiving £1 13*s* 11*d* [£1.70] compensation a week plus a 6*s* 1*d* [30p] *ex gratia*. His pre-suspension average was £4 3*s* 2*d* [£4.15] weekly.

illness. The company therefore adopted two approaches. The first was to find suspended workers—at least, those not totally disabled—another job in the factory, instead of simply firing them (as some American asbestos companies are said to have done).[17] Obviously, this had to be in a non-scheduled area. Between 1931 and the 1960s, dozens of sick workers at TBA and at other group factories were transferred to less-dusty asbestos jobs. Many were moved to the rubber-proofed goods department (where asbestos was mixed with various rubberized textiles); others were relocated to the warehouse or workyard.[18] One disabled worker, Harry Clegg, suspended in 1941, was even briefly found a job as Sir Samuel Turner's gardener! The latter also took a personal interest in the fate of William Duffy, a belt weaver, who had joined up in 1939 and had returned home from Dunkirk with respiratory problems. Whether this was due to the war or his job may be debated (as Bateman suspected asbestosis): however, Sir Sam thought him an ardent patriot and 'influence for good in the place' and arranged for private treatment from Bateman and then found him a light job.[19]

By the late 1960s, the transfer policy was still operating. Citing the case of one carder and spinner, who was suspended in 1967, a TBA manager explained how 'transferees have continued to remain in the staff pension scheme and receive all the other privileges appertaining to their original grade. This method of dealing with transferees does much, I feel, to protect the image of the company, and keep up the morale of staff employees in the "scheduled" areas.'[20] On the other hand, it had always been company policy that factory 'efficiency' was to be the determining factor in relocating suspended workers. They were still expected to earn their pay. As director Frank Bussy remarked: 'to employ a man at a higher rate of pay than his compensation, and at a rate he does not earn, is bad business.'[21]

The other approach adopted by Turner & Newall was to pay each worker at rates slightly above the statutory level, so that the injustices of the workmen's compensation law could be softened. One idea, which Turner & Newall adopted in 1940, was to pay suspended workers three-

[17] See D. Kotelchuck, 'Asbestos: "The Funeral Dress of Kings"—and Others', in D. Rosner and G. Markovitz (ed.), *Dying for Work: Workers' Safety and Health in Twentieth Century America* (1987), 192–207.

[18] Sometimes workers were transferred to these departments as a health precaution, even if they had not been suspended. See 66/2191: file on Agnes Allman (1902–61), who was passed fit by the Medical Board in 1957. However, TBA's chief medical officer decided she had asbestosis and she was moved from carding and spinning to cut-joints. 111/793. TBA board meeting, 19 Dec. 1957.

[19] Duffy worked until retirement in 1964. See 46/1314–41: Duffy file.

[20] 66/2314. I. Waters to RHP, 6 Feb. 1968. Quoting case of George Armstrong (1917–74).

[21] 351/928. Bussy to J. L. Collins, 15 Feb. 1936. See also 43/296. Asbestosis Committee Minute Book, 8 Apr. 1932, 19.

quarters (rather than a half) of the differential between their new and old wages. However, it was intended that this would only be paid to very serious cases of asbestosis. A more favoured method of extra payment was the *ex gratia*, a hand-out that was to become almost an institution at the company (see Chapter 5). It helped raise wages of disabled workers to more respectable levels (usually by paying half the difference between the worker's previous pay and his income in his new job). Sometimes it was paid to workers who had retired or to dependants after a death. The company did not publicize this policy; and workers were given to understand that any payment was discretionary and subject to annual review.

Within its narrow scope, the compensation scheme seems to have worked reasonably efficiently at the company. After suspension, the wheels began turning to compensate the disabled worker usually (though not always) without dispute. Turner & Newall made some effort to keep wages and other benefits up to former levels. In one fairly typical case, Clifford Butterworth was suspended in 1945 as partially disabled with asbestosis from his job in TBA's carding and spinning section. He was moved to the warehouse. The company calculated his pre-suspension weekly average at £5 16s 3d [£5.81]; while his wage in his new job was 81s [£4.05] weekly. This meant he was entitled to weekly compensation of 17s 7d [88p] plus 5s 10d [£5.04] supplementary allowance. This made his weekly wage £5 3s 5d [£5.17], leaving Butterworth out of pocket by about 13s [65p] each week.

Yet although the redeployment of workers and extra compensation payments sometimes provided important economic support for ill workers, one does not have to look far to find crucial defects within the system. The practice of moving workers to the warehouse or rubber department proved a mixed blessing. A cynic might say that this had the benefit of reducing or sometimes eliminating compensation payments and also allowing the company to extract some final productive effort from the workers whose health it had seriously damaged. At Washington Chemical Company, for example, in 1936 it was decided to move two suspected (but not officially suspended) asbestosis cases to other jobs, partly to prevent or delay them becoming official or 'full' disablement cases and therefore claimants on the Asbestosis Fund.[22] Ominously, even in the non-scheduled areas workers were still inhaling asbestos dust. To underline this point, it should be mentioned that TBA soon discovered that some workers developed asbestosis by working in the rubber or warehouse departments *alone*.[23] Transferring asbestosis sufferers may have retarded

[22] 53/352/364–5. WCCo Local Board Meetings, 21 Jan. 1936; 18 Feb. 1936.
[23] See, for example, 65/164: file of L. F. Griffiths (c.1891–1937), who died from TB/asbestosis after working in the TBA rubber department. John Binns died in 1969 from ca. lung/asbestosis after 23 years in the same department; Jack Ellis (c.1910–74) died from

the progression of the disease, but such a move was hardly likely to remove entirely the continued risk to their health.

Workers also found that it was all too easy to slip through the compensation net or become enmeshed in various technical and legal problems. Perhaps the worst example was that of William Presland. Employed as a disintegrator at Newall's Plaistow factory in east London, Presland was suspended as partially disabled in 1931 and ceased work in January 1932. Unable to find light work, his claim became mired in the bureaucracy of the Medical Board, Commercial Union, and the various outposts of the Turner & Newall organization. By January 1934, Presland had still received no compensation and was surviving on parish relief and small sums from a Friendly Society. Turner & Newall then began paying him full compensation: but there was another mix-up, when the company claimed that this was a mistake and attempted to reduce his payment to cover only partial disability. An exasperated Presland then hired a London solicitor to take his claim for total disability benefit to arbitration. In court in December 1935, Presland cut a sorry figure. He told the judge:

I feel pain every time I breathe and feel it more on the right—when I take in breath in a close or foggy atmosphere. Cough troublesome in the morning—it is worse—had it a long time—I wake up at night with a cough and suffocating feeling—affects nights occasionally. It is worse in the summer because of close atmosphere—I get phlegm in the throat. Exercise affects my right side—I feel a kind of drag. Cannot work because of shortness of breath—it causes this [pointing to chest] to ache. I appear to breathe more easily in a chair—I am sometimes better than others—the fog affected me this morning—coming from the warm into the cold.[24]

The judge ruled in Presland's favour and ordered Turner & Newall to pay him full weekly compensation.[25] Yet the company and Commercial Union still refused to believe that he was incapacitated. In September 1939, Commercial Union decided to 'have this man watched',[26] and for over a year they tailed and pestered the hapless man. In early 1941, the Commercial

---

bronchitis/asbestosis after 28 years' service. Casualties from the warehouse included Robert Rhodes (c.1884–1931) and Fred Whitham (c.1871–1942). Although coroners at the Rhodes and Whitham inquests returned verdicts of 'natural causes', both men had developed pulmonary fibrosis.

[24] 36/1870–1. Southwark County Court, before Judge Bensley Wells, 17 Dec. 1935.

[25] A similar case to Presland's occurred in London in 1934, when Cape Asbestos worker John Needham took the company to court to claim full compensation for asbestosis (the company had only offered him half). In what the newspapers described as the first court case of its kind, the judge ruled that he was 80 per cent disabled. See 8/1361–2. Cape to T & N, 4 May 1934; 8/1271–2. *Daily Herald*, 28 Apr. 1934; *Ilford Recorder*, 3 May 1934.

[26] 36/1947. CU to T & N, 19 Sept. 1939. It was T & N policy to monitor suspended workers closely by an 'annual verification' procedure. This involved visits to the worker's home and various observations, clandestine or otherwise. See 27/1671–85. E. W. John file.

Union spy told his bosses that he was satisfied the man was not working, but added:

Locally he is regarded as a semi-invalid and is apparently not expected to work again. I understand that his wife is in employment and is the mainstay of the home. I have kept observation on Presland, but he seldom leaves the house and when I called there on a pretext, he terminated the interview by saying that he could not stay at the door long because the weather affected his chest; he was continuously coughing whilst I was speaking to him. Apart from his cough the workman appeared to me to be quite strong and healthy and I can see no reason why he should not be gainfully employed in some indoor ARF or other war work which has become available since it was decided that he was an odd lot at the 1935 arbitration proceedings.[27]

Finally, Turner & Newall decided that the 'odd lot' was more trouble than it was worth and in 1943 they settled Presland's claim with an £800 lump sum, paid while he was still alive.

Almost as bad was the experience of William Bolton (1890–1940), who was suspended from his weaving job at TBA in 1932. The Medical Board judged him fit for moderately heavy work and the company found him a job in the rubber department. Because his new job was initially as well, if not better, paid than the old, TBA did not pay him compensation. Thus they did not feel obliged to compensate him when he began to deteriorate after 1933. Bolton pleaded with the works manager:

I have never had one penny of compensation on my wages or while I was away from work ill. Two years ago I was in a sanatorium at Grange over Sands for six months, and received nothing, only my insurance money. *I find my present* wage Mr Kenyon is *not quite enough to carry on with* as my wife has to buy me all kinds of Patent Medicines and foods, every week, to keep my body up, and *it cost more money than I can afford with my present wage*. Had I been at my own job in the cloth weaving section I would of [*sic*] been earning from *four to five pounds a week*, which I could do before I was suspended, but the last twelve months from my suspension we did very bad time, *three days a fortnight*. I worked one full week in all, and that the last week, before moving to the Proof Goods my wage was *a shilling short of five pounds*, so that is the reason I am writing to you *to see if you could not give me an increase of wages*. I have not been found any light job or anything like that. *I do the same as other men, and perhaps more than some*, so I hope you will look into my case, and give it careful consideration, or grant me an interview.

I remain your humble employee, Wm. H. Bolton.[28]

TBA thought Bolton a 'very decent type', agreed to an interview and also started to look for a better job for him. However, a year later his position had hardly altered and he was now virtually incapacitated. His claim for

---

[27] 36/1902. Memo by C. Addington, 3 Jan. 1941.
[28] 66/1078–80. Bolton to P. Kenyon, n.d., May 1935.

full compensation was blocked by the Medical Board, which until March 1938 maintained that his condition was 'unaltered'. Eventually, Bolton recruited a local solicitor to press his case. By arguing that the Medical Board's diagnosis was 'not prophetic', the solicitor forced TBA to refer Bolton to Dr Bateman. At the subsequent examination, Bateman found an emaciated and anxious man. Bateman noted:

Shortness of breath. Cough, worse in morning. Not much sputum. When he walks his heart 'bumps badly'. He sleeps badly 'because he is all of a dither'. His weight is now 8 stone 10 lbs, but he has been 10 stone 3 lbs. His chest is $31\frac{1}{2}$ and 33 and gives the typical clinical signs of a severe degree of asbestos fibrosis in the lungs. The heart is enlarged, especially on the right side and the pulse is 144 and very irregular, the condition being one of auricular fibrillation.

Bateman concluded: 'This man is totally unfit for work.'[29] Full compensation followed, though Bolton did not long survive and died in 1940.

Similar problems befell Elsie Shears, who had worked at TBA for many years in a scheduled occupation. Suspended as partially disabled in 1935, within two years her condition had deteriorated and she was unfit for any work.[30] Initially, her unfitness seems to have been due to a condition not associated with asbestosis. Turner & Newall therefore resisted the claim for full compensation, while Commercial Union argued that the onus was entirely upon the worker to prove her case. This was a difficult job, when Turner & Newall did not accept the medical findings of any other doctor than their own and the only other recourse was more expense for another examination by the Medical Board. Eventually, Shears also instructed solicitors to take her demands to arbitration. At this point, Turner & Newall backed down and agreed to pay full compensation. They complained about Shears's absenteeism after they had found light work for her, and then haggled about the costs incurred by their opposition to the claim. Turner & Newall were to prove equally unsympathetic to her family when she died from asbestosis in 1947.

Another interesting case was that of Fred Greenwood, a TBA weaver, who had worked for the company since 1913. He was suspended as partially disabled in 1935, when he was about 46, after over eighteen years in the scheduled areas. He was offered partial compensation at 13s 5d [67p] a week, but Greenwood applied for full compensation because of severe stomach trouble and his greatly reduced circumstances. He asked Turner to reconsider his case:

Dear Sir,

I now write a few lines to you to see if you can tell me why I cannot draw my 30/- [£1.50] per week like my other work mates are doing. I don't know if my case

---

[29] 66/1011. Bateman to TBA, 27 June 1938.   [30] 38/1185–1220. Shears's file.

[h]as been before the directors. I have been told it has. You know I have been suspended with my asbestosis since Sept. 28th 1935. Mr W. M. Ellison said a week or two ago my case was not a straightforward one with my other complaint that was stomach trouble. Well I have worked at Turner Bros. for 18 years and never lost a day's work through my ailment . . . Now the truth is Mr Turner I am getting more behind every week with only drawing [illegible—12/-?] per week. My rent is weeks behind and the things I have to pledge come to about £3.10.0 [£3.50] now. I have only what I stand in now and my wife [h]as been at home from work since October under the doctor. So will you please try a[nd] let me know soon what they intend doing with me one way or the other. I remain your late asbestos cloth weaver. F. Greenwood.[31]

To settle the matter, Greenwood was sent to Bateman for another medical examination. Bateman was sceptical of his gastritis and implied that if Greenwood had a stomach problem then it might be caused partly by drink: 'He admitted he took a few gills of beer.'[32] TBA then agreed to raise his compensation to 22s 6d [£1.13] per week, which was closer to the 30s maximum, basing this on Bateman's assessment of 75 per cent asbestosis disability. Commercial Union then offered the advice that Greenwood might well win a claim against the company in the courts. By 1937, Greenwood appears to have been receiving full compensation, but by then it made little difference: he died from asbestosis in November of that year. After the autopsy, Bateman remarked that it was the clearest case of asbestosis he had ever seen.

The fact that compensation was not legally extended to those outside the scheduled areas also caused problems. In 1947, Wilfred Cavanagh, a TBA maintenance fitter, was suspended. Unfortunately, this was not a scheduled occupation and all that he received initially was £2 10s 0d [£2.50] *ex gratia* a week. Cavanagh's average earnings had been £5 10s 5d [£5.52] weekly and TBA thought that this was a case where more than the legal entitlement might be paid. Yet he evidently had to fight for compensation through his solicitors, who hammered out an agreement with the firm that he should receive £2 10s 0d [£2.50] compensation, plus £2 7s 0d [£2.35] *ex gratia*, and 10s [50p] weekly from the Turner & Newall Welfare Fund. This brought his income up to a more acceptable £5 7s 0d [£5.35] a week, but still below his old earnings.

The careers of suspended workers had effectively ended, even if they had a warehouse job: not only was their ability to earn extra money through piece rates, shift work, and overtime badly affected, but also there was no upward mobility. As carder and spinner Clifford Butterworth pointed out to TBA in 1952, by basing his compensation on his pre-suspension rates the company was taking no account of the likelihood that he would have been promoted. Commercial Union, however, pointed

---

[31] 65/225–8. Greenwood to Turner, n.d.   [32] 65/263. Bateman's report.

out that as the Workmen's Compensation legislation stood it was impossible to take this into account.[33]

Older workers, such as those approaching retirement, were especially vulnerable. John Jenkins, a TBA yarn trucker, was suspended, but 'fit for light work', in 1936, when he was 65. Even if he had been able to take up the alternative work the company had offered, he was clearly at the end of his career. All he could then claim was partial compensation: but this had to be based on his earning capacity in the open labour market (which would certainly be very low for an unfit elderly man). If Jenkins retired, then he could enjoy a non-contributory pension of 10s [50p] a week (which was only paid to workers with twenty years' service), but Turner & Newall were entitled to take the compensation into consideration and deduct it from the pension. A small *ex gratia* was the only other income a worker such as Jenkins could enjoy. Eventually, he received neither pension nor *ex gratia*, but was paid weekly compensation of only £1 7s 0d [£1.35] when he retired aged 68. He died in 1939 from asbestosis.

No amount of pension, hardship allowance, or *ex gratia* could compensate for the ravages of the disease itself. Very few suspended workers continued through to a normal retirement. Analysis of 180 or so Turner & Newall workers who were suspended with asbestosis (or who died from the disease) between 1932 and 1948 shows that on average they died in their mid-fifties. Usually workers retired prematurely. To give only one example from the dozens on record: George Armstrong worked only four years in the rubber department and then took early retirement in 1972. Totally disabled, he died at his home in Royton two years later from lung cancer and asbestosis. Retirement, enforced or otherwise, could greatly reduce living standards. Workers at most had a pension and a small *ex gratia*. James Hamilton (1886–1948) had been a foreman at the Washington Chemical Company and was classed as totally disabled by asbestosis in 1946. However, his disease was 'unofficial', as under the Asbestosis Scheme the company did not send foremen in the Insulation Division for medical examination. At the time of his premature death from asbestosis, Hamilton was receiving each year £130 compensation, £44 pension, and an £86 *ex gratia*. His total income was £260: yet he had earned £405 a year as a foreman.

Workers who survived into retirement in their sixties often found their final years clouded by illness and destitution. Vernon Richardson retired from TBA in 1969, when he was 65. In 1975 he was a certified asbestotic, with 30 per cent disability. He rapidly descended into dementia and incontinence, placing an intolerable burden on his aged wife, who was forced to beg social services and Turner & Newall for financial help.[34]

[33] 65/1991–2. CU to TBA, 7 Oct. 1952.
[34] 46/1502–41. V. Richardson (1904–c.1977) file.

The company had one final alternative in compensating workers—it could give them a lump sum as a final payment during their lifetime. Turner & Newall rarely adopted this course of action under the Asbestosis Scheme: so rarely, that in well over 200 claims, a lump sum settlement during the life of a suspended worker was only made on about *nine* occasions before 1970. Most of these cases were in the late 1930s and 1940s, when Sir Samuel Turner was concerned at the bad publicity generated by asbestosis.[35] For some of these workers—Herbert Trueman, George Theobold, John Grimshaw, and James Isherwood—the case-files give a detailed insight into Turner & Newall's (and Commercial Union's) attitudes to compensation.

Herbert Trueman had joined TBA in 1923, working first as a weaver and then as a loom tackler—two jobs that were broken by a brief spell at the US Ferodo factory in New Jersey. He was suspended with asbestosis in 1944 (when he was about 43) and through his solicitors pressed for a lump sum. Trueman was clearly anxious about his condition worsening (he was certified as totally disabled in 1947) and hankered for an open-air life. The company secretary, John Collins, brushed aside Trueman's fears, suggesting that the Medical Board's policy of suspending workers sooner meant that life expectancy was not necessarily affected.[36] Collins stated that even if Trueman left his job at the factory, Turner & Newall would still prefer to pay weekly compensation. Commercial Union agreed and emphasized Trueman's 'favourable position'. He had once earned £8 8s 0d [£8.40] a week and Turner & Newall had found him an office job that paid £5 2s 0d [£5.10] a week and £2 4s 4d [£2.21] compensation, which was tax free. As far as Turner & Newall and Commercial Union were concerned, the job was congenial and 'this is a case of very early asbestosis. No great harm has so far been done to the lungs and the workman is leading a comparatively sheltered life'.[37]

Commercial Union told Turner & Newall privately that if a lump sum was paid to Trueman, £850 to £1,000 would be a bargain. Trueman's solicitors wanted £1,400 and disagreed with the description of his new job, telling the company that his present job was not 'quite as congenial as you suggest. We understand that he has to go into the scheduled part of the works periodically and however regrettable it may be, Mr Trueman (to use his own word) "dreads" having to go into such part of the works.'[38] Finally, a settlement of £1,000 was agreed, plus a claim for 25 guineas legal costs, over which Turner & Newall quibbled.

With George Theobold, Turner & Newall were more forthcoming about

---

[35] 161/287. TBA Directors' Meeting, 2 Mar. 1944.
[36] Collins must have realized that there was no evidence for this in the late 1940s.
[37] 66/1432. CU memo, 23 Jan. 1945.
[38] 66/1442. Hudson & Taylor to CU: letter stamped 10 Mar. 1945.

why they opposed lump sum settlements and why they believed they were 'usually not advisable in the employees' own interests'.[39] A brake-band lining weaver at TBA, Theobold had joined the firm in 1923 and was suspended in 1942 with medium impairment. By 1947 he was totally disabled and asked for a lump sum. Turner & Newall believed that the income from a lump sum would be only small and that weekly compensation would be of greater advantage for the worker. However, as TBA director Ronald Soothill admitted privately, it was also in the company's interests.[40] With many asbestotics dying within only a few years of suspension, it was often cheaper to pay compensation for a few years (or avoid it entirely by finding the worker another job) rather than one big payment. This was more so, as the lump sum at death was usually not large (see Chapter 5) and it could be reduced by up to £100 by deducting compensation already paid.

Turner & Newall's attitude was paternalistic: they did not trust workers with large amounts of money and, when a big payout was envisaged, demanded to know all the details. Theobold wanted to buy outright his wife's grocery business. Turner & Newall and Commercial Union began weighing up the relative costs. According to Collins:

there is *prima facie* no reason to depart from the decision previously made that a lump sum payment should not be agreed to, unless we are satisfied that the purchase of the business by Theobold's wife does represent a reasonably sound business proposition, though in addition there is the second point that as Theobold is comparatively young [53] it might well be that the weekly payments of compensation would continue for a long time, and it might pay us from the financial point of view to make a lump sum settlement.[41]

Based upon their prognosis that five or six years was Theobold's probable lifespan, Commercial Union thought that a payment of £750 to £800 would be on 'the generous side', for a man, 'who must surely be an unsound vessel'.[42] Theobold's solicitors demanded £1,500. However, gradually Turner & Newall began softening their position and admitted the possibility of a lump sum, but only if the solicitors provided information on Theobold's private financial circumstances. The Commercial Union representative paid them a visit and found the solicitors 'quite prepared to give us information'.[43] He then visited the shop to assess its worth. After Theobold had turned down an initial offer of £750, Commercial Union revised their assessment to £1,000. They explained to Turner & Newall: 'Valuing an asbestosis case for settlement really requires

[39] 38/0787. Collins to Asher & Banbridge, 26 May 1944.
[40] 38/0766. Soothill to Smith, 27 May 1947.
[41] 38/0745. Collins to Chadwick, 6 July 1949.
[42] 38/0742. CU to T & N, 15 Nov. 1949.
[43] 38/0731. Report of CU representative, 2 Feb. 1950.

an answer to the comparatively simple question, namely, what is the expectation of life of the workman.'[44] The case was settled at £1,000— easily the largest single payment Turner & Newall had ever made.[45] Commercial Union's prognosis proved accurate: Theobold died in 1956.

The only other asbestosis sufferer who was successful in a lump sum claim during his lifetime was John Grimshaw. A weaver at TBA between 1928 and 1944, Grimshaw was suspended in 1944, aged 56, and left the firm. The Medical Board had certified Grimshaw as 'fit for light work'; but this was a most optimistic assessment, as it was soon evident that he was virtually incapacitated. Grimshaw immediately left Rochdale and planned to find a gardening job in Nottingham. His letters to the company make sad reading, as he encountered problems in gaining weekly compensation payments (which in his case would have only been for partial disability). In August 1944, he wrote to TBA that he had visited a doctor: 'he says I must not think of work yet. When I do commence I will certainly notify you at once. Pleased to hear you are getting on with my claim. It is three months since I had a wage, so you will realise I am getting rather low financially.'[46] Eventually, Grimshaw found a job as a caretaker at £2 for a 45-hour week; but his prospects were grim. In December 1944, a doctor notified TBA that Grimshaw was seriously disabled with asbestosis: 'His capacity in the open labour market is nil compared with a healthy man. He is able to do a little light work out of doors, in good weather, e.g. gardening, but quite unfit to do any heavy gardening work, and is dependent on the weather.'[47] The caretaking job proved too much and he then entered private service, before moving to St Helier in Jersey in 1945. He continued to write to Turner & Newall and asked them if they would consider a lump sum payment. He told the directors:

The climate here is much warmer than at home in Rochdale, and coupled with the clearer atmosphere I find that I am enjoying much better health here than I have done for two or three years past. But the snag is, that, although I have applied all over the place, I am unable to find suitable employment. There are plenty of jobs going in the building and demolishing line, also plenty of farm work to be had, but the work is much too heavy for me. On the other hand there are lots of opportunities to open a small business, such as tobacco and sweets, or a small boarding house. Or, if I had the capital, I would very much like to start a small poultry farm, for which there is plenty of scope here.[48]

Soothill agreed to the payment. Grimshaw's letters seem to have struck a sympathetic chord with the company and there was little argument over

[44] 38/0729. CU memo, 8 Feb. 1950.
[45] At 1996 prices, this was equivalent to about £17,000.
[46] 65/2189–90. Grimshaw to Fox, 3 Aug. 1944.
[47] 65/2167. W. T. Rose medical report, 11 Dec. 1944.
[48] 38/0554–6. Grimshaw to Fox, 8 Nov. 1945.

the sum, which was immediately settled at £750 (though this was Commercial Union's initial offer and they would have been prepared to go higher). Grimshaw's ultimate fate is unknown, though presumably he did not live long.

James Isherwood (*c*.1895–1948), on the other hand, was to prove much more troublesome. A weaver at TBA since about 1918, he had been suspended in 1935 as partially disabled with asbestosis. Unhappy with partial compensation, in 1936 he threatened to take Turner & Newall to court. This was a slightly worrying prospect for the company, who noted that they had recently lost two such cases. Widespread unemployment (which meant that the partially disabled could not find alternative work) and the way in which the courts were interpreting compensation law meant that, from the Turner & Newall viewpoint, it was 'only too easy for these partial cases to become total disablement cases'.[49] Isherwood won full compensation of 30*s* a week, but then immediately raised the question of a lump sum payment of £400. The board opposed this, even though Turner & Newall felt Isherwood had made 'himself a nuisance to all concerned'.[50] 'I do not see why we should do anything more for this man', Frank Bussy scribbled on a communication from Isherwood.[51] By 1938, however, Isherwood wanted another job at TBA. Bussy told him: 'I cannot promise anything definite at the moment, but if we did ultimately find you a job it would only be on the distinct understanding that the annoying actions you have practised in the past would cease and that you would do all in your power to follow the instructions of those in control.'[52]

Isherwood then drifted into the Defence Corps, though he still continued to plague Bussy, who told him not to call round at his house: 'We have done so much for you in the past and you have obviously not appreciated what we have done and we shall now just treat the case on a legal basis.'[53] However, the war meant that Turner & Newall were short of weavers and so Isherwood was exempted to work on wet weaving. In 1941, however, he was still arguing with the company about his compensation, claiming that it was obstructing him and preventing him from drawing his money. By 1942, Isherwood had become permanently incapacitated and his entreaties to Turner & Newall were becoming even more pressing. He again raised the question of a lump sum and this time Turner & Newall agreed. Explained William Ellison, after the board had agreed a figure of about £200: 'The great advantage would be that we should get rid of further liability in what has been, and is likely to be, a very trou-

[49] 66/1746. Collins to Kenyon, 20 July 1936.
[50] 66/2078. Ellison to CU, 16 Nov. 1936.
[51] 66/1775. Isherwood to Ellison, 24 Mar. 1937.
[52] 66/2057. F. Bussy to Isherwood, 18 Oct. 1938.
[53] 66/2024. Bussy to Isherwood, 6 Dec. 1939.

blesome case. The disadvantage would be that the man would go through the money very quickly and afterwards pose as one of Turner's outcasts.'[54] Isherwood, however, had little time to spend his money: he died from asbestosis and lung cancer in 1948, aged 53. Such a relatively early death was the common fate of suspended workers.

[54] 66/1896. Ellison to Bussy, 6 July 1942.

5

Death by Industrial Disease

we can safely say that [Turner & Newall] are one of those firms who
treat their employees, and in particular their compensation cases, on
a very fair basis.

66/1443. Commercial Union to Hudson & Taylor (solicitors), 23
Feb. 1945.

For most suspended Turner & Newall workers, death from an asbestos-
related disease followed with depressing regularity. Their suffering, at
least, had ended. However, the misery of their relatives and dependants
could be prolonged by the dismal formalities of a post-mortem, inquest,
funeral, and Medical Board verdict. The most that they could now expect
was a lump sum settlement for 'death by industrial disease', either
through the Workmen's Compensation Act or by bringing a common law
action against Turner & Newall.

POST-MORTEMS, INQUESTS,
AND THE MEDICAL VERDICT

The usual prelude to a settlement was a post-mortem and then the ordeal
of an inquest, though this did not always happen. In the same way
that many cases of asbestos-related disease escaped medical surveillance,
not all former asbestos workers had a post-mortem and inquest. For
example, no post-mortem or inquest was made on Joseph Macbeth, a
suspended Roberts' spinner, who died in 1949 from broncho-pneumonia
and heart failure, and the underlying cause of his death was never ascertained. In cases where the deceased worker had tuberculosis or some
other severe chest complaint (such as bronchitis), often no further investigations were conducted. In 1969, when Evan John, a TAC worker, died
in Rhoose, there was no post-mortem or inquest. His death certificate
recorded broncho-pneumonia and chronic bronchitis and no attempt was
made to assess the part that asbestos had played in his death, despite the
fact that he had been suspended in 1949. Other workers were simply
missed, even to Turner & Newall's surprise. One example was Joseph
Cowlam, a suspended Roberts' worker, who died in 1949 in St James' Hospital, Leeds. The death certificate stated that death was due to bronchial

carcinoma, but there was no inquest and so asbestos was never implicated.[1]

Coroners could dispense with an inquest if they believed that the post-mortem had revealed the cause of death. In 1962, for example, the Rochdale coroner declined to call an inquest for Edith Shears—a suspended TBA spinner and doubler—as the post-mortem showed no naked-eye evidence of asbestosis.[2] The fact that there was no post-mortem (or inquest) could sometimes mean that dependants faced severe and unjustified hardship. William Seddon, a TBA manager who retired early with ill-health in 1942, subsequently died in 1951 from lung cancer. There was no post-mortem; yet Knox intimated some years later that 'had there been a PM, asbestosis would have been mentioned'.[3] The company discovered the consequences of this oversight in 1960, when a chance visit to the widow in Shrewsbury revealed that she was living in poverty with two semi-invalid offspring. TBA arranged for an *ex gratia* of over £100 a month, for which the widow was profusely grateful. However, the situation should never have arisen.

Post-mortems and inquests were often waived in workers who died suddenly from a heart attack or stroke. Accidents and other events also conspired to hide the extent of asbestosis at death and limit the company's liability. One suspended TBA weaver, Stephen Williams, had retired in ill-health and had moved to his son's home in Huntingdonshire. When he died there in 1969, his doctor wrote on the death certificate: 'broncho-pneumonia and stroke'. But a TBA manager noted later: 'Had he been resident in Rochdale at the time of his death, I feel sure that the coroner would have arranged a post-mortem examination and that there would have been an "odds-on" chance of an industrial disease verdict being recorded. As things were there was no post-mortem, no inquest . . .'.[4]

Even suicide could obscure the facts. Joseph Hartley took his own life

---

[1] Roberts paid £15 funeral expenses to Cowlam's son and daughter, who were not classed as dependent by the firm. His daughter recalled: 'There were two men [at Roberts] who said they were sorry to hear about our father's death. They said that they had a copy of his death certificate which said that the cause of his death was carcinoma of the lung. They said that they felt they should warn us that if we were thinking of claiming compensation from the company, that we should lose and it would cost us money, as cancer had no connection with asbestos. They asked us to accept £18 with their sympathy. At the time we did not know what they were talking about or the significance of them giving us the money.' Evidence of Kathleen Oldfield in *Margerson/Hancock v. Roberts & T & N*, High Court Leeds. Trial transcript, 26 June 1995.

[2] Pulmonary congestion, pneumonia, and heart disease were found at the post-mortem. Chadwick remarked that this was 'quite a remarkable case', as Shears had worked in the scheduled areas for twenty-five years and was in receipt of 30 per cent disability benefit. See 122/2172. Chadwick to J. Kemp, 12 Jan. 1962.

[3] 123/4437. Chadwick to J. Waddell, 12 July 1960.

[4] 38/1328. J. Arnold to J. Kemp, 16 Jan. 1970.

in 1939 by gassing himself in bed. He had been suspended as totally disabled in 1932 after fifteen years as a TBA weaver. Witnesses at the inquest told the coroner how the illness had preyed upon his mind and induced depression.[5] Yet the verdict—suicide whilst 'the balance of his mind was disturbed'—did not mention asbestosis. As there were no dependants, TBA could close its file on the case. A terse scribbled sentence on a letter to Commercial Union, read: 'Nothing further to pay.'[6] Henceforth, TBA did not even categorize Hartley as an asbestosis case—simply listing the dead man as a suicide.

Some coroners preferred to avoid an inquest from the best of motives, as it removed an ordeal for a bereaved family. The Medical Board and especially Turner & Newall had no such sensitivities in complicated cases. At the inquest of Edward Butterworth in 1937, the coroner told the jury that the proceedings were 'quite unnecessary', and then pulled employment manager William Ellison aside and expressed his annoyance at the whole business, as the worker had been suspended with asbestosis and had been compensated for years. Noted Ellison: 'He did not think it was right that the relatives should have the painful experience of an inquest just because it was hoped that the Pathologist might "fish up" something other than asbestosis.'[7] Ellison admitted as much by pointing out that autopsies sometimes did indeed turn up other diseases, such as lung cancer. Thus, there was the possibility that the Medical Board would refuse a certificate and the company escape any costs.

Ellison's comments hint at the fact that even if a post-mortem and inquest were conducted, the outcome was uncertain. Turner & Newall had plenty of opportunity to defend its position. Company doctors Bateman and Knox were first on the scene at the post-mortem. They were not allowed to wield the knife, though the Medical Board did allow them later to take away and examine any specimens (such as the lungs). This gave them and their directors the chance to prepare for the inquest in advance. Even if the verdict went against the company and an 'industrial disease' death was recorded, coroners and jurors were not allowed to attribute blame and the verdict did not determine liability.

One might have expected that post-mortems would have brought home to the firm the full horror of the health problem at the company. Hundreds of post-mortem reports survive in the company files and they make harrowing reading. 'Looks older than his age'; 'thin emaciated man'; 'a spare subject' are typical comments. The state of the lungs inevitably attracted the most attention and the effects of breathing asbestos were

[5] 35/1117. *Rochdale Observer*, 1 Feb. 1939.
[6] 36/1240. W. M. Ellison to CU, 2 Feb. 1939.
[7] 66/1707. W. M. Ellison to Bussy, 29 Dec. 1937.

often all too readily apparent. A typical post-mortem report in 1952 on a 51-year-old Roberts' worker recorded:

Lungs: In addition to being bound by thickened pleurae, which [were] thickened up to 1/8th-inch in some parts in the intercostal spaces on the right side, the several lobes were also adherent one to another. The lungs throughout were of soft india-rubber consistency and this increased density was practically uniform. The lungs were so firm that it was impossible to breach the tissue by pressure of finger and thumb.[8]

Nevertheless, the company continued its approach from the Nellie Kershaw inquest by using its medical officers and managers to challenge any view that workers had died from asbestosis. Turner & Newall's Rochdale solicitor, Geoffrey Collins, agreed with the company secretary's remarks 'as to the desirability of giving the coroner advance notice of any conflict of medical opinion'.[9]

During the Second World War, TBA directors decided they that would need a more heavyweight medical man than Bateman. Someone was needed to counter pathologists, such as Dr Charles Jenkins at Salford, who 'too easily gives an opinion that death was due to asbestosis'. Ellison thought that the company's own pathologist could also turn up evidence that 'would influence the Medical Board in giving or withholding a certificate'.[10] They did not have to look very far. They had been friendly with Matthew Stewart at Leeds University for some fifteen years and he had often advised Roberts' directors on cases that came to inquest. Stewart was now one of the leading pathologists in the country—important enough to have been runner-up for the Oxford University chair in pathology that went to penicillin pioneer, Howard Florey. Not only was Stewart a hearty dinner companion, but he also took a more sceptical view of the evidence of asbestos disease at post-mortems than other pathologists, which no doubt recommended him to the company.

In 1943, Stewart was appointed as Turner & Newall's consultant pathologist. He visited the works and was instructed how to liaise with the company's legal counsel, who was also hired to appear with Stewart at each inquest. As far as Turner & Newall were concerned, the coroner's verdict was 'of no consequence whatsoever', but the company were concerned at the way in which coroners had often 'dragged in asbestosis when there was nothing in the evidence to justify doing so'. Turner & Newall told its counsel:

[8] 61/527. PM report on Joseph Thompson, Leeds mortuary, 6 Oct. 1952. Thompson had spent less than eight years carding at Roberts, having joined in 1932.
[9] 65/470. G. Collins to J. L. Collins, 16 Jan. 1948.
[10] 65/412. W. M. Ellison to Bussy, 16 Feb. 1939.

The main purpose of instructing [you] to appear at inquests . . . is to restrain the coroner from fostering the local prejudice against employment in the asbestos industry and, if the opportunity arises for [you] to do so, to emphasise the prevention measures which have been adopted and the large extent to which these preventive measures have been successful. [You] will appreciate that under present conditions, it is against the national interest that shortage of labour should cause any restriction on the company's output.[11]

At the first inquest at which TBA was represented by its barrister, a verdict of meningitis was recorded, 'with no traces of asbestosis'. TBA felt that legal representation was already having its effect.[12] Meanwhile Stewart proved valuable in an alleged asbestosis death (Mary Fahy) in 1944, which it later transpired was due purely to tuberculosis. Stewart's report confirming this fact, was 'gratifying' to the TBA directors, who felt that his views should be publicized at Rochdale Employment Exchange to counter the firm's recruitment problems.[13]

Stewart's knowledge and authority, however, did not always prove persuasive. In 1949, he was asked to represent the company at the inquest of TBA carder Thomas Butler, who had died aged 58 after only six years or so in the scheduled areas. Stewart travelled over to see Collins and the company directors at Rochdale, where he was 'regaled with an excellent lunch, soup, turkey and extra, and a sweet, with sherry, Bass and coffee'.[14] He was then driven back into town for the inquest, where a disagreement with the local pathologist, John Oddy, threatened to spoil Stewart's digestion. Oddy had found lung fibrosis and asbestos bodies after 'work in a department said to be free of asbestos dust'; and did not believe that Butler's other lung problems—bronchiectasis and emphysema—precluded a verdict of asbestosis. Stewart disagreed and thought that Butler's asbestosis was insignificant. Despite Stewart's greater experience in these cases (Oddy admitted he had never conducted an asbestosis postmortem), the coroner evidently gave Oddy's report the greater weight and an asbestosis verdict was recorded.[15]

Coroners (who were not always medically qualified) found such cases troublesome. A meeting was soon arranged between the Rochdale coroner, A. S. Coupe, and Turner & Newall solicitor, Geoffrey Collins. The latter reported after the meeting: 'I got the impression that the coroner was very anxious indeed to avoid a clash of medical testimony . . . [and]

[11] 301/893–5. TBA Instructions to Counsel, Jackson & Co., Rochdale, 1943. This was where Geoffrey Collins—John Collins's brother—practised.
[12] 161/278–9. Inquest on Stanley Wild, directors' meeting, 29 July 1943. Later it was decided to hold the barrister in reserve for only particularly difficult cases.
[13] 305/1275–6. TBA employment manager (Mr. Chew?) to Juvenile Employment Bureau, Rochdale, 13 Oct. 1944.
[14] Brotherton Library, Leeds University, M. J. Stewart Diary, 27 Apr. 1949.
[15] See 111/603–4. Thomas Butler file.

... in order to avoid this ... the coroner would like the two pathologists to meet and discuss these cases *before the inquest* [Collins's emphasis]. He would welcome the closest liaison between Dr Knox and Dr Manning [his pathologist] and he assured me that Dr Knox must consider himself entirely at liberty to discuss these cases frankly with Dr Manning at any stage.'[16]

The company knew from previous experience that time spent liaising with the coroner was not wasted. To be sure, Turner & Newall's relationship with the coroner was sometimes prickly. At the inquest of Alfred Buckley in 1942, for example, the coroner had brushed aside William Ellison's implication that the victim's age (he had turned 70) was to blame for his death from asbestosis. However, other coroners proved more helpful. In 1928, at the inquest of 34-year-old Roberts' worker, Margaret Marsden, the coroner (Sir William Clarke) announced that he would visit the Midland Works. Predictably, having given advance notice of his visit, 'he found very little dust in the air of any of the rooms', and that 'every suggestion made by the Government Department for the elimination of dust had been adopted'.[17] At the inquest of asbestosis sufferer Thomas Tattersall in 1944, Soothill found it 'gratifying' that the coroner had referred to the great safety improvements at Turner & Newall and that the company intended to reduce asbestosis to very negligible proportions. His remarks were reported in the *Rochdale Observer*, which according to Soothill showed that 'the attention paid by the company to this question was having the desired effect'.[18] Similarly, at the inquest of TBA spinner James Murphy in 1948, the jury was evidently not entirely happy with the post-mortem findings of lung cancer and pressed many questions about asbestosis. The widow stated that three local doctors had told her husband that he was suffering from the disease and on their advice he had left his job in 1944 to work in the open air. According to a TBA manager, the coroner 'explained in great detail that vast sums had been, and were still being spent on improving ventilation, etc., during the processing of asbestos, and that the cases that were now coming to light were really the result of ignorance of the past'.[19] A lung cancer verdict was returned. The coroner at the asbestosis inquest of Mark Tweedale in 1955 also put in a good word for the company and 'went to considerable length to explain to the widow that cases such as this were due primarily to the lack of knowledge and effective preventative measures many years ago,

[16] 302/1355. Collins to Morling, 24 Mar. 1950.
[17] *Yorkshire Evening Post*, 29 Aug. 1928, 4 Sept. 1928. Coroners were similarly soft-handed with Cape Asbestos, one of whose workers died from asbestosis in 1930. The coroner was said to have been 'rather favourably disposed to Cape in his summing up'. 8/1318–19. J. A. Cann to J. Carter, 18 Nov. 1930.
[18] 38/0661. Director's minute No. 2952, 2 Mar. 1944. Tattersall file.
[19] 123/4388. Chadwick to N. A. Morling, 18 Feb. 1948.

and that he knew from personal contact that the company had, and still were, continually striving to improve working conditions'.[20] Such interventions show Rochdale operating as a company town.

The same ethos prevailed at other locations, such as Chapel-en-le-Frith. At an inquest into a Ferodo worker's death from mesothelioma in 1967, the coroner emphasized that the company's dust control was exemplary and that 'no criticism could be levelled at the firm'.[21] It may be significant that the only occasion when the coroner criticized Turner & Newall was in London at an inquest in 1946.[22] Apart from this solitary occasion (when the criticism was purely verbal), coroners made no use of their power to make recommendations to prevent the occurrence of asbestosis deaths.

Turner & Newall, backed by its counsel and pathologist, and aided by sympathetic coroners (some of whom were friends of the Turners), presented a forbidding presence for relatives. The latter usually attended inquests without legal representation and sometimes without any clear idea of the true cause of death. Unlike the company, they were not entitled to any advance notice of evidence. The medical investigations did not always bring enlightenment. In any disputes on the post-mortem table or at the inquest, Turner & Newall were aided by the fact that the diagnosis of asbestos disease was a medical minefield of conflicting views. This was mainly because asbestosis was always linked with other conditions, such as heart failure, stroke, pneumonia, and lung cancer, any of which could sometimes cloud the issue. In the 1930s and 1940s, other major bronchial conditions—notably tuberculosis—occurred alongside asbestosis; and asbestos cancers were already presenting problems for pathologists and coroners.

One thing is evident from the Turner & Newall claims files: the role of asbestos as a cause of death was constantly played down by the company; and whenever asbestosis occurred with other diseases, the company usually placed the greater weight on the latter (see Table 5.1). Turner & Newall's medical officers, who invariably attended the inquests, made much of the fact that there was often, what John Knox termed, 'no naked eye evidence of asbestosis' in the lungs. The phrase occurs in the notes of several post-mortems. This implied that asbestos had played little role in the death of a worker and enabled blame to be subtly shifted to some other cause. In the case of TBA carder and spinner Ernest Hawkyard, who died in 1963 from lung cancer and asbestosis, the company believed lung

---

[20] 65/0805. G. Chadwick to J. Waddell, 27 Nov. 1955.

[21] 27/805. *Daily Telegraph*, 15 Feb. 1968. Frank Pearson file. Yet only a year later, an internal Ferodo report admitted to a dust problem at the company since at least the 1950s. See 27/846–964. Jack Hibbert file.

[22] Cf. 61/130: Frank Watkins Jnr file.

cancer was the main cause of death, comforted by Knox's verdict that there was little visual evidence of asbestosis. Yet it should have been apparent from previous experiences that visible inspection of the lungs was often no guide to the underlying cause of death. Often asbestosis was easily established by microscopic examination after autopsy. For example, in the Grindrod case (discussed in Chapter 3), 'vast numbers of asbestos bodies' were found in the lungs, despite the normal naked eye appearance. The case of Ernest Kershaw (1904–42) shows the company's blinkered outlook on this subject. Despite the fact that Kershaw had been suspended with asbestosis and this was confirmed at the post-mortem, William Ellison, clearly straying beyond his administrative duties into medicine, thought fit to inform Commercial Union that the man had died of broncho-pneumonia and 'a few asbestos bodies were found only after a search'.[23]

When Lawrence Griffiths died, in 1937—the first casualty outside the scheduled areas—Bateman could not accept that asbestos was to blame and instead criticized the pathologist. He told TBA:

This man died from pulmonary tuberculosis and neither clinically nor pathologically, by the naked eye, was there any evidence of fibrosis. I understand that, on pressure by the coroner and somewhat reluctantly, Dr Pooley [the pathologist], who had found a few asbestos bodies and some slight increase of fibrous tissue, put down asbestos fibrosis as a contributory cause or an aggravation of the tuberculosis. I am not in a position to dispute this as I have not seen the microscopic sections but from my own clinical examination . . . and from what Dr Knox tells me of the post-mortem examination I am convinced that the asbestos fibrosis had nothing whatever to do with the cause of death.[24]

Even William Ellison found Bateman's reasoning impossible to understand, especially the questioning of Pooley's integrity. However, Bateman insisted on contacting Pooley himself and gave TBA a report of their conversation, adding a new twist on the inquest: 'The death was due to pulmonary tuberculosis and the amount of fibrosis in the lungs was very slight and had nothing to do with the death. Dr Pooley did however find asbestos bodies in the lungs, and this fact, together with the presence of a slight increase in fibrous tissue, evident only on microscopical examination, made it impossible for him to say there was no evidence of fibrosis.'[25] Now Ellison was able to proclaim that the whole inquest had been grossly unfair to Turner & Newall.[26]

Even after microscopic examination of the lungs (the usual procedure in asbestosis cases), the coroner's final verdict was often subtly qualified.

---

[23] 38/872. W. M. Ellison to CU, 24 Mar. 1942.
[24] 65/0174. Bateman to TBA, 1 Oct. 1937.
[25] 65/0171. Bateman to TBA, 18 Oct. 1937.
[26] 65/0170. W. M. Ellison to Bateman, 19 Oct. 1937.

Table 5.1. *Turner & Newall or Commercial Union assessment of causes of death*

	Autopsy/Medical Board verdict	Turner & Newall/Commercial Union view
Edmund Ashworth (1864–1937)	bronchitis/emphysema due to asbestosis	'natural causes'
Thomas Butler (1890–1949)	heart failure/asbestosis	bronchitis
Alexander Caldwell (?–1948)	asbestosis	previous employment in coal industry
George C. Cryer (c.1886–1960)	cor pulmonale and asbestosis	'small degree' of asbestosis
Nora Dockerty (1918–50)	asbestosis/TB	TB/asbestosis
Kathleen Dougan (c.1921–48)	TB/asbestosis	'no sign of asbestosis'
Jane Duggan (c.1887–1959)	stroke accelerated by slight fibrosis	not listed as asbestosis case
Fred Dowling (c.1877–1951)	ca. lung/asbestosis	ca. lung
Lawrence F. Griffiths (c.1891–1937)	TB/asbestosis	'slight fibrosis . . . nothing to do with death'
James Grindrod (1892–1933)	pneumonia/asbestosis	no 'naked eye' asbestosis, but signs of bronchitis
Barker Greenwood (1880–1935)	pericarditis/asbestosis/lung cancer	'heart condition;' Medical Board certificate doubtful
Mary J. Hagerty (c.1888–1943)	Bright's disease accelerated by asbestosis	Bright's disease independent of asbestosis
Ernest Hawkyard (1904–63)	ca. lung/asbestosis	'death was primarily due to cancer'
Ashworth Haworth (c.1881–1950)	asbestosis	fibrosis 'of little significance'
James Holt (c.1879–1934)	silicosis/TB/asbestosis	fibrosis due to previous work in quarry
James F. Hoyle (1893–1955)	heart failure/asbestosis/lung cancer	'asbestosis was not the prime cause of death'

Ernest Kershaw (1904–42)	pneumonia/asbestosis	pneumonia
Saville Kershaw (c.1894–1935)	pneumonia aggravated by asbestosis	'appears to have died from pneumonia'
Joseph Lowe (c.1875–1935)	heart failure/lung cancer/asbestosis	'death not due to asbestosis'
Joseph Osbaldeston (c.1901–65)	coronary thrombosis/asbestosis	'heart failure'
Mark W. Rush Snr (1883–1942)	ca. lung secondary to asbestosis	'death not due to asbestosis'
John J. Scott (1900–72)	heart attack/asbestosis	'asbestosis ... present to a very minor extent'
George Scully (c.1892–1941)	lobar pneumonia accelerated by asbestosis	'death due to lobar pneumonia'
Bernard Stevenson (c.1887–1942)	asbestosis	'cause other than asbestosis'
Thomas Tattersall (c.1888–1944)	heart failure/asbestosis	bronchitis
Samuel Taylor (c.1888–1941)	lung cancer accelerated by asbestosis	'death due to carcinoma of lung'
George J. Teens (c.1889–1933)	cerebral embolism/cardiac failure/asbestosis	cerebral embolism/cardiac failure
Dorothy Thirlaway (c.1908–45)	lung cancer/asbestosis	cancer
Lawrence W. Wallis (1873–1955)	asbestosis	asbestosis present to a 'minor degree'
Frank E. Watkins Jnr (c.1928–46)	TB/asbestosis	TB. No asbestosis
William Wood (1890–1944)	ca. lung/asbestosis	'asbestosis ... not the cause of death'
Thomas A. Woodhead (c.1892–1933)	pneumonia/aggravated by lung fibrosis	'death not due to asbestosis'
James W. Wren (c.1899–1947)	ca. lung/asbestosis	'no evidence death due to asbestosis'

Source: Turner & Newall compensation files.

Asbestosis was rarely stated as a straightforward cause of death, because of other associated conditions (albeit ones that had often been caused by asbestosis). The medical terminology invariably spoke of death being 'accelerated by asbestosis', while conditions such as lung cancer and heart failure were said to be only 'associated' with asbestosis. Sometimes undisputed evidence of asbestosis was discounted if other conditions appeared more important. According to a pathologist's report, the death of TBA warehouseman Robert Rhodes in 1931 was due to 'cardiac and arterial degeneration'. Asbestos bodies and 'some degree of fibrosis' had also been found in the lungs, but the pathologist argued at the inquest that this was not enough to cause death. A 'natural causes' verdict was returned.[27] In the early 1950s, Knox reported that four TBA workers had died suddenly (mostly from heart failure). All had asbestosis, albeit 'slight' or 'minimal', yet at inquest were not deemed to have died from industrial disease.[28]

Turner & Newall fastened on such subtleties to convince themselves and others that their product was blameless.[29] When Washington Chemical Company worker Dorothy Thirlaway died of lung cancer and asbestosis in 1945, Collins told the subsidiary: 'resist any suggestion that death was due to asbestosis . . . [and] adopt the attitude that it was due to cancer.'[30] Commercial Union also tended to interpret inquest and other medical findings in favour of Turner & Newall.

The company were often quick to point to other industries as responsible for their workers' respiratory conditions. Indeed, John Collins believed that the general term pneumoconiosis, which had been introduced by the government in the 1940s, was most unsatisfactory. The term did not differentiate between asbestosis and any other form of pneumoconiosis, thus denying the company the chance to blame another employer.[31] The fact that several Washington asbestotics in the late 1940s had once been coal miners was enough for Turner & Newall to argue that it would be best not to employ such men in the future.[32] In the 1960s, the company was still blaming everyone but themselves. James Steen, an ex-TBA worker died in 1967 from lung cancer and diffuse fibrosis of the lungs. He had spent eighteen years in the scheduled areas, before leaving

[27] 305/1158. *Rochdale Observer*, 24 June 1931.
[28] 301/802. J. F. Knox, 'Report on Medical Arrangements Scheme', 1953. Such cases, of course, would never be listed in official asbestosis statistics.
[29] In the Taylor case, the widow only received a £1 a week *ex gratia*.
[30] 61/1171. Collins to A. W. Cole, 29 Nov. 1946.
[31] 9/1133–5. 'Miscellaneous Points', Dec. 1954.
[32] 55/1163. WCC/Newalls Directors' Minutes, 9 Sept. 1947. Interestingly, one of TBA's workers, Thomas Chapman, got the worst of both worlds—he was a mason at an asbestos works! Not only did he suffer from silicosis, but the pathologist's report suggested that his death in 1942 was accelerated by asbestosis. No compensation is recorded for either him or his dependants. See 305/879. Chapman file.

TBA in 1941 to start a job in an iron foundry, where he worked until retirement in 1964. When TBA directors agreed to pay his widow a meagre *ex gratia* of 30s [£1.50] a week, one director stated: 'I believe his time—22 years—in the iron foundry contributed very substantially to his lung condition. Shouldn't his last employer make a contribution or split the cost with us'.[33]

Turner & Newall also contested any claims if tuberculosis was involved with asbestosis—not an unusual occurrence, especially in the first decade of the Asbestosis Scheme's operation. Between 1932 and the end of the 1950s, about thirty-seven Turner & Newall workers were found to have had tuberculosis and asbestosis at death. For example, Gladys Hinchcliff, a Roberts' yarn spinner, was diagnosed with tuberculosis in the 1930s. However, she was never suspended and therefore received no compensation when she became too ill to work. At least part of her problem was caused by asbestos, for when she died in 1940, the coroner decided that she had died from tuberculosis accelerated by inhaling asbestos dust. However, Turner & Newall secretary Collins argued, typically, that the inquest verdict was 'insufficient evidence' for a claim, unless a Medical Board certificate was produced. Commercial Union then wrote unsolicited to the Medical Board to highlight the fact that Hinchcliff's work had been highly intermittent (thus implying that her six years at the job was really not enough to cause asbestosis) and reminding the Board that it had passed her as fit in 1938.[34] The claimants recruited a solicitor, but no certificate appears to have been issued; and there is no record that Turner & Newall made a lump sum payout.

Kathleen Dougan, a 27-year-old TBA weaver, was another victim of asbestos and tuberculosis in 1948. The company disputed the inquest findings of 'tuberculosis accelerated by asbestosis' and no Medical Board certificate appears to have been issued. Her mother wrote to TBA in March 1948: 'For the greater part of the last three years owing to her health, as no doubt you well understand, I have been in receipt of no income from her, indeed it has rather been a time of no small expense to me, this being brought to an end by her death (to my deep sorrow) . . . Whether or not your firm will see their way to grant me financial aid is a matter of some concern to me.'[35] The personnel manager replied, in words that echoed those used after Nellie Kershaw's death: 'I would at the outset like to say how sorry we were to hear of your daughter's death, as she was a very conscientious and popular member of our staff. You will realise that to make a grant to you would be rather creating a precedent, and in view of

---

[33] 122/395. J. Arnold memo, 20 Jan. 1967.
[34] 61/999–1000. CU to Silicosis Medical Board, 22 May 1940.
[35] 65/0466. M. C. Dougan to TBA, n.d., Mar. 1948.

this I regret to advise you that the directors have not been able to grant your request.'[36]

Turner & Newall's resistance to any negative medical verdict was not pointless. They knew that whatever the coroner's verdict, the dependants still needed a Medical Board death certificate confirming asbestosis as the cause of death. This was another expense for claimants, who had to pay £2 2s 0d [£2.10], of which £1 10s 0d [£1.50] was refunded if the certificate was issued. For Turner & Newall the cost of each certificate was £10, a sum of which neither the company nor Commercial Union were unmindful. It says much for the mentality of Turner & Newall that, when dealing with the few cases that were classed as straightforward liability cases, the company could still derive some satisfaction that proceedings could be concluded without paying the £10 certificate fee. Even when cases were settled without a successful claim against the company, the fee was still regarded as a significant saving if a certificate could be avoided. The £10 sum assumed even more significance if—as was often the case—the final payout to the relatives was only £15 or so for funeral expenses. Such procedural matters worked in Turner & Newall's favour in at least one case: that of belt-weaver Edmund Ashworth in 1937. Commercial Union urged TBA to wait on a Medical Board certificate, arguing that the death was due to natural causes (although the inquest decided it was an asbestosis case). During the delay, Ashworth's widow died and since she was the only dependant no lump-sum payment was made.

Without a certificate, Turner & Newall almost invariably denied liability. As John Collins arrogantly remarked in 1946: 'the verdict at the Inquest ... is of course immaterial ... as ... we do not accept statements that deaths are due to asbestosis unless we receive a certificate to that effect from the Medical Board itself.'[37] Of course, Turner & Newall's opinions themselves were 'immaterial' if the autopsy report and the Medical Board certificate confirmed an asbestosis death. At this stage, the Board's role was more positive in its defence of the worker. Turner & Newall had little direct influence over its decisions and had no access to its files (much to their annoyance). For better or worse, it gave a final decision as to the cause of death. Yet its certificates were remarkably rare. As Table 5.2 shows, for the whole of the asbestos industry only sixteen death certificates for asbestosis were issued before 1940; eight of them relating to TBA workers.[38] Meanwhile, in the same period the Factory Inspectorate had listed well over a hundred deaths directly attributable to asbestosis. One

---

[36] 65/0465. 17 Mar. 1948. Other asbestos companies seem to have had exactly the same attitude. The secretary of Cape Asbestos, W. A. Godfrey, wrote to Shepherd in 1932 concerning an inquest on one of its workers. The verdict had been 'asbestosis accelerated by tuberculosis'. Godfrey believed 'the verdict would have been more correctly given as tuberculosis accelerated by asbestosis, if indeed the latter existed'. 9/671. Letter, 8 Apr. 1932.

[37] 61/1171. Collins to Cole, WCC, 29 Nov. 1946. Dorothy Thirlaway file.

[38] A few were also issued for asbestosis and tuberculosis.

Table 5.2. *Medical Board (and TBA) asbestosis death statistics, 1931–40*

Year	Deaths			
	Applications		Certified	
1931	**1**	?	**1**	?
1932	**2**	–	**2**	–
1933	**5**	*1*	**1**	*1*
1934	**2**	*1*	**2**	*1*
1935	**2**	*1*	**1**	*1*
1936	**1**	–	**1**	–
1937	**–**	–	**–**	–
1938	**1**	–	**–**	–
1939	**3**	*2*	**4**	*2*
1940	**6**	*3*	**4**	*3*
Total	**23**	*8*	**16**	*8*

Medical Board figures in bold; TBA in italic.

Source: Home Office, *Workmen's Compensation Statistics* (London, 1933); 113/1,668. F. Bussy memorandum, 16 Feb. 1942.

reason for the low number is that certificates were only issued on *application* and payment by relatives. Another is that, although the Medical Board usually rubber-stamped the verdict of the inquests (which its representatives rarely attended), it could also occasionally reverse decisions. Again, this highlights the rule of thumb element in medical diagnosis and no doubt it gave an unpleasant surprise to dependants. In 1933, for example, Thomas Woodhead, a suspended TBA worker, died after a bout of influenza. The pathologist, Dr J. S. Pooley, reported to the inquest that Woodhead had died of broncho-pneumonia. However, he had also found asbestosis and large numbers of asbestos bodies—evidence which influenced the jury. They agreed with Pooley that the death was due to pneumonia, but believed that asbestosis had worsened the condition. William Ellison was furious with the verdict, arguing that Pooley's evidence 'had contained no suggestion whatever of such a possibility and it therefore seems to be quite wrong that a jury of ignorant laymen should be allowed to adjudicate upon a matter which only the medical profession could decide'.[39] Ellison need not have distressed himself: the relatives had their request for a Medical Board certificate rebuffed.

---

[39] 305/1009–10. W. M. Ellison to P. Kenyon, 9 Feb. 1933.

In 1946, the inquest on Roberts' weaver Florence Fairbourn had returned a verdict of death by 'pericarditis, following asbestosis of the lungs and pleura'—yet the Medical Board refused to issue a certificate confirming that death was due to asbestosis. How the Medical Board reached this decision is unknown, because its files have not survived: yet it had important repercussions for the family, as Fairbourn supported her husband (a clerk, who was said to have been a semi-invalid), a young daughter and widowed mother. There is no record of any lump sum payment to the family.[40] In 1947 the Medical Board reversed another inquest's asbestosis/lung cancer verdict, by stating that the deceased did not have asbestosis.[41] Similarly, after TBA asbestos weaver Charles Crewe's death in 1953, the inquest's finding of sudden heart failure seems to have influenced the Medical Board more than the fact that he also had significant asbestosis. They refused to confirm that death was due to industrial disease.

ASBESTOS WIDOWS

Once a Medical Board/PMP certificate had been issued, one might have expected that dependants would receive a lump sum settlement as a formality. This sum was set by the Workman's Compensation Act at a maximum of £300 (though extra amounts for dependent children could raise this to £600). Why £300? This was the figure that had been set by the Compensation Act of 1897 and it was clearly regarded as set in stone.[42] These sums did not represent punitive damages, which have never been awarded against British firms (even in common law actions). They were certainly not very generous for families that had often lost their main breadwinner. By the late 1930s and during the 1940s, the average earnings of Turner & Newall workers ranged between £200 and £350 a year. For most, £300 was much less than two years' wages. By the 1960s (when a £400 limit was in place), death benefit for the dependants of workers suspended with asbestosis had clearly fallen far behind the rate of inflation.[43] For example, the family of TBA weaver William Fletcher received

[40] As noted above, Florence Fairbourn had been frequently examined by the Medical Board, but never suspended. Did the Board feel that they were unable to change their verdict and admit their mistake?

[41] 66/2340. G. H. Ashman file. Ashman's employment record was interesting, as he had only worked at T & N for 16 months. However, his previous employment had been with a brake-lining manufacturers in Bury for 13 years. Did this previous occupation, which was not 'scheduled', influence the Medical Board in believing that this worker (who was never suspended) could never have developed significant asbestosis?

[42] In 1943, however, the basic figure was raised to £400.

[43] To appreciate better the worth of lump sum payments, if 1996 is taken as a baseline for the value of £1, then its purchasing power would have been about 40× in 1935, 20× in 1946, 17× in 1950, and 12× in 1960. Thus a £300 lump sum in the 1930s would be worth about £12,000; in 1960, about £3,600.

only £300 in 1960, in what the company admitted was a straightforward asbestosis case. Moreover, dependants rarely received the maximum payout. This can be demonstrated by analysing the company's claims files, upwards of 1,500 of which have survived. Approximately 400 files relate to pre-1970 claims and these show that only a quarter of claimants received *any* lump sum payment. Only 77 cases merited a payment of £300 or more (and no payment before 1960 exceeded £1,000). Even allowing for the fact that some claims may have been legitimately rebuffed or that some payments may not have been recorded in the files, or paid by the state, this was still a scandalously low figure.

Numerous factors hindered dependants receiving the full sum. The first was that the payment was calculated by a statutory formula. This allowed the firm to deduct from the lump sum the compensation already paid to any suspended worker up to a maximum of £100. Effectively, this meant that in the case of suspended and compensated workers, Turner & Newall were partially reimbursed for its costs and the maximum that dependants could claim was often £200.

Compensation was also far from automatic. Dependants and relatives not only needed a Medical Board certificate, they also still had to *claim* by the formal channels (in which, of course, few of them were expert or even knew about). Some relatives evidently never claimed. When brake-band weaver Samuel Taylor died in 1941, he was living with (and probably supporting) his 60-year-old sister: but she never made a claim. Bereaved families who believed that a personal letter to the company informing them of their plight would elicit a sympathetic response and start the compensation wheels turning were to be sadly disappointed. Such letters were likely to be ignored. In 1935, the family of Dorothy Keily, a 32-year-old Newalls' worker, wrote to the company to inform them of her death after 'terrible suffering'. The letter was not acknowledged.[44] When Washington Chemical worker James Kay died in 1938 from asbestosis, his widow (who had five children) asked for compensation. But the company, which denied liability because Kay had left within days of the Asbestosis Scheme's enactment, was reluctant to reply to her letter and eventually decided to ignore it. Joseph Buckley's widow failed initially to make a claim when her husband died of asbestosis in 1942, a fact which Commercial Union found surprising. A Rochdale manager scribbled on the Commercial Union letter: 'It can only be assumed that the widow expects the issue of a certificate will automatically bring compensation. Presumably we should tell CU that no further steps should be taken if we do not get a claim.'[45] Both Turner & Newall and Commercial Union knew that

---

[44] Keily died from asbestosis and TB. The final payment was a £25 *ex gratia*.
[45] 66/2454. CU to TBA, 6 May 1942.

claims needed to be registered within six months to count within the Compensation Acts. In one instance—the asbestosis case of Washington worker, Bernard Stevenson—the widow did not make a formal claim until 1947. This was five years after the man's death. The company eventually paid a £200 settlement, but not before it had tried to wriggle out of payment by invoking the six-month rule. Collins felt that the claim should be resisted entirely: 'After all, the widow has apparently existed during the five years since the death without any help from us.'[46]

Claimants who persisted, however, soon came up against Turner & Newall's contentious attitude to compensation. Certainly, the company occasionally behaved relatively reasonably towards workers and their families. When cardroom jobber Edwin Holden died of asbestosis in 1943, Turner & Newall admitted it was a straightforward case and paid the widow a £397 lump sum and also 25s [£1.25] a week *ex gratia*. When Frank Travis died in 1962 from a stroke, Turner & Newall accepted that there was a 'moral' argument that the death was due to asbestosis and paid £300 to the widow, even though there had been no inquest and no certificate issued.[47] Indeed, in one case that was settled in 1948 for £360, a solicitor wrote to Commercial Union that it was 'so refreshing to find an employer behaving so reasonably'.[48]

However, these cases were exceptional. The Turner & Newall compensation files generally tell a depressing story of how the company often managed to escape its financial liabilities. The documents show the company following the attitudes laid down by the founders: 'that doctors' opinions and judgements should be challenged; that the interests of the company, as understood by the board, were paramount; and that the appropriate defensive tactics were denial, a legalistic view of the situation, and litigation.'[49]

The company was helped by the small print in the legislation. Workers who had left the industry by 1931 were not eligible for compensation. For example, Robert Kershaw, a TBA employee, had ceased work in September 1930 due to illness and survived on welfare hand-outs. Turner & Newall kept him on their books and no doubt the sick worker was expected to return. However, when he died in June 1931 from asbestosis (a fact confirmed by the Medical Board), the company resisted any claim for him, because he was not actually working when the Scheme came into

[46] 36/2085/6. Collins to CU, 24 Jan. 1947.
[47] Significantly, the amount was paid direct and not via the Court Registrar.
[48] Wilfred Cavanagh file: 38/1277. W. H. Thompson to CU, 28 July 1948. This comment, though, may have been made ironically, in view of Thompson's previous experience with T & N over the Lancaster case. See below.
[49] D. J. Jeremy, 'Corporate Responses to the Emergent Recognition of a Health Hazard in the UK Asbestos Industry: The Case of Turner & Newall, 1920–1960', *Business and Economic History* 24 (Fall 1995), 254–65, 258.

operation on 1 May 1931. The company went to the expense and trouble of seeking the opinion of a barrister, which proved inconclusive. However, Turner & Newall never paid a lump sum to the widow, though after some deliberation they paid her medical and legal bills and also began paying her an *ex gratia*.[50] At least seven other TBA workers—Arthur Butterworth, John Butterworth, Richard Hardman, Thomas Stott, John Torkington, Marion Trevor, and Herbert Wright—had also ceased work by 1931 or died within months of the Scheme's launch. All these workers died from asbestosis; yet neither they nor their dependants received official compensation, apart from the occasional *ex-gratia* payment.[51] Many more similar deaths must have passed unrecorded in the early 1930s.

Workers who had left a scheduled occupation for more than three years were also outside the scope of compensation.[52] Although the company had agreed with the Home Office that in straightforward asbestosis cases they would *not* take advantage of the time-limit rule,[53] these promises were later forgotten. John Lancaster had worked in the scheduled processes at TBA between 1931 and 1936 and had then left. He had developed asbestosis by 1943 and three years later, when he was aged about 40, the disease killed him. His dependent widow made a claim against Turner & Newall through her London solicitors, W. H. Thompson. However, the company denied liability and invoked the three-year rule. Frustrated by the Rochdale management, Thompson took the unusual step of writing to Sir Samuel Turner at his home in High Wycombe (where Thompson also lived). The solicitor expressed puzzlement as to why a successful company such as Turner & Newall would want to make an issue of an unjust rule and asked Turner whether the company was prepared to do anything apart from legal obligations.

Turner was outraged by this unsolicited letter. Ignoring Thompson, he wrote to TBA director Soothill in terms which belied his image as a caring employer:

I enclose a letter I have received from W. H. Thompson, Solicitor, about whom I know nothing.

What I don't like about this letter is the suggestion that we take advantage of

[50] 161/77. Directors' Board Minutes, 9 Oct. 1931. The board noted that Kershaw died 'from what was presumed to be asbestosis'.

[51] Besides Kershaw, the mother of Marion Trevor is known to have received an *ex gratia*.

[52] Time-limits also bedeviled workers' claims for diseases in other Lancashire trades. An example is mule-spinners' cancer, a painful scrotal disease caused by engineering oils, which also has a very long latency. Only those spinners who had been employed in the industry within a year of contracting the cancer could claim compensation. See T. Wyke, 'Mule Spinners' Cancer', in A. Fowler and T. Wyke (eds.), *The Barefoot Aristocrats* (1987), 184–96.

[53] WCC/Newalls board meeting 22 Oct. 1946: minute 2659. The time limit was increased to five years in 1939 and abolished in 1958.

the victims of asbestosis. In your reply I think it might be well to inform this man that it has been our consistent practice to pay far more to the victims of this industrial disease, than is prescribed by law, but also to tell him if you can, discreetly, that in practice there has been much abuse in administering the law, as we have many cases of death obviously caused by the usual diseases to which man is heir, but if by any chance a few particles of asbestos happen to be found in the lung, then coroners invariably bring in a verdict which involves a claim.

I don't like writing to a man of this sort, and if you could arrange for someone to see him some time I think it would be better, because he may be one of the type of solicitors who take up such cases on a percentage basis and he might very well make an improper use of anything you might say in a letter.[54]

Finally, Turner & Newall agreed to an *ex gratia* of £450, but not until—as a point of principle—they had forced the family and Thompson to withdraw their threat of legal action.

The biggest obstacle to many claimants was that the Asbestosis Scheme applied only to workers within the scheduled areas: those outside that pale were largely denied the benefits of medical monitoring, dust reduction measures, and any claim against the company for asbestos-related disease. More than a dozen deaths in the Turner & Newall files before 1948 relate to factory workers who had the misfortune to work outside the scheduled areas. The first at TBA was Lawrence Griffiths, a 46-year-old rubber-proofed goods worker, who died in 1937 of tuberculosis and asbestosis—a verdict that, as we have seen, Turner & Newall had great difficulty in accepting. The widow was told there could be no claim as her husband had worked outside the scheduled areas.

Predictably, the Asbestosis Scheme resulted in many similar injustices. Joseph Buckley had worked at TBA for over twenty years, when he retired aged 65 in 1941. At least ten of those years had been spent as an asbestos mixer and weaver, but in 1938 (perhaps because of ill-health) he had become a hoist attendant—a non-scheduled job. It proved an unfortunate move for his widow, because he died from asbestosis (accelerated by tuberculosis) in his first year of retirement. Initially his widow made no claim, but when she did (and a Medical Board certificate was issued), she was told that her husband had not been employed in a scheduled area and so Turner & Newall were not liable. By 1946, however, the widow was a chronic invalid, living on 10s [50p] a week widow's pension (which was about to expire) and 9s [45p] from her son's services pay, which was also due to end. Eventually, in 1946 Turner & Newall awarded her an *ex-gratia* payment of 10s a week.

The manufacturers, of course, had given a definite promise to the government in 1932 that non-scheduled cases would be treated 'broadly'. What this meant in practice can be seen in the case of Fred Whitham, a

---

[54] 38/1377. 5 Mar. 1947.

chargehand in the TBA warehouse between 1910 and 1938. His local doctor diagnosed asbestosis in 1941 and Whitham died, aged 70, in the following year. The post-mortem revealed broncho-pneumonia and diffuse fibrosis of the lungs, but this finding did not lead to an industrial disease verdict at the subsequent inquest. The pathologist had found no asbestos bodies present in the lungs and argued that Whitham's death was unrelated to his work. William Ellison's testimony was also influential. Whitham had in fact been exposed to dust for several months as a bag-carrier in the disintegrator room before he began his warehouse job. Before the inquest, Ellison suggested to Bussy that it would be best 'to leave the relatives [at the inquest] to raise the doubtful points . . . [and] If questioned I would say that Mr W. had never been engaged in any [scheduled] asbestos process'.[55] Ellison testified accordingly, a 'natural causes' verdict followed, and no compensation was paid.[56]

The Medical Board, aware of weaknesses in the legislation, had written to Turner & Newall in 1944 underlining this treatment along 'broad lines'.[57] However, the company's attitude does not appear to have altered. Thomas Tattersall, who died in 1944, had worked in TBA's moulded goods department since 1926 and was not a scheduled worker; on the other hand, he had worked as an asbestos weaver for the company between 1919 and 1926. He had never been examined by the Medical Board, so clearly it was not government or company policy to monitor workers who had once been in what were now scheduled areas. Collins thought that Tattersall was obviously 'bronchitic . . . and any suggestion by the Coroner that asbestosis was a contributory cause should be resisted'.[58] But the inquest returned a verdict of death from asbestosis (the same conclusion reached by the company's consultant pathologist, Stewart). Since Tattersall had left a widow and an 11-year-old daughter, the board decided to treat the case 'sympathetically'. The family received death benefit of only £50 and an *ex gratia* of 25s [£1.25] a week for the child, which was to be reviewed when she was 15; but there was no lump sum.[59]

Workers at TAC, Newalls, and Washington were particularly vulnerable, as many of their jobs were unscheduled. For example, Turner &

---

[55] 305/868–9. W. M. Ellison to Bussy, n.d.
[56] 305/862. 'Death Not Due to Employment', *Rochdale Observer*, 11 Mar. 1942.
[57] Director's board minute, 31 Mar. 1944.
[58] 38/670–1. Collins to Mr Chew, TBA, 16 Feb. 1944.
[59] A similar case occurred in 1941, when Edgar Shires, a 37-year-old textile manager at Roberts died from extensive asbestosis and tuberculosis. When he became departmental manager, he had technically moved outside the scheduled areas and so was never examined by the Medical Board (and therefore never suspended). His widow, Emily, and his son, did not receive a lump sum, only £1 a week *ex gratia* at the company's discretion. Ironically, a lump sum would have saved the company money, as Emily Shires collected her company pension until her death in 1979—by which time she had received nearly £3,000.

Newall fought to exclude from compensation TAC worker William Lythgoe, who died from asbestosis in 1948. Collins argued that his dependants had to *prove* he was employed in a scheduled process—something the company made difficult by arguing that the deceased had encountered 'no dust' in any of his jobs. Collins continued: 'I think that as a matter of principle we ought—in a case where the deceased was never engaged in a Scheduled Process—to see that the claim made against us is abandoned before we make an *ex-gratia* payment.'[60]

In particular, Turner & Newall doggedly contested any claims from the largest high-risk group outside the scheduled factory areas—the laggers. A Newalls' manager wrote in 1939, after the suspension of lagger Bernard Stevenson: 'We have never previously admitted a case of asbestosis at Newalls Insulation Co. . . . [so] . . . Stevenson may establish a precedent.'[61] The company feared that 'unscheduled' asbestosis cases might cause the government to widen the regulations; and this would also alarm 'bystander' workers (such as painters and electricians) in the shipyards. This meant that sick laggers and their dependants faced a tough fight for compensation, as the Watkins family discovered. Ernest Watkins had worked alongside his son (Frank) as a London-based boiler lagger for Newalls Insulation. The father worked for Newalls between 1929 and 1946 (with a previous stint with Cape Asbestos). He had plenty of opportunity to inhale asbestos dust, when fitting mattresses, cutting up asbestos sections and mixing asbestos paste (which soon dried out, leaving dust on his clothes). The son had helped his father mix paste for only two years between 1942 and 1944, yet had also probably been inhaling fibres for many years at home from his father's dusty workclothes.

In a double tragedy, both father and son died in 1946 from asbestosis and tuberculosis—facts confirmed at the two inquests. At 18-year-old Frank's inquest, the coroner—who had the unique experience of having three asbestosis cases in court on the same day[62]—criticized Turner & Newall and suggested that a 'little more precaution could have been taken' by using respirators. Yet Turner & Newall disputed the findings. Despite the medical evidence of asbestosis that was presented at the inquest by the respected London Chest Hospital pathologist, Dr Stephen Gloyne, Collins refused to believe that the son had asbestosis. He first stated that the boy's actual exposure was less than 8 hours a week (thus excluding him from the Scheme), arguing that the dust in Watkins Jnr's lagging job was 'either non-existent or quite negligible . . . [because] as soon as the mixture is wet there is no risk'.[63] Collins argued that the 45-

[60] 36/1588–9. Collins to CU, 9 July 1948.   [61] 36/2095–6. Letter to CU, 18 Dec. 1939.
[62] The other two workers were at Cape Asbestos, Barking.
[63] 61/1354–5. Collins to CU, 20 May 1946. Collins could hardly plead ignorance. A Washington manager told him—if he needed telling—that, although plastic was applied wet, 'a considerable amount of the material is left on the workmen's clothes and soon dries out'. See 61/1440. W. L. McClure to Collins, 22 Oct. 1946.

year-old father's job also fell outside the scheduled areas. Here the argument was that as a chargehand, the father was not a mixer, like his son. Watkins Snr's solicitors were incredulous: 'He most certainly did from time to time personally handle and mix asbestos . . . Surely the employers are not suggesting in this case that the deceased had not on many occasion during the five years had occasion to personally handle and mix asbestos.'[64]

Turner & Newall, however, decided to dispute liability in both cases (despite the issue of a Medical Board certificate for Frank). Under attack from two different solicitors, Turner & Newall did eventually offer to look at the two cases in 'a broad-minded way'.[65] This meant admitting liability for the son, whilst at the same time continuing to deny liability for his father. Turner & Newall then insisted that the two cases should be considered together, causing confusion among the two sets of Watkins' solicitors as to who should handle the claim. Collins wrote contemptuously: 'This seems rather stupid . . . Delaying tactics on our side would therefore appear to be advisable.'[66] Commercial Union then suggested offering £300 to 'get rid of both cases'. Eventually, a settlement of £450 was reached for both men, but this was far less than the £1,100 demanded by the family.

Turner & Newall escaped with even lighter costs when a Newalls' boiler lagger, 58-year-old James Wren, died from lung cancer and asbestosis in 1947. At the inquest, a company manager stated that the lagging material contained mostly magnesia and only 15 per cent asbestos; he also emphasized that cases of asbestosis on such work were 'rare'. Wren had asked the firm, shortly before his death, whether they had a pension fund or could provide compensation, but no payment was forthcoming. His widow could not afford the cost of making a formal claim and received only £50 death benefit.[67] Wren's asbestosis was not even listed in the company records.

The experience of a Glasgow insulation worker, Charles Coyle, was even more shocking. This man had been a Newalls' sprayer for about nine years between 1945 and 1954. In only his late forties, he was then suspended with pneumoconiosis and his solicitors made a claim for negligence in November 1955. Turner & Newall, through their Manchester solicitors, Chapman's, greeted this claim with scepticism ('it is clear that every precaution was provided for your client'). A doctor's letter in March 1956, saying that Coyle would not survive longer than a few months also received little sympathy. Under Scottish law at that time, the death of a claimant virtually killed the claim, too, and relatives could only expect greatly reduced damages. Chapman's noted: 'If the man does not survive then there will be obvious difficulty in establishing any claim in

[64] 61/1431. L. Bingham & Co. to CU, 16 Jan. 1947.
[65] 61/1435–6. Collins to CU, 25 Oct. 1946.
[66] Collins to CU, 19 Mar 1947.   [67] 61/1113–22.

negligence because in all cases of this kind the man's own personal evidence is vital.'[68] Turner & Newall told Chapman's: 'Our records suggest that it is very rare indeed for a man to acquire recognisable symptoms of asbestosis within nine years . . . and it is quite extraordinary that Coyle should have become so bad as his doctor's report suggest in so short a time.'[69] On the copy of this letter, someone at Turner & Newall ringed the words 'very rare indeed', and wrote in the margin: 'Too strong!' In fact, by this date several workers at Turner & Newall had developed asbestosis within ten years, including some sprayers.

The company considered blaming Coyle's previous job and also hired its own doctor to examine him at home in May 1956. But this doctor only confirmed that Coyle was dying from asbestosis. Chapman's then recommended that Turner & Newall should 'continue to deny liability on the short ground that the disease was not contracted by reason of any breach of duty on the part of the employers'.[70] Then, as Coyle's health declined, Chapman's sat back and waited: 'The man has a very poor expectation of life, and if he does succumb the claim will not be any more expensive, and without his evidence the solicitors will be in greater difficulties. In short, I do not think tactically we have anything to lose by leaving the matter in abeyance.'[71]

In February 1957, Chapman's solicitor, Arthur McKenna, at last met Coyle's legal representative, only to be informed that the worker had died from asbestosis in the previous November (his widow had been slow to inform the solicitor). The tragedy made no impression on McKenna, who noted that Coyle's solicitor, 'had approached this case as so many people do by assuming that merely because the workman had contracted pneumoconiosis he was of right entitled to damages . . .'.[72] McKenna added: 'he really does not understand this case because he has never properly applied his mind to the real issues and conducted investigation, but has been content to take some notes of evidence from the workman, obtain a medical report and do very little more apart from write some formal letters'. Privately, Chapman's calculated damages at a minimum of £4,000, but having browbeaten Coyle's solicitor into believing that the widow and two children might be lucky to receive £500, and only then if Turner & Newall decided it was a 'deserving case', he terminated the interview with a warning: 'if this sympathetic approach to the case was misunderstood and proceedings were instituted then both he

[68] 9/923. Chapman's to Arthur D. N. Jones, 27 Mar. 1956. See generally, Tommy Gorman, 'Hidden Hazard/Forgotten Victims: Some Aspects of Asbestos Abuse in Britain', Glasgow Caledonian University BA, 1997.
[69] 9/922. A. D. N. Jones to A. E. McKenna, 28 Mar. 1956.
[70] 9/915. McKenna to Jones, 5 June 1956.
[71] 9/908. McKenna to Jones, 25 Aug. 1956.
[72] 9/904–9. McKenna to Jones, 13 Feb. 1957.

and his client would have a hard fight on their hands.' With the widow having been suitably 'conditioned' by this treatment, the case was soon settled with a £500 *ex gratia*, with no admission of liability. Even the costs of Coyle's solicitor were less than expected (£42, compared to Chapman's bill of £133). The company secretary felt it had all 'turned out very satisfactorily'.[73]

The biggest stumbling block for the victim's survivors was the issue of dependency. As we have stated, the lump sum payment was not a punitive award against the company; it was intended to compensate a family for the income forfeited by the death of its main wage-earner. Again, it was not an automatic payment, as a lump sum was only payable to those who could *prove* dependency. A bereft unemployed widow with a baby was obviously dependent on her late husband's income; but what if that widow was working part-time, or her offspring had started work? Or what if it was the unemployed widower who survived? Having undergone the suffering of loved ones, the ordeal of the inquest, and the costs, inconvenience, and uncertainty of obtaining a Medical Board certificate, dependants often found themselves in another round of correspondence, negotiations, and costs (this time for birth and marriage certificates) over their claim for dependency. Turner & Newall and Commercial Union, who never assessed the costs to the family of what could be years of medical caring, were at their most punctilious when assessing dependency in the aftermath of a death.

The framers of the compensation regulations envisaged a simple world in which each family was composed of a stable couple. However, real life was inevitably not so tidy. When Barker Greenwood died in 1935, the company ascertained that he was married with two adult daughters. However, he had not lived with his widow for eight years and instead resided with a sister, who was on assistance. TBA and Commercial Union, who were disputing the medical diagnosis, decided that there was no dependency and so the company merely paid £15 for funeral expenses. Even crueller was the case of Clifford Butterworth, who retired in 1955 after forty-three years with TBA (thirty-three of them in the scheduled areas). He died in 1956 from asbestosis and it seemed a straightforward case as regards dependency, since the diagnosis was not disputed and he left a widow. Turner & Newall were about to make a £300 lump sum payment, when Commercial Union pointed out that Butterworth had remarried two years before his death and since this person was not married to him at his time of suspension (in 1945), technically the company had no need to pay. The outcome: Butterworth's widow got only £15 in funeral expenses and a small pension! Marital circumstances

[73] 9/881. Arthur Jones to Chapman's, 29 July 1957.

also came into the reckoning when Geoffrey Hesford, a suspended TBA worker, died in 1959 from asbestosis and lung cancer after twenty-five years at the company. A lump sum should have been paid, but in probing into his family circumstances the company found that Hesford's first wife had left him in about 1930. The company reported that since about 1940, 'Mr Hesford has lived with another lady, who has now assumed the name of Hesford and in fact she gave evidence at the inquest'.[74] Commercial Union immediately advised that under the law Hesford's partner had no claim to compensation, apart from £50 in funeral expenses, which 'more than settles our liability under the Workman's Compensation Acts and no further payments are envisaged at the present time'.[75]

Turner & Newall and Commercial Union were thorough at obtaining information regarding workers' and claimants' income and assets. In one instance, involving Ernest Kershaw, who died in 1942, Commercial Union had assembled within four months a complete employment record on the widow and also information on her pregnancy (substantiated from a medical certificate).[76] Information was collected by various channels. Sometimes solicitors would provide the information; though Commercial Union and Turner & Newall—as the Presland case has shown—also used more informal means, such as discussions with neighbours, employers, and friends. Commercial Union made 'discreet enquiries' to ascertain the income of the widow of John Clegg in 1946.[77] Thus, lump sum payments were almost means-tested—a humiliating process for claimants. Knowledge was then power in the hands of the company. When James Grindrod died in 1933, Turner & Newall not only disputed a routine medical verdict of asbestosis, but Commercial Union's investigations into the widow's background revealed that she had worked between November 1932 and March 1933, no doubt to support herself and her dying husband. This fact was used to undermine her claim for total dependency and her lump sum payment was halved to £150. Even on strictly technical grounds, Commercial Union's arguments were unfair: dependency had to be assessed only on the situation at the worker's death (which in Grindrod's case was in May 1933).

Exactly what claimants were up against is demonstrated by the case of John Oddie. The latter was a disintegrator at Roberts, who 'cracked up suddenly' in 1931, and died the following year from asbestosis (or 'misadventure', as the coroner termed it). His widow recruited a solicitor to claim her £300. The family background was unfortunate: the widow had two children aged 16 and 23, but one was partially paralysed in both arms

[74] 38/718. G. Chadwick to J. Kemp, 2 Feb. 1960.
[75] 65/81. Chadwick to Kemp, 25 Apr. 1960.
[76] 38/0866. CU to TBA, 18 June 1942.   [77] 38/1489. CU to TBA, 25 Jan. 1946.

(though at work) and the other—like his mother—had no proper job. Commercial Union's investigations discovered the following: 'The widow is earning the sum of 4/– [20p] per week for one day's charring. We have seen the person who employs her, and the payment she receives is more in the nature of a charity.'[78] Nevertheless, this fact was used as evidence of partial dependency and Commercial Union suggested a settlement of £208, 'to make payment as small as possible'. This proved too low for even the registrar at the County Court who made Turner & Newall increase their offer, so that the final total cost to the firm was £262—a sum significantly below the £300 claimed.

The fact that a surviving widow had a pension was also enough for Turner & Newall to avoid, or at least reduce, the lump sum. Turner & Newall's attitude after the asbestosis death of John Jenkins in 1939 is instructive. As the hapless Jenkins was 70, the company immediately objected to the lump sum payout since the worker was obviously at the end of his working life. William Ellison complained: 'This case, I think, shows one of the directions in which the Workmen's Compensation Act should be amended in the employer's favour. Provided the Medical Board gives a certificate, it would appear that the widow, an old lady, is entitled to receive £200 as compensation for the death of her husband at 70 years of age.'[79] Commercial Union suggested that since the widow had a pension she was not truly dependent; and she also had two daughters at home, both working. The Manchester solicitors Whittle, Robinson & Bailey were enlisted by the family and eventually the widow agreed to settle for £125 plus costs. Commercial Union thought this was 'slightly on the high side', but believed that a court might award more. TBA agreed the amount was high, but pointed out to Commercial Union that there were 'other considerations'.[80] Jenkins, had once brought five workers to the firm and his son, Edward Jenkins, had died recently (within a day of his father)—no claim being made in respect of his death.[81]

Even if Turner & Newall paid a lump sum, it was usually not given directly to the dependants. Unless there was a reason to act otherwise— and there was at least one case where payment was made directly to the family[82]—the money was invariably paid into the court. The company

---

[78] 38/337–8. CU to T & N, 4 Apr. 1932.   [79] 65/412. Ellison to Bussy, 16 Feb. 1939.

[80] 65/384. W. M. Ellison to CU, n.d.

[81] This implies that the company felt that the son, Edward John Jenkins, may have suffered from asbestosis. There had been no inquest, as the coroner accepted that the cause of death was heart trouble. See 'Family Tragedy: Son Dies Day after His Father', *Rochdale Observer*, 11 Feb. 1939; 353/607–10. Correspondence on death of E. J. Jenkins, 1939.

[82] George Scully's widow, for example, was handed a £50 cheque in 1941, after the company claimed that death was due to pneumonia (despite the inquest verdict of pneumonia and asbestosis).

favoured this, as it made any settlement more legally binding, though Registrars could sometimes be awkward and ask Turner & Newall to raise its offer.[83] In certain circumstances, the court could hold the money over and retain control over it. The widow of John Lancaster received a £450 *ex gratia*, but only £125 was paid as a lump sum: the balance of £315 was to be paid monthly until 1958, when Lancaster's daughter was 15. This procedure—heavy with overtones of Victorian paternalism—was obviously to safeguard the interests of children, but it could increase the problems of the family. After her husband's death in 1937, Harriet Greenwood had been awarded £232, but it did little to alleviate her immediate poverty. She wrote to William Ellison:

I am just writing to you not because I want you to think that I [have] any claim on you for anything because I have never thought that. I never liked having to draw Fred's money when he was ill, it is because I am asking if you can give me any advice, as I am making myself ill with having so much worry that I have had of late. My children have been doing very bad . . . and now they are without anything proper on there [*sic*] feet and back. In fact I have not been able to get to eat what they should have. I have not been having 30/– [£1.50] a week for months now through bad times. My oldest girl had to come home ill last week and she has never been strong. She is still under the doctor, and Harriet age 16 [h]as been out of work for 8 weeks now. I am getting off her from the labour and 11/– [55p] for my boy Fred, so you can see what I get them. I have been like this now almost since there [*sic*] Dad died. I had not quite enough insurance to bury him. My trouble started from then as I had to let the club go bad at the time when he was only getting 13/5 [67p] at the time of him first finishing work, and I was not able to do anything. Then I was under the doctor for nearly 4 months. That is something I shall never forget. He went without food often then to let his children have it, before he would ask for help. I can't tell you how I feel to have to ask for anything out of my husband's money at court. I feel I have no right to it. They did let me have something to put myself straight for what I was in up to Fred dying. But there is nothing I have got since, not one penny. Having had to be paid through court [h]as made me feel like one of those women that would do nothing only waste and drink everything they got hold of, something I have never done in all my life. When I draw my £4.0.0 next Wednesday [get] myself straight in my rent and coal and insurance there won't be much left for anything. So do you really think Mr Ellison that if I ask for something out of that money they would allow me anything . . . I am afraid to ask them as they make me feel that I have no right. Surely they will be able to bring me more in later on. I don't know how my other little girl will go on when she leaves school. I know I have no right to be bothering you, but I just thought your advice was worth asking, for just of late I have seemed to be at the far end.[84]

---

[83] An example was the claim made by the relatives of weaver Arthur Slater (1877–1941), to whom Roberts intended paying a £100 lump sum after characteristically quibbling over dependency. The Registrar made them increase the sum to £166.

[84] 65/0202–5. H. Greenwood to Ellison, n.d., 1938.

Ellison sympathized with the fact that she was having 'some little difficulty' and promised he would have a word with the clerk at the county court, but there was no lump sum payment.

There were a number of other small concessions to dependants. A non-contributory pension scheme, introduced by the company by 1936, provided some support for those with more than twenty years' service. It provided 10s [50p] a week when the worker reached 65. A death benefit of £50 was payable to the widow if death occurred before retirement; and if death occurred within five years after retirement, then the widow continued to receive a pension for that five-year span.

Another payment that appears repeatedly in the Turner & Newall compensation files is the *ex gratia*. This hand-out was paid either as compensation during the worker's lifetime, especially if an individual had been forced into early retirement, or as a death benefit. *Ex gratia* payments began—surely not coincidentally—in 1924, at about the time of Nellie Kershaw's death. The first *ex gratia* recorded was paid in February 1924 to William Hoyle, a hoist-tenter at TBA, with thirty years' service. He died in April, aged 53, with 'chronic bronchitis' on his death certificate. Certainly by 1931, TBA were using such payments to meet some of the inequalities created both by the Asbestosis Scheme and their own parsimony. In that year, the *ex-gratia* book recorded the payment of 12s [65p] a week to the widow of Robert Kershaw, the TBA cardroom employee who had the misfortune not to be actually working when the Asbestosis Scheme became operational (he was dying of asbestosis).[85] Jane Trevor, the widow of another 'border-line' case, was awarded 7s 6d [38p] a week by 1933. *Ex gratias* were also used to raise a worker's compensation payments if they fell below the poverty level. By 1938, about forty individuals were being paid a small weekly *ex gratia*, with annual payments ranging from £26 to £65.

Other *ex gratias* were made to cover solicitor's costs or other expenses. Lump sum *ex gratias* at death were relatively rare and were usually only paid in asbestosis cases that the company believed were not clear cut, or where they did not wish to accept liability. The payment was made on sympathetic grounds if it was decided that 'officially' there was no claim, but that there were mitigating circumstances. This meant that Sir Samuel Turner could claim that the company paid more than was prescribed by law. On the other hand, Turner made it clear that any payment was entirely 'without prejudice' and discretionary. Thus, for example, when the widow of Robert Kershaw was awarded a weekly allowance, Bussy told William Ellison: 'You must make it quite clear . . . that this payment is purely *ex-gratia* and is not to be looked upon as compensation . . . and

[85] 355/299. *Ex-Gratia* Payments Book, 30.

further that it will be subject to investigation from time to time. Also, we are not binding ourselves to pay it for any definite period. It is purely at the pleasure of the Board.'[86] It was also sometimes made clear that legal action from relatives could result in the complete withdrawal of an offer.

Meanwhile, to circumscribe any further claims, the company occasionally asked dependants to sign away their rights. This policy seems to have begun as early as the 1930s, when workers could be asked to promise that compensation would not lead to future action. For example, when TBA worker Harold Tildsley was in a sanatorium in 1933, the company paid him compensation in an 'unofficial way'. They then asked him for a letter saying that he was accepting the money without prejudice and would not bring it up against the insurance company at a later date. In 1952, when Joseph Thompson was paid a £500 *ex gratia* (a sum which included £100 supplementary allowance) during his lifetime, the agreement he signed with Turner & Newall stated that the sum was 'in full satisfaction and discharge of all claims for further compensation'.[87] Consequently, when he died four years later, his dependants received only £30 funeral expenses.[88] In the Charlie Coyle case in 1957, the final agreement signed by his widow, Margaret, rubbed more salt into the wound: it discharged the company from 'all further claims arising out of the death'.

The *ex gratia* was thus a classic paternalistic device. It assuaged any guilt feelings that the company may have had about its asbestosis victims; it sometimes aroused gratitude in the recipient; and it also acted as a disincentive for those contemplating legal action. The *ex-gratia* policy was maintained throughout the 1950s and 1960s, and even into the 1970s.

THE ASBESTOSIS SCHEME: HOW MUCH DID IT COST?

Obviously, the government Asbestosis Scheme never adequately compensated workers—though it did have one positive element. Since asbestos was not covered by compensation legislation before 1931, any benefits were an improvement. That said, the legal parameters set by the government meant that there was never any commitment to compensate sick workers fully. The methods of calculating partial and total disability benefit, the maximum figures set for lump sums, and the small amount prescribed for funeral and other costs (which was all that some relatives received) ensured that most sick workers and their dependants only

---

[86] 354/162–3. Bussy to Ellison, 6 Nov. 1931.

[87] 61/538. Leeds County Court agreement, 25 Mar. 1948.

[88] If one assumes that the company would have paid the £500 as a lump sum at death, then the arrangement was a bargain for T & N. It meant that the company had effectively saved the cost of paying Thompson any compensation during his lifetime.

received a nominal sum for giving their health and, in some cases, their lives for the industry. This was aside from the nightmare of laws and conditions that stood in the way of claimants.

Turner & Newall's main concern was to drive down costs, a rational economic response in 1931 when the future costs of the Asbestosis Scheme were unknown and when the company feared that the cost of each claim could top £500. Some directors were worried that during the Depression this amount might give competitors an edge—especially if Turner & Newall had to carry higher insurance charges than other firms. They also believed that trade unions would exploit the 'scheduled' status of asbestos to demand danger money.[89]

Yet these fears about crippling asbestosis costs must have been quickly dispelled. First, the original Asbestosis Fund subscriptions—$7\frac{1}{2}$ per cent for Fund A and $2\frac{1}{2}$ per cent for Fund B—were hardly burdensome or particularly generous. Second, from the outset the Fund began accumulating a surplus and the levies on the unit companies were soon reduced (see Table 5.3).[90] In January 1933, contributions to the Fund were slashed by half, though a year later the Fund still had a large surplus. By 1936, contributions were over £20,000, compensation was about £5,000, and the surplus was over £15,000. In April 1937, contributions to Fund A were reduced from $3\frac{3}{4}$ per cent to $2\frac{1}{2}$ (though it was increased for Roberts to 5 per cent, a reflection of its greater asbestosis rate); while the rate for Fund B was reduced from $1\frac{1}{4}$ to $\frac{1}{2}$ per cent. By 1939, it was even suggested that payments into the Fund should be temporarily suspended. The contribution rate was again reduced in 1941, and though a rise in compensation cases after the war caused the rates to be restored somewhat, levies fell again in 1953. Thereafter the Fund was almost dormant. By 1961, it had accumulated £47,200 and half of that was ploughed back into the group's revenue.[91]

Turner & Newall board papers give more detail on the compensation picture. It is difficult to provide a precise figure for compensation payments paid by the company over a long period—say, from 1931 to 1969—partly because the records are incomplete. Turner & Newall's recorded lump sum payments over that period total about £270,000, but that does not include the cost of *ex gratias* or compensation paid during a worker's life. A more revealing method is to look at payments under the Asbestosis Fund until 1948 (when the National Insurance Act took over new cases of asbestosis from the employers). In this period, the company alone was responsible for compensation.

[89] 10/1977. George Carter to W. W. F. Shepherd, 30 June 1931.
[90] 36/1531–67. Correspondence re. Asbestosis Contributions, 1933–61.
[91] The death of the last worker within the Asbestosis Scheme occurred in 1979, when Frank E. Edwards, a TBA weaver suspended in 1937, suffered a heart attack.

Death by Industrial Disease

Table 5.3. *Turner & Newall: Profits, Asbestosis Fund contributions, and compensation costs, 1931–48*

Year	Profits after tax	Asbestosis Fund: contributions	Asbestosis Fund: balance	Compensation
	£	£	£	£
1931	360,879	–	–	–
1932	305,671	5,700	4,936	548
1933	406,656	3,792	27,779	842
1934	714,228	3,769	10,231	1,200
1935	780,625	4,095	12,934	1,278
1936	1,163,308	4,373	15,524	1,675
1937	1,333,489	?	?	?
1938	1,361,694	4,602	21,727	2,010
1939	960,615	?	?	?
1940	1,015,214	?	?	?
1941	506,000	?	?	2,441
1942	530,840	2,464	23,708	3,193
1943	553,292	2,655	22,525	3,731
1944	545,665	2,992	19,388	6,022
1945	629,462	3,059	15,552	6,787
1946	209,787	3,044	11,049	7,440
1947	727,058	7,475	11,293	7,124
1948	2,602,361	10,401	14,772	6,815
Total	14,706,844	73,941	–	57,476

Source: Turner & Newall, *Annual Reports*, Board Papers and Asbestosis Fund.

The data are presented in Tables 5.3 and 5.4. These show that between 1931 and 1948 Turner & Newall spent £57,476 in compensating 140 registered asbestosis victims (plus £15,690 on workers' medical examinations). By 1948, the Asbestosis Fund had a surplus of £14,772. Compensation was about £410 a head, though 63 of the 140 cases were still alive and within the Scheme. These compensation costs can be compared with Turner & Newall's profits after tax: between 1931 and 1948 these totalled nearly £15 million—of which £9 million was distributed to the ordinary shareholders (among them the Turner family and other directors).[92] Put another way, the sum of £73,166 (actually spent on medical examinations and

---

[92] G. Tweedale and D. J. Jeremy, 'Compensating the Workers: Industrial Injury and Compensation in the British Asbestos Industry, 1930s–1960s', *Business History* 41 (April 1999), 102–20.

Table 5.4. *Asbestosis Fund: contributions, claims, compensation, and medical costs, 1948*

	Contributions			Claims			Compensation			Medical costs		
	£	s	d	Submitted	Settled	Outstanding	£	s	d	£	s	d
TBA	44,325.	14.	10	84	50	34	34,650.	9.	8	10,562.	19.	6
JWR	17,540.	17.	6	35	15	20	13,440.	15.	0	2,591.	16.	6
Ferodo	700.	11.	2	–	–	–			–	32.	3.	0
WCC	4,358.	12.	8	8	4	4	2,779.	2.	11	699.	4.	0
Newalls	2,964.	5.	11	6	6	–	3,681.	9.	10	78.	14.	0
TAC	4,052.	16.	1	7	2	5	2,923.	16.	1	1,725.	10.	6
Total	73,940.	18.	2	140	77	63	57,475.	13.	6	15,690.	7.	6*

*Total includes an additional payment for disablement and death certificates.

Source: Turner & Newall Board Papers.

given to victims or their next of kin) represented ½ per cent of profits and under 1 per cent of ordinary dividends.[93] Little wonder that John Collins could view the asbestosis problem as one of 'small dimensions'[94]—for the company, at least.

[93] With bizarre logic, the cheapness of the compensation bill was used by T & N as a pretext to argue that the cost of medical examinations (relative to compensation) was 'very high'. In 1940, the company suggested abolishing the exams altogether (or at least lengthening the period between appointments)—a suggestion rejected by the government. See 37/608–9. Shepherd to Under Secretary of State, 2 Aug. 1940; and 37/603–4. Home Office reply, 23 Oct. 1940.

[94] 8/1368. JLC to Refractories Industries Compensation Fund, 20 Feb. 1946.

6

Dust, Mortality, and the Cancer
Hazard: 1940s to the Early 1960s

evidence already accumulated seems to favour a causal connection
between asbestosis and pulmonary cancer and humanitarian motives
may decide the public conscience not to wait for scientific proof before
insisting on more stringent safeguards against dust inhalation.

> H. Wyers, 'That Legislative Measures Have Proved Generally
> Effective in the Control of Asbestosis' (Glasgow University MD
> thesis, 1946), 89–90.

the only really safe number of [asbestos] fibres in the works
atmosphere is nil . . .

> 6/347. D. W. Hills (T & N) to R. L. Moore, Raybestos–Manhattan,
> 27 Oct. 1961.

The period after the Second World War was the most successful in
Turner & Newall's history, when the company emerged as the 'Asbestos
Giant'. An era of unbroken commercial success lifted profits after tax
from about £½ million in 1945 to over £7 million by 1960 (with ordinary
dividends averaging 20 per cent in the 1950s). Asbestos production
expanded at a new factory at Hindley Green in 1949, where the firm also
made non-asbestos industrial and transmission belting. Old plant,
such as Roberts' Leeds factory, was shut and Turner & Newall diversified
into new materials. In 1955, it acquired Glass Fabrics, an Irish fibre
glass business in Dungannon; and then in 1961 purchased Stillite, a
mineral wool company in Middlesbrough. In the 1950s, Newalls also
began making fibre glass insulation; while during the same period,
Roberts (with its business switched to Hindley Green and Horwich)
introduced polyester resins reinforced by glass fibre (Feroglas). These
materials were complementary to, and in some cases competitive with,
asbestos. However, the magic mineral still reigned supreme and the
African mines had never been busier. In 1949, the company's head office
was moved to Manchester and named, appropriately, Asbestos House.
However, this expansion was bought at a price. More asbestos meant
more dust and continued risk for Turner & Newall staff. It gradually
became apparent that the risk included not only asbestosis, but also
cancer.

CONTINUED DUST PROBLEMS AND RISING MORTALITY

The reorganization discussed by Turner & Newall in 1945 had taken several years to get underway. Detailed planning was still taking place in 1949, when an internal survey revealed a dreadful picture at TBA: 'The fibre preparation plant at Rochdale is all at least 30 years old (much of it is probably a great deal older), and is virtually worn out. Undoubtedly but for the war it would have been replaced several years ago. It is costly in maintenance, inefficient in operation and cannot be adequately ventilated as a protection against asbestosis.'[1] The situation at Roberts' cramped factory was even worse and was described as 'well below current standards'.

Turner & Newall had preserved these 'extremely serious' health hazards against the recommendations of the Factory Inspectorate. Indeed, the Inspectors wanted a closure order on the old Harridge Mill, which Commercial Union had criticized in 1932. Even the company admitted it was unhealthy and uneconomic. However, with the large-scale reorganization being planned at Hindley Green, the Inspectorate allowed short-term violations of the law in exchange for a permanent solution. However, the Hindley Green factory was not fully commissioned until 1958.

In the late 1940s, Dr John Knox readily admitted (at least privately) that dust was still a health hazard. In 1954, when discussing the government dust regulations, he remarked that these had been devised to ensure that 'dust cannot escape . . . into the air of the workroom', though he knew that this 'counsel of perfection [was] not attained'.[2] He believed that the dust was much less than before 1932, but pointed out that no one knew in the early 1950s how to take accurate dust measurements.

TBA had started to give dust counting more serious consideration after the 1949 reorganization, by which time it had recruited its first industrial hygienist, Dr Stephen Holmes (1914–91). The quest to count the impossible—the number of asbestos fibres in a specific volume of air—began in the crudest fashion with the idea of simply suspending a small petri dish from the rafters and then counting the fibres that settled on it. During the 1950s, more scientific methods were introduced at TBA, beginning with thermal precipitators—devices which captured dust by a combination of heat and settlement.[3] In 1961, TBA tried the membrane filter method—a

---

[1] 2/1355–80. 'TBA and JWR: Reorganization of Textile Manufacture', 31 Oct. 1949.

[2] 301/50. Knox's observations on draft of Doll lung cancer paper, 31 Jan. 1954.

[3] I. J. Selikoff and D. H. K. Lee, *Asbestos and Disease* (1978), 71–94, have an excellent discussion of dust counting methods. See also C. G. Addingley, 'Asbestos Dust and Its Measurement', *Annals of Occupational Hygiene* 9 (1966), 73–82; S. T. B. Beckett, 'Monitoring and Identification of Airborne Asbestos', in L. Michaels and S. S. Chissick, *Asbestos* (1979), i, 207–45; and S. Holmes, 'Developments in Dust Sampling and Counting Techniques in the Asbestos Industry', *Annals of the New York Academy of Sciences* 132 (1965), 288–97.

technique that by the mid-1960s had become the standard at the company and had been adopted by the industry's own research body, the Asbestosis Research Council. Sampled air was passed through a porous cellulose ester membrane, which could then be 'cleared' (made transparent) with a solvent so that it could be placed on a microscope slide. A count could then be made with an optical microscope using transmitted light and phase contrast techniques to enhance the visibility. Counts were eventually expressed as fibres per cubic centimetre of air (f/cc).

The membrane filter was to be used through the 1960s and 1970s, but, like all dust-counting techniques, it had drawbacks. Counting a microscope slide of asbestos fibres—many of which were split, clumped together, or stuck to background contamination—was so laborious and difficult that the count error could, at best, be +/−50 per cent.[4] Even worse, most fibres remained invisible, because the resolution was limited to no more than 500×. Transmission electron microscopy could magnify up to 100,000×, but this method was never considered (even though the Washington factory had such a device by 1947).[5] This was not only due to the expense and lack of portability of the electron microscope, but also because it was argued that very small, unobservable particles were harmless. The industry had agreed on the convention that only fibres greater than 5 microns long and having a length/diameter ratio of at least 3/1 were to be counted. These fibre dimensions were adopted mainly for practical rather than medical reasons—counting was greatly simplified and these longer fibres were more easily removed by contemporary dust-control technology. It was assumed that relatively long fibres were the most dangerous, but the medical evidence for this was slim. Indeed, the ARC had admitted in 1959 that as regards particles under 5 microns, 'it has not been conclusively shown that such particles are not dangerous'.[6]

While it began counting dust, Turner & Newall continued trying to suppress it. The Regulations of 1931 had required exhaust ventilation on carding engines and looms, but this was to be supplemented by various improvements that were to be introduced on the company's initiative (or

---

[4] HSC, *Asbestos: Measurement and Monitoring of Asbestos in Air: Second Report by the Advisory Committee on Asbestos* (1978), 9. An electronic automatic particle counter (the Royco) was used at TBA between 1964 and 1974 to speed up dust counting. It could be calibrated to give equivalent membrane filter readings, but it did not entirely supersede the membrane filter. Light-scattering instruments such as the Royco 'see' all dusts—a disadvantage in areas with mixed dusts, such as asbestos cement factories.

[5] In 1949, Soothill agreed that the electron microscope at Washington might be used for ARC research into asbestosis, but the experiments were short-lived. The researchers involved believed that only the larger particles were hazardous.

[6] 401/767–76. Minutes of 7th Meeting of Research Committee of ARC, 29–30 June 1959. An ARC secretary was later unable to discover the medical rationale of the fibre-dimension standard. However, he added disarmingly, 'this decision was made with the agreement of the late Dr John Knox . . . [and] . . . presumably he had no objection to this arbitrary figure'. See 303/1298–1300. R. Sykes to W. H. Walton, 25 June 1980.

due to government pressure). Most were commissioned at TBA and were not necessarily adopted at other unit companies. They were as follows:[7]

- 1942 dust settling chambers in the ventilation system were replaced by fabric sleeve filters
- 1946 damping, already in use since 1939 for weaving, was extended to yarn doubling
- 1952 mineral oil was introduced into the fibre mixture to suppress dust
- 1953 the ventilation system of the carding engines was improved
- 1958 blending and mixing fibre on the floor were replaced by enclosed drum-mixing
- 1964 bags with paper and plastic linings were introduced within the factory
- 1965 damping was extended to intermediate spinning
- 1968 dust-suppressed textiles were devised in which fibres were 'locked in' by polymers or resins.

The company also stepped up health surveillance. The TBA directors thought that periodic health and safety conferences would be helpful, though Ronald Soothill saw the 'danger of having too open a meeting, with representatives present who were not fully familiar with the problem [asbestosis]'.[8] Those deemed not familiar enough with the problem included the workers and their trade unions, who were never invited to attend discussions on health. When a formal TBA Health Committee began meeting regularly after 1950, it included only the management and John Knox.

The result of these measures could only be seen many years later in reduced mortality from asbestosis. Meanwhile, Knox decided to compare Merewether's 1931 data with his own interpretation of TBA trends in 1952. The statistics in Table 6.1 were presented to the company, with a commentary from Knox. As with much of Turner & Newall's mortality data, the pint pot could be seen as half full or half empty. Knox found the comparison between the two sets of data 'very satisfactory'. The overall incidence of asbestosis was 26.2 per cent for the Merewether group; 3.4 per cent for the Rochdale group. This certainly demonstrated a great improvement in working conditions, but Knox said nothing about the other conclusions that could be drawn from the Rochdale data: workers in the survey who had been in the scheduled areas more than twenty years had a nearly 10 per cent chance of developing asbestosis; over thirty years and the risk was 40 per cent.

---

[7] W. P. Bamblin, 'Dust Control in the Asbestos Textile Industry', *Annals of Occupational Hygiene* 2 (1959), 54–74.
[8] 302/1346–7. Memo of Meeting held at TBA, 28 Mar. 1949.

Table 6.1. *TBA asbestosis comparison, 1931–52*

(a) Merewether and Price, 1931

Years employed	Number examined	Cases of fibrosis		
		Number	Group incidence %	Average age
0–4	89	0	–	–
5–9	141	36	25.5	36
10–14	84	27	32.1	40.4
15–19	28	15	53.6	43.4
20+	21	17	80.9	52.7
Totals	363	95	26.2	41.4

(b) TBA workers, 1952

Years employed	Number examined	Cases of fibrosis		
		Number	Group incidence %	Average age
0–9	566	0	–	–
10–14	120	8	6.6	53.4
15–19	89	3	3.47	42.3
20–24	22	2	9	41.5
25–29	34	5	14	49.4
30+	29	11	38	49.0
Totals	860	29	3.4	47.2

Source: 302/1372–3. Report on Medical Arrangements Scheme, 8 Jan. 1952.

Knox was sometimes less upbeat. In 1953, he alerted the company to a number of recent deaths, which had not been classed by the coroner as asbestosis deaths (because heart failure had usually been the leading cause), but had nevertheless shown some signs of asbestosis. All had been exposed since 1931. Knox called for a 'new ideal' in factory conditions. 'We are getting near to safe conditions', he informed his bosses, 'but we have not yet arrived there.'[9]

Knox's letters and medical reports show his continued anxiety:

On my return to Rochdale I felt a sense of the magnitude of the problem of the prevention of dust disease in the textile section of the asbestos factory, where each

[9] 301/800–3. J. Knox, 'Report on Medical Arrangements Scheme, 1953'.

area and machine has its own special problem of design and maintenance. No other section of the asbestos industry operates under such a conscious sensation of potential danger everywhere. No other section of the industry has had so many reminders of the realities of these hazards. [1959[10]]

Further pressure for improvement in dust conditions continues to come from the Factory Inspector . . . The cards come in for particular mention with the obviously visible droppings and the tendency for fibre to float against the exposed oily surfaces of the card framework . . . my own view is that fibre count levels are higher than desirable. [1963[11]]

As far as our principal hazard is concerned we cannot claim to have reached finality yet. The occasional case which arises, even since employment in the 1940s, is enough to prevent complacency . . . If I were to point to the areas where problems are most urgently awaiting solutions I would name the card room, waste chopping areas, and all the points at which asbestos is bagged, poured into hoppers, or otherwise dealt with by hand in a loose condition. [1964[12]]

Knox's worrying picture of conditions at TBA is corroborated by independent evidence. For example, one worker recalled that in the early 1960s fibre was allowed to accumulate on the floor under carding machines and then had to be shovelled into bags.[13] A Factory Inspector in 1963 had also seen a 'considerable quantity' of dust under the cards and urged that the company rapidly introduce its promised and overdue system of vacuum cleaners.[14] Some operations at TBA had hardly changed since the 1920s. The Regulations had specified the use of impermeable bags within the factories: yet even in the early 1960s, poor quality hessian bags were used, and fibre was still transported into and out of the factory in them. The company admitted that 'short fibres and dust easily filter through the hessian during handling', and that as regards unloading crude fibre, 'we don't need dust counts or even photographs . . . to see that this stuff is bad'.[15] Prompted by Knox and government pressure, the search began for superior bags, but cost was to be the primary consideration.[16]

Disappointingly, even new plant was plagued with dust problems. In 1959, the Hindley Green factory was singled out by the Factory Inspectors because of problems in the asbestos textile department,

[10] 13/62–3. Knox, 'Visits', 22 June 1959. See also 301/647–52: Knox's remarks to the board meeting, 5 Aug. 1960, when he admitted no area of the works was completely safe.

[11] 01/673–5. 'Report by Chief Medical Officer', 2 Aug. 1963.

[12] 301/679–80. 'Report of Chief Medical Officer', 4 Sept. 1964.

[13] 355/1420. *Donald Robinson v. TBA*, report, 22 July 1982.

[14] 355/1384. J. R. Allen, HM District Inspector of Factories, 25 June 1963.

[15] 22/1847. T. Berry memo, 1 Sept. 1964; 22/1844. H. Slater letter, 7 Sept. 1964.

[16] 22/1843. Research director, David Hills, commented, 7 Sept. 1964, that unit companies were 'well aware of this dust problem arising from the use of hessian bags, but I don't think we would get very far by tackling this problem at this stage on a wide front'. Hills became joint managing-director and chairman of TBA between 1969 and 1976.

especially with carding machines, which were spewing dust into the air.[17] The inspector wanted total enclosure, but Turner & Newall did not believe that this was feasible. The company was not punished for these and other violations. Dust extraction at Hindley Green was still a problem in 1963, when its ventilation system compared unfavourably with Rochdale.

However, conditions were even worse elsewhere. At Roberts'—described as clean and healthy by Bateman and Robert Turner in 1932—almost all the processes were dusty.[18] Until the factory's closure in 1958, Armley workers still stuffed mattresses with loose asbestos and then beat them flat with wooden paddles. They risked developing asbestosis after about two years' exposure.[19] The dust extraction system designed to cope with such conditions was still modest. In litigation in the 1990s, dust control at Armley was analysed in detail and it was shown that extraction made no more than a contribution to dealing with the dust. For example, in the 1950s, suction pipes removed the bulk of the dust from the disintegrator, but one worker has stated that 'they could not take away all the dust and there was fine dust on the floor which accumulated to about two inches in depth . . . There was dust in the air like fog all day and every day.'[20] A carder, whose five-year exposure at this time was enough to cause asbestosis, claimed that sometimes 'it was difficult to see from one end of the room to the other end'.[21] Dusty workers were dubbed 'abominable snowmen' and the asbestos on their trousers also led to a nickname for the Armley factory—'featherlegs'.

Management reports confirm these impressions. One director recalled that after the Second World War:

The two points of greatest risk in terms of dust were at the blending points where crudes and/or processed crudes were blended on the floor where they were turned over by hand implements and shovelled into and out of crushers and into bags or other machines. A further danger point was at the dust collecting chambers which were regularly cleaned out . . . There were undoubtedly areas where the dust count exceeded our 'norm' [67 particles/cc] by a wide margin . . . but in my years at Armley we did not once receive any official adverse criticism from the Factory Inspectors who made regular visits sometimes five or six a year.[22]

[17] 20/1560–1. N. Gregson to T & N re. visit, 16 June 1959.
[18] G. Tweedale, 'Management Strategies for Health: J. W. Roberts and the Armley Asbestos Tragedy, 1920–1958', *Journal of Industrial History* 2 (1999), 72–95.
[19] 114/585–607, 619–21: J. C. Seget (1920–72) file. See also 115/158–99 and 114/641–57: Biddle file.
[20] Evidence of Elmars Knabe, in *Margereson and Hancock v. J. W. Roberts and T & N*, High Court of Leeds, 23 June 1995. Trial transcript, 79–94.
[21] 114/797. Confidential report, *F. A. Bentley v. JWR*, 16 Feb. 1979.
[22] 82/109–10. A. R. Milnes to A. N. Marshall, 6 Oct. 1971.

Roberts' managers accepted dust as a fact of factory life. The 1931 Regulations were regarded as 'impracticable' and the only defence workers had against the dust (apart from the deficient exhaust systems) was the issue of equally inadequate respirators in the scheduled areas. The Turner & Newall board also accepted the situation, even though by the 1950s this tiny factory—only 2 per cent of the group workforce—was responsible for nearly a quarter of the compensation payments from the Asbestosis Fund. Only when the company realized it would have little defence against breaches of statutory duty did it respond. One of Roberts' directors was John Waddell, a robust, no-nonsense university-educated engineer, who had formerly been a Factory Inspector.[23] In a common law action brought against the company in 1951, Waddell considered calling his old Factory Inspectorate friends to testify that controlling asbestos dust was impossible. To head off future claims, in March 1952 John Collins arranged a meeting with Sir George Barnett, the Chief Inspector of Factories. Before that meeting, a revealing series of letters passed between Collins and Waddell. The latter attempted to find some 'statistical ammunition' for the company, but after reviewing all the data on suspensions, Waddell concluded: 'we can hardly claim that [these figures] prove that complete prevention of dust is not essential in order to eliminate the disease'.[24]

Collins eventually drew up a memo for the meeting, which included some candid comments on the dust situation:

When it is remembered that an appreciable proportion of common asbestos dust is smaller than 1 micron is size and that asbestos can divide into particles below the limit of visibility of optical microscopes, the impossibility of preventing the escape of any particle of dust even from fully enclosed machinery hardly needs to be stated. But the Regulations as worded require even more than that, since some of the machines and processes specified in Regulation 1 cannot by their very nature be fully enclosed; for example, carding machines in normal operation, the cleaning and grinding of the cylinders of such machines, and workplaces where the filling or emptying of sacks is effected by hand.[25]

The argument was that, because the Regulations were unworkable and because (according to Collins) experience had shown that there was a level below which asbestos disease did not occur, the rules should be amended. Turner & Newall did not want to tighten the safety measures, they demanded a qualifying clause. Exhaust equipment was to prevent the escape of dust only *'so far as reasonably practicable'* [original emphasis].[26] Fortunately for the workforce, no such amendment was ever passed.

[23] Waddell became chairman of TBA (and a T & N director) between 1963 and 1968.
[24] 9/1462–6. Waddell to Collins, 5 March 1952.
[25] 57/801–2. J. L. Collins, 'Memo . . . for discussion with Sir George Barnett', 17 Mar. 1952.
[26] 9/1540. Chapman & Co. to J. L. Collins, 31 Oct. 1951.

Dust at the company's asbestos cement plants also continued to cause asbestosis and cancer. At Trafford Park, workers recalled that 'there had been a great deal of dust around'.[27] The complaint is supported by statistics of the plant's asbestosis cases, some of which occurred in about a decade or less. Some workers developed asbestos diseases from simply unloading asbestos fibre.[28] One victim of asbestosis had been only a clerk at the company, albeit for forty-two years.[29] One Widnes worker, who finished asbestos-cement sheets and also acted as a beaterman (mixing asbestos fibres with cement and water), recalled working in 'a very dusty environment . . . in a large building which covered about four acres. For many years [after 1941], there was no dust extraction . . . [and] . . . face masks were first provided . . . in 1969.'[30]

Documents in the Turner & Newall archive show that not only was dust extraction ineffective, but also that other protective aids, such as respirators, offered little protection. Face masks were routinely provided for the dustiest operations by the 1960s and company rules were laid down for their use. However, writs served against Turner & Newall from the 1960s regularly alleged that the rules were more honoured in the breach than in the observance. Respirators were often poorly maintained, difficult to use, and were often discarded even in the dustiest conditions. An asbestotic TAC sprayer, who had worked for the firm for about six years, testified in 1975 that it was usual to remove masks during spraying so that workers could talk with each other and move scaffolding; and that the filters in the masks were not cleaned or maintained.[31] A Roberts' sprayer, who developed asbestosis after five years, claimed that although he was provided with a mask, he had no overalls and not enough replacement filters. No one warned him of the dangers of inhaling asbestos. Obviously, Turner & Newall often counterclaimed worker negligence, though privately it was admitted that the cleaning and inspection of masks were 'ineffective'.[32] Of course, blaming workers was simply evading responsibility, as even the best respirators did not keep out all respirable fibres.[33] As Waddell admitted: 'respirators are always the last resort; prevention of dust emission in the first place is the aim.'[34]

Some of the gravest dangers were experienced by insulators. By 1948,

[27] 114/1744. J. F. Dark Medical Report, 1977. George Forsyth file.
[28] 27/1688–90, 1700–13: W. Willows file.   [29] 79/2190: R. Vost (1900–76) file.
[30] 114/1830. Medical Report, 6 Apr. 1981. R. Carman file.
[31] 114/886–8. Walter Sutton and TAC claim, 1975.
[32] 114/813–34. G. Swinney file. See especially 114/820. R. D. Lunt memo, 27 June 1972.
[33] Siebe–Gorman's micro-filter ori-nasal respirators, introduced in about 1951, claimed to give protection against dust particles down to 0.5 microns diameter—above the size of the smallest asbestos fibres. Siebe-Gorman filters also contained crocidolite.
[34] 9/309. Waddell to J. A. E. Clogg, 5 Feb. 1965.

the trade unions at Washington were becoming restive with conditions in the insulation division in the factory.[35] Two 'unscheduled' deaths had occurred and Collins thought he should see conditions for himself. He described the problem as 'largely a tactical or psychological matter for the management rather than a legal one',[36] and refused to extend the medical scheme. However, he did ask Hirst Bateman to examine some six employees and tour the factory. Bateman found that only one man—John Robson, a felt-packer—had definite asbestosis; two others were 'doubtful'.[37] However, implicit in Bateman's comments was the view that conditions at the factory could be greatly improved. He recommended periodic medical examination of all workers handling asbestos, closer general monitoring of workers' health, and constant vigilance to avoid unnecessary dust.[38] Collins saw no problem in implementing these recommendations: however, as he pointed out, the 'strict letter of the Regulations' meant that the company could not ask the Medical Board to examine workers. They would have to apply themselves for an examination. In the event, John Robson was not suspended until February 1950.

That working conditions at Washington Station were far from ideal is revealed in several sources. One is the testimony of the workers. A mesothelioma victim, who spent his childhood in a house polluted by emissions from the works, recalled that until the 1960s 'asbestos dust in the atmosphere at the factory . . . was rife. You used to go into the factory and inside it looked just like a snowstorm.'[39] Further evidence can be found in the biennial visits of the Factory Inspectors as reported in the company minutes. In November 1948, after an extensive tour of the works, they made several recommendations regarding dust suppression after failures to comply with the Regulations. In 1950, a Factory Inspector was sufficiently concerned with dust in the fibre store to argue that its personnel should be brought within the 1931 Scheme (a 'serious issue' for the company, though the views of the Inspector were not implemented). In 1951, the room of an 'unscheduled' cutter of asbestos cloth was found

[35] A Washington director informed Collins that one trade unionist had been invited to lecture in America on industrial disease. He added: 'Personally I believe he is out of his depth in dealing with such a subject, but as you will appreciate that is most often the person who causes most trouble.' 160/161. A. W. Cole to Collins, 15 June 1948.

[36] 55/1374. WCC/Newalls Directors' Minutes, 13 July 1948. Presumably, the two dead workers were James Hamilton and Alexander Caldwell. See Table 6.2.

[37] Of the workers Bateman examined, two appear in T & N claims files: John Robson died in 1957 from lung cancer and asbestosis; Wilfred Rutter, whose X-ray Bateman found 'suspicious', was never suspended and died in 1966 from lung cancer and asbestosis ('carcinoma', according to T & N).

[38] 12/480–1. Bateman to G. Wilson, 25 Sept. 1948.

[39] 603/4–11. Testimony of Henry Kerton (1908–86), a blacksmith at WCC/Newalls, 24 Nov. 1984.

to be inadequately ventilated and not sufficiently isolated from the main factory.

Outside Washington, Newalls' staff were exposed to even greater peril. In 1952, a Factory Inspector visited the Newcastle premises of Newalls and noted that men using asbestos mixtures had not been wearing suitable respirators.[40] The failure to enforce safety standards for contract laggers seems to have been almost universal, judging from writs served on the company in the 1980s. As one doctor observed: 'the stories from employees are pretty consistent until about 1970. They all say that they were exposed to asbestos, whether white or blue, that there were no special precautions, that there was frequently a snowstorm of asbestos around them, and there is no question that they were exposed to dangerous quantities of asbestos.'[41]

The government was certainly aware of this problem, especially in the shipyards. In August 1950, the Ministry of Labour & National Service issued new draft Regulations for shipbuilding and ship-repairing.[42] The preface stated (not inaccurately) that the new code had been 'in contemplation for a considerable time', but had been delayed by the war. The twenty-seven-page document was circulated in advance to allow for discussion among interested parties. The asbestos provisions filled less than half a page and essentially resurrected the key suggestions of the Garrett circular of 1945 (see Chapter 2). The new code recommended the use of respirators for most asbestos jobs and argued that no young person be employed on such work. Anyone working in the vicinity of asbestos workers should also wear a respirator.

Turner & Newall's response was again written by Collins. He began by reminding the government of his previous letter of October 1945, in which he had stated that the proposals were needless and that no asbestosis had occurred among employees handling and applying finished goods: 'That, I understand, is still the case.'[43] Collins then underlined his belief that with Newalls' products 'there is no asbestos dust and no possibility of risk'. He continued:

We are under the impression that in general the references to asbestos . . . have been included because of the widespread use of the Asbestos Spray Process aboard ship . . . No suggestion has ever been made to us before that respirators should be worn in connection with the handling or application of the finished articles; on that basis every plumber, for instance installing Magnesia Insulation Sections anywhere in this country, should wear a respirator! . . . As regards the Spray

[40] 56/29. WCC/N Directors' Minutes, 7 May 1952.
[41] 603/2119–22. John Robertson report on James A. Morris, 7 July 1986.
[42] Ministry of Labour & National Service, *Revision of Regulations for Shipbuilding and Ship-Repairing: Preliminary Draft of New Code* (1950).
[43] 12/172–5. Collins to Ministry of Labour & National Service, 6 Dec. 1950.

Process itself, our spray operators have been provided with respirators for a number of years at the request of the Department, and I am informed that it is still a fact that no asbestosis cases have occurred amongst them . . .

Collins emphasized the new damping techniques that had made spraying even safer. He then quibbled over the word 'vicinity', arguing: 'Whatever the risk there may be from the Spray process can only exist (if at all) in the immediate vicinity of the work.'

Collins's denial of asbestosis at Newalls and Washington Chemical Company was again unwarranted. There had been twenty-six cases by 1949 and many of these had been laggers (some on ships): this was in addition to the case at a subsidiary company in 1944 (discussed in Chapter 2). These cases were especially significant as these workers were not covered by the Medical Arrangements Scheme and so were unlikely to be notified. Probably, the Factory Inspectorate would have known about some of them through its surveys. Yet, the government let Turner & Newall know that any revision of the regulations would not occur for some time.

In March 1950, twelve years after the first official interest in the subject, two Factory Inspectors visited Armley to examine dust concentrations when spraying Limpet. A report was later issued, but no ruling was made to restrict the use of spray.[44] Interestingly, Turner & Newall investigated spray dust levels in October 1949 and concluded that with adequate pre-damping, spray dust levels were 'substantially below that in a good flyer spinning room' (that is, below Merewether's magical dust datum).[45] Besides its tortured comparison with an old rule-of-thumb benchmark, the company also highlighted that dust concentrations could be higher in confined spaces and where spraying was conducted for a long period. At least one Factory Inspector regarded this report as unsatisfactory and atypical of working conditions.

In the early 1950s, the increase in asbestosis cases at Newalls began causing some concern at the company. In November 1954, an area managers' meeting discussed the new cases, which had occurred among employees working with asbestos cloth and mattresses. Worryingly, there had been two cases among sprayers.[46] Those at the meeting

appreciated that men fitting asbestos sections or asbestos slabs . . . might reasonably be expected to be just as much exposed to the danger of absorbing into their lungs as much asbestos as those employed fitting cloth or making mattresses. No

[44] 30/89. Dust and Respirators Data Sheet, May 1963.
[45] 301/410–12. J. S. Evans's report on Limpet Asbestos Spray Machines, 17 Mar. 1950.
[46] The first 'official' spray case may have been Prince William Apps, who was suspended with pneumoconiosis/TB in 1953 after less than three years' spraying. Apps launched a common law action in 1956, but later abandoned it. He died in 1963, aged 38, from a brain tumour. There was no inquest and his death certificate mentions neither asbestosis nor TB.

solution which was practicable could be found for men employed in this operation other than supplying them with masks, but it was appreciated that if this had
to be done all other personnel working in the same spaces, such as engine rooms,
boiler rooms, etc., aboard ships, would object and would refuse to work in the
same space as our men.[47]

Eventually, Newalls decided that it would arrange its own medical
examinations for both new and current staff (as far as this was practicable); that mattresses should not be made in the shipyards; and that
workers (including sprayers) should be issued with masks, for which they
should sign and regularly submit for inspection.[48] The laggers, though,
presented a problem. It was agreed that theoretically they should also
wear masks, but again this would throw up the question of 'other trades
people working in the same space refusing to do so whilst our men were
engaged in this operation'. Damping would lessen the danger, but
Newalls felt that 'for obvious reasons this is not really practicable'.

Not until 1957 was the shipyard problem raised again by the government, when the 1950 draft revisions were circulated again and Turner &
Newall directors were asked to attend a meeting to discuss them. Sales of
Limpet spray were now reaching a peak. Knox believed that safety precautions were adequate, but stonewalling the government was becoming
increasingly difficult. First, a Washington director in December 1957
began distancing himself from the board's pre-1950 enumeration of
asbestotics. He told Collins bluntly that the 'position is more difficult than
you had hoped would be the case'.[49] A bad crop of suspensions at Washington and among Newalls' contract workers had occurred in 1957:
sixteen in all. Second, by 1955 asbestosis had been reported in sprayers in
Sweden and Australia, albeit that Knox had blamed this on the company's
safety precautions not being followed.[50] However, in 1955 Knox himself
confirmed asbestosis in a sprayer in Victoria, Australia.[51] Here, too, the
company were battling to keep spraying outside any health regulations,
a task made difficult by 'left wing sections of the trade unions . . . using
the dispute for political ends'.[52]

In 1958, when Collins replied to the government, he finally had to shift
his ground on the prevalence of asbestosis in shipyard workers. He now
admitted that there had been *fifteen* cases among Newalls' workers: ten of
these were marine laggers, five 'land' workers, and there had also been
four spray cases. Yet he assured the government that nearly all these men
had started work before the Asbestos Regulations were introduced in

[47] 9/1142–3. J. A. E. Clogg, 'Asbestosis' memo, 6 Dec. 1954.
[48] 56/660. WCC/Newalls Directors' Minutes, 7 Dec. 1954.
[49] 57/1098–9. J. A. E. Clogg to Collins, 19 Nov. 1957.
[50] 301/760–1. Knox, 'Report on Medical Arrangements Scheme at Roberts, 1956–7'.
[51] 24/127–8. Knox to Waddell, 22 Sept. 1959. Knox argued that the man in question was
only 'considered to have asbestosis . . . no one has yet died to prove it as far as I know'.
[52] 24/99–102. R. M. Stratton, 'Asbestosis in Victoria', 6 Nov. 1959.

1932. This was sophistry, as the Regulations had never applied to ancillary trades and spraying only began in the early 1930s.

The figures that Collins supplied to the government were from a company survey in January 1958. However, as Table 6.2 shows, Collins again was only telling a small part of the story. The number of asbestosis and cancer cases at Washington Chemical Company and Newalls was not thirty-nine: it was at least sixty-eight. Again, it must be stressed that most of these workers were not medically monitored and undoubtedly many sick workers and deaths would have been 'lost'. What accounts for such a huge discrepancy? Evidently, Collins only counted what he regarded as 'pure' asbestosis cases. If workers had not been certified by the Medical Board (Keily, Kay), or had cancer (Wren, Thirlaway), or had worked in the mines (Dockerty, Jordan), or had tuberculosis (Watkins), they were excluded from the lists. Collins's exclusion of cancer cases is particularly revealing, as by now the company was aware of the lung cancer risk for asbestos workers (see below).

Despite these deaths, Turner & Newall's attitude (and that of other asbestos manufacturers) to the draft code had not altered: they argued that introducing respirators for shipyard asbestos workers would lead to a 'very wide extension of the Regulations'.[53] Waddell particularly objected to the phrase 'working in the vicinity', which he believed should be 'strongly resisted'.[54] Indeed, Turner & Newall's stance when they and other interested parties met the government in March 1958 was that this clause should be withdrawn.

Collins felt reasonably satisfied with that meeting, though one Factory Inspector—Dr Arthur 'Mac' McLaughlin—was unimpressed. An expert in occupational chest diseases, well known for his short temper, McLaughlin knew the dangers of asbestos and believed that respirators should be worn wherever there was an asbestosis risk.[55] In April 1958, McLaughlin was invited to watch Newalls spray a tanker at Wallsend. McLaughlin, who had not seen asbestos sprayed since a previous Turner & Newall demonstration in 1940, was said by one manager to have been surprised at the 'cleanliness' of the procedure. However, McLaughlin said he still 'did not like spray processes', and believed that 'the spraying of asbestos could be highly dangerous'.[56] The visit was stage-managed by the company, with Waddell particularly keen that the spraying machine had a pre-damping drum.[57] At one point, McLaughlin had asked to see other parts of the ship—partly, the Newalls' man felt, in the hope of

---

[53] 12/264–6. Collins to Ministry of Labour & National Service, 21 Jan. 1958.

[54] 12/276–9. Waddell to G. Alderson, 10 Feb. 1958.

[55] 12/309. Collins's memo to T & N Board Meeting, 20 Mar. 1958.

[56] 12/335–7. G. Wilson memo, 17 Apr. 1958.

[57] 59/1782–3. J. Waddell to G. Alderson, 24 Mar. 1958. Behind the scenes, T & N were continuing with experiments to reduce the dust levels by adding oil and chemicals to the spray mixture.

Table 6.2. *Asbestos disease in Washington Chemical Company/Newalls employees to 1957*

Name	Occupation	Service (years)	Suspended/ died	Cause of death
William Presland (c.1892–?)	Disintegrator	$12\frac{1}{4}$	1931	?
Dorothy Keily (c.1903–35)	Mattress maker	6	1932	Asbestosis/TB
Henry Coggan (c.1886–1946)	Fibre mixer	8	1933	Asbestosis
Florence Watts* (c.1902–42)	Magnesia and slab machinist	23	1936	Asbestosis
Edward Roberts (?–?)	Mixer	6	1938	?
Charles Jenkins* (c.1896–1938)	Foreman Compo Division	19	1938	Asbestosis/TB
James Kay (c.1892–1938)	Plastic packer	17	1938	Asbestosis
Mary Keegan* (c.1892–1939)	Slab cutter	26	1938	Asbestosis/TB
Bernard Stevenson* (c.1886–1942)	Marine lagger	22	1939	Asbestosis
Job B. Bordess* (c.1907–65)	Fibre treater	17	1944	Coronary artery disease
George Wilden* (c.1901–?)	Labourer Insulation Division	29	1944	?
John J. Benson* (c.1888–1946)	Lagger/fibre treater	9	1946	Asbestosis
Dorothy Thirlaway (c.1908–45)	Insulation division	7	1946	Lung cancer/asbestosis
James Hamilton* (1886–1948)	Foreman Insulation Division	21	1946	Asbestosis
George F. James* (c.1900–54)	Fibre mixer/treater	18	1946	Asbestosis
John R. Scorer* (c.1891–1946)	Goods loader	26	1946	Asbestosis/endothelioma of the pleura
Ernest T. Watkins (c.1901–46)	Lagger	20	1946	Asbestosis/TB
Frank E. Watkins (c.1928–46)	Lagger	2	1946	Asbestosis/TB
Alexander Caldwell* (?–1948)	Felt maker/packer	17	1947	Asbestosis
William McMann* (c.1901–59)	Fibre treater	18	1947	Asbestosis
James W. Wren (c.1889–1947)	Lagger	42	1947	Asbestosis/ca. lung
William J. Clark (c.1903–49)	Lagger	27	1949	Asbestosis
William T. Griffiths* (c.1905–53)	Marine lagger	24	1949	Asbestosis
Henry J. House* (c.1885–1951)	Labourer	27	1949	Ca. lung
John Larkum* (c.1888–1950)	Fibre labourer	12	1949	Asbestosis

Table 6.2. *(cont.)*

Name	Occupation	Service (years)	Suspended/died	Cause of death
W. J. Smith* (c.1903–51)	Marine lagger	23	1949	?
Thomas A. Beaty (c.1903–1953)	Lagger	32	1950	TB/ca. lung/asbestosis
Thomas Jordan (c.1890–1950)	Labourer	10	1950	Pneumoconiosis
John W. Robson* (c.1908–57)	Labourer Insulation Division	22	1950	Ca. lung/asbestosis
Joseph Meanen (?–1951)	Lagger	32	1951	Asbestosis
John Smith* (c.1898–1964)	Lagger	$22\frac{1}{2}$	1951	Asbestosis
Charles H. Bartley* (c.1904–?)	Lagger	24	1952	Cancer
Richard Chisholm* (1897–1962)	Moulder	34	1952	Asbestosis/ca. lung
Robinson Peacock* (c.1907–55)	Foreman Insulation Division	23	1952	Asbestosis
Michael Pratt (?–?)	Labourer	20	1952	?
Prince W. Apps* (1925–63)	Sprayer	$2\frac{1}{2}$	1953	Brain tumour
George Bain (c.1893–1953)	Marine lagger	42	1953	Asbestosis
Edward Nelmes* (c.1890–1966)	Fibre treater	$9\frac{1}{2}$	1953	Coronary occlusion, asbestosis
Robert W. Pearson* (1916–70)	Marine lagger	12	1953	Peptic ulcer (DCe)
William L. Whitelaw* (1915–?)	Marine sprayer	$5\frac{1}{2}$	1953	?
Andrew Anderson* (c.1892–1956)	Products Loader	34	1954	Ca. lung/asbestosis
Peter Dockerty (1893–?)	Labourer Magnesia Division	$13\frac{1}{2}$	1954	?
John S. Fletcher* (c.1900–60)	Lagger	41	1954	Asbestosis
Charles Coyle* (1907–56)	Marine sprayer	9	1954	Asbestosis
George Galbraith* (c.1903–61)	Marine lagger	36	1954	Asbestosis
Hugh Goldie* (c.1895-?)	Labourer/unloader	$12\frac{1}{2}$	1954	?
Alexander Paisley* (c.1905–57)	Marine lagger	31	1954	Asbestosis
Frederick Turnbull* (c.1898–1957)	Marine lagger	39	1954	Asbestosis
William Brown (c.1904–55)	Fibre mixer/packer	23	1955	Asbestosis/'carcinoma'
James Conway* (c.1892–1961)	Mixer/fibre treater	40	1955	Ca. rectum
Charles W. Bauer* (c.1885–1968)	Lagger	44	1956	?

Table 6.2. *(cont.)*

Name	Occupation	Service (years)	Suspended/ died	Cause of death
Andrew Carnegie* (c.1915–?)	Marine sprayer	18	1956	?
John Gallagher (?–?)	Lagger	10	1956	?
Mary J. Gibson* (c.1910–63)	General worker	24	1956	Asbestosis
George Thompson (c.1904–62)	Lagger	30	1956	Asbestosis
William Wright* (1901–57)	Lagger	35	1956	Asbestosis
Arthur J. Bell* (c.1901–61)	Marine lagger	$19\frac{3}{4}$	1957	Ca. lung/asbestosis
Utrick C. Bright (c.1906–?)	Packer	21	1957	?
Emily L. Curran (c.1903–?)	Magnesia labourer	15	1957	?
Alfred A. Embley (?–1960)	Lagger	35	1957	Asbestosis
Francis A. Fergusson (c.1906–59)	Lagger	37	1957	Asbestosis
William Jamieson (?–1960)	Labourer/sprayer	11	1957	Asbestosis
James Laughlin* (c.1921–?)	Marine sprayer	24	1957	?
John S. Mason (c.1900–61)	Blanket/Magnesia Division	$18\frac{1}{2}$	1957	Ca. lung/asbestosis
Frederick F. Parsons (c.1919–62)	Sprayer	$9\frac{1}{2}$	1957	Asbestosis
Thomas Sergeant (c.1914–65)	Lagger	25	1957	?
D. Evans (?–?)	Lagger	12	1957	?
T. McCutcheon (?–?)	?	17	1957	?

*Cases listed in John Collins's correspondence with Ministry of Labour, 1957–8.

Note: Length of service covers the period up to suspension.

Source: T & N compensation claims files and death certificates (DCe). (File data is not always complete.)

finding spraying going on elsewhere—but this had been 'carefully taken care of and there were no other spraying machines operating'. Generally, McLaughlin was sceptical of pre-damping and did not believe that the conditions that he had seen were typical.[58] Documents in the Turner & Newall archive show that he was right. Spray guns were prone to clogging; hopper flaps were left unbolted in operation; and unused fibre in

[58] 59/1864–5. Waddell to G. Alderson, 2 May 1958.

machines created dust. Some workers had been reported sweeping asbestos waste into the cavities on railway carriages.[59] The much-vaunted damping drum and continuous damping device, which had been introduced between 1948 and 1950, were never widely used. The equipment was bulky, awkward to operate in a confined space, and increased costs. Neither system found favour in the building, engineering, and marine fields, and the only substantial use of the damping drum was in railway carriage shops.

Despite McLaughlin, by May 1958 it was evident that the asbestos companies had won their hoped-for concessions from the government. More water was to be applied to the new draft regulations than to the fibre. The rules for respirators would now only include spraying, the removal of asbestos lagging, the cleaning of sacks, and the scaling of boilers and smoke boxes. The clause requiring protection for bystander workers on the ships had been abandoned entirely. As Collins argued, this would 'no doubt have caused continual difficulties with other contractors and with the shipbuilders and might well have led to a substantial loss of asbestos insulation business'.[60] Whatever the reasons for the government's surrender—Waddell mentioned the departure of McLaughlin for a research post at the London Hospital as 'largely responsible for the smooth manner in which our recommendations were accepted'[61]—the final regulations gave the industry very little reason for complaint.

More tinkering with the wording followed, so that the Shipbuilding and Ship-repairing Regulations did not become law until October 1960. It had taken fifteen years for the government to achieve a very modest extension of the 1931 Regulations and most asbestos jobs in the shipyards were still not protected by the medical and compensation scheme.

However, government pressure had not been entirely without its effect on Turner & Newall, despite Collins's machinations. In August 1958, the company had decided voluntarily that it would introduce initial and periodic medical examinations for its sprayers—a move that Collins felt was unnecessary.[62] Yet nine sprayers from 135 operatives examined were immediately suspended, most with early signs of asbestosis.[63] By the early 1960s, the company was also monitoring the wearing of respirators more closely, partly as a response to visits by the Factory Inspectors and partly on advice from the company's solicitor (who was now liaising with

[59] 39/1321. 'Technical Information on SLA', 18 Mar. 1955. See also 9/48–51. Knox's letter to J. A. E. Clogg, 23 Sept. 1960.

[60] 12/338. Collins's memo to T & N Board Meeting, 26 June 1958.

[61] 12/342. Dolbey to Waddell, 25 July 1958. A. I. G. McLaughlin (1896–1983) later became an expert witness in asbestos-related disease cases involving the Royal Dockyards.

[62] 30/1423–6. General Instruction L. M. 17, Aug. 1958; 160/183–4. Collins to Waddell, 21 Apr. 1958. This, of course, did not cover spray licensees.

[63] 24/65. 'Details of Employees Found Unfit for Spray Work', 5 May 1960.

Knox).[64] Nevertheless, this was only one asbestos company and generally, as Nick Wikeley observes, 'the wider battle for the protection of shipyard workers' health had long since been lost'.[65] Only the Royal Navy followed a more stringent line in protecting its workers. At Devonport by 1968, the removal of old lagging was conducted with impervious overalls and air-lines; and asbestos workers were given annual medical examinations and chest X-rays.[66]

Turner & Newall could not keep the lid on asbestosis cases indefinitely. Asbestosis and cancer cases among Washington and Newalls' workers were rising inexorably. Between 1958 and 1966, there were ninety-two sus-pensions, mostly amongst laggers and sprayers.[67] These cases were now apparent to those outside the company. In 1963, a Newcastle industrial health physician observed that he had personally seen eighteen cases of asbestosis among north-east insulators (whom he believed numbered about 500) and concluded: 'asbestosis is relatively common amongst insulators'.[68]

By the early 1960s, the Factory Inspectorate were becoming increasingly concerned. They were particularly worried about stripping asbestos and one Inspector gave Turner & Newall a friendly warning that asbestos insulation might be banned. Waddell thought the Inspector concerned was 'inclined to allow his zealousness to run away with him';[69] but another director warned against complacency:

The awkward thing about this is that even if we succeed in perfecting a way of applying the material by dustless and 'safe' method (and that is a big 'if'), we are still liable to come unstuck according to [the Inspector] when somebody eventu-ally comes to rip out the asbestos. I cannot see much hope of rendering this 'safe' from a health point of view so that reliance would still have to be put on protec-tive measures.[70]

The Inspector advised the company to start looking for asbestos substi-tutes. Yet there is no indication that the company pursued this option seri-

[64] See, for example, 59/1812–13. Memo on a Visit to a Newalls' office by Dr James Tombleson, 15 Sept. 1958. Tombleson later told Knox that he was paying particular atten-tion to the asbestos industry, especially WCC. See 9/92. Knox to Clogg, 26 July 1959.

[65] N. J. Wikeley, 'Asbestos in the Shipyards: Dust, Disease and Drafting Regulations', Inaugural Lecture, University of Southampton, 4 Feb. 1997. Typescript.

[66] Harries, 'Dockyards', 140. The Navy had abandoned the spray process in 1963, though this was largely due to reasons of weight.

[67] 9/1975–98. Asbestosis Statistics.

[68] G. L. Leathart and J. T. Sanderson, 'Some Observations on Asbestosis', *Annals of Occu-pational Hygiene* 6 (1963), 65–74, 68. Leathart estimated the total number of UK insulators at about 5,000 (with 18,700 employed in the asbestos textile and products industry). Leathart had also visited the Washington works and later told Knox that he had seen workers feeding fibre into machines by hand without respirators. 9/48–51. Knox to J. A. E. Clogg, 23 Sept. 1960.

[69] 24/1218–19. Waddell to A. N. Marshall, 24 July 1962.

[70] 24/1216–17. Marshall to Waddell, 25 July 1962.

ously until at least the 1960s. One might imagine that this was because asbestos was unique, but this was far from the case. Asbestos's fire resistance is not as great as is popularly believed and its thermal insulation qualities can also be duplicated. In any case, in some products—especially 85 per cent magnesia—asbestos was merely a *reinforcing* agent. Substitutes were available even before asbestos was pushed onto the world market in the 1880s. Robert Jones's technical treatise, *Asbestos and Asbestic* (1897), contained a whole chapter on 'substitutes and similarities' for asbestos. The chief of these was slag wool (known as mineral wool in the US), which was produced after 1840 by dispersing blast furnace slag into tiny particles and fibres. Rock wool was a similar fibrous mineral that was available at this time. Slag wool, like asbestos, was incombustible and indestructible; it was also a superior insulator. Above all, it was cheaper.

How then did asbestos gain its hegemony? Partly, it seems, because of its all-round qualities in actual use. As Jones highlighted, slag wool had disadvantages: it lacked flexibility and lubricity; and sulphides in the wool could cause metal corrosion. Mattress makers such as Turner & Newall also complained that slag wool contained 'shot'—small particles that could shake down in the mattresses and cause them to lose their shape. Ironically, it seems that the tendency of mineral wool to irritate the skin counted against it, especially when compared to silky asbestos. Jones warned that slag wool might cause 'serious mischief', while Royal Navy surgeons reported that it caused skin irritation and chest problems.[71]

Meanwhile, in the inter-war period, asbestos was trumpeted as a wonder product. Turner & Newall absorbed competing insulation companies and swallowed market share from substitute materials (sometimes by using unfair and secret price agreements). With business expanding so rapidly and profitably, asbestos makers had little interest in substitutes, despite the emerging asbestosis problem. In 1930, when the government legislated for asbestosis, other fibrous minerals were appearing, such as 'Zonolite' (based on mica) and, above all, fibre glass. Both these products were discussed at Newalls' local board meetings in 1931, though not from a health viewpoint.[72] Fibre glass was soon in demand in the shipyards where it was found acceptable. Robert H. Turner, on a trip to North America in 1930, found that the ocean liner 'Bremen' had boiler mattresses made from asbestos cloth filled with German fibre glass, which did their job well.[73] When the company ran trials on spun glass, they too found that it was as efficient as magnesia.[74] However, although Newalls was

[71] R. H. Jones, *Asbestos and Asbestic* (1897). 324; D. S. Wright, 'Man-Made Mineral Fibres: An Historical Note', *Journal of the Society of Occupational Medicine* 30 (1980), 138–40.
[72] 231/2048. Insulation Executive, 24 Sept. 1931.
[73] 102/906. R. H. Turner Visit, 1930–1.
[74] 231/2074. Insulation Executive, 27 Jan. 1932.

initially interested in developing the product themselves, it eventually decided that a 'neutral attitude' should be adopted—neither pushing fibre glass, nor preventing its sale.[75] The firm could make more money from asbestos.

During the Second World War, however, substitutes began gaining in popularity. The trend was most marked in the USA, where Roberts hoped to market Limpet. By 1945, rock wool was sufficiently important for Turner & Newall to consider launching its manufacture in America. Meanwhile, fibre glass had made such serious inroads into the American spray business that Roberts had trouble in marketing Limpet. Fibre glass proved well suited for acoustic and insulation work; it was also more economic and much less messy; and it was vigorously marketed. By 1950, fibre glass firms were the sole suppliers of spray to the US Navy.[76] In Britain, Roberts had found that by 1948 a satisfactory spray blend could be mixed from mineral wool and asbestos (indeed, such a mixture was later sold to TAC), though amosite remained the material of choice for economic reasons.[77] However, mineral wool makers continued to improve their product by reducing the shot content and making wool easier to mix with water and cement. By 1957, Roberts and Keasbey & Mattison agreed that rock wool spray was both feasible and cheaper.[78] On the Continent and in Australia asbestos insulation was soon losing out to mineral wool and fibre glass (and also vermiculite and perlite). Yet Roberts refused to countenance shifting its strategy. It had a mineral wool spray blend ready for France by 1958, but its sale was to be restricted to avoid causing 'embarrassment' in countries where Roberts was not offering such an alternative.[79] In Britain, products such as fibre glass were regarded as 'complementary to, rather than competitive with, our existing range of insulation products'.[80] The arguments were strictly economic: no mention was made of the health benefits of substitutes. This was unfortunate, as by then a new asbestos hazard had emerged—cancer.

ASBESTOS AND LUNG CANCER

Since the 1950s, lung cancer has become such an 'epidemic' that it is now the commonest cause of cancer death. Smoking cigarettes is primarily

[75] 53/1943–4. Newalls' Local Board, 28 Jan. 1938.
[76] 40/1690–1722. N. L. Dolbey, 'Spray—USA', Nov.–Dec. 1950.
[77] Roberts's use of amosite in the 1950s was a reversal of its policy in the 1930s, when the Leeds company had promised the Rochdale board to cease using the material because of its adverse health effects. See 36/1548–9. Directors' minutes, 27 Apr. 1937.
[78] 112/1778–9. Rockwool memo, 10 July 1957.
[79] 156/18–21. A. N. Marshall to N. A. Morling, 21 Oct. 1958.
[80] 14/1161–4. Marshall to Morling, 11 Nov. 1959.

responsible for this dramatic increase in a disease that was hardly known in 1900; however, some lung cancer deaths are due to asbestos.

Asbestotics—if they live long enough—have an increased risk of lung cancer. The risk in heavily exposed workers with asbestosis can be as high as 50 per cent, though how cancer develops in such individuals is still not entirely clear. Asbestos fibres are inert and not chemically carcinogenic. One suggestion is that the microscopic fibres—especially those that possess the 'correct' physical properties of straightness, diameter, and length—traumatize cells, beginning a cascade of biological responses that later cause cancer. Another possibility is that the fibres 'skewer' cells so that they are vulnerable to the action of other carcinogens. If this is true, then asbestos is doubly dangerous: it can act not only as a cancer agent in its own right (probably without first causing asbestosis), but also as a promoter of cancer. This may explain why asbestos is especially potent when combined with cigarette smoke. The two factors appear to be synergistic: one multiplying rather than adding to the risk of the other. Heavily exposed asbestos workers who smoke can have over *fifty times* the incidence of lung cancer when compared to non-smoking individuals in the ordinary population.

Certainly the latency for lung cancer—like asbestosis—is long. Lung cancer from asbestos or smoking (or both) does not usually appear in less than twenty years after exposure. Yet once it develops, the disease is painful, difficult to treat, and has a bleak prognosis: death usually occurs within a year or so of the first symptoms and few sufferers survive longer than five years.

A connection between lung cancer and asbestos was first highlighted in the early 1930s in European and American medical journals.[81] In 1934, pathologists in east London reported cases of carcinoma of the lung among their asbestosis autopsies. Sometime before 1935, one of those pathologists, Dr Stephen Gloyne, suggested to Merewether the possibility of an association between the two diseases.[82] A German medical authority reported further examples of asbestosis and lung cancer in 1938 and, after reviewing the literature, stated for the first time that lung cancer was a specific disease of asbestos workers. In 1943, the German government became the first in the world to recognize asbestos-induced lung cancer as a compensatable occupational disease.[83] In Britain, the Factory Inspectorate, first alerted to the trend in the late 1930s, featured the rising

---

[81] Selikoff and Lee, *Asbestos and Disease*, 6–8; B. I. Castleman, *Asbestos: Medical and Legal Aspects* (1996), 49–158.

[82] W. Burton Wood and S. R. Gloyne, 'Pulmonary Asbestosis', *Lancet* 227 (22 Dec. 1934), 1383–5; W. D. Buchanan, 'Asbestosis and Primary Intrathoracic Neoplasms', *Annals of New York Academy of Sciences* 132 (31 Dec. 1965), i, 507–18, 508.

[83] R. Proctor, *The Nazi War on Cancer* (1999), 107–13.

incidence of asbestosis/lung cancer deaths in its publications in the late 1940s.

Yet it is not clear how widely this knowledge was disseminated or to what extent contemporaries regarded such case reports—if they knew about them—as scientific evidence. One medical authority has recalled that in the early 1950s he regarded much of the early evidence as suggestive, but anecdotal and not widely known.[84] Another has agreed, describing the case data as 'numerators, without denomination and not a basis for action'.[85] However, this assumes that the asbestos industry learned about its cancer problem by reading articles in medical journals. But as a leading South African chest physician, who was involved with asbestos-disease research at this time, has observed: 'The industry discovered the problem directly through seeing their workers and some of their executives die of cancer and through the research results of studies funded and controlled by the industry.'[86]

Turner & Newall workers began dying from asbestosis *and* lung cancer at least as early as 1932. As Table 6.3 shows, during the next twenty years at least eighteen scheduled TBA employees were found at post-mortem to have had lung cancer (usually combined with asbestosis). This was to present another occupational health challenge to the company. It also meant a difficult problem for sick workers as the 1931 regulations had been formulated to deal only with asbestosis. Not until the 1980s was lung cancer prescribed as a compensatable asbestos-related disease, and even then only in conjunction with asbestosis.

In the earliest occurrence of lung cancer in suspended Turner & Newall workers, it proved difficult for the medical experts to decide upon its significance. In none of the early cases of lung cancer/asbestosis—Flood, Gullen, and Lowe—did the company admit any liability; and the Medical Board never issued any asbestosis death certificates. For example, pathology reports after the death of Peter Flood in 1932 did not implicate asbestos. Although the pathologist had found fibrosis in Flood's lungs, he told the inquest that death was due to the lung cancer he had observed.[87] However, at the inquest of John Greaves in 1938 the doctors were more divided. Although Greaves had been classed as totally disabled by asbestosis and this was confirmed at the post-mortem, the investigation also revealed heart failure and cancer of the lung. When questioned by the coroner, Salford pathologist Dr Charles Jenkins stated that it had 'not yet been established that cancer of the lung is more prevalent in asbesto-

[84] Sir Richard Doll, interview with author, 25 Sept. 1996.
[85] R. Murray letter, *British Journal of Industrial Medicine* 48 (1991), 431–2.
[86] G. W. H. Schepers, 'Changing Attitudes and Opinions: Asbestos and Cancer 1934–1965', *American Journal of Industrial Medicine* 22 (1992), 461–6, 464.
[87] 305/1140. *Rochdale Observer*, 14 Dec. 1932; 305/1141–4. Pathology Reports.

Table 6.3. *Lung cancer cases at TBA, 1932–52*

Name	Death	Age	Occupation	Exposure (years)	Cause of death
Peter Flood	1932	70	Bag carrying/ fiberizing	30	Asbestosis/ca. lung
Alice Gullen	1932	50	Rover in spinning	35	Asbestosis/ca. lung/ ca. pancreas
Joseph Lowe*	1935	62	Weaving	13	Asbestosis/ca. lung
Barker Greenwood*	1935	54	Weaving	23	Asbestosis/ca. lung
John R. Greaves*	1938	47	Weaver	19	Asbestosis/ca. lung
James Pickstone*	1940	52	Disintegrating	22	Asbestosis/ca. lung
Samuel Taylor*	1941	52	Weaving	20	Asbestosis/ca. lung
Mark W. Rush*	1942	59	Bag carrying	28	Asbestosis/ca. lung
Fred Smith*	1944	36	Weaving	2	Ca. lung
George H. Ashman	1947	57	Weaving	$1\frac{1}{3}$	Asbestosis/ca. lung
S. Brown*	1948	48	Spinning	26	Asbestosis/ca. lung
Wilfred Cavanagh*	1948	65	Maintenance	29	Asbestosis/ca. lung
Joseph Dorber*	1948	53	Weaving	32	Asbestosis/ca. lung
James W. Isherwood*	1948	53	Weaving	13	Asbestosis/ca. lung
James Murphy	1948	42	Spinning	4	Ca. lung
Louisa F. Roney*	1950	51	Spinning	27	Asbestosis/ca. lung
J. Aughey*	1951	43	Fiberizing	9	Ca. lung
Fred Dowling*	1951	74	Fiberizing	26	Asbestosis/ca. lung
Edmund Leach*	1951	60	Weaving	27	Asbestosis/ca. lung
William Seddon	1951	59	Departmental manager	12	Asbestosis?/ca. lung
T. Chadwick*	1952	51	Weaving	7	Ca. lung

*Cited anonymously in R. Doll, 'Mortality from Lung Cancer in Asbestos Workers', *British Journal of Industrial Medicine* 12 (1955), 81–6, 82. It should be noted that Doll's listing (based on an analysis by J. F. Knox) differs slightly from the above table. Firstly, I have included two cases—Flood and Gullen—not counted by Doll/Knox , who were only concerned with post-1932 mortality (i.e. the period after government regulation). I have also added three other cases, not listed by Doll/Knox—Ashman, Murphy, and Seddon. These were lung cancer deaths, which for some reason the 1955 article did not include. None seems to have been suspended workers and the limited exposure (in two cases) may have led Knox to ignore them. On the other hand, Ashman had worked for fifteen years for a brake-linings manufacturer. In the Seddon case, there was no post-mortem, but Knox later acknowledged that it was a lung cancer/asbestosis case. Doll/Knox, however, did enumerate two probable mesothelioma cases as ordinary lung cancers—Pennington and Pilling—and these I have transferred to Table 6.4.

Source: Turner & Newall compensation claims.

sis cases than in ordinary cases of lung trouble. He said the cancer may
have been caused by asbestosis in this case or it may not. He was not prepared to say.'[88] The jury first found that Greaves's death was due to industrial disease, but the coroner rejected that and the jury eventually agreed
that he died from heart failure and cancer accelerated by asbestosis. The
Medical Board refused to issue an asbestosis death certificate and Turner
& Newall denied liability and payment. The same events were repeated
in 1940, when a TAC worker died from lung cancer and asbestosis.[89]

However, lung cancer cases among suspended TBA workers were
growing. This was at a time when the disease was still relatively uncommon. In 1941, TBA weaver Samuel Taylor died from lung cancer 'accelerated by asbestosis', and Jenkins was the pathologist in that case too. By
the following year, he was clearly having second thoughts. At the inquest
of Rochdale asbestos bag-carrier, Mark Rush Snr, he reported on the post-
mortem findings of lung cancer/asbestosis and told the coroner: 'There
have now been so many of these cases in Rochdale that I must say I think
the cancer was produced by the asbestosis.'[90] However, Turner & Newall
disagreed and were bolstered by the Medical Board's decision not to grant
a certificate. Rush's widow received no compensation. Moreover,
Jenkins's views did not evidently signify a new consensus. At the Leeds
inquest on a Roberts' worker in 1944, the coroner returned a verdict of
death due to 'sarcoma of bronchus accelerated by inhalation of asbestos
dust during the course of his employment'. A Roberts' manager was able
to argue: 'It is still a point which is not decided. Some medical men have
the view that asbestos does produce carcinoma and others [do] not.'[91]
Turner & Newall inclined to the latter view. In the same year, a Roberts'
mattress maker, William Wood, died from lung cancer and asbestosis. His
widow received no lump sum, after the company had made her drop her
claim by arguing that 'asbestosis was not the cause of death'.[92] However,
it is noteworthy that pathologists in Leeds were now adopting the view
that asbestosis and lung cancer were linked. Turner & Newall's consultant pathologist, Matthew Stewart, had attended the inquest on Roberts'
worker Arthur Stead, who died in 1945. Stewart later noted in his diary:
'Polson made the PM . . . and expressed the view that the asbestosis had
been a factor in the development of the cancer. I concurred.'[93]

[88] 65/1797. Bussy to Ellison, 29 Sept. 1938. Jenkins took a similar stance in the Edmund
Pilling pleural mesothelioma case in May 1939 (see below). When asked by the coroner if
asbestos had caused the lung cancer, he replied: 'Nothing is known on that point, irritation
may or may not have caused the growth.' 123/3791. Bussy to Ellison, 25 May 1939.
[89] 38/1231. James Pickstone file.
[90] 123/3970. Ellison to Bussy, 14 July 1942.
[91] 61/760. Fred Stringer case. Coroner's report, 21 Sept. 1944.
[92] 37/2139. Collins to J. W. Roberts, 26 Apr. 1945.
[93] Brotherton Library, Leeds University, M. J. Stewart diary, 4 June 1945.

Turner & Newall's experience was mirrored at other firms. In 1946, Dr Hubert Wyers, a physician at Cape's London factory, completed a doctoral thesis on asbestosis among its workforce. A major section looked at lung cancer. Wyers not only highlighted a high cancer rate generally at Cape (about 20 per cent in nearly a hundred post-mortems), but also an excessive incidence of pulmonary cancer: 15 cases in 98 autopsies (15.3 per cent). He suggested that improved safety measures might be warranted even without greater scientific proof.

By the early 1950s, although some inquests on Turner & Newall workers were returning verdicts of death due to lung cancer accelerated by asbestosis, usually medical opinion gave the company the benefit of the doubt. This meant compensation claims could be rebuffed. Yet while it vigorously denied the asbestosis/lung cancer link in public, Turner & Newall's private stance was far less certain and assured. In 1942, as we saw in Chapter 2, the company was attempting to quell a 'scare' in Rochdale about the dangers of working at TBA. This had been triggered by publicity over asbestosis deaths, some of which had involved lung cancer. Certainly TBA director Frank Bussy had tried to brush aside the cancer problem when he circulated his memorandum to the workforce— though the fact that he had mentioned the disease was significant. In February 1942, Bussy copied to Sir Samuel Turner an extract from the *Report of the Chief Inspector of Factories* for 1938, which noted the 'suggestion' in the medical press of a relationship between the two diseases and provided statistics showing a significant difference in the number of lung cancer cases in asbestosis sufferers compared to those in silicosis cases.[94] The *Report* urged that 'extended inquiry and collection of data' were needed.

Turner & Newall were already collecting information, not only from the experiences of its own workers, but also from America.[95] From the early 1940s, the firm was linked with the work of the Saranac Laboratory in upstate New York. This research facility had been founded as part of the famous Trudeau Sanatorium for tuberculosis at Saranac Lake. By the interwar period, the Laboratory had begun investigating the relationship of mineral dusts to tuberculosis, drawing increasingly on corporate funding for its experiments and symposium programme. By the late 1930s, its director, Dr Leroy Gardner, had begun a new line of research—the effects of asbestos inhalation—with the support of the leading American firms. Among Gardner's sponsors was Turner & Newall's American subsidiary, Keasbey & Mattison. Reports of Gardner's research, which were confidential and not for publication, were also sent to Rochdale.

---

[94] 113/1670–1. Bussy memo, 16 Feb. 1942; Ministry of Labour & Factory Inspectorate, *Annual Report . . . for 1938* (1939), 80–1.

[95] David E. Lilienfeld, 'The Silence: The Asbestos Industry and Early Occupational Cancer Research—A Case Study', *American Journal of Public Health* 81 (June 1991), 791–800.

Initially, Gardner's work appeared to go well: the research suggested that asbestosis might be amenable to treatment. Turner & Newall happily forwarded details to the government to show the company in a favourable light. But some findings proved far less welcome. Gardner was already aware of lung cancers among asbestos workers from the published literature and from his medical contacts. He was 'most sceptical' of such a link,[96] but some of his animal experiments on white mice startled him. They showed an excessive incidence of pulmonary cancer—enough to convince him that further research was required. Gardner proposed a follow-up study and also wanted to include a chapter on lung cancer in a projected monograph on asbestosis.[97] Notification of Gardner's work and book proposal were sent to Turner & Newall through Keasbey & Mattison president, Ernest Muehleck, who told Walker Shepherd: 'we feel that reference to the question of cancer susceptibility should be omitted from the report since it is inconclusive.'[98]

Turner & Newall's response to Gardner's work is not known in detail. However, a TBA director commented: 'The reference to the possibility of producing cancer of the lung by inhalation of asbestos fibres is disconcerting, but Gardner may be right in this since I understand that there have been one or two cases of deaths due to cancer accelerated by asbestosis, or vice versa.'[99] Predictably, rather than circulate Gardner's preliminary experiments, TBA preferred more palatable scientific truths. In Rochdale in the same year, TBA instead publicized the results of their privately funded research from the British Postgraduate Medical School, which happily was said to show that asbestos was not toxic. Eventually, the Saranac sponsors agreed that Gardner's references to cancer should be omitted from the final report, which appeared in 1951.[100]

John Knox became occupied with the cancer issue when he joined TBA in 1949. By then, the lung cancer/asbestos link first highlighted in the Chief Inspector of Factories' *Annual Report* for 1938, was beginning to crystallize into greater certainty in the *Annual Report* for 1947.[101] The latter found lung cancer at post-mortem in 13.2 per cent of workers with

[96] 30/1543–4. Gardner to Vandiver Brown, Johns–Manville, 9 June 1943.
[97] 30/1521. 'Outline of Proposed Monograph on Asbestosis', 1943.
[98] 30/1536. Muehleck to Shepherd, 8 Mar. 1943.
[99] 8/1967. 'Notes made by Dr W. Francis after Perusal of the Outline of the Proposed Monograph by Dr Gardner', n.d. 1943.
[100] It might be argued that Gardner never discovered anything significant—in other words, that his cancer studies were 'inconclusive'. However, that is not the view of one of the physicians who was an insider to the events at Saranac Lake and has since examined Gardner's surviving specimens. See G. W. H. Schepers, 'Chronology of Asbestos Cancer Discoveries: Experimental Studies of the Saranac Laboratory', *American Journal of Industrial Medicine* 27 (1995), 593–606.
[101] Ministry of Labour and Factory Inspectorate, *Annual Report . . . for 1947* (1949), 79–80. Publication was delayed until Jan. 1949, due to a squabble between Merewether and Sir George Barnett.

asbestosis compared with only 1.3 per cent for workers affected by silicosis. This evidence was duly considered by Knox, who was initially inclined towards scepticism.[102] This was characteristic Knox conservatism; other members of the medical community were far less doubting. In 1949, an editorial headed, 'Asbestosis and Cancer of the Lung', in the *Journal of the American Medical Association*, accepted the data in the *Annual Report* for 1947 as strong evidence of a causal link and urged that 'increased attention' to the problem was desirable.[103] In that year, Wyers published the results of his study of Cape Asbestos workers, which showed a pulmonary cancer rate of about 15 per cent in 115 cases—a percentage close to the government's figures.[104] Of course, TBA's directors may have been unaware of this literature: however, that seems unlikely. At about this time, the company's research team at the Postgraduate Medical School at Hammersmith wrote up a detailed report on their asbestosis work. It included a referenced section on asbestosis and carcinoma (including pulmonary cancer), noting a 'suggestive' relationship between the two.[105]

Although Gardner's cancer findings were never published, there was continued interest in the cancer/asbestosis question in North America. The Canadian asbestos industry asked Turner & Newall for information and so Knox examined TBA's post-mortem reports. From a hundred autopsies he found ten cases of lung cancer—an incidence that he did not think particularly significant.[106] However, in 1952 (the same year that Merewether published data showing an 18 per cent incidence of lung cancer in asbestos deaths) Knox attended the Seventh Saranac Symposium at Saranac Lake. The Symposium programme and Knox's notes show that the subject of pneumoconiosis (including asbestosis) and its link with pulmonary cancer were discussed during a whole day.[107] This prompted Knox to have another look at the problem, when he returned to Rochdale. He re-examined the hundred or so TBA post-mortem reports, noting all the lung cancer cases. The cancer percentage now seemed higher than it should have been, though Knox believed that this was a post-mortem artefact (in other words, when looking for one thing, pathologists found something else). Still, as Knox recognized, the matter would only be settled by a professional statistical study.

Knox decided to contact Richard Doll at the London School of Hygiene & Tropical Medicine. Doll was a 40-year-old medical statistician, who was

[102] 302/1330. Memo of Meeting Held to Discuss the Future Direction of Asbestosis Research, 13 July 1950.

[103] *Journal of American Medical Association* 140 (13 Aug. 1949), 1219–20.

[104] H. Wyers, 'Asbestosis', *Postgraduate Medical Journal* 25 (Dec. 1949), 631–8, 637.

[105] 117/702–26. 'Experimental Asbestosis: Work Carried Out at the Postgraduate Medical School, 1946–8.'

[106] 303/1369. Board meeting, 8 Jan. 1952.

[107] 101/1288–1306. See also 2/1388–9. Knox's itinerary, 27 Aug. 1952.

to become one of the world's foremost investigators of the epidemiology of cancer (mainly due to his pioneering work establishing a relationship between smoking and lung cancer). It was this work that had recommended him to Knox, who in 1953 wrote:

Dear Dr Doll,

As a medical adviser to a large asbestos works in Rochdale I have been reviewing my accumulated reports on autopsies conducted on workers here who were alleged to have died of asbestosis. This series goes back to 1930 when asbestosis was given official status and numbers 115 cases to date. In the present instance I am anxious to contribute to the carcinoma lung question in association with asbestosis and I would like your opinion on the material . . . My statistical ability is nil and I have the approval of my firm, Messrs Turner Bros. Asbestos Co., to approach a statistical authority to discuss this question.[108]

The approach was timely. Having started his research into cigarette smoking and cancer, Doll was already wondering whether asbestos had the same effect. He had been alerted to the possibility by an article in the *Lancet* in 1951 by Stephen Gloyne, who had analysed male pneumoconiosis necropsies and, like the Factory Inspectorate, had noted the differing incidence of lung cancer among silicosis and asbestosis cases.[109] Nevertheless, Doll—like Knox—still awaited what he regarded as adequate scientific proof. In early 1953, he had approached Cape Asbestos (where Wyers had already suggested a lung cancer risk), but was rebuffed. When Knox wrote to him, therefore, Doll readily accepted.

The two men devised a study in which the lung cancer incidence from TBA's scheduled workers was compared with the death rate from the disease in the general population between 1935 and 1953. Within a matter of months, Doll had concluded his analysis. The results were striking. Of 105 scheduled TBA asbestos textile workers examined at autopsy, 18 showed evidence of lung cancer, 15 times in association with asbestosis.[110] Asbestos was indeed associated with a heavy risk of lung cancer; and the order of risk—in those exposed twenty years or more—was estimated to be *ten times* that in the general population.

Knox and Doll expected to publish their results in a medical journal. Sometime at the end of 1953 (or early in 1954), Knox informed the board of the findings and requested approval for publication of the jointly authored work. The directors evidently took some months to reach a decision, but in June they refused to allow the report to be published. Knox

[108] 9/0414–15. Knox to Doll, 12 Apr. 1953.

[109] S. R. Gloyne, 'Pneumoconiosis: A Histological Survey of Necropsy Material in 1205 Cases', *Lancet* 260 (14 Apr. 1951), i, 810–14.

[110] The individual case files survive in the T & N archive. Interestingly, there are some indications Knox undercounted. See Table 6.3. As the figures only relate to TBA workers, it should be noted that lung cancer cases also occurred in other group factories.

lamented to an American colleague: 'The headline news about lung cancer has scared people over here and it was thought that we might attract undesirable publicity in our own area.'[111] The high-level board discussions surrounding the company's decision have not survived, though Collins was brought in to wield the hatchet. In the same way that tobacco companies were to dismiss as 'unscientific' any evidence linking lung cancer with their products, Collins argued that the report's conclusions were 'inaccurate'.

Knox professed 'surprise' at his directors' attitude. Doll was 'shocked' and told Knox: 'I feel that any positive findings with regard to the cause of cancer must be available to all research workers in the subject . . . I would not, of course, have undertaken the work in the first place, had I imagined that there would be any attempt to limit the dissemination of scientific data.'[112] Turner & Newall were equally determined that the results should not be published. Until then, the company's sponsored research had been private, limited in scope and usually inconclusive. Inconvenient findings were either not disseminated (as with the Saranac work) or appeared in obscure foreign journals.[113] However, the directors got more than they had bargained for in Doll: not only was he a skilled epidemiologist, whose analysis clearly demonstrated a lung cancer risk, but he was less easy to censor.

Turner & Newall tried all the same. In July 1954, the board drafted a barrister's letter to bully Doll into withdrawing the paper. It stated that a published article 'would be wholly premature and undesirable from all points of view'. This was never sent and a visit from the tactful Knox was relied upon instead to extricate the company from a difficult situation. However, Doll was unshakeable. He had signed no pre-conditions and had followed his normal practice of working for no fee. More significantly, he also had the backing of a major medical institution. He sent the article to the *British Journal of Industrial Medicine*, still hoping that Turner & Newall would allow its publication, but determined to press on regardless.

The Turner & Newall directors were aghast to find that even before the report had been published, it had leaked into the national press, via the annual report of Doll's institution. In reporting this, *The Times* on 19 February 1955 not only mentioned Knox, but also detailed the main conclusions of the research. By March a Bristol MP was asking questions in

[111] 506/715–16. Knox to W. Smith, 2 June 1954.

[112] 35/1104. Doll to Knox, 8 June 1954.

[113] M. J. Stewart, T & N's consultant pathologist, also published in 1955 a paper highlighting excess lung cancers among asbestos workers. However, the article was published in America and aroused no interest. See Georgiana Bonser and M. J. Stewart, 'Occupational Cancer of the Urinary Bladder in Dyestuffs Operatives and of the Lung in Asbestos Textile Workers and Iron-ore Miners', *American Journal of Clinical Pathology* 25 (Feb. 1955), 126–34.

Parliament and demanding a special inquiry.[114] This could not have come at a worse time for Turner & Newall, with profits in the 1950s on a steep upward trend. No asbestos firm in the world had ever admitted publicly that there was a cancer risk. Desperate to prevent bad publicity, the company tried another approach. Richard Schilling, the *BJIM* editor, later recalled that he was visited at his office at Manchester University by a 'man with dark hair' from Turner & Newall. The visitor tried to persuade Schilling to reject the article.[115] Appalled at the suggestion that he suppress such important findings, Schilling refused and Doll's paper on 'Mortality from Lung Cancer in Asbestos Workers' duly appeared in 1955, shorn of any citation of John Knox as co-author and any mention of TBA.[116] The paper was immediately recognized as a landmark case-study, which firmly established the link between lung cancer and asbestos (which was to be even more fully confirmed in the early 1960s by American research on insulation workers).

The article had an unexpected sequel. Doll's work did not make the wider splash the company had feared and the bad publicity never materialized. With the crisis over, Turner & Newall directors began taking another look at the paper. Suddenly, it did not look too bad. Of the fifteen cases that Knox had identified with asbestosis and lung cancer, all had joined the industry before 1923 and had at least nine years' exposure before dust control had become more effective. Moreover, Doll had assumed, like most doctors, that asbestosis probably triggered lung cancer and the company's apparent success in reducing the former also led him to write that the lung cancer risk at TBA had been greatly reduced—even perhaps eliminated. This was to prove a controversial part of the paper. As a critic of Doll has remarked, in 1955 he had 'no way of knowing how much the cancer risk would come down with reduced exposure—or how much it would rise with the decline of asbestosis as a competing cause of death . . .'.[117] This was because the follow-up period under the new conditions was only twenty-one years; whereas for the fifteen cases of lung cancer and asbestosis in the survey, the average number of years for the development of the malignancy from first exposure was over twenty-six years. To be sure, Doll had added an important proviso: 'Whether the spe-

---

[114] *Bristol Evening Post*, 4 Mar. 1955.

[115] Schilling deposition, *Chase Manhattan Bank v. T&N* (1995). Trial transcript, 900–54. Schilling (1911–97) was Reader in occupational health at Manchester University.

[116] R. Doll, 'Mortality from Lung Cancer in Asbestos Workers', *British Journal of Industrial Medicine* 12 (1955), 81–6.

[117] Castleman, *Asbestos*, 98. Doll's private opinion appears to have been more guarded than that expressed in his article. He wrote to Schilling: 'If, on the other hand, the survival rate is not yet normal (and I doubt if it is), the sooner the firm are made to realize it the better. Unless I offer them quid pro quo, we may never find out.' 506/1857. Doll to Schilling, 3 Dec. 1954.

cific industrial risk of lung cancer has yet been eliminated cannot be determined with certainty: the number of men at risk, who have been exposed to the new conditions only and who have been employed for a sufficient length of time, is at present too small for confidence to be placed in their experience.'[118] However, Turner & Newall ignored this comment and only accepted the positive tenor of the report. One of the directors thought that there were 'several encouraging features of the analysis' and also saw the advantage of continuing to work with someone of Doll's standing.[119] The upshot was that Doll was quickly forgiven and invited to continue his work.

By 1958, Doll had updated the cancer study and he informed the company that there was still no excess mortality from lung cancer. However, he added: 'Even if an excess risk of lung cancer still persisted we could not expect to have had, as yet, any clear evidence of it. From past experience we know that very few cases appear under 20 years from first employment and few of the employees in this group have been observed for that length of time.'[120] In any case, Doll's data was from a select group of workers: nationally, the picture for asbestosis and lung cancer should have given Turner & Newall less comfort. The proportion of lung cancer cases among asbestotics listed by the Factory Inspectorate was rising throughout the 1950s and 1960s (see Table 8.2).

Doll's article made little immediate difference to dependants claiming compensation, as it was to be another thirty years before lung cancer was recognized by the government as a compensatable disease—and only then in association with asbestosis.[121] This was bad news for workers and their relatives, since asbestosis and lung cancer deaths among TBA's workers continued, even among those who had started work after 1932, and it was soon apparent that neither disease had been entirely eliminated. A recent review of Turner & Newall's medical files has found that by January 1959 at least fifty of its employees had died of lung cancer.[122] By then, an even more frightening asbestos cancer had appeared.

---

[118] Doll, 'Mortality', 86.

[119] 9/382–3. J. Waddell to J. L. Collins, 16 May 1958. Waddell thought that the 'increased cancer risk appears to be mainly linked with asbestosis, although it is of course very difficult to establish which disease came first . . .'. 9/366–7. Waddell to Collins, 19 Nov. 1958.

[120] 9/378–9. Doll to T & N, Sept. 1958.

[121] In 1956, a TBA lung cancer victim (Harry Kershaw) was found at inquest to have died of 'natural causes'. This was despite pleural thickening, some evidence of asbestosis and asbestos bodies in his lungs. Noted a manager: 'In view of this verdict, there will be nothing we can do for the widow, and the pension paid to Mr Kershaw will now, of course, cease. This is just one more of those very hard cases where a widow is left at an advanced age, and her husband had worked here for 33 years, but I just don't see what we can do as there have been many similar cases in the past.' 123/4439. G. Chadwick to F. Wood, 1 Aug. 1956.

[122] *Chase* v. *T & N* transcript, 631–4.

MESOTHELIOMA

This dread disease is a highly malignant tumour of the pleura (the lining of the chest) or the peritoneum (the lining of the abdomen). Once a rare condition, it is now (alongside asbestos-induced lung cancer), a leading cause of asbestos-related deaths. Its only known occupational cause is asbestos.[123]

By the 1950s, it was known that asbestos could cause pleural responses, such as adhesions, effusions, thickening, and the formation of plaques (whitish, raised areas, which sometimes calcified). Such plaques came to be regarded as 'markers' of asbestos exposure, but they were benign and usually asymptomatic. They gave little indication that a new asbestos disease was on the horizon.

Even the most hardened doctors regard mesothelioma as one of the most extraordinary of all cancers. Only very recently has it been identified as a distinct disease. Although a few cases of unusual pleural cancers had been noted since at least the 1920s (when the term mesothelioma was first used), pathologists rarely saw this tumour: when they did, they assumed it must be due to secondary deposits from an unidentified cancer elsewhere. Certainly, there seemed little reason to suspect asbestos. That linkage was masked by mesothelioma's extended latency: the cancer seldom appears in less than twenty years after exposure, and more usually latency is forty years or even longer. The exposure itself can be remarkably transient—a matter of weeks or months rather than years—and does not even need to have been occupational.

The physical appearance of the tumour itself is remarkable. It develops as a dense white or grey–yellow sheet, which can encase and constrict the entire surface of the chest or abdomen. Its consistency varies, but it has sometimes been likened to leather. An experienced pathologist recalled his first sight of a pleural mesothelioma at necropsy:

On opening the thoracic cavity, I was amazed to find a huge gelatinous tumour, which filled the right thoracic cavity, and infiltrated into the parietal pericardium. The mediastinum was displaced, with congestion of the left lung. On slicing into the mass a greatly contracted right lung was found. I had never seen a mesothelioma . . .[124]

Mesothelioma is also one of the most virulent cancers. It is untreatable, highly painful, and invariably fatal—usually within a year.

As with lung cancer, the biological mechanisms by which asbestos triggers mesothelioma are not understood. Evidently not all mesotheliomas

---

[123] Unlike lung cancer, mesothelioma is not linked to smoking.

[124] J. C. Wagner, 'The Discovery of the Association between Blue Asbestos and Mesotheliomas and the Aftermath', *British Journal of Industrial Medicine* 48 (1991), 399–403, 399.

are due to asbestos, as there is a slight 'background' rate of the disease (even among young children), which is difficult to link with asbestos. One 'outbreak' of mesothelioma in an obscure Turkish village in the 1970s seems to have been caused by a different fibrous mineral, erionite. However, one thing is certain: mesothelioma does not show a clear dose–response relationship. With asbestosis, the more asbestos a worker inhales, the greater the risk. Malignant processes, however, have a basic all-or-none response; or, as one expert, has explained:

One may speculate that a certain trigger dose is required for the initiation of car-cinogenesis . . . but once this has been supplied further dosage will not affect the ultimate appearance of the tumour [mesothelioma], provided that the individual lives for the required period of development . . . The trigger dose may be small, in some cases extraordinarily so.[125]

In other words, no safe level of asbestos exposure could be predicted for the cancer risk: theoretically, some would argue, a single fibre could kill.

Mesothelioma's link with asbestos did not emerge fully until the 1950s in South Africa. In 1952, Dr Christopher Sleggs (1906–87), a physician at a hospital in Kimberley, Cape Province, became aware of a number of unusual pleural malignancies. In 1955, he began work in a clinic in Kuruman, situated in the heart of the asbestos mining territory, where he found more such cases. Unsure about the nature of the disease, Sleggs and a colleague (Paul Marchand) passed biopsies to Dr Christopher Wagner, a young pathologist in Johannesburg, who was working as an asbestos research fellow. In 1956, Wagner had diagnosed a single case of mesothe-lial tumour where asbestos bodies had been found in the lung. A con-nection was made and it was suddenly realized that asbestos might be responsible for all the other cases. With this insight, the trio began exam-ining their patients' life-histories in detail. Marchand recalled how they toured the poverty-stricken mining areas, where there was so much asbestos waste everywhere that it was not surprising that most of the doctors and old inhabitants were well aware of the fatal disease.[126] The industrial and residential case histories revealed that many of the indi-viduals had lived near, but not necessarily worked in, the asbestos mines and mills in the North West Cape.

While evidence accumulated, in September 1957 Wagner took sabbati-cal leave to tour European pneumoconiosis centres. Asbestos disease was not his only concern, though he thought it worthwhile to pursue the mesothelioma problem by visiting the leading asbestos firms.[127] In 1958,

---

[125] Selikoff and Lee, *Asbestos and Disease*, 262.

[126] P. E. Marchand, 'The Discovery of Mesothelioma in the Northwestern Cape Province in the Republic of South Africa', *American Journal of Industrial Medicine* 19 (1991), 241–6.

[127] Wagner, 'Memorandum on European Tour, Sept. 1957–Apr. 1958'. Chase hardcopy document from Pneumoconiosis Research Unit Library, Johannesburg.

Wagner arrived in Rochdale, where he met John Knox. Wagner later recalled:

We went to lunch . . . where I was introduced to senior managers, and, I think, a director of TBA. I was questioned on my work and future interests. I explained about the investigations into the possible association between crocidolite and mesotheliomas, and the nature of the tumours. They felt further work in this field was unwise, and advised against it . . . Their final opinion was that I was being foolhardy and wasting my time.[128]

However, in the following year Wagner and Sleggs publicized their findings at the International Pneumoconiosis Conference in Johannesburg. Then in 1960 came the bombshell. The South Africans published their research in a British medical journal. They had found forty-seven cases of mesothelioma and had established a possible association with exposure to crocidolite in all but two.[129] News of the disease and its link with asbestos spread around the world and the article became the most cited paper in industrial medicine.

The reaction of the Turner & Newall board is not known in detail. The minutes of TBA's Health Committee for some of the crucial 1950s' meetings have not apparently survived. The directors, though, were fully aware of Wagner's work. John Waddell read his draft paper from the Johannesburg Conference in 1959 and told Knox that it should not be circulated to the Health Committee, because it was 'incomplete' and 'highly technical'.[130] Overall, the response was to minimize the problem. Knox himself only slowly came round from what he described as a position of 'frank disbelief' to one of 'qualified acceptance' regarding mesothelioma, and even then he did not believe that the disease affected TBA workers.[131] In February 1964, he reported on a meeting of the Medical Research Council that had discussed the emergence of mesothelioma. The consensus of this meeting—which was chaired by Dr John Gilson, the chairman of the Pneumoconiosis Research Unit—was that a new asbestos cancer had appeared. However, Knox told his directors reassuringly that: 'as far as my knowledge goes, no tumour of this type has yet been recognised in Rochdale either before or after death. There are, however, certain differences between pathologists as to the exact criteria required to confirm the diagnosis.'[132]

Certainly, it was true that some debate surrounded the identification of

[128] J. C. Wagner, letter to author, 27 Oct. 1998.
[129] J. C. Wagner *et al.*, 'Diffuse Pleural Mesotheliomas and Asbestos Exposure in the North-Western Cape Province', *British Journal of Industrial Medicine* 17 (1960), 260–71.
[130] 1–3/598. Waddell to Knox, 4 Aug. 1959.
[131] 11/0067. Knox to RAW, 18 Jan. 1967.
[132] 6/1765–7. JFK's notes on a meeting of the Occupational Health Committee of the MRC, 24 Feb. 1964.

mesothelioma; however, Knox's belief that no mesotheliomas had occurred at the factory is difficult to understand. As Wagner himself pointed out, Knox and Doll in their 1955 lung cancer paper had listed an 'endothelioma of the pleura'. This was William Pennington, who died in 1936.[133] Knox and Wagner had discussed the case at their meeting in 1958, when the latter was told that the original specimens had been destroyed (though Knox did have an old photograph). Besides Pennington, three other pleural cancer deaths—Edmund Pilling, James Hoyle, and Fred Butterfield—had occurred at TBA (see Table 6.4). Butterfield had died in 1957 only months before Wagner's visit, so it seems extraordinary that Knox professed ignorance of this case—especially as he had personally filed the post-mortem details of an 'endothelioma of the pleura' that had all the tell-tale signs of mesothelioma. Knox also made no allowance for the fact that some former workers might have developed mesothelioma. Two such cases had occurred between 1958 and 1959—one of them a sister of Louisa Roney, who was one of Knox's lung cancer cohort. These cases did not come to light until 1971.[134]

Knox also did not investigate the files of other unit companies. These would have shown that between 1936 and 1964 several Turner & Newall workers died from diseases that could have been mesotheliomas.[135] Obviously—then as now—it would have been impossible for Knox to confirm these cases scientifically after so many years. However, it is significant that Professor Stewart in Leeds recognized mesothelioma as an independent entity. In 1949, when conducting the post-mortem on Roberts' worker Frederick Fallowes, he found that the right pleural sac was almost completely obliterated by an unusual growth. Later that day, he wrote in his diary: 'tumour a pleural mesothelioma?'[136]

During 1964, not even Knox could ignore the growing evidence. In August, a mesothelioma was confirmed at the Ferodo factory at Chapel-en-le-Frith; in September, another case came to inquest at Roberts (though it was never acknowledged by the company). TBA's first 'official' mesothelioma followed in December 1964, when a worried personnel

[133] The case was listed in the classic Doll/Knox study. Pennington died, aged 65, after twenty-two years in the scheduled areas. See *Rochdale Observer*, 31 Oct. 1936; 305/1085 Pennington file.

[134] 71/1839. Medical Officer's Report, 2 Aug. 1971.

[135] Mesotheliomas can also be identified at other companies, retrospectively. Plate 6 in Wyers's thesis, 'Legislative Measures', is a striking photograph of an 'endothelioma of the pleura' from a Cape Asbestos autopsy.

[136] Brotherton Library, Leeds University, M. J. Stewart diary, 30 Mar. 1949. When Stewart's asbestos lung cancer cases were written up by a co-worker, Dr Georgiana Bonser, and published in America, it is interesting to note that reference was made to primary malignancies of the pleura and peritoneum; apparently Stewart did not insist on the term mesothelioma, though the excess of peritoneal cancers was emphasized. See Bonsor and Stewart, 'Occupational Cancer'.

Table 6.4. *Mesothelioma cases (confirmed and suspected) at Turner & Newall, 1936–64*

Name	Death	Age	Occupation/department	Location	Exposure (years)	Cause of death
William Pennington	1936	65	Mixing/fiberizing	Rochdale	23	Asbestosis/endothelioma of pleura
Edmund Pilling	1939	49	Disintegrating/winding	Rochdale	29	Asbestosis/pleural ca. of one lung
Edith Parish	1945	57	Mattresses	Leeds	20	Peritoneal carcinomatosis
Annie E. Robinson	1945	44	?	Leeds	?	Malignant peritonitis
Joseph Greensmith	1946	61	Carding	Leeds	10	Asbestosis/carcinomatosis of peritoneum
John Scorer	1946	55	Insulation goods loader	Washington	26	Asbestosis/endothelioma of pleurae
Frederick Fallowes	1949	46	Fibre opener/fan duct cleaner	Leeds	10	Asbestosis/sarcoma of pleura
Harold S. Kaye	1952	49	Carding	Leeds	15	Asbestosis/ca. peritoneum
James W. Hoyle	1955	62	Weaving	Rochdale	7	Asbestosis/pleural ca. of one lung
Fred Butterfield	1957	74	Weaving/carding & spinning	Rochdale	39	Asbestosis/endothelioma of pleura
Ian Howarth	1958	59	Proofed goods/Weaving	Rochdale	16	Pleural mesothelioma (suspected)
Catherine Fairclough (née Roney)	1959	61	Textile piecing	Rochdale	5 months	Pleural mesothelioma (confirmed)
James Ilott	1961	64	Bag shaking/cleaning	Erith	16	Pleural mesothelioma
Vivian Richard John	1962	55	Beating/drawing office	Rhoose	18	Pleural mesothelioma
Archibald Vernon	1964	65	Inspection	Chapel-en-le-Frith	38	Mesothelioma
Sydney Hall	1964	60	Carding	Leeds	22	Peritoneal mesothelioma
Frank Brooks	1964	57	Warehouse/rubber/carding & spinning	Rochdale	37	Pleural mesothelioma

Exposure = total service in scheduled and non-scheduled occupations.
Source: Turner & Newall compensation claims files; death certificates.

manager told director David Hills and Knox about an inquest that he had attended. The dead worker was Frank Brooks, a long-serving employee from the warehouse and rubber departments, who had spent only a year or so in the scheduled textile areas. The inquest was very much a Rochdale affair, with Coupe as the coroner and his son as the hospital pathologist. Brooks did not have asbestosis (though asbestos bodies were present): the cause of death was a 'malignant pleural tumour'. Yet although the pathologist knew what this meant, he declined to verify that Brooks had died from mesothelioma. He stated: 'There are certain malignant tumours which are *said* to be associated with asbestos bodies, but he had not been able to decide whether the pleural tumour in this case was that type of tumour.'[137] Further investigations were needed, but Coupe Snr decided that these would hold up the funeral. Because further investigations were 'in the good hands of Dr Knox and certain expert colleagues and that any obligations that the company felt they should honour as a result of such findings would be duly carried out', he returned an open verdict.[138] This disqualified the widow, who also worked at TBA, from any increased company benefits for an 'industrial disease' death and she never filed a claim against the firm.

Mesothelioma, besides its devastating impact on individuals, sounded the death knell of the UK asbestos industry. With no safe threshold, even relatively trivial amounts of dust could be lethal—a fact demonstrated by Turner & Newall's own mesothelioma cases. A woman piecer at TBA died from a pleural mesothelioma in 1959, having been exposed for only five months during the First World War. Mesothelioma proved no respecter of the scheduled areas: the disease began appearing at all Turner & Newall plants—for example, at the various TAC sites—many in unscheduled occupations. A draughtsman at TAC in Rhoose died of mesothelioma in 1962, after about seventeen years in the offices. Previously, he had worked as a beaterman there for ten months.[139]

For a brief period in the 1960s, the company was relatively safe. While it held on grimly to its asbestos business—including even the crocidolite trade, which had been implicated in many cases of mesothelioma—the situation with workmen's compensation remained unaltered. Mesothelioma did not become a prescribed asbestos disease until 1966, so there was little chance that the dependants of workers would succeed with claims. William Pennington was not a suspended worker (as he had been repeatedly cleared by the Medical Board); and the pathologist at the

[137] 83/1045–6. J. Arnold memo, 11 Dec. 1964.
[138] TBA had confirmed Brooks's mesothelioma by Jan. 1965. Knox told Waddell: 'One case does not prove anything, but it is a straw in the wind.' JFK to JW, 21 Jan. 1965.
[139] 114/1531–55. V. R. John (1906–62) file. John's widow and a dependent son did not make a claim until 1972, when the media first alerted them to mesothelioma's link with asbestos. They later abandoned their action.

inquest in 1936 listed heart failure and pleural endothelioma as the first two causes of death. Pennington's asbestosis was stated as the third cause (as his lungs were honeycombed with fibrosis), but in view of this verdict it is not surprising that no compensation was paid by the company. Similarly, in 1939, at the inquest on Edmund Pilling, a 49-year-old TBA cheese-winder and disintegrator, the pathologist reported that one of the deceased's lungs was covered with a pleural cancerous growth and that there was some asbestosis. But he gave greater weight to the former, leading the court to decide that asbestosis had neither caused nor accelerated the cancer as a cause of death. The Medical Board, in turn, declined to certify death due to asbestosis and the widow was unable to make a claim.[140] Similarly, in 1946 the inquest on 61-year-old Roberts' carder Joseph Greensmith found 'widespread carcinomatosis of the peritoneum' and 'mild asbestosis'.[141] However, a 'natural causes' verdict meant that Turner & Newall did not need to pay a lump sum.[142] No doubt, the company—had they known of future events—would have argued that it was impossible before 1960 to have known of the mesothelioma risk and so their actions in denying liability were reasonable. However, this is not a view that has been endorsed in asbestos litigation in the 1990s. In any case, Turner & Newall denied liability in mesothelioma cases, even after 1960.[143]

---

[140] 123/3812. Pilling file. See 'Cancer of the Lung: Inquest on an Asbestos Worker. Death not Due to Work', *Rochdale Observer*, 24 May 1939. The Medical Board's rebuttal was unfortunate, as the widow (who partly supported two daughters) was in poor health and straitened circumstances. T & N must have felt some responsibility, as they paid her a small *ex gratia* of about 10s [50p] a week until 1944.

[141] 61/798–9. Cyril Polson PM report, 8 July 1946.

[142] Of the other mesothelioma cases in Table 6.4, only Scorer and Kaye elicited a £300 lump sum.

[143] In 1967, for example, when Roberts' worker Margaret Hick (116/2190–2229) died from mesothelioma/asbestosis after less than five years in the scheduled areas, her widower received £25 towards legal expenses, without admitting liability.

7

Countervailing Forces

We never complained about the [Roberts'] factory. We could not complain. We would have been too frightened of our father losing his job.

Testimony of Pauline Hannah, daughter of asbestosis victim John
Cromack (1906–78), in *Margerson/Hancock v. J. W. Roberts and T & N.*
Trial transcript, 26 June 1995, 20–1.

This chapter sheds more light on the central question of this book: why it
took so many decades for the full implications of the asbestos health
problem to be realized and acted upon. So far this book has demonstrated
the low priority given to health and safety in one British industry. It has
also confirmed the adversarial nature of industrial compensation, where
most claims resulted in a battle between employer and employee—a most
unequal contest. Turner & Newall and its insurers, aided by flaws in the
government regulations and biases in the medical system, held nearly all
the trump cards. The picture before the 1960s shows a powerful industry,
only lightly constrained by social and legal pressures.

The Medical Board provided some support for workers in scheduled
areas, but that help has been shown to be highly variable. Only rarely did
the PMP scrutinize factory conditions. That was the job of the other main
linchpin in the regulatory system—the Factory Inspectorate. Only a few
records in the Turner & Newall archive relate to the activities of this
department, a fact that seems to reflect the Inspectorate's level of activity.
Certainly, the Factory Inspectors monitored the implementation of the
1931 Regulations. Visits to Turner & Newall factories, such as Trafford
Park, seem to have been reasonably thorough and presumably helped to
rectify some of the worst excesses of dust.[1] At Washington, Factory Inspectors visited at least twice a year in the 1930s and did complain about
breaches of the Regulations. After one visit in 1936, Inspectorate complaints about a defective exhaust machine led to two local directors
promising to keep 'a close watch' on compliance with the Regulations.[2]
On the other hand, the TBA directors' minute books show that visits by
the Inspectors were rarely on the agenda. Even when workers died, the
government showed little interest. In 1939, for example, one Inspector

---

[1] 37/279–301. Factory Inspectorate visits. 1932–3, 1945.
[2] 53/389–90. WCC Local Board meeting, 2 Apr. 1936.

visited TBA after an asbestosis death, but in the directors' words, 'made no recommendations as to the precautionary measures which the company adopts, nor did he make any criticism whatsoever'.[3] Similarly, in 1939 a Home Office doctor and a Factory Inspector visited Washington Chemical Company after the death from asbestosis of Mary Keegan. They asked to see the Insulation Division where she had worked for twenty years, and inspected the saws she had operated. According to the company, they were 'pleased with what they had seen'.[4]

In wartime, the Factory Inspectorate, like the rest of the country, bowed to the priorities of the time. This meant considerable convergence in thinking between the government and the Rochdale firm. Relations between the latter and Edward Merewether were very cordial during the war. In 1942, Merewether and Sir Samuel Turner indulged in a mutual bout of back-slapping. Merewether asked Turner for a letter of introduction to Keasbey Mattison and other American plants. After Turner had readily complied, Merewether thanked Turner effusively, telling him that

we have progressed in the great task of preventing asbestosis quicker than anyone would have expected. This has been very much due to the remarkable way in which the whole industry led by yourself, has thrown itself wholeheartedly into the solution of the very complex problems involved. While we have . . . a long way to go yet, deaths, the result of very short exposure, do not occur nowadays.[5]

Turner replied grandly: 'You may rely on me to do anything regardless of cost, to overcome the calamity of asbestosis'; and he told the Americans that Merewether had 'the most profound knowledge of anyone in this country'.[6] As one writer has commented, on examining this correspondence: 'It is clear that Merewether believed the sincerity of Turner, but anyone reading the contemporary papers could not be blamed if he expressed the view that Turner's concern was somewhat hollow and Merewether somewhat gullible.'[7] Certainly, Merewether's assertion that 'short-exposure' asbestosis cases did not occur at that time is not true: the Turner & Newall claims files show several cases that resulted from exposure of less than six years.

Other Factory Inspectors who came to Rochdale were similarly uncritical. In 1943, a Miss Vickers visited TBA to examine its labour problems, which had been caused partly by fears of asbestosis. The directors noted:

---

[3] 161/223. TBA board minutes, 17 July 1939.

[4] 54/413–4. WCC/Newalls directors' minutes, 28 Dec. 1939.

[5] 8/1224. Merewether to Turner, 22 Sept. 1942.

[6] 8/1225–6. Turner to Merewether, 18 Sept. 1942; 8/1233–4. Turner to E. Muehleck, 12 Sept. 1942.

[7] B. N. Barker, 'The History of Turner & Newall . . . [and] . . . its Dealings with Asbestos-related Diseases and its Employers' Liability Coverage with the Midland Assurance Ltd' (Feb. 1989), 16. Typescript courtesy of Clydeside Action on Asbestos.

'The Inspector asked what measures we were taking to counteract the asbestos "bogey" and was given details of our efforts towards improved conditions; she agreed that propaganda in connection with what we have done . . . did not appear advisable as it might tend to make the existence of this disease more widely known.'[8] Clearly, few obstacles were placed in the way of the production of such a strategic material.

In 1946, however, the north-east divisional Inspector of Factories (H. M. Carter) and the Medical Inspector of Factories (Dr A. T. Doig) became concerned after the deaths from asbestosis of Dorothy Thirlaway and John Benson.[9] Both these Washington workers had been exposed to dust for less than ten years (Thirlaway for only seven years as a machinist) and neither had apparently worked with asbestos again. In the case of Benson, the Insulation Division manager remarked:

The Inspectors asked to see the operation carried out by the operatives in that department and they were not at all satisfied with the conditions as they exist today. They thought there was too much evidence of fine dust and thought it advisable that some further dust extraction plants should be installed at points indicated . . . Whilst in the fibre-treating building they also paid a visit to the dust chamber and the medical officer, after various enquiries recommended that no man should be employed in the dust chamber for a period of more than six months.[10]

Carter stated in passing that he expected tighter regulations would be introduced, though this did not happen until 1969. The company was never fined or censured for violating dust regulations and killing workers. In 1946, a Factory Inspector wrote to Washington with a list of various breaches of the Factory Acts at the company's Barrow-in-Furness site. These included employing two juveniles for more than 44 hours a week, failure to keep records, and not reporting a disabling accident. The board thought there was no risk of prosecution.[11] This seems to have been one of the few occasions when an Inspector visited an outside site.

In Benson's case, the visit of the Inspectors seems to have been influential in Turner & Newall paying the dependants £200 *ex gratia*, despite the fact that he had left the job more than the statutory three years. (In the Thirlaway case, no claim was made and no liability admitted.) There was another occasion when the Factory Inspectors visited a Turner & Newall plant to check on a worker. After a Trafford Park fibre unloader was

[8] 161/266. TBA Directors' Minute Book, 4 Feb. 1943.
[9] Sandy Doig (1906–83) was a Medical Inspector of Factories for the Scotland area between 1943 and 1970. An expert in occupational diseases, he was a close friend of A. I. G. McLaughlin, and throughout his career was more aware than most Inspectors of the dangers of asbestos. See Doig, 'Asbestos Disease', *Health Bulletin* 26 (Jan. 1968), 24–9.
[10] 61/1182. A. W. Cole to J. L. Collins, 1 Nov. 1946. Collins scribbled across the letter: 'Thirlaway: scandalous pathologist said asbestosis—died from *cancer*'.
[11] 55/864. WCC/Newalls directors' minutes, 26 May 1946.

suspended with asbestosis in 1960 (and also had a lung removed), the Inspector asked to interview him and also examine his working conditions.[12] On the other hand, it may be significant that in the hundreds of claims files, these appear to be the only cases that invited the attention of the authorities.

In the data disseminated in the annual reports of the Chief Inspector of Factories (collected and written by, among others, Merewether), the Inspectorate did provide important insights into the dangers of asbestos for those who cared to look. These reports also show how the Factory Inspectorate saw its role and how it perceived the asbestos hazard. In the early 1930s, the Inspectors praised the high standards achieved by manufacturers in meeting the Regulations. They tried to present a similarly upbeat picture in the *Annual Report* for 1956, but a far less reassuring picture emerged. In the 1950s, working conditions evidently varied across the country, but in many asbestos mills manual bagging and shovelling were still practised; hazardous paper and hessian bags were still used; and mattresses were still beaten without proper ventilation. The removal of old lagging—mentioned for the first time in the *Annual Report* for 1956—was another hazard. Compliance with the Regulations was said to be sometimes 'extremely variable' and enforcement by the Inspectors 'difficult' and at times 'impossible'.[13] Yet only two prosecutions were logged under the 1931 Regulations: that was in 1935 and 1936, when two separate convictions brought total fines of £23 plus costs.

The culture of the Factory Inspectorate militated against dealing effectively with severe industrial hazards. Matters of health and safety involved a dialogue between the Inspectors and the bosses—a dialogue from which the workers were invariably excluded. Some Inspectors tried to counter the problems in the dustiest asbestos factories. Dr Morris Greenberg was one Inspector who was especially sensitive to the problems in the insulation trades and did his best to protect workers.[14] However, such inspectors were constrained by government secrecy, which meant that health hazards could not be publicized and even routine information was subject to the Official Secrets Act. Workers had no right to information and the Factory Inspectors could not warn them independently. As one Inspector remarked, when discussing the asbestos problem in the early 1970s, the main constraint was 'this very odd relationship that had been built up by the Factory Department with the employers over the past 150 years, a very friendly relationship. Armed friendliness, if you

[12] 156/291–2. E. Wilson to J. P. McCormick, 11 Apr. 1968. His only recommendation was that long-serving workers might be X-rayed.

[13] Ministry of Labour & Factory Inspectorate, *Annual Report . . . for 1956* (1957), 141–5.

[14] 30/425–7. D. C. Smith to J. C. Byrom, Trafford Park, 26 May 1967. Dr Greenberg's criticisms of spray operation at a London multi-storey flat were said to be 'so critical . . . to the point of being practically impossible to achieve on a building site'.

like, but nevertheless friendly. Things should be done voluntarily and not because employers were made to do them. That is still, I may add, departmental policy.'[15]

No doubt there were other reasons for the Factory Inspectorate's failings. It was often chronically understaffed. In about 1970, some 700 Inspectors had to scrutinize thousands of industrial establishments—a job that has been likened to painting the Forth Bridge. The volume of work was sometimes overwhelming, especially in dusty trades such as coal, where the death toll in accidents and lung fibrosis was numerically far higher than asbestos. A perspective is provided by one prominent Factory Inspector, who was active between 1949 and 1957. He recalled how he 'visited 10,000 or 12,000 factories in that first period, [and] there were quite a number of asbestos factories in that group . . . Of course, at that time I had no real reason to pay any particular attention to asbestos factories, more than perhaps factories manufacturing cyanide or anything else.'[16] Mounting a prosecution in every situation where the rules were violated was clearly impossible, especially since Inspectors took on their own prosecutions in the courts. As Morris Greenberg has pointed out, Inspectors were in an unenviable situation: if they lost a case it would be a black mark; if they won, the courts would impose only a trivial fine.[17] This explains why the general strategy of the Inspectors was to persuade and negotiate rather than exhort and convict.[18] Moreover, before the 1970s, Inspectors often lacked the specialist skills and laboratories required to tackle the asbestos problem. The Inspectorate's expertise in dust counting undoubtedly lagged behind the industry itself: indeed, between 1931 and 1969 the government showed no more inclination to count dust in the factories than it did to survey workers' health. The Turner & Newall records make plain that some Inspectors were on a learning curve. Even when they acquired expertise in one area, a change of job or location within the Civil Service soon took them elsewhere. In these circumstances the failure to police the asbestos Regulations becomes more understandable, if not completely forgivable.

What other countervailing forces could workers or claimants use or rely upon against Turner & Newall? One decision was in their own hands: they could refuse to work at Turner & Newall in the first place. Evidently, many workers in Rochdale did make this decision, as by the early 1940s the reputation of the asbestos industry was causing the company labour problems. In 1938, William Ellison wrote:

[15] 70/1114–25. BBC TV, 'The Right to Know—An Investigation into Secrecy', 23 Apr. 1974. Remarks of Mr Cronin.

[16] 507/2301–85. J. G. Luxon deposition in *J. L. May v. A. C. & S. Inc.*, 14 July 1992.

[17] M. Greenberg, interview with author, 17 Aug. 1998.

[18] See generally H. Jones, 'An Inspector Calls: Health and Safety at Work in Inter-war Britain', in P. Weindling (ed.), *The Social History of Occupational Health* (1985), 223–39.

There is difficulty in obtaining the requisite number of young girl recruits for our spinning departments. This is due to the reluctance of parents to allow their children to enter what is regarded as a dangerous trade. Constant efforts are made to dispel unfounded fears, but there exists a very considerable prejudice which is fed by the Home Office regulations regarding frequent examinations and inquests. Also we are compelled by Home Office regulations to supply each new entrant to the asbestos industry [with] a 'Worker's Register' which contains a few pages of printed matter related to disease and death. The entirely wrong impression formed by young people and their parents on reading this information may well be imagined.[19]

In 1945, fear of asbestosis was identified as the biggest single obstacle to recruitment. Job applicants refused outright to work 'in the asbestos', unemployed workers at the Labour Exchange declined to be sent to TBA, and headmasters were reluctant to send their pupils for interview. In Rochdale, one manager discerned a general feeling that 'there is something rather inferior in working at Turner Bros.; it is a fact which one hides rather than displays'.[20]

On the other hand, many workers did accept a job at TBA and other factories, and were loyal to their employers. As regards compensation, the attitude of victims and claimants themselves is hard to gauge from the extant correspondence, much of which is official in nature. One thing is certain, however: Turner & Newall's workers rarely complained before the 1960s and their typical attitude was one of quiescence and acceptance. As one Roberts' worker remarked: 'It is a miserable life to live always coughing, but I will have to make the best of it.'[21] If anything, many employees and their dependants often expressed gratitude to their bosses, no matter how small their compensation. When Thomas Stott, a TBA carding jobber, retired prematurely with asbestosis in 1929 after about twenty-seven years' service, the company authorized a 20s [£1] a week *ex gratia*, which was paid until he died from the disease in August 1930. Employment manager William Ellison noted: 'When I visited Mr Stott to hand him the first payment, he seemed to be completely taken by surprise, and the money was very gratefully received. He wished me to convey to the directors his best thanks for the allowance. He further remarked, "Turners is a grand firm, and I hope they continue to prosper. I am only sorry that I cannot carry on working for them".'[22]

The widow of Edward Butterworth, after her husband had died from asbestosis in 1937, wrote to Ellison: 'I am very sorry you could not find time to attend my late husband's funeral. Mr Hartley gave me the money

[19] 305/1670–1. W. M. Ellison's 'Observations', 12 Feb. 1938.
[20] 301/903. 'Asbestosis' memo, by M. E. Oliver, 30 July 1945.
[21] 115/1664. J. R. Cooker to Roberts, n.d., *c*.1959. Cooker died from asbestosis in 1962.
[22] 354/135–6. W. M. Ellison to Bussy, 28 Dec. 1929.

which you sent me & I thank you very much. Wishing the firm and your-self a happy and prosperous New Year.'[23] She later received a miserly £100 lump sum (and only after union intervention). Mark Rush's widow, who was denied any lump sum payment after her husband's death from lung cancer and asbestosis in 1942, wrote to Turner & Newall's directors to express her gratitude at their 'kindness' in extending her 10s [50p] per week *ex gratia* when she remarried in 1950.[24] When John Thompson was suspended as totally disabled through asbestosis in 1946 and received an *ex-gratia* payment of £1 6s 6d [£1.32] a week (which the company stressed, 'must not be considered by yourself as permanent'), he thanked TBA for their 'kind help'.[25] Lily Taylor, who died in 1957 from asbestosis, left a sister, Elsie Rush, who had cared for her during her final illness. After deciding 'there really is no liability', Turner & Newall paid her £100. Elsie Rush accepted this with 'grateful thanks . . . as some recompense to me for my sister'.[26]

Others harboured no trace of bitterness towards their employers. Dorothy ('Doris') Child, a Roberts' spinner who by 1952 was totally dis-abled with asbestosis, was perhaps the most forgiving. She was unable to work and even unable to write easily due to finger-clubbing. Yet, while her friends around her succumbed to the disease, she nevertheless kept in friendly contact with the Roberts' managers through letters and wished she was 'sometimes back [there] in the good old days'.[27] When she died in 1971, aged 59, from lung cancer and asbestosis ('misadventure', accord-ing to the coroner), her husband informed Roberts of the date of the funeral and expressed gratitude for her *ex gratia*: 'You will never know how grateful Mrs Child and I were for the monthly payments you made . . . from the bottom of my heart, a more than grateful thank you.'[28] Sen-timents such as these explain why many dependants never even submit-ted a claim. Another worker delayed making a claim for several years after his retirement in 1960, because, as he explained: 'I always felt should anything happen to me the company would do the right thing by my wife.' The meagre *ex gratia* the worker received, when he was eventually certified with asbestosis in 1969, showed that his hopes had been misplaced.[29]

Apparently only once did a sick worker under the Asbestosis Scheme show any real fight against his treatment. That was in May 1946, when lagger Ernest Watkins—whose son had died only weeks before from

---

[23] 66/1690. Mrs Butterworth to Ellison, 24 Dec. 1937.

[24] 123/3991–2. Mrs J. Wilson (formerly Rush) to Chadwick, 3 Aug. 1950.

[25] 65/927–8. Thompson file.   [26] 122/1333. Rush to TBA, 18 Dec. 1957.

[27] 115/943. Letter to Roberts, n.d.

[28] 115/838. A. Child to Roberts, 11 Jan. 1971. A manager wrote on the letter: 'No action for flowers or representation for these cases.'

[29] 46/756. Jimmy Waldron to J. Arnold, Jan. 1970.

asbestosis and tuberculosis—had received no compensation. He wrote to a Newalls' manager:

Please note that with the wife's careful nursing and my doctor's special attention I shall now live quite a number of years, 15 to 20 years or more, so I would advise you to release that compensation form, and don't put me off with the Newcastle stunt, that's too old now. I am also going to warn you, actually I shouldn't, now follow this, Our Labour MP has become interested in my case, and has five sheets of the case. He is disgusted at the charlady's rate of pay, and he is going to take up my case to Parliament and he is going to ask if Sir Guy Newall knows anything about this side of his million pound firm. Now, as you know this will cause trouble, so it's up to you. I'm claiming and expecting compensation from when I left work, so Mr Hornsby send that form and clear up the arrears. Perhaps you think this is bluff. Well you shall be the judge and take what comes either way or the other. A little later on I may come up to see you.[30]

The manager sent this Kafkaesque reply three days later:

I would . . . ask you to refrain from communicating with me respecting the financial side of your claim . . . as I am unable to help in any way, the matter being entirely out of my jurisdiction. As I understand it, a claim . . . is being dealt with by the official machinery which has been set up to attend to such cases. Therefore, officially, there is nothing that I can do in the matter, although personally I am glad to hear that you are improving and wish you a speedy relief from your many troubles, in which you have my deepest sympathy.[31]

The wheels of the official machinery moved too slowly for Watkins: his letter was the bluff of a very ill man and he died three weeks later. The company then refused to accept liability for his death.

Why were workers and their relatives so meek? The culture of the textile and asbestos industries—paternalistic, deferential, and relatively weakly unionized—obviously played a part. Then there was the Lancastrian temperament: tough, self-reliant, and given to understatement of personal travails.[32] In Rochdale, workers had traditionally turned to cooperation rather than trade unionism to better their lot (after all, the town was the home of the Rochdale Pioneers and the Co-operative movement). Despite all the asbestos health problems, TBA enjoyed a good level of worker loyalty. Turner & Newall itself noted that historically Rochdale workers had been very reluctant to launch legal proceedings, due mainly to the *ex-gratia* policy, which TBA had utilized more than any other unit company.[33]

Workers were also kept in the dark and Turner & Newall did little to publicize the health hazards of asbestos. The quarterly staff magazine,

[30] 61/1466. Watkins's letter to Hornsby, 12 May 1946.
[31] 61/1465. Hornsby to Watkins, 15 May 1946.
[32] These characteristics were noted by occupational health physician Richard Schilling, in *A Challenging Life* (1998), 89.
[33] 500/262–71. 'T & N Asbestos Disease Litigation in the UK'.

Firefly, which was launched in 1952, contained no mention of asbestos disease or any health warnings during its entire publication run until 1968. Its pages regularly listed obituaries, many of them of workers who had died from asbestosis. Yet this was never mentioned, though the company's internal documents allow us in retrospect to find a sinister meaning in phrases such as 'died after a fairly long period of illness'.[34] More distressingly, in its Christmas 1952 issue *Firefly* profiled on its cover and inside story Roberts' longest-serving employee, Bill Jagger, a 47-year-old storekeeper. It did not mention why he was working in the stores— he had been suspended in 1946 with asbestosis. The next issue carried brief news of his death in January 1953 from asbestosis and lung cancer— another fact not mentioned.

Ignorance was a factor in workers' deference—then, as now, many workers (and even their medical advisers) did not know their rights. Another key factor was economic circumstances. In the 1930s, when government regulations came into force, workers were often grateful for any job (especially one that was relatively well paid), thus giving the firm a very strong bargaining position. Some workers seem to have accepted an element of risk for extra money, though this was not based on complete information about the hazards. An old Roberts' mattress-maker recalled:

The pay we received at the factory was more than that I would have received had I had a sewing job. The reason I went to Roberts was because I wanted to earn more money to get married. It was generally thought that working there was a little bit dangerous, but no one had any idea it was as dangerous as it is now known.[35]

The close community and workplace network in Rochdale allowed TBA's managers to monitor closely workers' attitudes and stamp out any heresy. In 1941, a Liverpool worker at TBA asked William Ellison if three girls, whom he had recently brought to the factory, could leave. The reason: he had heard about the dangers of asbestos from another worker. Ellison soon found out the culprit's name and ordered him to his office. It was the father of Mary Mitchell, an 18-year-old spinner, who had recently died from tuberculosis. Her father had broadcast to other workers that asbestos had killed her. Ellison spoke to him 'severely about spreading what amounted to a libellous statement'. The father, no doubt suitably chastened, was sent on his way: since he worked at TBA, too, this rebellion was no doubt nipped in the bud.[36]

---

[34] *Firefly* obit. of Mark C. Tweedale, d. 14 Aug. 1955 from asbestosis.

[35] Evidence of Eliza Shaw, *Margereson/Hancock v. J. W. Roberts and T & N*, High Court Leeds, 1995. Trial transcript, 28 June 1995, 21.

[36] 123/3941–2. Ellison to Bussy, 8 Aug., 6 Sept. 1941. Ellison was comforted by the fact that this was not an official asbestosis case. Mary Mitchell had been suspended with tuberculosis in 1941. However, no inquest took place after her death to ascertain whether asbestos had played any part in accelerating her condition.

The asbestos industry fed and then killed more than one member of several families, as it was not unusual for whole households to work at Turner & Newall. Dr Ian Grieve's study of asbestosis sufferers at Roberts' factory gives an insight into these family networks in the 1920s. One of his patients, Edith Parish (aged 37), had asbestosis: her mother also worked at the factory and suffered from chest trouble; while Edith's two sisters (aged 37 and 32) had also developed asbestosis. Caroline Cowlam, a mattress-maker, was another Grieve patient: she died in 1939, aged 48, from asbestosis. Her husband, Joseph, worked at the same job and was suspended with asbestosis in 1944 (later dying from lung cancer in 1949). One of their daughters had developed asbestosis by 1992—apparently a non-occupational ('bystander') case. Arthur Dobson was a cashier at Roberts and by 1934 had worked there for thirty years: two of his four sons also worked at the factory, one of them—Akrill—a manual worker in the carding departments. The managers regarded Akrill as 'one of the heaviest, and for his stature, strongest men we had in the factory, and generally of exceptional physique'.[37] It made little difference: Akrill died aged 30 in 1934, the same year as his father: both from asbestosis and tuberculosis.

Ominously, Turner & Newall's dust spread beyond the factory gates. In the streets around the Armley factory, the pavements and even the insides of houses (including the lofts) were coated with asbestos, while children played among sacks of blue asbestos that Roberts had carelessly stacked outside the factory. In the words of one resident, it was 'as though we were practically eating dust. I remember dust and fibre all round the streets near the factory. You could see the dust in the air. I have seen it blow around like a snowstorm.'[38] However, local residents did not complain, fearing that family members would lose their jobs.

Roberts' workers also brought dust home on their clothes, which was to cause bystander asbestosis and mesothelioma deaths. This lay some way in the future. For the moment, after the asbestosis scares at Roberts and TBA in the late 1920s and early 1940s, the steady drip of deaths may not have been enough to trigger real alarm among the workers. Some died from disputed causes, others passed away in retirement, and contract staff such as laggers were widely dispersed. Many workers did not become sick at all, especially those that had only worked for the company for only months or a few years. After the 1940s, even workers who succumbed to asbestosis were living longer, thus giving their mates a false sense of security. Moreover, the number of Turner & Newall workers who became sick within only a few years may have been counterbalanced by those few who seemed able to work with asbestos for decades. To be sure, most of

[37] 38/0267. Akrill Dobson 'History'.
[38] Evidence of William Parker, *Margereson/Hancock* transcript, 27 June 1995, 3.

them succumbed to asbestosis or cancer eventually: however, it highlights a personal susceptibility that is still not understood. At TBA, Mark Rush Jnr (1912–75) spent forty-three years in a scheduled carding and spinning job and forty-eight years with the firm until he was suspended in 1974 with asbestosis (the same disease that had killed his father in 1942).[39] Joseph Duffy (1906–78) completed over forty-five years in carding and spinning until his suspension in 1970 (he later died from cancer and asbestosis). The record seems to have been held by Erith asbestos cement worker, Leonard Goodwright (1901–76), who had a non-scheduled labouring job for fifty-three years until his death from lung cancer and asbestosis.

In these circumstances, it is perhaps not surprising that trade unions had little impact before the 1970s. As regards the cotton industry generally, the prevailing judgement of the performance of British trade unions in occupational health has been largely negative, though some have emphasized that cotton unions did spearhead some health campaigns.[40] In the early 1930s, TBA employees through their Workers' Committee *were* concerned about health and safety and also compensation. In 1932, for example, the Committee, responding to 'widespread dissatisfaction' in the works, pressed the management for a meeting to discuss the terms of Robert Turner's legacy. The directors later used this bequest to establish a pension scheme; the workers wanted to use the money to improve compensation payments. They also asked to meet Samuel Turner to discuss the Asbestos Regulations. William Ellison brushed aside these requests: they were matters, he argued, solely for the board to decide.[41] As might be expected, a striking feature of the Turner & Newall case files is that trade unions rarely seem to have been involved in occupational health negotiations before the 1960s. Apparently in only a few cases—perhaps four or five—did the worker's union fight hard for adequate compensation, and even then their success was mixed.

Before the 1960s, perhaps the only example recorded in the files of a union trying to use any muscle was in the case of Edward Butterworth, who died in 1937. The deceased worker's union, the Rochdale Weavers' Association, had recommended that his widow consult a local solicitor. For this straightforward asbestosis case Turner & Newall offered £50 compensation, which the solicitors succeeded in raising to what they considered an acceptable £75. The Weavers' Association were not satisfied with that and one of its members, Mr Nuttall, had a quiet word with Ellison, who noted their conversation:

---

[39] Mark Rush Jnr died from pancreatitis, though both lungs showed evidence at postmortem of asbestosis. Mark Rush snr, who was suspended in 1941, died from lung cancer and asbestosis.

[40] See A. McIvor, 'Health and Safety in the Cotton Industry: A Literature Review', *Manchester Region History Review* 9 (1995), 50–7.

[41] 305/1442–7. Letters between W. M. Ellison and Workers' Committee, May–June 1932.

Mr Nuttall stated to me that they were out to get £150 for Mrs Butterworth if possible. He used the argument that the widow had worked hard and if we stick to the strictly legal aspect we are penalising thrift. The woman has been thrifty and has not battened upon her husband's resources. 'A life has gone and it is a small amount we are asking for.' Mr Nuttall went on to quote the firm's profits for last year and said: 'You would not like to go to court for £150 for a life.'[42]

Commercial Union believed that £150 was quite unreasonable and Turner & Newall felt that the union was bluffing. Eventually, the firm offered £100 and it was accepted.

The only other occasion when a union appears to have swung matters the way of the relatives was when Washington worker Mary Keegan died from asbestosis in 1939. The National Union of General & Municipal Workers paid for the Medical Board certificate and may have been instrumental in securing a small *ex gratia* of £50, which was paid by the company 'on sympathetic grounds with a denial of liability'.[43]

Unions did not make a big issue of working conditions before the 1960s. The only example of such concerns in the Turner & Newall files relates to Ann Buckley. When she was suspended in 1937 and moved to a job in the rubber department in the Rochdale factory, the NUGMW representative wrote to Commercial Union: 'I am given to understand that the Rubber Shed is only divided from other departments in which asbestos is handled by a partition which does not completely fill the space from floor to ceiling and, therefore, particles of asbestos dust travel into the Rubber Departments.'[44] This complaint was dismissed by Ellison who told Commercial Union that Buckley was 'employed in an area which is non-scheduled and is approved as such by the Home Office authorities'.[45] She continued in the rubber department for another ten years, eventually dying in 1964, apparently after a heart attack (so there was no inquest).

Sometimes the union virtually begged Turner & Newall for the funeral costs, as in the Barker Greenwood case where the union appealed for £20 (the relatives later got £15). Similarly, when Elsie Shears died, in 1947, the Weavers' Association wrote to a director:

On our behalf our solicitor attended the inquest and advised us that although she died from asbestosis there is no legal claim, other than £15 for funeral expenses, against you because dependency cannot be proved. I have had Miss Shears' brother down to see me at my request and I have shown to him our solicitor's letter and pointed out that we cannot make any legal claim. But in the past I know you have dealt far more generously than the law requires with cases of this kind. Might I ask you to give your most generous consideration in this particular case. I think it reasonable to assume that during the period of her incapacity her com-

---

[42] 66/1685. W. M. Ellison to Bussy, 23 Mar. 1938.
[43] 61/1651. WCC letter, 18 Sept. 1940.   [44] 66/1220. J. Cooper to CU, 23 Mar. 1937.
[45] 66/1216. W. M. Ellison to CU, 25 Mar. 1937.

pensation has been insufficient to maintain her, and the funeral expenses would certainly be in excess of £15. That I can ask for your sympathetic consideration I feel sure.[46]

The company were 'sympathetic' in this case, agreeing to pay the full funeral cost.

This supports a recent study, which has suggested that the unions were largely ineffective in modifying the provisions of the 1931 legislation and gave health and safety a low priority.[47] However, the evidence from Turner & Newall also highlights the difficulty trade unions faced in opposing a powerful commercial organization. The files are not always complete and unions may have performed a more pervasive low-key role, by perhaps providing general support and advice, which has not always been recorded. They may also have advised claimants with regard to solicitors (as happened in the Butterworth case), who undoubtedly wielded more influence. The payment of the £750 lump sum to John Grimshaw, for example, was brokered by his union (albeit through the intermediary of a solicitor). In the Henry Hodgeon case in 1946, the union paid the legal fees, as Commercial Union told Turner & Newall they were not obliged to pick up the bill. Before the death of Nora Dockerty in 1950 (see below), the NUGMW helped to reverse Knox's medical diagnosis of 'bronchitis', so that she could enter a tuberculosis sanatorium; and then after her death the union appears to have put the family in touch with solicitors. After Alec Franks died in 1966 from asbestosis contracted at Trafford Park, the TGWU initiated legal action against Turner & Newall, arguing that no dust extraction was used in Franks's workplace.[48]

However, the involvement of solicitors was not typical of asbestos compensation cases before the 1960s. For some workers and their families the idea of actually threatening their employers with any legal action was too much to contemplate. The risk of incurring major expenses would be a major impediment for many families (unless a union underwrote the costs), so that solicitors rarely make an appearance before 1940, though their activity became rather more marked after 1950. Given Turner & Newall's (and Commercial Union's) frequent denial of liability, a solicitor was a very useful asset for dependants. A few solicitors evidently acquired expertise in asbestosis cases: Whittle's in Manchester, Hudson's in Rochdale, and Thompson's in London appear the most regularly in correspondence.

[46] 38/1186. Letter to N. A. Morling from Ernest Thornton, Secretary, Rochdale & District Weavers, Winders, Beamers, Realers & Doublers' Assoc., 22 Dec. 1947.

[47] N. Wikeley, 'Asbestos and Cancer: An Early Warning to the British TUC', *American Journal of Industrial Medicine* 22 (1992), 449–54. On trade unions and asbestos, see also M. Greenberg, 'Knowledge of the Health Hazard of Asbestos Prior to the Merewether and Price Report of 1930', *Social History of Medicine* 7 (Dec. 1994), 493–516.

[48] 27/1717. TGWU to T & N, 25 Jan. 1967.

Generally, solicitors had a positive impact on the outcome of a claim—though of course they did not work for free and the question of legal costs was another bone over which Turner & Newall and Commercial Union were prepared to argue at great length. In the Watkins's case, concerning the father and son laggers, the solicitors (originally one represented each man) were important in securing a settlement, even though the final sum was below the claimant's target. Whittle's seem to have been successful in the Alice Morris claim in 1940 in winning £100 for an infant child. Solicitors working on behalf of the widow of Washington worker James Kay in 1938 were persistent enough to win her 30s [£1.50] a week pension and some legal costs. When non-scheduled Washington worker John Scorer died from asbestosis in 1946, the widow was represented by Crute's. This Newcastle firm pressed for a substantial settlement, despite Turner & Newall's denial of liability. A manager at Washington noted: 'We know of course that Mr Crute has a very wide experience of compensation cases, and he frequently acts for certain of the Allied Offices. His opinions always merit consideration, and it certainly seems to me that there is quite a lot in what he has to say'.[49] The widow eventually won a £300 *ex gratia*, a sum she would almost certainly have never received but for legal intervention.[50] In the case of William Lythgoe—a non-scheduled TAC worker—a solicitor secured a settlement in 1948 of £250 (which he thought 'exceedingly generous on Turner & Newall's part').[51]

Solicitors were usually recruited to make the best possible deal under the Workmen's Compensation Act. Under that Act claimants had the right to elect between using the compensation scheme or proceeding to sue their employer in the ordinary courts. Yet the first common law actions against Turner & Newall were not lodged until 1950. The first, by a TAC worker in Dalmuir, was later abandoned. The second was on behalf of Nora Dockerty née Kelly (1918–50), a TBA carder and spinner, who had died from tuberculosis and asbestosis.[52] John Collins confidently told the Turner & Newall board: 'the chance of a common law asbestosis claim being made against us successfully . . . on the score of negligence or of breach of statutory duty is slight.'[53] However, the action was settled for £375 plus costs. In 1951, a second common law action was launched by the widow of a Roberts' worker, Thomas McDonald, who had died from

[49] 61/1295–6. J. W. Simpson to T & N, 7 Nov. 1946.
[50] Crute's also represented the widow of George James, a Washington worker, who died from asbestosis in 1954. She was awarded £300 and an *ex gratia*.
[51] 36/1581–2. CU to T & N, 7 Sept. 1948.
[52] N. J. Wikeley, 'Turner & Newall: Early Organizational Responses to Litigation Risk', *Journal of Law and Society* 24 (1997), 252–74; Wikeley, 'The First Common Law Claim for Asbestosis: *Kelly v. Turner & Newall* (1950)', *Journal of Personal Injury Litigation*, 3 (1998), 197–210.
[53] T & N board papers: Asbestosis Fund Report, 10 Nov. 1950.

tuberculosis and asbestosis. Collins again was 'not at all worried about the fact that there was some dust in the atmosphere. It is obvious that in no asbestos factory can the whole of the dust be extracted and I think that the plaintiff would find it difficult to prove negligence or breach of statutory duty on that score.'[54] This view was quickly disabused by Chapman's, the firm's Manchester solicitor, and Collins was soon telling the board exactly the opposite: that the company, in fact, had no defence. To avoid publicity that would encourage a crop of similar claims, the company had to settle out of court for £1,000. The year 1951 was a bad one for Turner & Newall, as the widow of Newalls' lagger Joseph Meanen also filed an action. Despite the lack of a post-mortem and PMP death certificate, the widow was awarded an Industrial Injuries pension and—to the company's dismay—granted legal aid for her claim. Again, the company had to settle for £1,000, since there was no adequate dust extraction where Meanen had worked at John Brown's shipyard.

In view of these relative successes, it seems a pity that more claimants did not resort to the common law. However, their reluctance is understandable. In effect, they had to transfer themselves from the arms of one vested interest (the asbestos industry) to another (the legal profession). Even then success was not guaranteed, no matter how just the case. A major impediment was the limitation period for tort claims—six years for personal injury actions after 1939; three years after 1954. The time period ran from the last relevant exposure (unlike today when the period runs from when the plaintiff first knew of any significant injury), which meant in practice that most claims were 'statute-barred'. The plaintiff also had to prove that that Turner & Newall had been negligent, again not an easy matter, especially before 1948 when companies could claim contributory negligence by the worker. In the UK plaintiffs have never had extensive rights of 'discovery' of relevant documents (as they would have in America), so hindering a successful claim. Thus, even with a solicitor it was not always easy to establish liability. In the Keily case in 1935, solicitors threatened exhumation, but Turner & Newall called their bluff and they had to settle for a small *ex gratia*. The company, naturally, had their own solicitors, Chapman & Company, who—as the Coyle case highlighted—were usually much more experienced than any legal firm hired by a claimant. Thus, solicitors probably only had a minor impact on the overall Turner & Newall bill for industrial compensation: most families did not employ them and even solicitors were at a disadvantage when dealing with a large company.

Surprisingly, in view of its key role in so many stages of diagnosis, treatment and prescription, the medical community offered victims and their

---

[54] 9/1568. Collins to CU, 10 Oct. 1951.

dependants relatively little support (except in an indirect way through the Medical Board). Doctors have traditionally been reluctant to become involved in court proceedings, except on behalf of companies. They also seem to have played a limited role in alerting patients or their relatives to their rights. This was in marked contrast to Canada, where doctors could initiate a claim on behalf of their patients. In only three cases from about a thousand Turner & Newall compensation files examined in the research for this book was there any evidence that doctors urged patients to claim industrial injury benefits. In one example, a Charing Cross Hospital physician, who had treated a TAC mesothelioma sufferer, wrote directly to TBA in 1962, asking if the company was willing to pay compensation.[55] The company replied that they were 'disinclined' to take any action.

Except for one or two experts in occupational health—such as Donald Hunter at the London Hospital[56]—Turner & Newall generally had little to fear from the medical community before the 1960s. Occupational health was a relatively specialized calling; epidemiology was still developing. The chances of any unwelcome publicity appearing of the type that had almost surfaced after Doll's work were very slim. In the 1950s, relatively little research was being conducted into asbestosis; what little was taking place was controlled by the industry. In 1957, Turner & Newall, Cape and British Belting & Asbestos joined forces in founding the Asbestosis Research Council. Key factors in this move were the continued incidence of asbestosis, the emergence of lung cancer (the implications of Doll's paper had not been entirely dismissed after all), and the evident need for better dust control.[57] For Turner & Newall, funding asbestosis research was not new—it had sponsored work at Hammersmith, Cambridge, and Reading since the early 1940s—but the ARC placed this support on a more formal footing. Turner & Newall had the main controlling interest in the organization, which was launched with a modest budget of £4,100.

Internally, the Council was dominated by the three member-companies, who controlled funding and vetted publications. In public, the image that the ARC tried to present to the world was of a conscientious industry doing all it could to protect its workers from a health hazard. Its sponsored scientific work was conducted by qualified health physicists and doctors, who helped the ARC amass a substantial 'portfolio' of published research. However, none of the work was of a type likely to generate headlines. Most ARC research was in the mould of Matthew Stewart's work

---

[55] 27/1722. Dr C. E. Warner to TBA, 27 Apr. 1962.

[56] Donald Hunter (1898–1979) was Britain's leading occupational health physician. First editor of the *British Journal of Industrial Medicine*, he was often critical of the asbestos industry and once described the spray process as 'murderous'. He advised dockers when they became concerned at the dangers of unloading asbestos. He was later joined at the London Hospital by Arthur McLaughlin, another doctor with few friends at T & N.

[57] 361/1174–80. 'The Asbestosis Research Council: The First Thirty Years', draft typescript.

with guinea pigs in 1930. Animal experiments had continued with the TBA-funded research at the British Postgraduate Medical School in the 1940s. Earl King's work with animals was said to have shown that experimental asbestosis was more readily produced by fibres of 5 microns and upwards. This research mantle had then passed in the 1950s to Professor John Beattie (1899–1976), a research physiologist at Cambridge University, who was also Knox's brother-in-law. Beattie, too, believed that particle size was the dominant influence on the development of asbestosis (with the larger particles—the type which could be more easily removed from a factory—being the most hazardous). Specialized laboratory work with guinea pigs and rats, microscope studies of fibres and asbestosis, and chemical analyses of asbestos bodies—these were the type of studies that were the staple of Beattie and other ARC researchers. Underlying some of this work was the assumption that with increased knowledge the harmful constituents of asbestos might be identified, so that it could be made less harmful, or that a medical treatment could be found for asbestosis. This was a worthy aim, but never a remote possibility, and meanwhile workers continued to inhale dangerous levels of fibre.

Like the Council for Tobacco Research, funded by the tobacco industry and also established in the 1950s, the ARC performed a public-relations function and provided a measure of political and legal protection.[58] The ARC would come into its own in countering government regulation in the 1960s; and its existence would also be used by Turner & Newall as a defence in litigation. As with tobacco, the ARC continually suggested that lengthy research (rather than common sense) was needed to clear up various controversies, even though its commitment to wide-ranging epidemiological study was limited. It was not in favour of projects that looked outside the laboratory or asbestos textiles. When Gilbert Leathart, a Tyneside industrial health physician, suggested a field study of lagging operations in a power station, Stephen Holmes told him: 'The committee has considerable resources of its own for carrying out experiments of the kind you propose and has a working group responsible for the insulation side of the industry. Would it not be better for you to make your views known to this body rather than do your own experiment?'[59]

Truly independent studies might attract the attention of the countervailing influence that Turner & Newall feared most—the media. Despite (or perhaps because of) Turner & Newall's authority and influence in the local community, it still feared bad publicity, especially by newspapers. Workers in Rochdale, Leeds, and other localities may have been in a weak position, but they were not fools and the dangers of working at Turner &

[58] On the tobacco industry's secret research and suppression of information, see S. Glantz et al. (eds.), *The Cigarette Papers* (1996).
[59] 45/620. Holmes to Leathart, 14 Mar. 1969.

Newall were known. Newspapers spread the bad news. Inquests, for example, were often reported in local newspapers, such as the *Manchester Guardian*, the *Rochdale Observer* and the *Yorkshire Post*. Turner & Newall were represented at inquests, but obviously it was the verdict and the remarks by the coroner and witnesses that carried the greatest coverage. Sometimes these were favourable to Turner & Newall, but more often they were critical. When Walter Leadbeater died in Leeds in 1928, the newspaper report of the inquest quoted a specialist in asbestosis who had emphasized the dangers of the minute particles of asbestos dust (against which masks were ineffective) and argued strongly for greater powers to enter and examine factories for the public good.[60] Walker Shepherd thought this press reporting 'distinctly unfair, consisting as it does largely of the evidence of a man who was not called [at the inquest] by anybody, but was allowed to make a big noise, apparently because he was a local pundit'.[61]

In 1932, soon after the launch of the Asbestosis Scheme, the company noted that it was having problems 'getting the best type of young people', mainly because their parents did not wish them to work with asbestos. TBA's works manager highlighted the fact that it might be due to 'a scare in the town . . . caused [by] reports in local newspapers in connection with an inquest dealing with an asbestos worker's death'.[62]

In another example, the *Rochdale Observer*, under the heading 'Mill Worker's Death Query: An Asbestos Factory Employee', reported on 25 September 1937 the inquest on Lawrence Griffiths. It noted the verdict— death due to tuberculosis and asbestosis—and highlighted that he had never worked in the scheduled areas. In a fascinating exchange, the question was raised as to whether people who had never worked in an asbestos factory could have the fibres in their lungs. The pathologist Dr Pooley stated that in Leeds he believed that asbestos had been found 'in people living in houses adjacent to such a factory'. William Ellison thought that the employer 'might have been given the benefit of the doubt', and added:

The press reports of these cases convey a very unfortunate impression to our workpeople. An electrician left our employ on Saturday last. He stated that he had got really scared of working in our factory since he read of the report of the Griffiths' case, so he had obtained work elsewhere although he was very reluctant to leave our employ.[63]

[60] 38/513. *Yorkshire Post*, 31 Mar. 1928. Remarks of H. de Carle Woodcock.
[61] 61/445–6. Shepherd to S. Turner, 2 Apr. 1928.
[62] 43/304. Asbestosis Committee Minute Book, 28 June 1932, 27. The works manager further stated that when T & N sent to the Labour Exchange for two 14-year-old girls, the vacancies 'were offered to fifteen girls before one would come for interview. It was stated that the Secretary of the Juvenile Employment Committee had said that in each case the parents would not consent to their children being employed in the industry.'
[63] 65/0172. Ellison to Bateman, 18 Oct. 1937.

When the case of Fred Greenwood was settled in the same year, fear of the press was a significant influence on Turner & Newall. In a letter thanking Commercial Union for its legal advice, Ellison explained why a slightly softer stance was being adopted: 'it seems to us that if [the case] was brought to a hearing we should have some difficulty in establishing a case for settlement on a partial dependency basis . . . Further, we should not welcome the appearance of this case in court owing to the undesirable publicity which would be given to it in the local press.'[64]

The impact of bad press was felt acutely during the Second World War, when TBA had its biggest problems recruiting staff. Fear of asbestosis was one of the major impediments to recruitment, caused partly—so the company believed—by inquest reports in the local newspapers. According to TBA: 'Even if the coroner's verdict does not give asbestosis as the cause of death or as having accelerated death, the company usually suffers owing to the publicity in the *Rochdale Observer*.'[65] Compared to the human casualties, however, the company suffered little at the hands of the press until the 1960s, when the balance of power between the company and various countervailing forces began to change.

[64] 36/1186. Ellison to CU, 26 Nov. 1937.
[65] 301/893. TBA Instructions to Counsel, 1943.

8

Lighting the Powder Trail

We have over the years been able to talk our way out of [asbestos-disease] claims or compromise for comparatively small amounts, but we have always recognised that at some stage solicitors of experience assisted by legal aid certificate or financed by a union would, with the advance in medical knowledge and the development of the law, and being prepared to undertake the work involved in a detailed investigation, recognise there is no real defence to these claims and take us to trial.

506/1702–5. James Chapman & Company (solicitors) to Turner & Newall, 10 Sept. 1964.

In retrospect, it seems remarkable that the asbestos industry should have declined so swiftly. In 1967, it was still possible for *The Times* to run a supplement on asbestos which included a glowing portrait of a successful industry. The newspaper's medical correspondent discussed the 'challenge of dust' and mesothelioma, but discouraged any alarmist thoughts about the industry disappearing.[1] However, within a decade the whole picture had changed, as various scientific, legal, social, and economic pressures caused a seismic shift in the fortunes of the industry. It was the 1960s—especially the mid-1960s—when the tide turned.

The first force for change was economic. Turner & Newall's profits hit a peak in the mid-1960s (see Graph 1.1) and then dipped as technology and the company's manufacturing profile changed. Turner & Newall were now involved increasingly in the production of fibre glass, mineral wool, and plastics. TBA had started the manufacture of asbestos reinforced plastic (Durestos) in 1948; and during the late 1950s and early 1960s, it also began researching and marketing polytetrafluorethylene (PTFE), thermoplastic resins, and PVC sheet. The acquisition of British Industrial Plastics (BIP) in 1961 underlined this change of direction. These materials augmented the company's growing business in glass fibre. The magic mineral remained the major source of profit, but by the late 1960s non-asbestos products accounted for 40 per cent of home turnover and 25 per cent abroad.

The other catalyst for change was the rising trend of suspensions and deaths. After 1931, it had been hoped that the suspension rate would fall

[1] 'Asbestos', *The Times*, 28 Nov. 1967.

as less dusty conditions made asbestosis a disease of the past. For a while—in the 1930s and early 1940s—it had seemed as if this might happen: then in the 1950s and early 1960s, the number of new cases of asbestosis in the UK began rising (see Table 8.1). At Turner & Newall, the number of cases between 1950 and 1965 was 235—nearly half of the UK total—whereas only 156 company employees had been suspended between 1929 and 1949. Obviously, the increasing size of the industry, the wartime relaxation of dust control, and better medical knowledge had played a part in this rise. However, the evidence also suggested that the dust Regulations were inadequate and that the flaws in the 1931 legislation were coming home to roost. After 1955, some 67 per cent of new asbestosis cases had started work after 1933; and over 40 per cent of the

Table 8.1. *UK asbestosis cases and deaths, 1950–70*

Year	Suspensions	Deaths
1950 (9 months)	17	12
1951	17	18
1952	15	12
1953	23	15
1954	31	12
1955	48	21
1956	31	16
1957	56	21
1958	27	20
1959	37	21
1960	29	31
1961	43	21
1962	52	38
1963	67	37
1964	83	44
1965	82	64
1966	114	64
1967	168	82
1968	130	112
1969	134	84
1970	153	107
Total	1,357	852

Source: H. C. Lewinsohn, 'The Medical Surveillance of Asbestos Workers', *Royal Society of Health Journal* 92 (Apr. 1972), 69–77, 70; Ministry of Labour & Factory Inspectorate, *Annual Reports of Chief Inspector of Factories* (London, 1951–71).

total was from the insulating trades (in other words, among workers who were still not covered by the statutory medical scheme).[2] Again, the trend was reflected in Turner & Newall figures. Between 1950 and 1965, 122 Newalls' workers had been suspended, over half the group total of 235. The days when John Collins could deny that asbestosis existed at that company had passed. In 1967, one director wrote to a colleague that Newalls' asbestosis 'experience is frightening and . . . we must do something and quickly'.[3]

The exposure needed to produce asbestos disease was often alarmingly short. My review of the company's compensation cases up to about the end of the 1970s—an exercise which can only provide an underestimate— shows about 120 individuals who became sick after being exposed for only ten years or less (in about 40 of these cases exposure was five years or less).[4] Such figures demolish Turner & Newall's oft-repeated assertions that 'asbestosis . . . can only develop as a result of long exposure after many years'.[5] The exposure needed to trigger mesothelioma was often much shorter than for asbestosis. The incidence of this cancer was also rising ominously among Turner & Newall workers—with at least thirty deaths between 1960 and 1970—and several cases showed the potency of even small doses of asbestos. TAC worker Charles Cheetham, who died in 1970, aged 56, from pleural mesothelioma (and asbestosis), had spent only seven months as a yard labourer at the Erith factory.[6] Mesothelioma was shattering the whole rationale of the scheduled areas.

The increase in disease had important implications for the company's compensation policy. As we have seen, Turner & Newall's compensation costs were so light that it never needed to insure for asbestos damages. Compensation for sick workers was paid by the state; death claims were usually soon settled with a £400 *ex gratia* or less; common law actions were anything but common and could usually be blocked or paid off for less than £1,000. In 1963, however, the government amended the Limitation Act for tort litigation. The old legislation had effectively barred actions by stipulating that they should be brought within three years of contracting the disease—an absurd requirement given the extended latency of asbestos disease. At last the government had seen this as grossly unfair. Now actions could be brought within a year of the plaintiff discovering any illness. Turner & Newall's solicitor, Chapman's, informed

[2] J. C. McVittie, 'Asbestosis in Great Britain', *Annals of the New York Academy of Sciences* 132 (1965), i, 128–38, 131 ff.

[3] K. Neve to G. R. Pushman, 25 Apr. 1967. *Chase v. T & N* (1995). Trial transcript, 3,001. According to Chase, there were 138 cases of asbestosis at Newalls between 1960 and 1969.

[4] For example: Prince William Apps, a sprayer suspended with asbestosis in 1953 after less than three years' work; Alexander Rennie, a Scottish lagger, who was suspended in 1962 after 2½ years; David Bell, a Washington fibre treater, who was suspended with asbestosis in 1965 after two years' exposure.

[5] 9/1032. A. D. N. Jones to TGWU, 22 May 1956.

[6] 114/1105–52. C. Cheetham (1913–70) file.

the company that this meant the loss of one of their 'strongest negotiating weapons'.[7] Medical advances which introduced greater certainty in diagnosis; the activities of trade unions; the availability of legal aid—all these factors made the legal outlook more threatening for the company. Chapman's estimated that future damages could reach £12,500 for each case. This proved to be somewhat pessimistic, as the industry was still in a powerful position and the legal hurdles for plaintiffs remained formidable. There was no sudden explosion in asbestos litigation or costs after 1963. On the other hand, although cases were still being settled for quite small amounts in the 1960s, there were a number of exceptions. In 1964, two claims had been settled for £3,500, another for £1,500 and one for £1,000.[8] These were hardly vast sums for a multinational, but the payments and precedents set an ominous upward trend which was to become steeper in the 1970s. Victims were becoming less inclined to accept the company's meagre payouts.

In the early 1960s, as suspensions rose, the medical community began to see the need for a new survey of asbestos disease, perhaps along the lines of the Merewether–Price report. The idea was first raised in 1959—not coincidentally the year when mesothelioma was identified. A medical officer at the Medical Research Council, Dr Joan Faulkner (Richard Doll's wife), arranged a meeting at the MRC in London. It was attended by, among others, ARC-funded researchers Earl King and John Beattie, John Gilson (the director of the Pneumoconiosis Research Unit), and John Knox. Discussion ranged informally over the whole asbestosis problem and the threat of mesothelioma. The survey idea was subsequently pushed forward by Gilson,[9] with the co-operation of the ARC. This was less than wholehearted, as John Waddell feared that an enquiry might stray beyond asbestos textile workers into the insulation industry. The ARC would also have no chance to control the results, though not co-operating could hardly be an option either. Not until 1962 did Gilson contact the MRC and the Ministry of Labour with a formal proposal for the 'Investigation of Asbestosis'. Knox told his directors: 'the scale and scope of this [enquiry] are not yet fully determined and . . . very slow progress will be made. There is, however, a certain inevitability in this matter.'[10]

A sense of urgency was to be injected into these deliberations by the spectre of cancer, which was beginning to register among the public. In

---

[7] 506/1072–5. Chapman's to T & N, 10 Sept. 1964.

[8] Company secretary Arthur Jones referred to two of these cases—both Belfast insulators—as a 'matter of concern to the whole industry'. The men had secured union backing and the company was worried about its defence, as it was not company policy for workers to wear masks during non-spray work. See 506/1343. Jones to Wm. Kenyon & Sons, 11 Feb. 1964.

[9] J. C. Gilson (1912–89) directed the PRU between 1952 and 1976. He took a particular interest in asbestos disease and was a government adviser.

[10] 301/725. CMO Report, 7 Sept. 1962.

1964, Turner & Newall described two 'sinister developments' it had noticed.[11] These sinister trends were, first, the fact that the link between lung cancer and asbestos was becoming more widely known; and second, that mesothelioma was attracting publicity. The MRC and PRU (and ARC) had appealed in the *British Medical Journal* in 1962 for information on mesotheliomas, and had stated that the disease could be caused by transient exposure.[12] This elicited an immediate response from a group of Belfast pathologists, who had re-examined a group of pleural tumours that had first been documented in 1958. Of fifteen cases, twelve had asbestos bodies in the lungs; most were linked to the shipyards; and exposure was often intermittent or transient.[13] This aroused no press comment at the time, but by 1964 mesothelioma was definitely in the news. For example, on 8 January 1964, the *Daily Telegraph* reported the death from mesothelioma of a London taxi-driver and former lagger. The report brought an immediate enquiry to Turner & Newall from West Somerset Water board officials, who were concerned at their men inhaling dust when cutting asbestos pipes.[14] This was merely a foretaste of what was in store for the industry.

In October 1964, the New York Academy of Sciences organized a major international conference on the biological effects of asbestos. What would normally have been no more than an obscure gathering of academics discussing recondite scientific issues, suddenly attracted the glare of publicity. Leading medical experts from around the world made up the programme—a veritable who's who in the world of asbestos disease research—with the proceedings filling a fat volume of over 700 pages.[15] The leading American asbestos companies did not attend the meeting, but the British industry was well represented. Turner & Newall sent Knox, Holmes, and Hills; and Cape were represented by Dr Richard Gaze, a director and research chemist, and Dr Walter Smither, its medical officer. They came with reassuring, if sometimes, eccentric messages—Smither, for example, helpfully suggesting that perhaps the asbestos industry should be engaged in only by older men![16] However, they were over-

[11] 152/424. Asbestosis Fund Report for Year to 30 Sept. 1964.

[12] 'Mesotheliomas and Asbestos Dust', letter signed by W. J. Smither, J. C. Gilson, and J. C. Wagner, *BMJ* (3 Nov. 1962), ii, 1194–5. Wagner had now joined the PRU at Gilson's invitation to investigate mesotheliomas.

[13] W. T. E. McCaughey, 'Primary Tumours of the Pleura', *Journal of Pathology and Bacteriology* 76 (1958), 517–29; W. T. E. McCaughey *et al.*, 'Exposure to Asbestos Dust and Diffuse Pleural Mesothelioma', *BMJ* (24 Nov. 1962), iv, 1397.

[14] Chase photocopy letter from West Somerset Water Board to TAC, 9 Jan. 1964.

[15] H. E. Whipple (ed.), 'Biological Effects of Asbestos', *Annals of New York Academy of Sciences* 132 (31 Dec. 1965), i, 1–766.

[16] W. J. Smither, 'Secular Changes in an Asbestos Factory', *Annals of New York Academy of Sciences* 132 (31 Dec. 1965), i, 166–83. Smither tactfully did not identify the factory (Cape at Barking) and described himself as a member of the ARC.

shadowed by a competing 'voice' from a group of doctors at Mount Sinai Hospital in New York. This group, with powerful backing from the US Public Health Authority, was the main influence in organizing the conference. Their team leader was Dr Irving Selikoff (1915–92), the director of the Environmental Sciences Laboratory at the hospital, for whom the conference was a personal triumph.

A New York-trained physician, Selikoff had begun his career in occupational medicine in Paterson, New Jersey, where he observed the adverse health effects of asbestos among local workers. Between the 1960s and the 1980s, he was to become the leading American expert on asbestos and health and a prominent critic of the industry. Often controversial—he argued that one asbestos fibre could initiate cancer—he was adept at publicizing his views to the public. American asbestos industrialists viewed him with bitterness and distrust, were jealous of his rapport with the media, and described him as a 'disturbing sore thumb'.[17]

Selikoff's approach differed from that of his medical contemporaries overseas. In Britain, research into asbestos disease had usually been conducted at the industry's behest. In the 1950s and early 1960s, the bulk of research into the health effects of asbestos had been funded by the ARC, or had drawn on industry-generated data. Thus Doll, the leading individual researcher in the UK, had relied upon TBA data to launch his well-known cohort study of cancer in asbestos workers. Apart from the 1955 débâcle, the work was generally untroubled by controversy. Doll, Knox, and others produced results which satisfied the industry and showed that the risk of lung cancer in asbestos workers was continually declining. Indeed, the results of the latest Knox–Doll collaboration on their Rochdale cohort, which had been publicized at New York, went so far as to say that 'it is possible that the specific occupational hazards to life have been completely eliminated. . .'.[18] This conclusion appeared inconsistent with government data—also reported at New York—that showed a rising incidence of asbestos disease and particularly an alarming rise of lung cancer among asbestos workers (see Table 8.2).[19] This difference can be explained by the Knox–Doll methodology, which had a crucial characteristic: it looked at cancer only among scheduled asbestos textile workers and only

---

[17] 5/77–8. Letter from W. M. Deckman, Asbestos Textile Institute, to D. F. Roberts, Rochdale, 18 Feb. 1966.

[18] J. F. Knox et al., 'Cohort Analysis of Changes in Incidence of Bronchial Carcinoma in a Textile Asbestos Factory', *Annals of the New York Academy of Sciences* 132 (Dec. 1965), i, 527–35. Another paper on this cohort soon followed, which stated: 'The results provide grounds for believing that the occupational hazard of bronchial carcinoma has been largely eliminated, but the data are insufficient to estimate the extent of the risk which may remain.' See J. F. Knox et al., 'Mortality from Lung Cancer and Other Causes Among Workers in an Asbestos Textile Factory', *British Journal of Industrial Medicine* 25 (1968), 293–303.

[19] Buchanan, 'Neoplasms'.

Table 8.2. *Death certificates recording intra-thoracic tumours among asbestosis cases*

	Males			Females		
	Asbestosis: all deaths	Asbestosis with lung cancer	% with lung cancer	Asbestosis: all deaths	Asbestosis with lung cancer	% with lung cancer
1924–30	13	–	Nil	7	–	Nil
1931–40	66	13	19.7	82	5	6.1
1941–50	92	21	22.8	45	5	11.1
1951–60	144	45	31.3	40	11	27.5
1961–64	113	62	54.7	26	7	26.9
1924–64	428	141	32.9	200	28	14.0

Note: A few mesotheliomas (15) have been included in these totals.

Source: Ministry of Labour & Factory Inspectorate, *Annual Report of HM Chief Inspector of Factories on Industrial Health* (1965), 39. Crown copyright material reproduced with permission of the Controller of Her Majesty's Stationery Office.

at TBA, where exposure had been mostly to chrysotile. By the 1960s, dust control in Rochdale (whatever its deficiencies) meant that the conditions for TBA workers represented 'best practice' in the industry. However, hardly anyone seems to have been inclined to look at 'worst practice'[20]— say, conditions at Roberts or among laggers.[21] On the subject of asbestos disease in the insulation trades (where the incidence was rising) the British medical community was silent.

In contrast, Selikoff did not rely on company data. He obtained the personnel and medical records of trade unions in New York and New Jersey, whose members worked every day with asbestos insulation. His results were shocking. He investigated 1,522 workers. Of 392 individuals examined after twenty or more years' exposure, 339 had asbestosis. Among those who had died, lung cancer was found to be at least seven times more common than normal; and there were several cases of mesothelioma.[22] More bad news would obviously follow as Selikoff continued to track these workers.

Selikoff's findings presented at the New York conference—alongside several papers on mesothelioma by other speakers—marked a turning

[20] An executive at Johns Manville believes that the failure to look at 'worst practice' offers one of the key lessons in the asbestos-disease story. See Bill Sells, 'What Asbestos Taught Me About Managing Risk', *Harvard Business Review* (Mar.–Apr. 1994), 76–89.

[21] The single exception seems to have been Surgeon-Commander Peter Harries's study of shipyard insulation workers, even though it was not truly independent (having been sponsored by the Admiralty).

[22] I. J. Selikoff *et al.*, 'Asbestos Exposure and Neoplasia', *Journal of the American Medical Association* 188 (1964), 22–6.

point in public perceptions of the asbestos hazard. The media seized on the cancer angle, even before the conference began. Particularly disturbing was the fact that pathologists were now commonly finding asbestos particles and bodies in random urban autopsies. A typical American headline ran: 'High incidence of cancer deaths found in asbestos workers; asbestos in environment also threatens city dwellers.' In vain did the British contingent—Knox, Hills, Gaze, and Gilson—complain about the sensationalist headlines.[23] News of the conference and the asbestos–cancer link were soon picked up at home.

In Britain a key moment was reached in the following year, with the publication of an article in the *British Journal of Industrial Medicine* by researchers Dr Muriel Newhouse and Hilda Thompson.[24] Again, the obscure subject-matter would have evoked no interest among ordinary readers at any other time. Using the superb pathology records collected over many decades by the London Hospital, Newhouse and Thompson had identified 83 patients who had died from mesothelioma between 1917 and 1964, and then began an exercise in medical detection to discover their full occupational and residential histories. It was possible to do so in 76 cases. Of these, over 50 per cent had a history of occupational or domestic (living in the same house as an asbestos worker) exposure to asbestos. Out of 31 patients with purely occupational exposure, only 10 had jobs scheduled under the Asbestos Regulations of 1931. However, even more disturbing was the fact that of those with no occupational or domestic exposure, nearly a third had lived within half a mile of an asbestos factory (in this case, Cape)—a figure obviously much too high to be merely coincidence. In an appendix, the article presented some laconic and chilling details of each mesothelioma victim:

- worked in close proximity to boiler repairer in dockyards
- husband railway carriage builder; lined compartments with asbestos sheeting; work clothes washed at home
- lived within $\frac{1}{2}$ mile of present site of asbestos factory
- worked as nursemaid to manager of gasworks in East London; asbestos insulation used in works.

The results were clear. Not only occupational exposure was dangerous. Casual and brief exposure through living near an asbestos factory, inhaling fibres from a relative's clothes, or working in a factory insulated with the material—all these could trigger mesothelioma. The fact that the latency period was usually so long—so much so that sometimes no

[23] 73/1525. Knox's Report on NY Academy of Sciences Conference, 16 Dec. 1964.
[24] M. L. Newhouse and H. Thompson, 'Mesothelioma of Pleura and Peritoneum Following Exposure to Asbestos in the London Area', *British Journal of Industrial Medicine* 22 (1965), 261–9. This research had also been presented at the New York Academy of Sciences meeting, but it was published in the *BJIM* before the NY proceedings appeared.

history of asbestos exposure could be traced—made mesothelioma seem even more menacing. A larger and better-equipped medical community soon began researching this disease intensively.[25] Among the studies in 1965 was an update from Belfast doctors on their cohort of pleural mesotheliomas, which further confirmed that most cases showed evidence of exposure to asbestos, sometimes of a very trivial nature and many years ago. Knox told his directors: 'this conclusion commands respect'.[26]

The media fastened on to this cancer with alacrity in a way that had not happened after Doll's research. The Newhouse–Thompson study triggered a spate of newspaper headlines, with the *Sunday Times* in October 1965 featuring a front-page article on the 'killer dust'.[27] According to John Waddell, this article 'set light to a powder trail, which had already been laid by the medical conferences and by the rising statistics of asbestosis from the insulation industry, with the result that MPs, trade unionists and many others with both good and bad motives began to fan the flames'.[28] Turner & Newall watched these developments anxiously, grateful that the study featured Cape workers in London, but also aware that the mesothelioma problem reflected on the whole industry.

Knox recommended keeping 'a look-out for any ill-informed follow-up correspondence'. This was not slow in coming, from both the public and asbestos users. A TAC manager informed the board in November 1965: 'I think you should know that TAC is receiving daily, enquiries from merchants, hospitals and customers which . . . indicate an outlook which could prove deleterious to the use of asbestos-cement.'[29] He cited, as an example, a Widnes laundry seeking an assurance that it was safe to continue washing factory overalls.

Turner & Newall's basic response was to minimize the risk and deny that a problem existed. Statements were prepared by TBA directors and by Knox reassuring the public and workers that there was no 'experimental proof that inhalation of asbestos dust can cause mesothelioma at all', and that it was an extremely rare disease.[30] The reply to a London manufacturer of engineering products, who was concerned for the safety of his own customers was emphatic:

---

[25] For a useful review of the situation in 1965, see J. C. Gilson, 'Health Hazards of Asbestos: Recent Studies on its Biological Effects', *Transactions of Society for Occupational Medicine* 16 (1966), 62–74.

[26] 152/418–19. Knox memo, 22 Feb. 1965, reporting P. C. Elmes *et al.*, 'Diffuse Mesotheliomas of the Pleura and Asbestos', *BMJ* (6 Feb. 1965), i, 350–3.

[27] 52/596–7. 'Urgent Probe into 'New' Killer Dust Disease', *Sunday Times*, 31 Oct. 1965.

[28] 11/2–11. J. Waddell, 'Paper for Managers' Conference', 15 Dec. 1967.

[29] 52/561–2. J. P. McCormick to R. M. Bateman, 9 Nov. 1965.

[30] 52/544–6. TBA Mesothelioma Statement, Nov. 1965. See also 52/575: Knox's statement, 'Asbestos and Health'.

There is no known health risk associated with the normal handling of processed asbestos goods, such as yarn, cloth, packings, jointing, asbestos cement goods . . . There is no *proof* that asbestos causes mesothelioma, and it is by no means the sole cause of this disease. The chances of anyone in contact with asbestos contracting this complaint are very small indeed, and it could not be over-emphasised that this is a rare condition.[31]

Others were told 'authoritatively', *inter alia*, that the dust generated in spraying asbestos was 'insignificant'; that the rise in asbestosis cases was due to the inclusion of insulation workers in the statistics (whom no one had known were at risk); that lung cancer only occurred as a result of asbestosis; and that *if* mesothelioma was connected with asbestos, then it would probably only be related to blue asbestos.[32] Plans were made to invite influential MPs to lunch and Knox reassured the Rochdale newspapers.[33] Meanwhile, Turner & Newall continued to admit to very few mesotheliomas before 1960. The directors were 'not particularly anxious that it should become common knowledge that we have quite a number of mesothelioma cases on the records now'.[34] When TBA medical data were published in 1972, the only pre-1960 mesothelioma case listed was Pennington in 1936.[35]

These reassurances had limited success. In 1967, British Rail publicized that it would no longer use asbestos insulation (switching instead to fibre glass) because of the danger to workmen. Crucially, mesothelioma struck at the heart of Turner & Newall's profitable business with the Admiralty and with other shipyards, indeed at the whole of its insulation business worldwide. Convincing these buyers that asbestos was safe was difficult. A number of trends suddenly converged. There was the Admiralty's and shipbuilding industry's growing awareness of the health risk, fostered by the studies of Surgeon-Commander Harries and others.[36] In the late 1960s, the naval dockyards alone employed some 50,000 civilians, with 17,000

---

[31] 11/676–7. Letter to E. D. Deykin, Witty & Wyatt, Romford, 2 Feb. 1966. Similar letters were sent to other makers of asbestos products.

[32] 20/1013–16. 'Asbestos and Health'.

[33] 52/543. 'Asbestos and Fatal Lung Tumours', *Rochdale Observer*, 6 Nov. 1965.

[34] 68/1901. D. W. Hills to Lewinsohn, 23 Dec. 1968.

[35] H. C. Lewinsohn, 'The Medical Surveillance of Asbestos Workers', *Royal Society of Health Journal* 92 (1972), 69–77. See also Table 6.4.

[36] P. G. Harries, 'Asbestos Hazards in Naval Dockyards', *Annals of Occupational Hygiene* 11 (1968), 135–42; Harries, 'Asbestos Dust Concentrations in Ship Repairing: A Practical Approach to Improving Asbestos Hygiene in Naval Dockyards', *Annals of Occupational Hygiene* 14 (1971), 241–54. See also G. Sheers and Ann R. Templeton, 'Effects of Asbestos in Dockyard Workers', *BMJ* (7 Sept. 1968), 574, who noted that the asbestosis rate among those continuously exposed (especially laggers and sprayers) was 28 per cent. Belfast pathologists had shown that laggers were dying prematurely, half of them from malignant disease, with a great excess of lung cancers, including mesotheliomas. See P. C. Elmes, 'Cancer Due to Inhaled Dusts', repr. of paper read before Health Congress of the Royal Society of Health (25–9 Apr. 1966), 6.

men at work afloat on the ships. Yet less than 450 men were classed as asbestos workers and only 50 men in the asbestos mattress shops were subject to government regulation. After the war, many of these individuals had been exposed to the increased use of amosite in sectional lagging (typically 90 per cent asbestos) and to sprayed crocidolite. The trade unions were becoming involved and demanding that asbestos be banned; a more literate workforce was complaining directly;[37] and substitutes such as glass fibre had appeared.

Dockers became especially vocal in their protests. Raw asbestos fibre was still shipped in porous hessian or paper bags of a type supposedly banned inside the asbestos factories after 1931.[38] The bags often became split or damaged in transit; asbestos was even shipped loose as ballast. For the dockers, removing asbestos from cargo-holds was laborious, hot, and dusty work. In 1965, when alerted to the risk, the dockers blacked asbestos cargoes and their union (the TGWU) became locked in a well-publicized battle with the Port of London Authority and the Ellerman Line. The PLA's medical department and various doctors (including the medical adviser to the TUC) dismissed the suggestion that asbestos bags were dangerous (providing they were impervious) and stated specifically that there had been no cases of injury to dockers who had worked with asbestos. Aside from the fact that this last statement was later shown to be wrong, there was already published evidence that handling permeable sacks of asbestos and transporting the fibre could cause mesothelioma.[39] Cases of mesothelioma and asbestosis among dockers themselves began appearing with increasing frequency after 1966, leading one journalist to comment dryly: 'It is odd that such cases started to occur, or at least to be recognised, as soon as the dockers themselves knew what they were dealing with.'[40]

As Turner & Newall predicted, the story was soon picked up by the media.[41] Its own initial reaction was to deny that a problem existed, and, if it did, imply that the dockers were to blame. Ignoring the fact that permeable bags had been recognized as dangerous in 1931 and that as recently as 1961 Turner & Newall had paid damages to one of its asbestos cement workers who had developed asbestosis from unloading

---

[37] 127/20. Letter from 'White Man', re. 'Killer Dust' in Belfast shipyards, *Belfast Telegraph*, 9 Aug. 1966. This lagger argued that 'trade unions should take a long hard look and do everything in their power to get asbestos banned.'

[38] Factory Inspectors had underlined this hazard in 1950. See Ministry of Labour and Factory Inspectorate, *Annual Report . . . 1949* (London, 1950), 146.

[39] Newhouse and Thompson, 'Mesothelioma'; W. Glyn Owen, 'Diffuse Mesothelioma and Exposure to Asbestos Dust in the Merseyside Area', *BMJ* (25 July 1964), ii, 214–21.

[40] Martin Stower, 'Dockworkers Land Asbestos-Related Disease', *Health & Safety at Work* (Apr. 1985), 36–8, 37.

[41] See 6/1629–38. 24 Hours (BBC TV), 'The Link Between Blue Asbestos and Mesothelioma', 19 Jan. 1967.

hessian bags,[42] chairman Ralph Bateman stated: 'We believe there is no danger to the health of the dockers who handle hessian bags . . . provided the bags are not split or burst by the careless use of hooks or some similar accident.'[43] But by 1967, despite more reassurances from the industry, every important port in the country except Avonmouth, Manchester, and Glasgow was closed to asbestos unless it was palletized or in containers.

The asbestos industry's confidential attitude to the dust problem, especially in the insulation trades, was unequivocal. A private report into the lagging trades, issued in 1965 by a sub-committee of the ARC, began with the words: 'Wherever asbestos dust is released into the atmosphere in such a form that it can be inhaled a hazard exists.' The sub-committee, which included Knox and Smither, admitted that mixing caused 'a considerable cloud of asbestos dust'; that stripping produced dust; that cutting and shaping insulation sections released fine particles; that during mattress-making 'considerable quantities of fine fibres can be found in the atmosphere'; and that in spraying, 'not only men engaged in asbestos spraying, but others in the vicinity are exposed to high concentrations of asbestos dust'.[44]

Medical men like Knox and Smither, however, did not run their companies. For the businessmen at Turner & Newall, these conclusions were soon tempered by economics. Faced with the loss of its business, the company dug in its heels and only reluctantly contemplated a switch to safer products. As regards crocidolite, Waddell believed that it was 'too big a trade to be thrown overboard in a hurry simply because there is fairly strong evidence that SAB [South African Blue] is more dangerous that chrysotile'.[45]

Another threat to the company's staple lines was emerging with the use of substitutes such as glass fibre. A key factor was that the Admiralty in 1967 had over 50 common law writs pending for asbestosis, though none had been publicized.[46] Nevertheless, welders had refused to work with asbestos cloth and a total ban by the Admiralty seemed likely.[47] Glass

---

[42] This was Walter Willows at TAC Trafford Park. He was awarded £500 damages before his death from asbestosis and cancer in 1968. Several loaders at WCC/Newalls had also been suspended (see Table 6.2).

[43] 9/10. Draft letter, 24 Aug. 1965.

[44] 30/168–71. 'Problems of Asbestosis Prevention . . . & Suggested Code of Practice', 22 Oct. 1965.

[45] 32/945. John Waddell memo, 25 Jan. 1966.

[46] The whole issue became so sensitive that after TBA medical officer, H. C. Lewinsohn, met Harries at Plymouth Naval Dockyard in 1967, they agreed to keep things off the record. However, Lewinsohn did note the reason why no asbestosis cases had appeared in the local newspapers: Harries had excellent relations with the local coroner! 72/390–1. HCL to TBA, 23 Nov. 1967.

[47] Asbestos cloth was banned by the Admiralty in 1969.

textile insulation (which Turner & Newall manufactured) had already been tried in steaming trials in HMS Sirius. In 1966, the Admiralty was arranging meetings to discuss the results with the manufacturers. The Turner & Newall archive is particularly rich on the dilemmas posed by this switch to substitutes. The directors spoke of 'fighting the cause of asbestos to the last ditch',[48] with the company 'flag nailed to the mast of asbestos cloth'. Newalls were already moving away from asbestos to glass, but too quick a move would be disastrous and hit short-term profits. Newalls had a turnover of well over £$\frac{1}{2}$ million a year in asbestos cloth in the mid-1960s, yielding about £200,000 gross profit. If asbestos was immediately replaced by glass, no more than £75,000 a year gross profit would be earned, and this was aside from re-equipment costs.[49] In 1966, one director argued that: 'we must make absolutely certain that Newalls add no impetus of their own to any move away from the use of asbestos cloth towards glass. It seems to me that T & N must recognize and bring forcibly to the attention of Newalls the very considerable financial stake which the group has in the continued widespread use of asbestos cloth.'[50]

Even the Factory Inspectorate was spreading the bad news. An Inspector from Wrexham was telling users in 1967 that asbestos was an insidious material and unsafe to be handled in any form.[51] Other Inspectors told TBA confidentially that they were 'very worried about asbestos' and intended to keep a strict watch on it.[52] By the late 1960s, the difficulty for companies such as Turner & Newall was that asbestos was no longer an *industry* problem. An awareness of the hazards and a fear of cancer had spread to the workforce and into society at large. The company now felt under siege. John Waddell told the board in 1967:

The allegation—mainly in regard to mesothelioma, and even this is very questionable—that quite slight exposure to asbestos dust could be very dangerous has led to alarm among dockers and also to very damaging and alarmist statements about the dangers of using asbestos products or even of living in asbestos-cement buildings. Much of this is ludicrous, but some of it is being put out by hospital and university authorities whose word carries weight, and the same distortions reverberate and are picked up and repeated with snowballing effect. The industry's products are being 'smeared' directly and indirectly in many ways and this is almost as difficult to combat as McCarthy's political smear campaign on indi-

---

[48] 11/657–8. A. C. Mann to D. W. Hills, 28 Feb. 1966.
[49] 11/630–1. K. H. Dixon to D. W. Hills, 1 June 1966.
[50] 11/563. E. B. Gates to A. C. Mann, 18 July 1966.
[51] 15/1534. J. D. Holt to TBA, 17 Mar. 1967.
[52] 73/1845–8. H. C. Lewinsohn memo on Aviemore meeting, 9 July 1969, reporting A. T. Doig's remarks.

viduals in the USA ten years ago. Every sub-editor now knows that the danger of asbestos dust is news, and unfavourable and alarmist headlines are appearing almost every day.[53]

The company decided to counteract this bad news with its own propaganda. In 1967, Turner & Newall, alongside Cape, British Belting & Asbestos, and Central Asbestos, founded the Asbestos Information Committee to act as 'spokesman' for the industry. Waddell was the first chairman of a body, which had the primary intention of combating and forestalling 'exaggerated' publicity. The London branch of the American firm Hill & Knowlton was recruited—a group which in the 1950s had helped the tobacco industry fight the growing evidence about the dangers of smoking.

The minutes of one of the first meetings of the AIC in August 1967 are revealing.[54] Attention was devoted to influencing the content of *The Times* supplement on asbestos (mentioned above), which from the AIC's viewpoint was no more than an industry handout. The editorial would be the newspaper's concern: however, the AIC would suggest subjects and authors and try to provide plenty of illustrations that emphasized manufacturing not health. The AIC was happy to pay the full cost of the supplement (£3,600), though it was keen to have the 'advertising' element made less apparent. Not surprisingly, the supplement extolled the virtues of asbestos and contained no 'alarmist' features. In the ports and docks, the AIC explored the possibilities of inserting favourable editorials in local papers. Meanwhile, press cuttings were collected and forthcoming conferences were monitored so that no opportunity would be lost for presenting the industry's viewpoint. Lobbying was increased. In 1968, Waddell told a meeting at the House of Commons: 'there is a risk to health only if substantial amounts of airborne asbestos dust are inhaled. Only in extremely rare cases has there been any suggestion that incidental exposure to asbestos dust has been harmful, and proof has been lacking.'[55]

In the 1970s, the AIC was to publish several reassuring booklets on the use of asbestos. Meanwhile, an internal AIC memo gave blunt guidelines about 'Putting the Case for Asbestos'. It advised members of its companies:

NEVER BE THE FIRST TO RAISE THE HEALTH QUESTION. If it is raised with you, then observe the following principles:

---

[53] 9/126–9. Waddell report to T & N board on 'Asbestos and Health—Publicity Problems', 25 May 1967.

[54] 36/121–7. AIC meeting at Manchester, 8 Aug. 1967.

[55] 125/424–39. Transcript of House of Commons meeting, 30 Jan. 1968.

- make clear our concern
- emphasize rarity
- stress that control is effective
- be positive
- mention indispensability.

With remarkable tactlessness, the AIC wrote to all the respirator manufacturers and distributors in the UK and told them: 'There is one way in
which your company could materially assist the work of this Committee,
namely by refraining in your publicity from making statements regarding the health risks associated with asbestos in connection with the sales
promotion of your products.'[56] The managing director of Martindale, a
leading respirator manufacturer, described the letter as 'quite the most
astonishing I have received during my 40 years' business experience'. He
added: 'My company has been built up on honest trading ... [and] ... it
has been made clear to us that the risks are in fact a great deal higher than
have ever been published in the Press or any trade announcements. As
we understand it, ultimately nothing short of 100% protection of the
workers in the industry will be acceptable.'[57]

The AIC also led the industry's opposition to the use of warning labels
on asbestos. In 1968, the UK industry had been panicked by the decision
of the Canadian Johns–Manville company to ship bags of asbestos with a
cautionary label about the harmful effects of inhaling the fibres. The J–M
sacks were destined for the US market, but as the chairman of the AIC
reminded the Americans: 'Dockers and seamen may see these labels in
the holds of ships intended for destinations other than Britain and draw
their own conclusions about the unlabelled asbestos cargo they were to
unload themselves.'[58] For this reason, 'the British industry would prefer
no labels to be used at all'.[59]

The AIC was intertwined with the ARC, which expanded its activities
after 1965. An ARC sub-committee began looking at the problems of the
asbestos insulation industry, the result of which was a published code of
practice. A series of these 'codes' or pamphlets started to appear, covering subjects such as the safe handling of asbestos and the use of respirators. In 1968, this committee was reconstituted as the Environmental
Control Committee and a new series of advisory 'Notes for Guidance' was
produced and published.

Similar organizations to the AIC/ARC were emerging across Europe
and America, with Turner & Newall often involved in their organization.
In Canada, for example, where Turner & Newall operated the Bell

[56] 36/1118. Wilfred P. Howard letter, 8 Jan. 1968.
[57] 36/1116. F. R. Stanley to W. P. Howard, 11 Jan. 1968.
[58] 500/172–3. W. P. Howard to Jack Solon, Johns–Manville, 30 Oct. 1968.
[59] 125/627–8. Howard to Solon, 11 Feb. 1969.

Asbestos Mines, the company was influential in the founding of the Institute of Occupational & Industrial Health (IOIH) in 1966. Based in Montreal, the Institute had no laboratories, but sponsored studies into asbestos disease in the mining areas. The first major project was at McGill University and was headed by Dr Corbett McDonald, whose work was mainly funded by the asbestos industry.[60] According to letters in the Turner & Newall archive, although the Canadian government was interested in supporting the IOIH, the main impetus in its founding came from the Quebec Asbestos Mining Association. As Waddell candidly admitted: 'The objective behind all this activity by the QAMA is, of course, to preserve their industry on which their business depends. [QAMA] were most anxious to avoid any undesirable publicity or any precipitate action by the USA or Canadian Federal Government which might be detrimental to the industry.'[61] Although the IOIH would accept funding from other sources, Turner & Newall envisaged that it would be 'independent of any other institution—university or governmental—so that its policy can be determined by the needs of industry'. Turner & Newall's Bell company was one of the smaller contributors to the QAMA and so its influence in the establishment of the IOIH was muted: however, they offered what advice they could, convinced that the Canadians were 'complete amateurs . . . and need good advice'.[62] Turner & Newall were particularly concerned at the lack of a similar organization in America, where the asbestos industry had to contend with Selikoff.

While it attempted to influence the media and improve the industry's image, Turner & Newall also faced problems closer to home. The end of an era in TBA's medical services was approaching with the retirement of its chief medical officer, John Knox, who had been with the company since 1949. Knox agreed to continue as a consultant, while the company looked round for his successor. In 1964, they settled on a 38-year-old GP, William Kerns, who had recently qualified in industrial health at Manchester University. Waddell found Kerns 'suitable, though . . . a little brash and very different from Dr Knox'.[63] For one thing, Kerns was more financially independent than his predecessor:[64] he had a number of small consultancies and only agreed to start at TBA part-time. He also brought with him new

---

[60] 76/1191–6. C. McDonald interview, CBC Radio, 7 Mar. 1975.
[61] 117/189–94. Waddell memo, 31 Dec. 1965. Waddell lamented the fact that in Canada there was no body like the Medical Research Council that functioned 'between state and private enterprise in a semi-independent way which can be very useful'. 117/68–72. Letter to R. Bateman 12 Apr. 1966.
[62] 117/195–6. Waddell to J. Beattie, 25 Jan. 1966.
[63] 36/995–7. Waddell memo, 31 Aug. 1964.
[64] TBA paid Knox £2,000 a year as consultant, which was increased to £2,500 in 1967—almost as much as his former full-time salary. He was promised £1,500 a year on retirement, with £1,000 to his wife if he predeceased her. In the event, he did so, in 1972.

ideas and a fresh vision, with no memories of the old days in the industry. Consequently, he was given a shock when Knox took him on a tour of the factories, beginning with TBA. Kerns later recalled being 'quite appalled at the amount of asbestos dust that was lying around and in the air . . . in most departments, not just what was called the scheduled areas'.[65] Knox, however, was unperturbed and was quite pleased with the appearance of the workshops. He told Kerns that previously the situation had been much worse and that once it had been impossible to see across some of the shops.

Kerns's introduction to the TBA Health Committee brought further surprises. When it was reported that a woman had been suspended after only seven years, Knox voiced the intention to write to the PMP 'to cast doubt on the diagnosis'.[66] The meeting also reported a worker's death from asbestosis, who had twenty-four years of exposure and a nineteen-year survival period. Kerns was staggered to find that the committee was congratulating itself on the fact that the survival time had increased: 'surely there was an improvement I agree, but nevertheless here was a fellow who died of asbestosis. I think that every death was regrettable, but regret wasn't being expressed.' Kerns felt that Knox and the management 'had been dealing with these things for a long time. It was new to me and the attitude was new to me'.[67]

Kerns rapidly concluded that TBA had 'tunnel vision'—a refusal by the company directors to accept what was happening around them. This was also illustrated by the company's methods of identifying mesotheliomas. Before accepting a new mesothelioma case, it was company policy to submit the details to a hand-picked international panel of seven experts. If anyone disagreed, the case was not listed. During Kerns's own stay with the firm, he identified three or four mesotheliomas, which the company did not acknowledge. Kerns wanted to publish these disputed cases so that the scientific community could decide, but permission to do so was refused. Kerns immediately resigned in 1965.[68] He had been with TBA only eighteen months, but had seen enough. Sensitive to the mesothelioma hazard, he later explained: 'I didn't want to put my family at risk from taking home asbestos fibres on my clothing. And I didn't want any further exposure to asbestos on a personal basis.'[69]

TBA soon found a replacement in the following year. He was Dr Hilton

[65] Kerns' testimony, *Chase v. T & N*, transcript, 1408–9.

[66] 153/393–4. Minutes of Health Committee Meeting, 11 Nov. 1964.

[67] *Chase v. T & N*, deposition, 20 Oct. 1993, 46. Adds Kerns: 'My own view that even one death was one death too many seemed to be beyond their comprehension.' Kerns to author, personal communication, 8 Apr. 1997.

[68] *Chase v. T & N*, transcript, p. 1344 ff. Kerns never did publish his cases, since his employment contract prevented him.

[69] *Chase v. T & N*, transcript, 1435.

C. Lewinsohn, a 37-year-old South African-born chest physician, with a wide training in his native country, the USA, and Britain. When he applied for the TBA job, he was a medical officer for the Pneumoconiosis Medical Panel in Manchester. The company was pleased to have found such a highly qualified individual and for family reasons Lewinsohn was happy with the prospect, too. Later his relationship with Turner & Newall would become strained, but for the moment the dusty conditions that Kerns had seen as a menace, Lewinsohn saw as a challenge.

With great energy, Lewinsohn set about reforming Turner & Newall's medical services, which needed modernization. His plans disconcerted the directors at the company, especially after Lewinsohn had recommended £$\frac{1}{2}$ million expenditure on revamping dust control and medical care. 'He has got to realise that this is a business—not just an opportunity to practice medicine and carry out research', confided one director.[70] However, Lewinsohn was not a traditional company-man like Knox. With his arrival a more critical note is evident in the dealings between the company medical officer and the board. Lewinsohn was a specialist in respiratory medicine, very much aware of the health problems presented by asbestos, and the fact that it could cause agonizing death to the longest-serving and most loyal employees. He also appreciated the threat posed by mesothelioma, recognizing that 'no [asbestos] dose, no matter how small, can at present be assumed to be safe'.[71]

One of Lewinsohn's first jobs was to draft a complete appraisal of the health problem at TBA, which he presented to the directors in 1968. His conclusions were blunt: 'In spite of all the engineering improvements and the highly efficient ventilation methods, [asbestosis] has not totally disappeared . . . [and] . . . it is obvious that a health hazard still exists in certain areas of the factory at Rochdale and that our present engineering standards have not adequately coped with the "high" dust levels in carding and spinning.'[72] Unless further changes were made, Lewinsohn argued, a 'trickle' of asbestosis cases would continue. He found the rising trend in mesothelioma deaths 'worrying', especially as he had been 'astonished' to discover 121 workers processing crocidolite on six carding machines at Hindley Green (the company having ignored Kerns's advice to banish the material). By 1967, he had already raised with the company the possibility of isolating and segregating crocidolite production, with the obvious intention of eliminating it. Lewinsohn also began a tour of

[70] 73/1696. D. W. Hills note, 22 Aug. 1968.
[71] 73/1716–17. HCL to D. W. Hills, 16 Oct. 1969. As Lewinsohn later remarked: 'I personally find little comfort from knowing the facts about mesothelioma, especially as I consider myself to have been exposed to all known varieties—*if only in small doses.*' 6/225. HCL to Holmes, 26 Apr. 1976.
[72] 21/50–67. H. C. Lewinsohn, 'The Health Problem in Perspective', 1 Oct. 1968

group factories to survey health hazards outside TBA. His reports demonstrate why Turner & Newall had not eliminated asbestos disease. The following comments give only a selection of Lewinsohn's criticisms and provide our first real insight into working conditions for asbestos jobs (many of which were not covered by the Regulations):

Exhaust ventilation at dust producing processes is often inadequate . . . Housekeeping is poor on the whole and careless handling has resulted in increased dustiness . . . Protective clothing was hardly in evidence and bags for transport of fibre inside the factory were handled carelessly . . . Not only are the drivers of tractors at risk but also the warehousemen, the office workers and others who use the roadway, as well as the community living in the neighbourhood of the factory . . . [TAC, Trafford Park][73]

The [fibre] platform was dusty and . . . a broken bag was lying on the platform unattended to . . . In the miracle mill area . . . the men were not wearing respirators and they were hand-shovelling fibres from the mill into bags . . . Respirators were carelessly placed on top of the box enclosure and were full of dust . . . The problem of coping with dust is enormous here . . . [TAC, Widnes][74]

In the fibre treatment area the hoppers are partially enclosed and the floor is covered with fibrous dust . . . On the horizontal saw, brushes were sweeping the saw dust onto the floor and the ventilation hood was leaking, puffing dust into the atmosphere . . . [TAC, Tamworth][75]

The [Limpet] spray was being directed upwards . . . The 'fall-out' from the spray was drifting downwards and settling on the face pieces of the sprayers' respirators and on their faces. One man was wearing a cap and overalls, the other was wearing neither cap nor any form of protective clothing. The 'fall-out' from the spray was falling onto the scaffolding platform, but there was no polythene sheeting laid out and no precautions whatever had been taken to isolate the area. All and sundry passing through the area had to be considered at risk . . . The man in question, when I asked him to take off his respirator was absolutely dismayed to find that the inside was full of dusty material . . . [Rolls Royce, Derby][76]

Lewinsohn also criticized the medical surveillance in these factories. Usually a part-time doctor was employed, who attended a day or so a week and had no real interest in industrial hygiene.[77] Apart from in a few scheduled jobs (such as fibre-treating and beating), the majority of the workers were neither examined by the PMP nor by the company.

[73] 2/903–6. Visit, 13 Nov. 1968.
[74] 72/960–4. Visit, 3 Feb. 1969. This description of Widnes can be compared with Knox's view a decade earlier. The latter's 'general impression was of careful planning with adequate control of the few points of risk . . . feeding and bagging operations were particularly well done'. 13/61–4. JFK Visits Oct.–Nov. 1958.
[75] 72/960–4. Visit, 3 Feb. 1969.
[76] 72/893–4. Visit, 10 Oct. 1969.
[77] For example, Trafford Park employed a semi-retired doctor, who lived in the Lake District and attended one morning per week.

Lewinsohn suggested nothing less than a comprehensive medical service for the whole of Turner & Newall, in which all the workers (including contract staff, such as laggers) would be examined. Each unit company should have a medical officer and a health committee, while at the centre an additional medical officer should be recruited. While this was considered, Lewinsohn began an overhaul of the medical department at TBA. The concept of 'classified' areas was introduced: these were sections of the factory which were non-scheduled, but which Lewinsohn felt should be brought within the medical scheme. He also established a lung-function laboratory and ordered more modern X-ray machines.

Lewinsohn's efforts took place against the backdrop of renewed government interest in asbestos disease. After over thirty years of inaction, a revision of the 1931 Regulations was now a possibility. The Chief Inspector of Factories' *Annual Report* for 1964 had noted the increasing concern about asbestos (particularly crocidolite) and mesothelioma, involving both occupational and non-occupational exposures. Cumulative data on asbestosis deaths between 1924 and 1964—shown in Table 8.2—demonstrated a significant proportion with intra-thoracic tumours (27 per cent). With the Newhouse–Thompson study and the publicity over mesothelioma adding to the pressure on the government, in July 1965 the Senior Medical Inspector of Factories convened an advisory panel to discuss the asbestos problem. Besides government officials and medical experts (such as Gilson and Newhouse), two industry representatives were invited— Knox and Smither.[78] In 1967, this body published a memorandum on *Problems Arising from the Use of Asbestos*. The panel recognized that the current Regulations were deficient; and also described the sudden rise in mesothelioma as relatively 'explosive'. A number of recommendations were made, including the setting up of a National Mesothelioma Register (now that the malignancy had become a prescribed industrial disease in 1966). The most important suggestion concerned the setting of a new threshold limit value (TLV). Privately, some members of the advisory panel believed that the only safe level for mesothelioma was nil: however, the following statement was eventually issued:

A biologically-based threshold limit for asbestos exposure cannot yet be defined but its establishment should be a long-term objective. Meanwhile a provisional standard or standards based on what can currently be obtained in the best factories should be given to industry.[79]

The 1930 meetings between the Home Office and the asbestos industry were to be played out again. In October 1966 the Ministry of Labour wrote

[78] 6/2017–18. Knox's notes on Meeting of Advisory Panel, 23 July 1965.
[79] Ministry of Labour & HM Factory Inspectorate, *Problems Arising from the Use of Asbestos* (1967), 29.

to TBA, the ARC, and other companies informing them that a review was underway which aimed at tighter dust control. The projected regulations would be wide-ranging—applying to *all* asbestos processes and premises—but the observations of the industry were invited. By the end of the year, the ARC and Turner & Newall had begun drafting their response, which picked holes in most of the government's suggestions. Waddell wrote: 'It is indeed only too obvious that if the Regulations were drawn up in the form outlined they would involve a crippling burden upon the industry and it is this we are trying to avoid.'[80]

One problem for the government in setting a TLV was that it had little data and expertise. In 1960, the Factory Inspectorate had half-heartedly listed an old American threshold—5 mppcf (5 million particles per cubic foot)—as a guideline.[81] But this had little credibility with British technologists, because the threshold was based on a particle count (which did not differentiate asbestos fibres) and used an American counting device that, they believed, gave 'meaningless results'.[82]

Soon the industry would devise its own threshold, with the help of the British Occupational Hygiene Society. This body had been founded in 1953 as a meeting ground for interested professionals, such as chemists, physicists, physiologists, and medical practitioners. Soon firms and organisations were invited aboard, including several from the asbestos industry. Knox had joined in 1959. The BOHS organized annual conferences (with the proceedings published in its journal, *The Annals of Occupational Hygiene*) and in the early 1960s held international symposia on inhaled particles and vapours. The Society had also begun formulating safety codes for industrial materials. Among the key players in the BOHS were industry representatives: indeed the Society had promised industrial members that they could share in the formulation of Society policy 'in all aspects of occupational hygiene, including the preparation of standards and advice on legislative proposals'.[83] In 1966, when the BOHS formed a sub-committee to consider a TLV for asbestos, it was conveniently timed: the committee solved the government's problem as regards technical and medical expertise; and it allowed the asbestos industry an opportunity to influence proceedings. Several asbestos industry doctors and health

[80] 30/1458. Waddell to A. D. N. Jones, 17 Nov. 1966.
[81] Ministry of Labour & National Service, *Toxic Substances in Factory Atmospheres* (1961). 5 mppcf was translated into 177 particles per cubic centimetre (equivalent to about 12 asbestos fibres per cc). See D. S. Egilman and A. A. Reinhart, 'The Origin and Development of the Asbestos Threshold Limit Value: Scientific Indifference and Corporate Influence', *International Journal of Health Services* 25 (1995), 667–96; and B. I. Castleman, *Asbestos: Medical and Legal Aspects* (1996), 265–384, for an excellent chapter on TLVs.
[82] 5/330–5. 'Asbestos Research', 9 Nov. 1956. See also Holmes's and Knox's complaint about the US TLV to Chief Inspector of Factories, 22 Sept. 1960.
[83] 69/1176–9. 'A Brief History of the BOHS'.

physicists had joined the BOHS by the mid-1960s. The asbestos sub-committee itself included Knox and Holmes from TBA, Smither from Cape, and Gordon Addingley from British Belting & Asbestos—all styled as members of the ARC.

The BOHS began grappling with the crucial question that had been side-stepped by Merewether and Price: what was the safe limit for asbestos exposure?

Turner & Newall became a major influence in setting this new TLV. It had the longest experience in using the membrane filter for counting fibres above 5 microns long and with a length/diameter ratio of at least 3:1; and in Rochdale it also had the world's largest community of asbestos workers, some of whom had been medically monitored since 1933. By evaluating these twin sets of data, the BOHS hoped to formulate an acceptable TLV. Although the precise mechanisms and discussions by which a decision was reached remain unknown,[84] it is plain that the BOHS hygiene standard was neither dictated solely by health factors nor by an overriding concern for the health of the workers. Stephen Holmes, the head of TBA's now expanding health physics department, explained:

In setting a hygiene standard we found the quantitative relationship between exposure and risk was not the greatest area of uncertainty. A much more difficult problem was to decide on what, in fact, was an acceptable risk. This depended upon the opinions of many different people.

Asbestos is very widely used and brings real benefits to the community at large. Now, asbestos workers share in these benefits. Also the asbestos industry provides employment for its employees and, indeed, a career for some. A standard may be made so stringent as to cost so much by way of dust control that the production and use of asbestos and asbestos goods cease to be economic, production and use is discontinued and the associated benefits are lost. The benefits gained by way of reduced risk of asbestosis through reducing air contaminant exposure have to be weighed against the possible loss of direct and indirect benefits to the community from the use of the material.

Any workable standard has therefore to be decided by consultation between industry and scientific experts in which both are involved in determining a standard—a standard acceptable to the industry as well as medical authority.[85]

The committee decided that a 'proper and reasonable' objective would be to reduce the risk of contracting asbestosis to 1 per cent in those who had spent a lifetime in the industry—in other words, a life-threatening

[84] One researcher was told in 1993 that the BOHS claims absolute confidentiality for its papers. See M. Greenberg, 'The 1968 British Occupational Hygiene Society Chrysotile Asbestos Hygiene Standard,' in G. A. and B. J. Peters, *Asbestos Disease and Asbestos Control. Vol. 14: Sourcebook on Asbestos Diseases* (1997), 219–55.

[85] 69/1096–1103. Holmes, '1968 Workshop on Threshold Limit Values', typescript.

illness in one long-serving worker in a hundred was deemed quite acceptable by a self-appointed committee which did not have a single trade union representative. To set the TLV, the BOHS received clinical and X-ray data on 290 TBA men, matched with the relevant dust measurements—the data (though not the X-rays) being provided by Knox and Holmes. The asbestosis risk was calculated from the observed relationship between dust exposure and the incidence of the disease in the men, who had worked in the factory for ten years or more since 1933. This itself was not an easy task, especially since the results from the various dust-measuring devices that had been used since the 1950s were not directly comparable. Of the 70 or 80 people working at 3–4 fibres per cubic centimetre (f/cc), Knox reported that only 1 had an abnormal X-ray. It was concluded that the risk of developing the early clinical signs of asbestosis would be less than 1 per cent for an accumulated exposure of 100 fibre years/cc. That is, a concentration of 2 f/cc for 50 years, 4 f/cc for 25 years, or 10 f/cc for ten years.

This hygiene standard of 2 f/cc (or 2 f/ml) was published in 1968 and immediately adopted by the government.[86] The latter assumed that the hazard for amosite was the same as for chrysotile and therefore made the limit for the two identical; but it was decided that the limit for crocidolite should be ten times more strict.

The report was also taken on board in America, where Holmes himself presented the British standard at a TLV workshop in Cincinnati in February 1968 and later recommended dust levels drawn from it to the US Department of Labor.[87] However, there were doubts. The BOHS admitted that, although it believed that inhaling 2 f/cc for up to fifty years could be tolerated without undue risks, the data were 'scanty'.

Knox's contribution hardly bears scrutiny. Not only had he sat on both the government advisory panel and the BOHS sub-committee, but he had also provided and interpreted data for those bodies. Yet he had no specific training as a statistician or even as an occupational physician. His study was based on the experience of a single asbestos textile plant (TBA), where dust conditions did not fluctuate very widely. The cohort (only men who had started work since 1933, had completed ten years' service, and were still employed in 1966) had excluded many workers from the survey. Crucially, the survey did not include women workers (a quarter of the total number of employees who had completed ten years' work in the scheduled areas); and no attempt was made to include workers who had left. On the other hand, Knox had used a very

[86] BOHS, 'Hygiene Standards for Chrysotile Asbestos Dust', *Annals of Occupational Hygiene* 11 (1968), 47–69.
[87] 500/40–9. Statement by S. Holmes to US Dept. of Labor: Occupational Safety & Health Administration Hearings on Standard for Exposure to Asbestos Dust, Washington, DC.

narrow diagnostic test for asbestosis—the presence of persistent basal rales (chest crackles). If X-ray changes had been used (employing the techniques then available), then more cases of asbestosis would have been found. A major flaw in the BOHS standard was that it only related to asbestosis, not cancer. The sub-committee freely admitted that it was unable to specify a safe limit for eliminating the cancer risk—indeed the whole report only discussed chrysotile. This was a huge irony when it was mesothelioma that was responsible for the government's review. As Lewinsohn stated: 'It is not asbestosis which has prompted the rapidity with which these new regulations are being prepared—it is the dreaded disease *cancer*'.[88]

Particularly significant in view of the cancer risk, was the way in which the dust had been counted and how many fibres were represented by the 2 f/cc limit. Two fibres in a cubic centimetre of air sounds negligible, yet as Castleman emphasizes it is important to recognize that even 1 f/cc is equivalent to 1 million fibres per cubic metre of air.[89] During an 8-hour day, a worker might breathe in 5 cubic metres of air (perhaps more). So a worker exposed to the BOHS 2 f/cc chrysotile limit for one day would risk inhaling over ten million microscopic fibres. This was bad enough, but these figures were gross underestimates, as they relied upon optical microscopes (prone to +/−50 per cent observer error). Electron microscopy, which was ignored by the BOHS and ARC,[90] had long demonstrated that most asbestos fibres were invisible with phase contrast optical microscopy.[91] Fibres below 5 microns would not be seen; more significantly, even longer fibres would be missed if their *diameters* were below the limits of the optical microscope. These long, thin fibres have been seen as especially dangerous in causing mesothelioma. In fact, only one fibre in 100 to 1,000 could be seen under the optical microscope, so—even at a conservative estimate—a worker might inhale a *billion* asbestos fibres in a day at the 2 f/cc limit. Most of these small fibres would be exhaled or

[88] 72/711. HCL, Medical Officer's Report, 12 Sept. 1967.

[89] Castleman, *Asbestos*, 333.

[90] A suggestion by Richard Gaze in 1959 that the electron microscope might be used by the ARC to look at small particles under 5 microns does not appear to have been followed up. See 401/767–76. Minutes of 7th Meeting of the Research Committee of the ARC, 29–30 June 1959.

[91] Holmes pointed out: 'There is, of course, a lot of medical evidence pointing to the view that longer fibres are of special significance biologically, but there is nothing about the figure of 5 microns. It was arbitrarily chosen many years ago and has continued as the lower limit for counting for historical reasons.' However, he believed that fibres above 5 microns represented more than 90 per cent of the weight of asbestos. Hence, only by 1970 was TBA taking a serious interest in the electron microscope. See 74/187. Holmes, 'Research Behind the UK Standards', typescript; 500/58–9. Holmes to E. M. Fenner, Johns-Manville, 18 Nov. 1969. Selikoff was to highlight the importance of the electron microscope in counting asbestos fibres in the early 1970s. See 'Electron Microscope Points to Wider Asbestos Health Hazards', *New Scientist* (14 Aug. 1975).

later removed by the body's defences, but given the mesothelioma risk the very high burden was hardly acceptable.

Another perspective on the BOHS standard is provided by examining data on dust levels at Turner & Newall (and among its customers). TBA did not systematically measure dust at all until 1951 and so very little data is available. Merewether's survey in 1930 had found that counts in the industry ranged between 506 and 6,324 particles/cc, with a count of 1,073 at the 'dust datum' in the spinning room (a reading that had been recorded at Roberts). When a Factory Inspector checked the count in 1938 in the same spinning room, he registered levels between 165 and 410 f/cc under normal conditions with no exhaust.[92] At Rochdale, retrospective attempts to provide a benchmark suggested that in 1952 the fibre count at TBA was 25 f/cc in 1952 (with a range of 12–80 f/cc); while between 1936 and 1946, the count was probably double this figure. However, these were no more than guesses and are probably extremely optimistic.[93] After 1965, when the modern era of dust counting began at TBA, the health physics department began generating more accurate readings. The data is sometimes not very easy to interpret in retrospect: however, the general impression is of working conditions that were far from safe.

In the Harridge Mill—a company health blackspot since the inter-war period—hessian bags of incoming crude fibre were still manhandled off conveyors and slid down planks. In 1966, dust concentrations up to 117 f/cc were recorded.[94] A TBA physicist stated that the Harridge Mill handling points 'must be considered as constituting a serious health hazard'. He observed that respirators were not worn by any of the men, and regarded their plea that 'the work was too heavy for their prolonged use' as an 'excuse'.[95] The hessian-bag problem was being addressed at this time and bags lined with paper or made of plastic would eventually be introduced, but as one manager put it: 'if we are sincere in our concern about high dust counts . . . all further deliveries should be suspended until the packaging is improved. I doubt whether our concern stretches so far.'[96] The Harridge Mill itself was not demolished until 1970—some forty years after Commercial Union had warned about its hazards.

In 1967, John Waddell noted that more progress was needed in other

---

[92] N. J. Wikeley, 'Measurement of Asbestos Dust Levels in British Asbestos Factories in the 1930s', *American Journal of Industrial Medicine* 24 (1993), 509–20. An attempt to recreate the 1938 counts concludes that the dust-datum by present-day standards was 10–20 f/ml, though this was only in the summer with windows and doors open. See G. Burdett, 'A Comparison of Historic Asbestos Measurements Using a Thermal Precipitator with a Membrane Filter-Phase Contrast Microscopy Method', *Annals of Occupational Hygiene* 42 (1998), 21–31.

[93] 301/1505. J. G. Morris, draft letter (apparently unpublished) to *Lancet*, Mar. 1968.

[94] Yet Knox *et al.*, 'Mortality from Lung Cancer', 296, reproduces a table of dust counts at 'a large asbestos factory', with no reading above 8 f/cc.

[95] 19/237–9. I. Harness, 'Airborne Dust Tests at Harridge Mill', 8 Nov. 1966.

[96] 19/239. T. Berry to NR, 22 Nov. 1966.

areas of the Rochdale factory, especially in carding and handling. TBA workers unloading from lorries and stacking manually experienced average counts up to 50 f/cc; so too did carding operatives.[97] The Hindley Green factory also had a continuing dust problem, especially in carding and spinning where dust counts were often over 20 f/cc and sometimes over 50 f/cc.[98] The problem led to the formation of a study group of Hindley Green managers and TBA physicists, such as Stephen Holmes and William Bamblin. In the 1960s, they began grappling with the high dust counts there, caused—it was thought—by the dustiness of asbestos crudes and higher machine speeds. Various sanding and sawing operations also raised levels over 2 f/cc, with some peak readings well above 40 f/cc. Most of the spray fibre preparation was conducted in dust over 10 f/cc with stacking bags being particularly dusty at 46 f/cc. Bagging 'dried' crocidolite raised very high dust concentrations up to 30 f/cc, albeit that the men were supposed to wear positive pressure respirators.[99]

Ferodo dust counts at Chapel-en-le-Frith also showed why some employees had developed asbestos-related diseases. Bag-opening and disc-brake preforming were dusty enough to be a health risk. Weighing-out asbestos in the stores—a relatively strenuous job—generated counts over 12 f/cc.[100]

The company's dust surveys demonstrated clearly the dangers of Limpet spraying. Between 1960 and 1968, an extended series of trials began re-examining the mainly reassuring picture provided by government surveys in 1938 and 1950, and the company's own assessment in 1949. The results of these trials were far less comforting. In one of the first trials in early 1962, using a test tunnel, the investigators found dust concentrations up to 1,827 f/cc—about two hundred times those in the scheduled asbestos textile divisions! Moreover, these dust concentrations persisted for about twenty minutes after spraying ceased. Ironically, the report recommended that respirators should be worn by everyone in the vicinity.[101] Generally, trials showed that spray operations, both near the sprayer and the machine-feeder, invariably exceeded 50 f/cc, even with pre-damping with oil and water. Later trials concentrated on improving pre-damping,[102] but they also confirmed that ripping

[97] 68/1983–5. Waddell memo, 7 Aug. 1967.
[98] 76/1002. I. Harness, 'Airborne Dust' memo to A. Spencer, 25 Feb. 1964.
[99] 73/837. I. Harness to AJH, 8 Oct. 1969. In 1967, conditions at Hindley Green attracted adverse comment for the Factory Inspectorate, who noted the low standard of cleanliness in the opening section and in the carding division, where some men were vigorously sweeping up asbestos dust with brushes. See 81/3013. G. Merga to TBA, 22 May 1967.
[100] 81/238–41. R. Sykes to Ferodo, 22 Dec. 1964.
[101] 301/2243–51. 'Interim Report', 2 Feb. 1962.
[102] 301/406–13. 'Evaluation of Airborne Dust Levels . . . at Belshill Swimming Baths', 2 Nov. 1965; 19/1845–50. 'Report on the Dust Levels . . . at the Film Theatre at TBA', 5 Oct. 1968.

out old spray insulation entailed an 'excessive health hazard', with readings over 100 f/cc.

Experiences with Limpet in field conditions showed the difficulties in controlling dust. In 1968, Manchester Central Library hired contractors to spray the inside dome of the main reading room with Limpet. Turner & Newall were not directly involved in the contract, but offered their expertise when the work began attracting adverse publicity. A TBA physicist, J. C. Byrom, arrived with a copy of the ARC *Code of Practice on Thermal Insulation*. This was useful, as the contractor had never seen a copy; and he did not wear a mask during spraying. When the work began in the daytime, Byrom recorded counts of 100 f/cc and this was not at the spray point—it was in the book stacks below the main reading room, where library staff were at work! TBA immediately advised the use of pre-damping and the operations were switched to the night-shift. This did improve matters, but the dust concentration during spraying still reached 20 f/cc in the reading room, and dust was still finding its way into the stacks.[103] Although spraying was conducted at night, dust continued to hang in the air throughout the day and was still detectable five months after spraying. TBA told the city authorities that there was 'no risk to health'.[104]

In the late 1960s, however, Turner & Newall claimed in public that fibre concentrations in spraying could be reduced to 4 f/cc or less if the fibres were pre-damped. The company continued to resist attempts by the Factory Inspectorate to improve personal protection for sprayers. One 'off-the-cuff' demand from the Inspectors for the use of airline respirators was dismissed by TBA as simply too 'inconvenient'.[105] Meanwhile, reports of asbestosis among sprayers continued to mount. Waddell was told of eleven cases (including some deaths) among a Swiss team in 1967.[106] The affected individuals included the spray-team leader, who wrote to the company with an account of his own problems and those of other 'sad cases'. The company believed that the man's experience was unrepresentative and partly due to the 'easy-going' health practices of sprayers.[107]

However, other insulation work was also monitored by TBA. The health

---

[103] 20/348–53. Manchester Central Library letters, Sept. 1968.
[104] 20/345–6. Holmes to City Architect, 23 Sept. 1968. Concerning one set of dust tests, W. P. Howard told Byrom: 'I think there would be no harm in divulging these results, which seem to me to be remarkably good, from a public health point of view, but I would suggest that we do not in fact go out of our way to take the initiative in this matter.' 20/776. Letter, 26 June 1969.
[105] 117/907–10. Correspondence between J. Graham (Factory Inspectorate) and TBA, 11, 20, 25 June 1967.
[106] 117/227–8. A. N. Marshall to J. Waddell, 5 Oct. 1967.
[107] 125/348–9. Marshall to Waddell, 22 Aug. 1967.

physicists took dust samples at Devonport dockyard and at various Newalls' sites. At Devonport, laggers using asbestos cloth generated dust levels up to 1,000 f/cc; while at Newalls, the majority of the readings were well over 2 f/cc and sometimes up to 60 f/cc. A TBA survey of dust generated by Admiralty welders at Plymouth, when they manipulated asbestos cloth during their work, showed some 'alarming' fibre counts up to 660 f/cc. Disturbingly for the company, this occurred with TBA's new 'dust-suppressed' cloths.[108] When local-government officers began commissioning private reports of fireproofing and insulating work, they also found that conditions were dusty enough to present a real hazard of asbestosis, besides the long-term cancer risk.[109]

More ominously, the new regulations would also apply *outside* Turner & Newall. As one TBA manager remarked: 'The range could be fantastic and be from large building contractors, shipbuilders, etc., down to the small garage needing to drill and countersink holes in brake linings.'[110] TBA physicists now found themselves involved in dust monitoring at the company's customers, one of whom had already reported a possible case of asbestosis in a worker using asbestos cloth for blankets.[111] As Holmes and his team toured the shipyards and engineering workshops, problems were apparent everywhere. One user of asbestos millboard for electric toasters gave two readings of 22 f/cc, and one at 14 f/cc. At a brake-linings manufacturer, most of the readings recorded were in the 2–12 f/cc range. A Manchester roofing contractor generated levels between 20 and 37 f/cc when unloading and sawing sheets.[112]

There was yet another asbestos risk with which the industry would have to deal—environmental exposure. This problem had several facets, ranging from asbestos dust in the general atmosphere to the dumping of asbestos waste. Ferodo's practice of dumping asbestos at a local quarry aroused the concern of residents, whose opposition eventually led to a public inquiry in 1966.[113] Even Ferodo's friction products became suspect. A prescient member of the public asked about the risk to motor mechanics, when blowing out brake drums. She was told by TBA that there was

---

[108] 81/598–9. Memos and letters by P. Harries and I. Harness, 3 Jan. 1968.

[109] 20/292–307. Prof. A. Mair *et al.*, 'Report on the Asbestos Dust Survey . . . at the Red Road Building Site, Glasgow, for the Corp. of Glasgow, May 1967'. This report concluded: 'every single dust generating operation produces asbestos dust levels in excess of the acceptable value'.

[110] 19/507–8. W. P. Bamblin memo re. 'Revision of Asbestos Industry Regulations', 26 Oct. 1966.

[111] 15/1349–50. Letters re. Croydon Asbestos Co., May 1968.

[112] See, for example, 20/398–9, Test at Besdek Roofing, Sale, 31 July 1968. Another firm recorded levels of 77 f/cc in a job with three men working full-time. See 20/363–4. Fabcol Distributors, Manchester, 21 July 1968.

[113] 35/169–82. 'Report of a Public Inquiry into . . . Permission to Use Land at Crist Quarry, Buxworth, for Tipping Inorganic Industrial Waste', Aug. 1966.

'very little asbestos dust' in this operation (though a vacuum cleaner should be used) and that mesothelioma was largely confined to blue asbestos, a variety not used in brakes.[114] But what of the risk to city dwellers exposed to the material shed during braking? By 1967, Turner & Newall—largely at the prompting of users such as the Ford Motor Company—was obliged to begin research into these problems. The company's view was that asbestos in brake linings (containing typically 50–60 per cent chrysotile) was either too degraded or too slight to constitute a health hazard. However, this was an area where many questions needed to be answered by further research.[115]

It was soon evident that buildings containing asbestos—especially those that had been completed recently—would be contaminated with asbestos. Anxiety about the use of asbestos in buildings had manifested itself as early as July 1966, when the Northern Ireland Hospitals Authority had instructed architects and builders to avoid the material in hospital buildings.[116] Knox and Holmes made a damage-limitation visit to counter this threat to the company's business. In Britain, a circular was sent by the Ministry of Education to architects advising them against the use of asbestos in educational buildings; and a similar university instruction (the 'Leeds University memo') was sent to buildings officers in those institutions.[117] But how much asbestos contamination was in buildings? No one knew. In 1968, the ARC launched a buildings' survey which monitored dust at various locations and eventually decided that the health risk could be ignored.[118] However, no consideration was given to the subsequent deterioration of asbestos materials, or the possibility that maintenance work or renovations could disturb the asbestos. The problem of bystanders inhaling asbestos during actual construction was not even broached.

For the moment, Turner & Newall had enough on its plate in its factories. In 1968, John Waddell felt that:

it is going to prove very difficult in many manufacturing operations and also in the insulation industry to get down to anywhere near 10 fibres/cc, much less to 5 or 2. The standards in the BOHS report are, of course, based on our TBA factories, and even we are going to find it extremely difficult and expensive to get below about 7 fibres/cc in the card room, although we are already down to about 3 or 4 in the weaving shed. In collaborating in the production of this report we have,

[114] 15/1469–70. Letters between Mrs D. M. Thorley and S. Holmes, 20 Oct., 17 Nov. 1967.
[115] 39/1165–73. Memo re. 'Asbestos in Brake Wear Dust—A Review' (3 Feb. 1970).
[116] 39/691. Northern Ireland Hospitals Authority memo, 20 July 1966.
[117] 39/1827–30. Leeds University Planning Office, 'Asbestos in Buildings', 28 Feb. 1967.
[118] J. C. Byrom *et al.*, 'A Dust Survey Carried Out in Buildings Incorporating Asbestos-Board Materials in their Construction', *Annals of Occupational Hygiene* 12 (1969), 141–5. See also C. Oliver, 'Asbestos in Buildings: Management and Related Health Effects', in M. A. Mehlman and A. Upton (eds)., *Advances in Modern Environmental Toxicology. Vol. 22* (1994), 175–88.

in effect, lent our support to the setting-up of target standards which will be a challenge to everyone and which our customers and competitors in overseas countries will consider wildly utopian and even catastrophic.[119]

A TBA review of its operations in 1968 showed that almost every textile process was over the 2 f/cc limit, with many in the 5–10 f/cc range. Expenditure on enclosure and ventilation was needed almost everywhere, with a projected cost of £400,000. Even then the time-scale to achieve a 2 f/cc target extended up to four years for some processes.[120]

However, the picture was not quite as stringent for the asbestos companies as Waddell made it sound. In 1969 the government placed the revised Asbestos Regulations on the statute book—the deletion of the word 'Industry' a sign that the asbestos health hazard had now officially spread outside the factories. However, the new rules did not come into force until 14 May 1970 to give the industry a year's grace to bring its processes into line. The new safety standards—2 f/cc for chrysotile and amosite and 0.2 f/cc for crocidolite—meant that the latter, believed to be the most potent cause of mesothelioma, would be legislated out of existence. A standard of 0.2 f/cc was virtually impossible to achieve and crocidolite therefore became uneconomic to produce. At Lewinsohn's insistence TBA had relinquished crocidolite between 1967 and 1969; while its import into the UK ended in 1970. This was hardly an economic disaster as its use had by then become very limited anyway. So limited, in fact, that the asbestos industry—recognizing that the government were 'gunning particularly for blue asbestos'—were amenable to a voluntary ban, in return for less stringent rules on chrysotile and amosite.[121] The latter became crocidolite's replacement, thus substituting one hazardous material with another.

As regards chrysotile and the 2 f/cc limit generally, Holmes noted: 'There is no doubt that the Factory Inspectorate regard the 2 fibre/cc limit as a goal to be aimed at eventually rather than a standard to be rigidly enforced.'[122] In March 1970, the government issued *Technical Data Note 13*, which was to be read in conjunction with the Regulations.[123] This *Note* advised that no enforcement was needed when the dust level was below 2 f/cc; that between 2–12 f/cc further readings should be taken to check

[119] 68/1873. J. Waddell to R. Murray, 6 Feb. 1968.

[120] 6/2097–8. Rochdale Factory Data Sheets.

[121] 30/1466. A. N. Marshall memo, 6 Dec. 1966.

[122] 500/40–9. Holmes's US Labor statement, 4. Holmes had been told by one of the Factory Inspectors, that the Regulations would 'not be too rigid . . . but should leave room for manoeuvre'. 76/1890–3. ARC Meeting with Factory Inspectorate, 25 June 1969.

[123] Dept of Employment: HM Factory Inspectorate, *Technical Data Note 13: Standards for Asbestos Dust Concentration for Use with the Asbestos Regulations 1969* (1970). The draft Regulations themselves had not set any TLV. See Ministry of Labour, *The Asbestos Regulations 1968: Draft Statutory Instruments* (1968).

for average concentration and duration of exposure; and that only when the recording averaged above 12 f/cc over a ten-minute sampling period should the Inspector (after attempting to confirm the accuracy of his data) advise the use of exhaust ventilation and respirators.

Meanwhile in the public arena, the government kept bad news at bay. In 1968 and 1971, a DHSS enquiry chaired by Sir Richard Doll accepted that there was a cancer risk to the public and that 'no amount of exposure is completely free from risk'. It made several recommendations: asbestos products should be labelled, waste tipping should be controlled, and local authorities should implement safety checks. However, neither the 1968 nor 1971 Reports were made public.[124] T & N managers read these signals accordingly. One of them wrote:

I consider that the introduction of the new regulations could result in an even more rapid reduction in the use of asbestos than anticipated. If, however, we demonstrate, by a token effort only of ostensible intention to comply with the regulations, it is conceivable that we can ward off the evil day when asbestos cannot economically be applied—i.e. 'hold on' until 1972/73.[125]

Other board members suggested that the company: 'Pay as little heed to the Regulations as would be necessary, but by the time they are in force be ready with a complete plan, reinforced by adequate stocks, for substitution of asbestos by mineral wool, and spend money to this end rather than in [complying with] every provision.'[126] Turner & Newall was buying time as it re-directed its corporate policy. It was still, as in the old days, exerting a large measure of control. In the 1970s, however, events would rapidly overtake it.

---

[124] DHSS. Standing Medical Advisory Committee: Sub-Committee on Cancer. SAC (M) SSC (68,71) 7. These reports were not released until 1975.
[125] 126/358. A. B. Boath to A. N. Marshall, 12 Aug. 1968.
[126] 126/305–9. J. R. Stevenson to Marshall, 27 Aug. 1968.

9

The Asbestos 'Bomb' Explodes

Within a period of about two months [in 1976] most people in the UK had received the message loud and clear that *asbestos is dangerous*.

20/203–4. N. Rhodes, 'The Impact of Adverse Publicity', 1976.

It is our policy to apply the British standard . . . in our factories throughout the world. We do this even when no local regulations exist.

Patrick Griffith (chairman), Turner & Newall, *Reports & Accounts* (1976).

REACHING THE 2-FIBRE THRESHOLD

The 1969 Regulations had for the first time set a quantitative limit for asbestos dust, yet neither the asbestos industry nor the government felt able to implement or enforce such a threshold immediately. The Factory Inspectorate stepped up its surveillance of asbestos factories and planned a new dust survey of the industry, but the demand for sampling was over-whelming. In industry itself, most of the asbestos textile factories in 1970 were operating over the 2-fibre limit and full compliance would clearly take some time.

Most of the dust counts between 1970 and 1972 in the carding and spinning sections at Hindley Green and Rochdale were above 4 f/cc (and some were over 12 f/cc). Nevertheless, this was regarded as 'extremely satisfactory', in view of the Inspectorate's decision not to enforce the Regulations below 4 f/cc.[1] Many cutting and insulating jobs also recorded similar counts at this time; and dust in the company's asbestos cement factories exceeded 2 f/cc.[2] Ferodo's operations were mostly below 2 f/cc, but the removal of machining and grinding dust from completed friction materials released local concentrations in excess of 100 f/cc.[3] By 1974, 50 per cent of counts at TBA and Hindley Green still exceeded the 2-fibre limit.[4]

---

[1] 26/2026–8. W. P. Bamblin memo, 30 Oct. 1970.
[2] 114/1817. C. J. Sutcliffe memo, 19 Nov. 1970.
[3] 6/250–1. T & N board meeting, 3 Feb. 1972.
[4] 85/741–4. Report on Personal Sampling at TBA, 7 Aug. 1975.

Dust-counting technology, though, was being improved by TBA's physicists. Although the electron microscope still had no place in setting standards, the membrane filter/optical microscope technique was steadily refined. In the early 1970s, it was appreciated that, instead of trying to count whole microscope fields of view in the scanning filter, restricting the field with an eyepiece graticule gave greater accuracy. By 1976, regular personal (instead of static) dust counts, using a portable device actually attached to the worker, had also become the norm. TBA estimated that these changes resulted in a fourfold increase in the count.[5] In other words, scientists could see more fibres, resulting in a *de facto* tightening of the threshold.

Turner & Newall continued to look for ways of reducing (though not eliminating) dust in its textile factories. By the mid-1970s, TBA's carding engines had been isolated from the main spinning areas and placed in group enclosures with no access permitted between the cards without personal protection. The air flow was reversed to prevent fibres from the dustier processes being drawn towards the cleaner locations and the incoming replacement air from the heated plenum systems was balanced to provide a slight negative pressure in the work areas. Unfortunately, dust control in spinning was still proving difficult.

In the early 1970s, Turner & Newall continued to extend its range of 'dust-suppressed' asbestos products, in which the fibre was 'locked in' by various polymers and resins. However, the ultimate breakthrough in 'cleaner' products came with the introduction of 'Fortex' at TBA in 1969. Licensed from Germany, the Fortex process involved mixing chrysotile into a chemical soup, from which spaghetti-like strands of asbestos could be drawn and then spun on specially adapted spinning frames. This eliminated mechanical opening and carding. It also promised much reduced dust shedding in use, as the yarn was virtually pure asbestos and the chrysotile was dispersed into tiny fibres.

However, Fortex proved a disappointment. Although many of the improvements were real enough, Fortex could only replace about 45 per cent of TBA's products. The innovation was also too late. Customers who had recently discontinued the use of ordinary asbestos cloth were not interested in another asbestos-based material and were wary of Fortex's 'dustlessness'. In 1971, for example, Shell would only consider buying Fortex if Turner & Newall could secure a recommendation from the Factory Inspectorate.[6] In fact, Fortex textiles in use released a high proportion of sub-microscopic particles—small enough to escape optical

[5] 509/35–48. S. Holmes, 'Asbestos', typescript, n.d., 10.
[6] 1/1111–12. E. B. Gates to R. A. Wells, 20 Oct. 1971.

viewing methods, but visible with an electron microscope.[7] When Fortex was marketed in Holland, the company had to admit that it could not be totally sure that such fibrils were safe.[8] TBA told Raybestos–Manhattan in 1972: 'Although produced by a wet dispersion process, you will see from this yarn that it is impossible to eliminate completely, any shedding of dust.'[9]

Fortex (the production of which was also not dustless) did little to alter the general picture at TBA and Hindley Green. As Lewinsohn highlighted in 1974, further dust control measures were needed and even the systems in use were not properly maintained. The standard of housekeeping was poor:

Fibre is left lying around machines without making any attempt to clean it up. Pieces of plant withdrawn for maintenance and repair are not cleaned down beforehand, thus exposing mechanics and others unnecessarily to asbestos dust. Although dry brushes are not permitted by the Regulations, long-handled brooms are still used for cleaning under cards and the progress towards vacuum cleaning is not yet discernible. The filter galleries are dirtier than they have ever been. Burst filter bags are now a frequent occurrence because they are used beyond their effective life—such happenings were formerly very rare. It is worthy of note that the general disregard for cleanliness is not confined to production areas but can be observed in corridors, lobbies, on staircases and even outside the factory walls. If conditions in the factory were entirely satisfactory no comment on the subject of personal protection would be necessary. As it is, the Asbestos Regulations, 1969, are being disregarded because of the failure to insist upon the wearing of head-gear and the proper use of overalls.[10]

In 1976—when 40 per cent of the counts were over 2 f/cc—the 2-fibre limit was thought 'just achievable' in carding and spinning at TBA, but reducing it further would be difficult and cost nearly £$\frac{1}{2}$ million.[11] This at a time when dust control plant at Rochdale was worth over £2 million and estimated to cost £200,000 a year to run.

However, the Factory Inspectorate's own sample surveys around the country in the early 1970s gave a much different picture. They reported in 1973 that 92 per cent of the samples were below 2 f/cc; by 1975 the

[7] 48/705–6. 'A Comparative Study of Dust from Fortex and Conventional Asbestos Textiles: An Interim Report', 25 Feb. 1971. Tests with a scanning electron microscope showed counts up to nearly 10 f/cc (fibres below 5 microns) when flexing Fortex cloth.

[8] Stephen Holmes told a Dutch scientist: 'I accept the point that we are not yet able to say with certainty that asbestos fibrils [from Fortex] are no greater a hazard to health than the optically visible fibre bundles. On the other hand, there is no firm evidence to the contrary and, on balance, one would expect the lung to deal more easily with these short, fine particles.' 81/918–21. Letter, 14 Feb. 1972.

[9] 78/1445–6. F. Ashworth to J. Hawkins, 15 Nov. 1972.

[10] 303/2230–1. Asbestos and Health at TBA: Medical Report, 1974.

[11] See 20/75–80. S. Holmes, 'Dust Measurement and Control', board presentation, 15 July 1976.

Table 9.1. *Factory inspectorate convictions and fines under the Asbestos Regulations, 1931–77*

Year	Convictions	Average fine
1931–69	2	£12
1970	0	–
1971	1*	£25
1972	40	?
1973	15	?
1974	39	?
1975	22	£79
1976	23	£45
1977	84	£182

*Turner & Newall prosecution.

Source: Chief Medical Inspector of Factories, *Annual Reports* (London, 1931–78).

figure was said to be approaching 95 per cent. This favourable picture appears to be boosted by evidence of much greater activity in policing the Regulations. In contrast to the feeble regulatory hand in enforcing the 1931 Regulations, the Inspectorate began issuing improvement and prohibition orders and it also convicted offenders. Between 1969 and 1976 there were 140 convictions under the new Regulations. However, the retribution meted out to offenders soon dispels the notion of a government department bearing down hard on the industry. Average fines were usually well under £100 (see Table 9.1).

In 1971, Turner & Newall had the distinction of becoming the first company to be prosecuted under the 1969 Regulations. The Factory Inspectorate had found dust concentrations of 84 f/cc at one of TAC's beater-floor operations. A TAC manager noted before the case went to court: 'I have had a word with the Factory Inspector . . . [and] . . . I obtained his assurance that he would present the case on the footing that TAC is a good firm which just happened to have slipped up badly in an isolated case. I think there is every reason to hope that he will not over-emphasise the length of time which the fault had continued and, in any event, his allegations will not go beyond April of this year although we know that it existed prior to that date.'[12] TAC pleaded guilty, though it cited several mitigating circumstances and tried to blame the media for the Inspectorate's action. The company was fined £25.[13]

---

[12] 7/68. I. Adaire to T & N, 28 Oct. 1971.
[13] 7/25–35. *HM Factory Inspectorate v. TAC Construction Materials*, 10 Nov. 1971.

The Factory Inspectors complained little about other Turner & Newall plants. They regarded TBA as a generally clean factory and, apart from a few criticisms, took no legal action.[14] The Inspectorate found that most TBA dust counts were below the 2-fibre limit in 1973, a fact which sheds more light on the Inspectors' dust-counting methods than it does on the dustiness of the factory. The Inspectors had no objection to the spray process, which, despite its proven track record in killing workers, survived the introduction of the 2-fibre threshold. In 1969, as part of its 'token' effort at complying with the Regulations, Turner & Newall dusted down (so to speak), the old pre-damping drum, which had never been used much anyway, and tried to improve its loading and efficiency. However, pre-damping remained awkward and messy. Fibre (either chrysotile or amosite) still had to be tipped and shoved manually into the drum (while the operator wore a compressed air respirator); and after wetting, the drum had to be discharged and the contents then fed into the spray machine. Turner & Newall found that loading the damping drum raised average fibre concentrations to 49 f/cc; whilst around the sprayer, levels of 74 f/cc were recorded—though it was claimed that most readings for the sprayer were under 10 f/cc.[15]

The government accepted these levels as safe. The Inspectors' *Annual Report* for 1971 repeated the Asbestosis Research Council's view on spray almost verbatim, when it stated that pre-damping could 'reduce respirable dust a hundred fold . . . [which] . . . enables members of the spray team to be fully protected by wearing simple approved dust respirators, and other tradesmen working outside the immediate area will not be exposed to concentrations above the hygiene standard'.[16] Yet the very same page of the *Report* warned that sprayed asbestos left measurable concentrations of dust in buildings for years, adding in 1974: 'Even relatively minor structural alterations involving disturbance of such coatings can give rise to concentrations of dust liable to cause danger to health.'[17] Turner & Newall had been aware of this problem since the 1960s.[18] However, further support for spraying came from the Medical Research

[14] 76/1582–3. Memo by S. Holmes, with attached letter and data from Factory Inspectorate, 8 Feb. 1973.

[15] 126/9–22. J. D. Pennington, 'Pre-Damping Equipment for Sprayed Asbestos', 27 Nov. 1969.

[16] Ministry of Labour & HM Factory Inspectorate, *Annual Report of the Chief Inspector of Factories 1971* (1972), 32. The Inspectorate's view was not shared by P. G. Harries, whose paper, 'Asbestos Dust Concentrations in Ship Repairing: A Practical Approach to Improving Asbestos Hygiene in Naval Dockyards', *Annals of Occupational Hygiene* 14 (1971), 241–54, had stressed the dangers of spray.

[17] Ministry of Labour & HM Factory Inspectorate, *Annual Report of the Chief Inspector of Factories 1974* (1975), 63.

[18] See chapter 6. Harries had told TBA in 1970 that birds nesting in a warehouse sprayed with asbestos had disturbed crocidolite that was falling on foodstuffs. He noted that the 300 women involved in packing the food could become an untraceable cohort of victims. See 500/64. HCL to E. A. Edmonds, 12 Nov. 1970.

Council, which, in a programme approved by TAC, had evaluated spray counts in 1972. The MRC regarded 7f/cc counts around the sprayer as acceptable and thought no part of the process involved a 'significant health hazard'. Yet the MRC investigators observed how asbestos contaminated the site, risking the health of unsuspecting tradesmen who later swept the debris up with brushes. Ironically, the test site was a hospital![19]

With the government's blessing, Turner & Newall continued to market asbestos spray vigorously in the early 1970s. Stephen Holmes visited New York in 1970 to emphasize the merits of pre-damped spray to city officials. He dismissed concerns about the dangers posed by future demolition, as this 'only occurred infrequently' and 'most of the insulation would be removed in large pieces and suitable precautions could be taken'.[20] Holmes did not regard mineral wool as a serious substitute. By 1971, however, New York and several other American cities had banned sprayed asbestos in buildings and within two years that ban was nationwide. However, spray was still used in the UK, where the AIC described it publicly as a product that could be 'used safely'.[21] In Europe, Turner & Newall used Factory Inspectorate reassurances to extol the virtues of sprayed asbestos in Holland.[22] Yet in the preceding month, Turner & Newall had already decided to 'phase out' spray in favour of mineral wool. This was to be done in the UK by April 1974 and overseas by April 1975. As that deadline approached, however, Turner & Newall were still supplying spray machines to places such as Northern Ireland—where the Asbestos Regulations did not yet apply[23]—because the company had realized that its timetable was too optimistic and would cut profits.[24] So the deadline was delayed for a year until 1975, when Turner & Newall, having maximized its profits from spray, sold the Newalls Insulation contract business to Cape Industries.[25]

It was almost the end of one of the most tragic episodes in the history of British occupational health. Yet even in 1975, spraying was not banned by the government, despite the overwhelming evidence of its dangers from as far afield as Australia and America. Spraying was not prohibited in Britain until 1985, a decade after the process had become defunct.

---

[19] 70/1959–76. J. W. Skidmore and J. S. P. Jones, 'MRC Report on Asbestos Spraying Project at the City Hospital, Nottingham' (June 1972).
[20] 170/1502–15. F. Howe and S. Holmes Visit to USA, 17–20 Aug. 1970.
[21] 81/323. W. P. Howard to *Guardian*, 16 Nov. 1971.
[22] 117/426–8. S. Holmes to Director-Gen. of Arbeidsinspectie, 20 Dec. 1972. See also A. A. Cross, 'Practical Methods for Protection of Men Working with Asbestos Materials in Shipyards', in International Labour Office, *Safety and Health in Shipbuilding and Ship Repairing* (1972), 93–101.
[23] 601/1277–8. H. Gomersall to D. J. Heaney, 17 Apr. 1974.
[24] 200/771–2. T & N board meeting, 7 Mar. 1974.
[25] The remainder of Newalls was sold in 1980.

In other areas, the influence of the Factory Inspectorate was less positive from Turner & Newall's viewpoint. Asbestos was straining the relationship between the employers and regulators. In their tours of the factories of asbestos users (not producers), the Inspectors often criticized asbestos. In 1970, a Rolls Royce rocket establishment decided to stop using Turner & Newall asbestos insulation after an Inspector had warned that it would require breathing apparatus and ventilation machinery. Turner & Newall found it 'quite monstrous that a local Factory Inspector should have produced this effect'.[26] Around the country, the Inspectors began following a consistent line: they complimented the industry on implementing government health measures, but they also recommended a switch to substitutes where possible.[27] Turner & Newall were infuriated by this advice, but could do little to counter it, as the Inspectors were only a barometer of a trend that was already well underway. For many users, pressure from insurance companies and trade unions was having a predictable effect. A Turner & Newall manager wrote to Rochdale: 'With these two forces bearing down upon them it is perhaps not surprising that some insulation contractors appear to be inclined to take the view that life is far simpler for them if they do not handle asbestos whether for primary or secondary insulation.'[28] By 1971, Turner & Newall had been told by the Admiralty that 'in no circumstances' would there be a return to asbestos primary insulation.[29]

At the centre of this troubled backdrop was Hilton Lewinsohn. In public, he was inclined to reassure workers that conditions at TBA were 'unlikely to affect the health of anybody'.[30] However, his annual medical reports to the board and his advice to the TBA Health Committee show that there was still much that worried him. In 1972, he emphasized that neither the 1931 Regulations nor the 1948 factory reorganizations could be regarded as watersheds. There had been thirty-two suspensions at TBA since 1948 and twelve had no history of exposure before 1948. Particularly disturbing were two cases from Hindley Green, which had supposedly benefited from Rochdale's dust control experience.[31] The two employees had started work in 1957 and 1959, respectively.[32] Looming over everything was the spectre of mesothelioma, which was occurring with increasing frequency at Turner & Newall companies. The case history of

---

[26] 45/2088. E. B. Gates to TJL., 11 Sept. 1970.
[27] 68/56–7. E. A. Edmonds to K. H. Dixon, 30 Nov. 1970.
[28] 45/2067–8. R. H. Cotter to E. B. Gates, 27 Jan. 1971.
[29] 45/2048. E. A. Edmonds to E. B. Gates, 15 Mar. 1971.
[30] *Rochdale Observer*, 23 Sept. 1972; and 73/950. 'An Assurance to Asbestos Workers', *Rochdale Observer* cutting.
[31] 301/528–40. CMO Annual Report, 6 Nov. 1972, 4.
[32] 153–249–53. TBA Health Committee, 65th Meeting, 12 July 1972.

Table 9.2. *Asbestosis suspensions, 1955–69*

Main occupation	Cases	Percentage
Opening/disintegrating	86	12
Insulating:		
Laggers	208	
Sprayers	28	48
Mattress-makers	26	
Others	83	
Weaving	30	16
Carding and spinning, etc.	88	
Slab and pipe-making	39	5.5
Brake-lining	14	2.1
Miscellaneous	118	16.5
Total	720	100

Source: 77/127–8. R. M. McGowan, Principal Medical Officer to H. C. Lewinsohn, 28 July 1972.

Margaret Chrimes illustrated that even clerical staff were at risk. She died of mesothelioma in 1973, having been employed as a switchboard operator at TBA between 1928 and 1936.[33] In some cases, exposure was so brief and so distant that victims and witnesses had difficulty in recalling the details. John Coshall died of mesothelioma in 1974—over fifty years since he had worked briefly for TAC's Erith plant as a beaterman, tipping chrysotile and cement into a mixer. The company had no record of Coshall and only the testimony of a friend confirmed that Coshall had worked there.[34] Several sprayers had now developed mesothelioma, often after less than ten years' exposure.[35]

Lewinsohn complained persistently about the bad housekeeping at TBA, but improvements were slow in coming. In 1973 he told TBA chairman David Hills of his frustration, especially with Newalls. By now the problem of asbestosis in the insulation trades could be seen clearly: as Table 9.2 shows, nearly half of the country's suspensions for asbestosis came from this sector. Besides Dr Peter Harries's studies of asbestos disease in the Admiralty shipyards, Turner & Newall were also being informed of major probes elsewhere. At Vickers' shipyard in Barrow-in-Furness, 12,000 men were employed in building ships. A preliminary

[33] See 128/2346. Lewinsohn believed that this case raised 'grave implications' and asked the directors to consider dust monitoring in TBA offices. Their response was non-committal.

[34] 114/1164–73. J. W. Coshall (*c*.1901–74) file.

[35] E.g. 114/567–84: Andrew Gledhill (1917–74) file. A TAC sprayer, William Allen (1918–72), apparently developed mesothelioma after about three years' exposure between 1955 and 1958. See 27/1737–84.

survey between 1967 and 1970, found that some 600 had X-ray abnormalities due to asbestos.[36]

In 1971, medical advisers at the TUC, Cape, and Turner & Newall met to discuss extending the medical monitoring system to insulation and contract workers.[37] But tracking such workers, as ever, would prove troublesome and costly. Lewinsohn wanted £25,000 spent on monitoring Newalls' workers, but although an X-ray survey was launched, a comprehensive medical service never appeared. Lewinsohn wrote to a Newalls' director in 1973: 'I find it difficult to restrain myself from asking why in the light of the suffering and the misery caused—Let me repeat that. "I find it difficult to restrain myself from asking why, in the light of the suffering and misery caused" . . . the company is so reluctant to reorganise its medical surveillance facilities.'[38]

At TBA, Lewinsohn had more influence. He continued the company's pre-emptive policy of transferring or retiring workers with suspected asbestosis, even though they had not yet been officially suspended by the PMP. By 1971 eleven cases were advised to leave the scheduled areas by Lewinsohn—a number that had risen to sixteen by 1973.[39] However, transferring workers to other jobs at TBA and Hindley Green was becoming problematical as the economic outlook for asbestos deteriorated in the 1970s and as the workforce began shrinking. In 1972, Lewinsohn noted that two individuals actually suspended by the PMP were still working with asbestos, and believed that the company might be guilty of negligence.[40] He also did what he could to alert employees to the dangers. By 1976, TBA workers were being treated to an 'Asbestos and Health' slide show with music and a commentary from Lewinsohn and the health physicists.[41]

Steps were also taken to involve the workers with health decision-making, though it was to prove difficult to overcome the culture of secrecy and mistrust. In November 1973, on Lewinsohn's recommendation, TBA decided to reconstitute the Health Committee to include senior trade-union shop stewards and factory supervisors. This was mainly a statutory requirement, though the directors accepted that it was time for a greater shop-floor involvement. However, this sentiment had its limits. It was decided that post-mortems and inquests on dead workers would be discussed at a separate meeting.[42] The result of this decision can be seen in the subsequent extant Health Committee minutes: when the trade

[36] 45/188–95. J. Edge to S. Holmes, 16 Jan. 1970.
[37] 77/124–6. Memo of Discussion between W. J. Smither, R. Murray, and HCL, 17 June 1971.
[38] *Chase v. T & N* (1995). Trial transcript, 3005–6. Lewinsohn to Proctor, 23 Nov. 1973.
[39] 153/275–6. TBA Health Committee, Minutes of 61st Meeting, 11 Mar. 1971.
[40] 153/254–60. TBA Health Committee, Minutes of 64th Meeting, 30 Mar. 1972.
[41] 20/171–82. 'Asbestos and Health', Jan. 1976.
[42] 153/242–7. TBA Health Committee, Minutes of 66th Meeting, 7 Nov. 1972.

unions were on board, the meetings became less candid, more routine, and ultimately less effective.

Lewinsohn was also concerned about workers smoking. As a physician, this would have worried him anyway, because of the lung cancer risk. However, by this time the multiplicative risk of smoking *and* working with asbestos (which greatly increased the risk of lung cancer) was also known. In 1972, the company agreed to Lewinsohn's request to withdraw cigarette machines from the factory. It caused immediate opposition. One director was unhappy because it would harm productivity and raise anxiety among the workers, especially in triggering 'alarming rumours' outside the factory.[43] The greatest opposition, however, came from the employees who were denied the opportunity to buy cigarettes at work. Faced with a strike, the cigarette machines were back on the walls within days. Much to Lewinsohn's chagrin, vending machines were *introduced* at TAC at Rhoose in 1974. There was even opposition later to the idea of pinning up warning notices about smoking.[44]

MULTINATIONAL HEALTH AND SAFETY

It would obviously not be long before the media and foreign governments began looking at Turner & Newall's overseas plants. By 1972, director Harry Hardie had launched a review of the firm's foreign subsidiaries to find out how closely they were complying with the targets set by the 1969 Regulations. He told the board: 'It is difficult to over-emphasise the potential threat which exists to our business in asbestos-based materials ... unless we ensure that our own house is in order.'[45] This would entail the introduction of UK standards around the world and closer liaison between British directors and overseas managers.

Our picture of Turner & Newall's huge multinational business is hazy. The financial performance of the various overseas companies seems to have been uneven—thus confirming the general picture of British overseas business that has emerged in the recent writings of business historians. However, most of Turner & Newall's foreign documentation appears to have been destroyed, particularly regarding the firm's mining activities in Africa. Some types of documentation never existed. Until at least the 1960s, asbestos health regulations simply did not exist in most of the countries in which Turner & Newall operated—a great advantage

---

[43] 72/2255–6. Norman Rhodes to HCL, 29 Nov. 1972.

[44] In 1978, a Ferodo manager opposed smoking warnings as it 'would only highlight the risks connected with working in our industry'. 69/1895. I. R. Duthie to M. C. Pretorius, 26 Apr. 1978. Not until 1984, did T & N introduce a no-smoking policy.

[45] 6/546–8. H. D. S. Hardie memo, 3 May 1972. Hardie was a T & N director, 1967–85.

for the company at the time, but a hindrance for the historian as there are no informative compensation files or autopsy records.

Of great interest at this point is Turner & Newall's overseas business strategy, which was masterminded for nearly thirty years by Walker Shepherd. The latter's activities as an international fixer began in the USA in the 1930s. During his visit to America in the summer of 1933, Shepherd was chiefly concerned with negotiating a scheme that would slice world asbestos markets between three groups centred in Russia, Canada, and the USA. The division had been agreed at a London conference of asbestos producers in 1932.[46] Within such grand cartels, Turner & Newall's international policy reflected its domestic arrangements—a highly devolved structure in which board policy was delegated to local managements with a high degree of independence. This structure was permeated with price-fixing agreements and holding companies, which were seen to their best effect in America. When the take-over of Keasbey & Mattison was planned in the early 1930s, Shepherd assured competitors Johns–Manville and Raybestos that his company would not upset any domestic arrangements and that it would always be prepared to fix prices and quotas alongside the Americans.[47] Such fixing was, of course, unlawful under anti-trust law, but American manufacturers dealt with this problem by using licencees as front-men, while the asbestos firms set prices in the background.[48] The US government eventually indicted the firms involved in 1944, but no companies were penalized, and Turner & Newall's other North American cartels persisted. In particular, Keasbey & Mattison—a wholly-owned subsidiary of the English firm—did not trade with Canada, while Turner & Newall did not compete with Keasbey in America. So that it would not run foul of US anti-trust legislation, Turner & Newall distanced itself from Keasbey by some complex corporate legal footwork. Keasbey's stock was held in Canada by a trust fund controlled by Turner & Newall Overseas (TNO)—a holding company. Under its aegis, Shepherd, as chairman of the Keasbey board, would eventually meet his fellow directors only in Canada. He was thus able to claim under oath to the US authorities that Keasbey was an 'independent corporate entity', and that TNO and Turner & Newall never did any business in the USA, nor had 'their names ever appeared on any door in the United States'.[49]

Such business practices—which were also used by other firms and industries—have usually been regarded by business historians as rational

---

[46] 103/1–60. W. W. F. Shepherd, 'Report on Visit to USA and Canada, 6 June 1933–1 July 1933'.

[47] 103/263–4. Shepherd's Report, 21 Oct.–6 Dec. 1933, 194.

[48] 103/1712–3. Shepherd's Report, 26 Apr.–30 May 1938, 43–4; 103/1768–9. Shepherd's Report, 15 Oct. 1938–23 Nov. 1938, 17–18. See also B. I. Castleman, *Asbestos: Medical and Legal Aspects* (1996), 37–8.

[49] 35/837–41. Affidavit, US District Court Eastern District of Pennsylvania, Aug. 1958.

economic responses to uncertain market conditions. The health perspective, however, provides another dimension to our understanding. Turner & Newall's business strategy might be of little interest if the product in question was a safe one, but it assumes greater significance with asbestos. Secrecy and unlawful business deals contributed to the hegemony of asbestos; while the whole devolved structure of Turner & Newall, with its overseas operations, holding companies, and decentralized UK administration provided a perfect breeding ground for the future asbestos health problem. Once that problem had been created, then the same structure also helped the company avoid its liabilities. The fact that Hardie evidently did not know the occupational health status of any of the firm's overseas factories and mines is comment enough on the company's attitude to its overseas workforce. After 1970, however, it was time for Turner & Newall to assess the health costs of this *laissez-faire* policy. The ghastly picture that began to emerge was to add greatly to the company's problems in the 1970s.

No one knows when asbestosis and asbestos cancers first became a problem for Turner & Newall in North America: whenever it was, the company could hardly claim ignorance. Walker Shepherd visited the USA at least once a year in the 1930s and his fellow directors and technical personnel were also frequent visitors. They toured plants and medical centres, and liaised with organizations of which Keasbey & Mattison was a member, such as the Asbestos Textile Institute and the Industrial Hygiene Foundation. In addition, Dr John Knox attended medical conferences and visited Turner & Newall subsidiaries.[50]

No documentation on health matters at Keasbey & Mattison has survived. Shepherd's voluminous American trip reports, which are extant, never mention asbestosis or cancer. This is intriguing when one considers that workers had developed asbestosis at Keasbey & Mattison by 1931 and six years later (when Turner & Newall had bought the business) the Department of Health in Pennsylvania investigated working conditions at the Ambler plant. State officials found that some exhaust ventilation had been installed, but other hazards remained, with the company evidently reluctant to do more.[51] By then the company was involved with other US firms in sponsoring asbestos-disease research at the Saranac Laboratory (see Chapter 6). By the late 1950s, when Keasbey & Mattison had over a thousand workers (and about 600 sales staff), several workers were filing asbestosis claims with the company's insurers, American Mutual Liability. The insurers' survey of Keasbey & Mattison plants found that, although dust concentrations were within the 'permissible' limits at

---

[50] See, for example, 31/1348–64. Knox's 'Report on Visit to USA, 25 July–17 Aug. 1960'.
[51] G. Markowitz and D. Rosner, *'Slaves of the Depression'* (1987), 124–6.

Ambler, conditions at another factory at Meredith, New Hampshire, left much to be desired. The company did little or nothing to improve dust control.

In 1961, Keasbey & Mattison were warned again by their insurers about dust levels and also about the dangers of spraying, for which the company acted as a licensee. An American Mutual Liability representative commented: 'It appears that the chickens are a little closer to coming home to roost. We must be very careful that they stay where they belong and don't roost on us.'[52] By then, Keasbey was again at the centre of a US government price-fixing probe, this time concerning the sale of asbestos cement products. Rochdale directors made the mistake of forwarding letters to Keasbey indicating that there had once been a cartel agreement between the two firms. This threw the American firm into such a panic that it destroyed the correspondence and then wrote to TBA to tell them that they should be 'wary of mentioning restrictive marketing agreements between our two companies'.[53] But the government's anti-trust action was soon rendered moot. By 1963, Turner & Newall had liquidated Keasbey & Mattison, selling the profitable asbestos-cement part to Certain-teed Products Corporation, in which it took an interest.

However, Turner & Newall were still mining and manufacturing asbestos in Canada, where the chickens would come home to roost. The company had maintained a significant presence there through the Bell Asbestos Mines in Quebec and the Atlas Asbestos factory in Montreal. The total workforce was about 1,300 by 1955, with over 450 miners and about 550 workers at the Montreal factory. In the 1970s, the Canadian asbestos mines still had the largest output of any country apart from the Soviet Union, with the Quebec economy still heavily dependent on the fibre. Perhaps appropriately, in view of the fact that (as John Knox had noted[54]) dust from tailings coated the environment, towns had been named after the mineral. *The Wall Street Journal* commented in 1969, that 'no place is prouder than Asbestos, where folks are willing to endure plenty to keep this industry going . . . [and where] . . . the risks of asbestosis don't get much attention'.[55] However, Turner & Newall would have been aware of the health problem by the 1930s, when Sir Samuel Turner admitted that 'dust conditions [in Quebec] . . . are really very bad indeed'.[56] In the mining area, the major companies had since 1940 funded the Thetford

[52] P. Brodeur, *Outrageous Misconduct* (1985), 203–5.
[53] 124/331. N. L. Barr to M. C. Bentall, 13 Jan. 1961.
[54] 101/1351–3. On 17 Dec. 1964, during a visit to Bell Mines, Knox expressed his concern at the 250-ton dump created by the company: 'Tailings contain, as well as crushed rock, some $\frac{1}{2}$–1% of fibres and from the numerous dumps in the area large amounts of fibre must blow all over the district.'
[55] 506/668. *Wall Street Journal*, 12 Sept. 1969.
[56] 9/1661. Turner to C. S. Bell, 5 July 1938.

Industrial Clinic under its head, Dr Paul Cartier. Until 1953, samples from asbestos-disease cases in the Thetford area were sent via Cartier for review at the Saranac Laboratory. Eleven of those cases came from Bell Asbestos Mines.[57] Knox had visited Cartier in 1964, when they discussed the incidence of disease in the region's mills. The lung cancer rate was particularly high, with Cartier admitting to 29 cases amongst 147 autopsies.[58]

A fuller picture emerged in the early 1970s, when Hardie asked his Canadian managers to provide a health review. Atlas Asbestos Company in Montreal (which was now a division of the Bell Asbestos Mines) replied that the factory was unable to comply with the 2-fibre standard. To do so would need expenditure of $\$\frac{1}{2}$ million, greatly raise operating costs, and destroy the insulation business.[59] A Turner & Newall director warned that, 'conditions in the factory . . . are below what T & N regard as an acceptable standard'.[60] This was underlined by Atlas's atrocious asbestosis record, which was the worst in Canada. In 1971, the company's part-time medical officer, Dr Philippe Landry, had accepted the government's offer to examine workers, with the result that forty-eight were immediately suspended. In Canada, compensation procedures were more favourable to claimants than in the UK, and often gave workers the benefit of the doubt. In 1972, the Quebec Workmen's Compensation Commission levied a $76,000 penalty on the company, which together with previous claims raised Atlas's compensation costs to over $220,000 a year. By the following year, these costs were expected to top $400,000. Turner & Newall's own detailed review of conditions at the factory described an appalling situation: unenclosed operations, poor dust extraction, torn bags, and workers covered in dust. The Montreal company had adopted the view that 'asbestosis is something to keep quiet about in case it spreads alarm'.[61]

In 1973, Lewinsohn visited Canada to see the gory details for himself. He confirmed the dangerous and dusty conditions and reported that there were 132 cases of asbestosis (by 1979 the figure was 207). The plant, which now had a workforce of about 350, had a disease incidence that would have made Merewether blanch: of 166 men exposed to asbestos for fifteen years or more, 91 current employees had asbestosis. Lewinsohn pointed to the reason: 'I cannot entirely accept management ignorance in the past . . . as asbestosis cases have been occurring at Atlas since at least 1959. The problem here would appear to be lack of communication with regard to

---

[57] Castleman, *Asbestos*, 235–6.
[58] 101/1351–3. Knox Report on Visit to Thetford Mines, 17 Dec. 1964.
[59] 76/1263–7. G. Barge to Hardie, 14 Mar. 1972.
[60] 35/71–2. K. Neve memo to Hardie, 5 Jan. 1973.
[61] 76/1276–89, 1290–305. R. W. Cooley, 'Safety and Health—Atlas Asbestos Co.', 15 Dec. 1972.

health matters between Atlas Asbestos Company, Montreal, and Turner
& Newall Ltd in the United Kingdom.'[62] Lewinsohn took a brief look at
the Bell Mine, without going underground. He found that the mill was
'old . . . congested, dirty and . . . unhealthy to work in', and added: 'if
urgent improvements are not made to the crushing mills and bagging
operations as well as to the dryers in the near future, Bell may well face
embarrassing situations with regard to the question of environmental
pollution.'

The Canadian situation was mirrored in Turner & Newall's extensive
African mining and manufacturing interests. The view that the company
presented in its trade literature of African working conditions and
workers was benign and patronizing (not to say racist). The opening shots
of a film the company planned to make in 1945 showed 'Swazis dressed
up . . . working in line to the antics of a leading nigger'.[63] Printed publicity material stressed the company's commitment to provide roads,
schools, and recreational facilities. A brochure for the New Amianthus
mines in the 1950s made the enterprise sound like a holiday resort, with
a cinema, tennis courts, and a golf course that was the venue for the
Swaziland golf championships. The brochure also extolled the well-
equipped hospital and claimed that 'an excellent standard of health is
enjoyed by all members of this mining community'.[64]

In reality, working conditions in the African industry were grim. Initially, the industry was characterized by many small mines, which
employed contract labourers on piece rates, who hand-cobbed asbestos
with the help of women and children.[65] Asbestosis had been reported in
the chrysotile mining districts of Rhodesia as long ago as 1928.[66] In the
late 1940s, a physician had observed children in the Transvaal being
whipped as they trampled amosite underfoot in bags: they had asbestosis and cor pulmonale before the age of 12.[67] Norman Dolbey visited
Rhodesia in 1950 and was driven along the 120 miles of strip-road to
Shabani, where the Birthday Mine supported a township of about 12,000
(of whom about 6,000 worked in the mines). The most noticeable feature
was waste dumps as big as the hills, which covered the whole country-
side in white dust.[68] Dolbey did not make a detailed report on conditions

[62] 76/1150–61. Lewinsohn, 'Report on Visit to Atlas . . . and Bell Mine', 14. Sept. 1973.
[63] Board meeting, 25 Jan. 1945. Synopsis of T & N film on asbestos.
[64] 222/163. African Mines brochure, *c*.1950.
[65] I am grateful to Jock McCulloch for making available to me his unpublished researches
on asbestos mining in South Africa. For important background on the asbestos mining industry, see L. Flynn, *Studded with Diamonds and Paved with Gold* (1992), 146–202.
[66] F. W. Simson, 'Pulmonary Asbestosis in South Africa', *BMJ* (26 May 1928), i, 885–7.
[67] G. W. H. Schepers's comments, *Annals of New York Academy of Sciences* 132 (31 Dec. 1965),
i, 246.
[68] 42/1318. N. Dolbey, 'Survey of . . . South Africa, the Rhodesias and Kenya', Sept.–Oct.
1950.

in the mine. However, Robert H. Turner did state in 1951 that 'dust conditions in the mills leave a lot to be desired . . . There is little one can do about the old mills, where the conditions are very bad'.[69]

The health hazards in these subsidiaries seem to have aroused no interest whatever in Britain, even when South African research linked asbestos with mesothelioma. By the late 1960s, reports of mesothelioma in South African workers (including one environmental case at the Havelock Mine, published in 1967) disconcerted TBA chairman John Waddell.[70] However, the company never launched a health survey of the South African operations, and with no health laws governing either dust control or compensation in Africa until the 1970s there was little official compulsion to do so.

After 1970 there was renewed interest in Africa by Turner & Newall. The 1969 Regulations provided the spur, but there was also pressure from the media, with Cape's African mines coming under scrutiny in 1971.[71] South Africa was now a political issue. In 1974, a government inquiry exploded the myth that British companies treated their African workers fairly. Turner & Newall were exposed as one of several companies that paid indigenous workers below the poverty level and operated wage discrimination.[72] The inquiry unfortunately did not mention health. However, after Turner & Newall had ascertained that most of the African subsidiaries had dust and health problems, in 1976 the indefatigable Lewinsohn was sent to investigate. His first stop was Durban in Natal, where Turners Asbestos Products and Ferodo had factories. In the Ferodo division, Lewinsohn found an 'obvious lack of safety consciousness . . . and the general housekeeping was of such a poor standard that it would have to be considered as constituting a hazard in some instances'.[73] The TAP factory was worse, because 'workers and supervisors . . . had obviously not been instructed in the rudimentary elements of working in a safe and dustless manner'. At tea-breaks, African workers simply sat on the shop-floor and consumed their food among the dust. Of 600 workers X-rayed, 82 possibly had asbestosis—in Lewinsohn's view, an 'epidemic'.

Lewinsohn next visited the Havelock Mines in Swaziland. These were at the centre of a township of about 4,500, of whom about 500 worked underground and 300 in the mill. The situation was no better

[69] 1/1660–3. R. H. Turner, South African visit, June 1951.
[70] 36/1507–8. Waddell to Knox, 8 Aug. 1967. Attached copy of T. F. B. Collins, 'Asbestos—The Lethal Dust', *South African Medical Journal* 41 (15 July 1967), 639–46.
[71] 18/158–9. A. Batty, 'South African Asbestos Workers', *Times*, 26 July 1971.
[72] HC Expenditure Committee, Sess. 1973–4, *Fifth Report . . . on Wages and Conditions of Africa Workers Employed by British Firms in South Africa*. HC 116, 78–9; *Memoranda* HC 21–IV, 754–63.
[73] 6/594–609. HCL, 'Report on Visit to TAP', 1–5 Mar. 1976.

than in Durban and conditions in the mill made Lewinsohn shrink. He recalled:

I was in two minds as to whether I should enter the grading mill without the protection of a positive pressure respirator. Going through the mill to the storage shed and then through the shed was frightening. The operative sitting in a glass box and operating the scoop which feeds fibre to the conveyor was covered in fibre. I was astonished to see a man poking at a blocked screw conveyor and creating clouds of dust all about him.[74]

No dust samples had ever been taken at the mines. When TBA health physicists assessed the situation later, they found it was 1920s Rochdale revisited. They estimated that pre-1976 dust exposures could have surpassed 100 f/cc, with most workers exposed to average levels of 50 f/cc. A TBA technologist observed:

An area which no longer exists, and had high dust exposures, was the 'old dusting and screening plant'. This area is difficult to assign to the technologies used, and ... the description of this area by the expression 'appalling; visibility less than two metres', is untranslatable into terms of meaningful dust levels. The 'worst job in the mill' has been described as cleaning out the main dust duct ... using hand shovels. Throughout the mill, however, job practices were crude by modern standards and all employees must have had significant dust exposures.[75]

However, there was no procedure for reviewing health hazards and the medical monitoring was inadequate. The medical officer at the mines suspected that twenty-seven individuals had asbestosis, though the statistics were unreliable. When sick African workers returned to their huts and villages, they were never tracked; death certificates outside the towns were rare; and so, too, were post-mortems. While Hardie was telling the media that asbestosis was in single figures and that the company had annual health checks,[76] Lewinsohn recommended that a full-scale epidemiological study should be started, despite the problems with follow-up. This was to be launched in 1978.

Much the same situation was apparent in India. In the 1960s, Indian health regulations failed to protect asbestos workers. Conditions at Hindustan Ferodo, for example, were regarded as acceptable locally, but only because those in most Bombay textile mills were so bad. However, the effects of blue sprayed Limpet, which had been used from 1956, were being noted. In 1966, Hardie told Turner & Newall that several Indian operatives had pulmonary problems and that 'the company had created ... a situation which cannot be solved easily'.[77] Spray work soon ceased.

[74] 6/588–90. HCL, 'Report on a Visit to Havelock Mines, Mar. 1976', 15 Apr. 1976.
[75] 68/442–3. A. L. Rickards memo on Havelock Mine, Mar. 1979.
[76] 6/626–8. Havelock Mines radio interview, 12 Apr. 1976.
[77] 43/1289. Hardie to W. P. Howard, 1 Mar. 1966.

Lewinsohn visited the Bombay factory in 1975.[78] By then, 1,800 were employed by Hindustan Ferodo (1,600 of whom were on the shop-floor), using chrysotile but not crocidolite. About 600 workers were then regarded as 'scheduled', though it seems that there were still no health regulations in India. Lewinsohn thought that the plant was not too bad, though dust levels in carding and spinning were high. With no follow-up and no long-term medical screening, Lewinsohn had problems in estimating the prevalence of disease, though he discussed with the Bombay directors the introduction of health and dust checks along Rochdale lines.

Our information on the health and safety record of other Turner & Newall overseas operations is, alas, slight. However, what there is confirms the picture presented here: wherever asbestos was mined or manufactured there was a health problem—sometimes a catastrophic one.[79]

THE SELIKOFF AFFAIR

In June 1971, Lewinsohn presented a paper at a regional meeting of the Royal Society of Health in Rochdale on the 'Medical Surveillance of Asbestos Workers'. It was a detailed epidemiological study of the TBA workforce which Lewinsohn had been preparing since he joined the company. The paper was published in the following year.[80] At its core was an analysis of the Rochdale workforce, which provided figures on abnormal chest X-rays and the incidence of asbestosis. For male workers, after 10–19 years' exposure, Lewinsohn reported that around 35 per cent had abnormal X-rays; for those exposed for 20–9 years, the figure was well over 50 per cent. As regards the incidence of asbestosis for these two groups, the figures were in excess of 20 and 30 per cent. Only passing mention was made of the BOHS standard for chrysotile and none at all to Knox's previous analysis of TBA workers. Yet the differences between the two studies were glaring. Knox had presented the BOHS with an analysis of the X-rays of 290 TBA employees with more than ten years' exposure, which he had interpreted as showing that eight had 'possibly asbestotic' changes—only 2.7 per cent! This begged an immediate ques-

[78] 23/2282. HCL, 'Report on Visit to India, 1–15 Nov. 1975', 5 Dec. 1975.

[79] For example, Ferodo had operated a factory in northern France since 1923. The company records do not appear to have survived. However, in 1964 Knox admitted that French Ferodo operations were responsible for the suspension of 63 workers from a national total of 84. See 5/134. Knox review of Congress International sur L'Asbestos, Caen, 29–30 May 1964; and A. Dalton, *Asbestos Killer Dust* (1977), 244.

[80] H. C. Lewinsohn, 'The Medical Surveillance of Asbestos Workers', *Royal Society of Health Journal* 92 (Apr. 1972), 69–77.

tion: why was there such a huge discrepancy if, as was obvious, many of the Knox workers must also have been examined by Lewinsohn?

Lewinsohn had perhaps succeeded only too well in presenting a 'truthful interpretation of the facts'. Few in Britain took much notice of this academic paper, but an alert Irving Selikoff in America read the findings with great concern. When Selikoff's worries about the paper were communicated to Lewinsohn, he did not accept that his group of workers was the same as Knox's and also defended the BOHS standard.[81] Later he reassured Selikoff that steps were afoot to reassess the Rochdale data with the help of John Gilson at the MRC Pneumoconiosis Unit (formerly the PRU). Lewinsohn also promised to visit Selikoff and discuss the whole problem when he visited the USA in August 1973. Before that meeting could take place, however, Selikoff raised the issue publicly at a conference in Boston in May 1973. Pointing out that the 2-fibre threshold was being recommended as a safe level in America, he told his audience: 'When we put these [Knox–Lewinsohn] sets of data together, we can find that as of 400 fibre years, Dr Knox had found that in reading the films that somewhere around 7 or 8% had abnormal X-rays whereas in the same population, a different film reader had found that somewhere between 40 to 50% had abnormal X-rays.' Selikoff concluded that, if the latest results were correct, 'then the asbestos standard of the Department of Labor places US asbestos workers at serious risk of irreversible, often fatal disease and, in my opinion, it should be immediately reconsidered'.[82]

Lewinsohn privately told David Hills that Selikoff had 'boxed clever' and that it would be difficult to deny his conclusions and concerns.[83] Lewinsohn also admitted to Hills his doubts about the BOHS data and pointed out that his X-ray reporting technique was far more stringent than Knox's. However, TBA's public pronouncements were to be different, for at this point the wider implications of the paper suddenly dawned upon the company. Not only did the new data shoot down the 2-fibre standard—which the industry had still not fully met—but it also made Turner & Newall vulnerable to adverse criticism from all sides, as they had provided the original data. To add to the embarrassment, the BOHS was about to publish a brief 'review' of the hygiene standard, which argued that any changes would be 'premature' and that 'no adverse comments ... have been received from any source'.[84] Lewinsohn had also thrown a spanner in the works of the American industry's negotiations

[81] 72/649–50. Lewinsohn to Selikoff, 15 Aug. 1972.
[82] 83/2198–21202. Lecture at American Industrial Hygiene Conference, 21 May 1973. Transcript.
[83] 72/639–40. HCL to DWH, 8 June 1973.
[84] BOHS, 'Review of the Hygiene Standard for Chrysotile Asbestos Dust', *Annals of Occupational Hygiene* 16 (1973), 7.

with its own government. The efforts of American firms to have the 2-fibre threshold adopted were being helped by Cape and Turner & Newall, and clearly these negotiations would be derailed if the data were deficient. Worst of all, Lewinsohn had now given Selikoff a stick with which to beat the asbestos industry.

This was all too much for TBA and it began a desperate effort to row back from Lewinsohn's published position. Animosity to Selikoff had now reached a crescendo. 'Dr Selikoff is going off his head,' wrote Hills, 'We really must get onto our friends in the AIA/NA; this man Selikoff has got to be stopped somehow . . . he almost needs certifying.'[85] In order to defuse the 'Selikoff affair', a letter was sent to the American in July 1973, signed by Lewinsohn and Stephen Holmes.[86] It was drafted at least four times. In essence, it made light of the differences between the two sets of data and endorsed the 2-fibre limit as providing 'an ample safety margin'. For good measure, the letter attacked Selikoff for divulging the contents of 'private correspondence', for trying to undermine the 2-fibre standard, and for mounting a 'political campaign'. TBA then sent copies of the letter to various American asbestos industrialists and lobby groups, including the AIA—an act which angered Selikoff greatly.

In response, Selikoff told Lewinsohn that he did not find the objections 'material or valid' and that 'the failure of your polemic to establish coherence and identity between Dr Knox's study and yours might make one all the more concerned that such identity does not exist'.[87] Selikoff continued: 'the problem is a serious one . . . [for] hundreds of thousands of men and women . . . [who] are at serious risk of irreversible, often fatal disease.' Selikoff argued that although differences did exist in the two studies, it was the same factory and largely the same older employees who were X-rayed. He suggested that the X-rays should be re-appraised by independent experts in Britain, a task made more urgent by the fact that the BOHS standard ignored the cancer risk.

Neither TBA nor asbestos physicians in Britain felt inclined to have their agenda and data hijacked by Selikoff. Lewinsohn decided that he would not visit New York after all while he was in America; and Selikoff would not be invited to England. As the English closed ranks, Gilson told Lewinsohn: 'We are all agreed here that this is not a matter likely to be solved by discussions with Selikoff in person or indeed by prolonged correspondence.'[88] The American was told only that a new BOHS survey would follow 'in due course'; and he was reminded that his compatriots had provided no data or comparable information.[89]

[85] 72/310. Hills to H. D. S. Hardie, 2 Mar. 1973.
[86] 72/2018–21. Holmes/Lewinsohn to Selikoff, 12 July 1973.
[87] 72/651–61. Selikoff to Lewinsohn, 13 Aug. 1973.
[88] 72/2006. J. C. Gilson to Lewinsohn, 18 Sept. 1973.
[89] 72/2004–5. Lewinsohn to Selikoff, 21 Sept. 1973.

In his quest to have the Rochdale X-rays re-evaluated, Selikoff then wrote in September 1973 to Dr Robert Murray, the TUC medical adviser.[90] Murray replied that he would be pleased to help and thought that Gilson would be very interested in a British and American examination of the X-rays. He added: 'I appreciate the need for urgency in view of the establishment of your standards. I must say that I always regarded the 2 fibres/cc standard as an adequate one for controlling asbestosis, but it is singularly difficult as you know to establish any realistic atmospheric standards in relation to cancer.'[91] Within a month, however, Selikoff received a much less positive letter from Murray, who wrote: 'I had a word with John Gilson recently and according to him the situation is now being fully investigated in this country. He does not see any immediate need to marry trans-Atlantic comparisons of X-rays, but when the present survey is finished I think it would be very helpful to make comparisons of corresponding data from our two countries.'[92]

Selikoff had done as much as he could, as with Gilson's opposition there was no way that the X-rays would ever be released. As Barry Castleman points out, Gilson's attitude was not surprising as he had been a member of the sub-committee which had set the 2-fibre standard—indeed, he had helped Knox evaluate the X-rays.[93] Meanwhile, Murray passed Selikoff's correspondence to Lewinsohn (who then transmitted it to his bosses). When Selikoff finally wrote to Murray agreeing that a transatlantic study was 'unwarranted', but emphasizing the cancer risk, the latter immediately wrote to Lewinsohn: 'I attach a copy of a letter I have had from Selikoff which would appear to scotch effectively the ideas he had about trans-Atlantic exchange of information. There is a bite in the tail of the letter, but otherwise I think we can forget about the ideas he has put up in his previous letter.'[94]

However, Selikoff's persistence had not been without effect. For one thing, it had made Lewinsohn take another look at the original 1966 cohort, using Knox criteria to assess the X-rays. However, this merely confirmed Lewinsohn's original findings: an asbestosis incidence of 3 per cent or so could be read as nearly 50 per cent! Obviously, either Lewinsohn had read the X-rays more critically than Knox, or the latter had grossly underestimated the problem by refusing to consider X-ray changes alone (without rales) as evidence of asbestosis.[95]

---

[90] Murray was a former Factory Inspector, whose 'constituency' of asbestos factories in the north of England included Cape's Acre Mill in Hebden Bridge. After a spell with the International Labour Organisation in Geneva, he joined the TUC in 1962. Murray was very friendly with TBA directors, who were delighted with his appointment.

[91] 72/615–16. Murray to Selikoff, 5 Oct. 1973.

[92] 72/612. Murray to Selikoff, 22 Oct. 1973.

[93] Castleman, *Asbestos*, 335–41, describes the Selikoff affair in detail.

[94] 72/584–5. 81 Nov. 1973.

[95] 73/1166–9. Lewinsohn to Jack Solon, vice-president Johns–Manville, 8 Nov. 1973.

Lewinsohn also updated the cohort. By 1972, there were 26 cases of asbestosis (a rate of nearly 10 per cent) and 65 individuals with X-ray changes. A total of 29 deaths had occurred from the 1966 cohort. Only 4 of these were considered to have had asbestosis and, according to TBA, none of them died of this disease. However, among the 29 deaths were seven cases of lung cancer and three of mesothelioma. Ten other individuals had died from cardiovascular disease; three from respiratory disease; and another from gastrointestinal cancer. When Stephen Holmes commented on the seven lung cancer deaths in an internal paper, he remarked that 4.8 deaths were expected in the general population—a difference he regarded as 'not significant', when the workers' ages were taken into account.[96] As regards the criticism that the BOHS standard did not take account of lung cancer, he argued that the latter only arose as a result of asbestosis and that the rate at TBA was no greater than the general population. As regards mesothelioma, the standard should be adequate against that too, though he added: 'we have no proof of this'.

However, the Selikoff affair had now been picked up by the media. In October 1974, ITV's 'World in Action' team screened 'Killer Dust—A Standard Mistake', which brought the Lewinsohn–Selikoff debate into the open. Made with the reluctant help of Turner & Newall, who regarded co-operation as the 'lesser of two evils', it featured interviews with Lewinsohn, Selikoff, and Holmes. It was the first of Turner & Newall's brushes with television and it did not prove a happy one. The company was put on the defensive, with Lewinsohn arguing that the X-ray changes he had seen did not necessarily denote that the individuals had any form of disease. 'If it's not asbestosis', observed Selikoff, 'then it would be a striking new discovery that workers in asbestos factories have lung scarring from some other cause . . .'. The overall tone of the documentary was highly critical of the industry and especially Turner & Newall, where it left a 'residual atmosphere of troubled minds' among the TBA workforce.[97]

TBA were furious with the programme makers. They disliked the 'sensationalized' approach, the lack of preview rights, and the fact that the company had been 'pilloried before a lay audience'. The BOHS were worried about raising 'unnecessary fears', with one of the committee chairmen (Ronald Lane) pompously declaring that he did not see how the programme could have been broadcast without reference to himself.[98] Even more galling for TBA was the fact that they were powerless to repair

[96] 78/47–8. S. Holmes, 'The Validity of the Hygiene Standard for Asbestos', 10 Oct. 1974.
[97] 32/180. R. H. Pearce memo, 17 Oct. 1974. The documentary was screened on 14 Oct. 1974. See 32/115–29. Transcript.
[98] 48/239–40. World in Action memo by R. J. Bishop, 13 Dec. 1974.

the damage. Lewinsohn considered returning to the fray in the pages of the *Journal of the Royal Society of Health* and drafted another rebuttal to Selikoff. However, it was decided that publishing a letter would be unwise.

As the messy episode came to an end, Lewinsohn began attracting criticism from his own directors. One of them, R. A. Wells, complained privately to David Hills, who responded that the comments were better made to Lewinsohn personally. However, Hills added: 'At the least, he will not be in a hurry to publish again and next time he wants to, I will ensure careful internal scrutiny of his papers (would you like to volunteer?!).'[99]

These patronizing comments did not augur well for Lewinsohn's future with the company. The Selikoff débâcle added to the strains from other directions. Lewinsohn was still frustrated at the company's failure to spend more on overhauling its medical provision within the group and his complaints were winning him few friends.[100] Much burdened by his duties at TBA and other unit companies, in September 1976 he resigned for a job as medical director with Raybestos–Manhattan in Connecticut. By 1978, the man who had done as much as anyone at the company to protect the workforce, was *persona non grata* at all Turner & Newall companies, and directors were instructed to deny him access to any facility or company information.[101]

COMPENSATION AND COUNTERVAILING FORCES

Lewinsohn had done much to improve medical services within TBA and, to a certain extent, at other unit companies. But in the wider community, sufferers from asbestos diseases still faced enormous problems in claiming compensation and death benefits.

It was still difficult to calculate factory mortality. In the early 1970s, the TBA Health Committee regularly noted what Lewinsohn termed 'lost souls'—asbestos deaths that had been missed. In March 1971, its members noted two colon cancers which might have been mesotheliomas; and a lung cancer case that might have revealed asbestosis had there been a post-mortem.[102] In August 1971, the Committee discussed two more probable asbestosis cases that had not had an autopsy.[103] In the same year,

[99] 72/1548–9. Hills to RAW, 4 Nov. 1974.
[100] By 1975, the annual spending on the medical programme at TBA was stated to have been £260,000.
[101] 301/371. S. Marks to JLB, 19 Dec. 1978.
[102] 153/276. TBA Health Committee Minutes, 61st Meeting, 11 Mar. 1971.
[103] 153/269 TBA Health Committee Minutes, 62nd Meeting, 2 Aug. 1971.

Lewinsohn identified two retrospective mesotheliomas: one in 1958 and another in 1959.[104] In July 1973, the Health Committee was 'surprised to see that there had not been an inquest in the case of a 62-year-old lady who had died of carcinoma of the lung due to asbestosis . . . [and] . . . also surprised to find that there had been neither post-mortem nor inquest in the case of a 66-year-old man who had worked over 23 years in Harridge Mill and had been observed to be suffering from a chest complaint'.[105] In 1975, James Hargreaves died, having retired early from TBA after thirty-one years in carding and spinning. The post-mortem revealed cancer of the mediastinum and stomach: but no inquest was held, despite the fact that Hargreaves had been suspended with asbestosis in 1971. Also in 1975, Sidney Johnson, a suspended TBA worker, collapsed and died from a heart attack, and yet there was no inquest. No lump sum payment was therefore made to his widow, Elizabeth, who also had asbestosis. Meanwhile, life's misfortunes continued to hide the prevalence of asbestos-related disease. In 1973, suspended worker Florence Turner died in a domestic fire and so it was classed as an 'accidental death'.

As in the 1930s and 1940s, the government Pneumoconiosis Medical Panel remained a stumbling block for sick workers. Chapter 3 highlighted the conservatism of its diagnoses—a feature that continued after 1970. An interesting sidelight on PMP diagnoses is shed by the TBA policy of suspending workers from their jobs with 'early stage' asbestosis. These individuals still needed to apply to the PMP for disability benefit (if they wished). Some workers were 'suspended' by the company, but refused a certificate by the PMP. Mary Barrett, for example, was a TBA carder and spinner, who was moved from her job in 1967 due to pleural disease, 'possibly due to asbestos exposure'. Yet the PMP rejected her claim in the following year. She died from asbestosis in 1982.[106]

PMP disagreements with pathologists and coroners also continued into the 1970s. An inquest on Enoch Stockton in 1971 decided that death was due to bronchitis with asbestosis as a contributory factor. The PMP decided the latter was *not* a factor. In the case of Roberts' sprayer Donald Sharp, the pathologist found that the main cause of death in 1974 was coronary artery disease, though she believed that the man's asbestosis (he had been suspended in 1970 after only about eight years' work) had made him less able to survive a heart attack. The Panel, however, ruled that this was not a factor in the death.[107] One asbestotic TBA worker, Arthur Mellowdew, died of lung cancer in 1976. However, despite the fact that

[104] 71/1839. Medical Officer's Report, 2 Aug. 1971.
[105] 153/216. TBA Health Committee Minutes, 68th Meeting, 25 July 1973.
[106] 46/1389–1401: Mary Barratt (1911–82) file; *Rochdale Observer*, 27 July 1982.
[107] 33/387: Enoch Stockton (1905–71) file; 116/873–6: Donald Sharp (1931–74) inquest depositions.

the pleurae over both lungs were thickened, the PMP decided that asbestosis was not a factor in the man's death.[108]

What of compensation? Turner & Newall remained locked into the culture of the *ex gratia*, which remained derisory. The widow of TBA worker Emile Moulin received a mere £1 a week *ex gratia* after his death from mesothelioma in 1970. When a suspended Roberts' worker, Walter Talbot, died in 1972 from a clear case of industrial disease (bronchitis, emphysema, and asbestosis), the company refused the solicitor's claim for a lump sum and paid the widow £2 per week *ex gratia*. The solicitor was asked to bear in mind that this was subject to annual review.[109] The habit of refusing to accept blame and liability also remained. A TBA joiner, Eric Fielding, had retired and moved to Norwich. He died in 1976, aged 74, and the coroner returned a verdict of 'broncho-pneumonia due to carcinoma of the bronchus with metastatic deposits in the brain due to the industrial disease of asbestosis'. A TBA manager commented: 'the cause of death has never been established and I think there was considerable doubt that his death has been caused by working in our industry.'[110]

The changing legislation for tort claims had altered the picture for claimants. Before the 1960s, common law actions against Turner & Newall were rare; after 1970, the number of such actions increased. Claims against the company almost doubled from 47 in 1973 to 89 in 1976.[111] Over 80 per cent of the claims were from Newalls' workers, especially contract laggers. The average cost of settlements also doubled in the same period from about £4,000 to about £8,000 (though part of this rise was due to inflation). By 1976, most claims were apparently being settled, though invariably out of court. As Turner & Newall's secretary remarked, regarding a Cape Asbestos settlement: 'We know very well the risks involved and the increasing awareness of plaintiffs of what might be achieved . . . [so] . . . all possible steps must be taken to prevent asbestosis cases reaching the courts.'[112] On the other hand, many plaintiffs remained very reluctant to take legal action: one widow actually wrote to Turner & Newall in 1974 apologizing for the fact that she was employing a solicitor after her husband's death from mesothelioma.[113] The legal costs could be daunting. One personal-injury solicitor, who began taking on asbestos cases in this

---

[108] Bilateral pleural thickening was not prescribed as an asbestos-related disease until 1985—the same year as lung cancer.

[109] 115/2131. TAC Construction Materials Ltd to Hepworth & Chadwick, 16 June 1972.

[110] 32/1872. I. Waters to SM[arks?], 30 June 1980. In 1970, a common law claim settled this case for £750 plus costs.

[111] 500/263. 'Asbestos Disease Litigation'.

[112] 160/289. A. D. N. Jones to J. A. E. Clogg, 14 Aug. 1963.

[113] 113/2007–8. Mrs A. T. Knott to TBA, 12 Oct. 1974. She wrote: 'I feel mean I have done this to your company as I appreciate how they were good to my husband in the past, but with me not being able to go out to work . . . I won't be able to manage.'

period, recalls: 'People were terrified of the cost. It gets through to you and you start keeping awake at nights. It was a horrible atmosphere.'[114] Nevertheless, workers and relatives were now becoming more active in seeking recompense.

Even some doctors were beginning to push relatives in this direction. In 1972, a doctor advised the relatives of asbestosis victim Sidney Sharratt to see a solicitor after TBA had offered only a yearly £104 *ex gratia*. In this instance, the relatives—shocked at the inadequacy of the offer and still numbed with grief—did not take legal action, partly because of the expected high legal costs. In another case, in 1973, a consultant physician told a Ferodo worker's widow to claim after an inquest verdict of industrial disease. The widow told Turner & Newall she did not want 'any trouble over money matters', while the company advised her to take an *ex gratia*. With a solicitor's help, she eventually received £750 in 1977.[115]

At TBA, the relatives of carder and spinner Joby Owen, helped by solicitors Whittles, won a £6,000 settlement in 1975 after his death from lung cancer and asbestosis. The rise in mesothelioma cases seems to have triggered even higher awards. For example, after the mesothelioma death of John Morris (1920–76)—a TBA worker for only five years—his relatives enlisted the help of solicitors and Roger Stott MP. Turner & Newall denied liability, but settled for £10,000. In 1976, Whittles won a settlement of £15,000 (and costs) on behalf of disabled TAC warehouse packer Leonard Lythgoe, who died in the same year. This seems to have set a record, though there could be wide variations in death payments and out-of-court settlements. Overall, the amounts were not large for such a big company, but the trend in payments and claims was steadily upwards.

The pressure on the company was increasing. Asbestos was an international industry, in which bad publicity could have worldwide repercussions. Particularly damaging for the UK industry was the situation in America, where the leading asbestos firms were unable to counter Selikoff's constant criticisms. Turner & Newall became so concerned about the feeble American response to Selikoff that in 1970 they sent Stephen Holmes and M. F. Howe to New York to acquaint Johns–Manville with the work of the ARC and also foster an American equivalent of the AIC. Accordingly, an Asbestos Information Association was formed in the US in November 1970. However, its immediate impact was limited and it could do little to deflect the impending American ban on asbestos spray. Meanwhile in Sweden, one of the main shipyards had virtually banned asbestos by 1970 and there was trade union pressure for a complete ban. In Denmark, asbestos insulation was prohibited in 1972 and other countries, such as Holland, were moving in the same direction.

---

[114] Author's interview with John Pickering, 8 Sept. 1997.
[115] 33/235: E. Bradley (1904–73) file.

Turner & Newall, as the linchpin of the ARC and AIC, played an important role in organizing the counter-attack. The AIC launched major press campaigns from its London base (situated in the offices of Hill & Knowlton, who also represented tobacco companies). In 1970, industry-funded advertisements with the theme, 'where would we be without asbestos', appeared in leading journals and national newspapers. A film 'Why Asbestos?' was produced and distributed to universities, schools, architects, and engineers, and a special leaflet was prepared for school children. The AIC published articles minimizing the cancer risk and dismissing concerns about casual and environmental exposure. Workers were told that new regulations would ensure that the risk of asbestosis in long-serving employees would be only 1 in 100. No mention was made of the long-term cancer risk. Workers already ill would be helped by 'good' medical care and 'fair' compensation: 'This responsibility the asbestos industry has willingly undertaken and many millions of pounds have been paid both in direct compensation and in maintaining the earnings of employees transferred to lighter less exposed work.'[116] Another activity was the publication of booklets which stressed the word *safety*. Titles included: 'Asbestos—Safety and Control', 'Asbestos—Public not at Risk', and 'Safety of Buildings Incorporating Asbestos'. These publications disseminated the industry's sacred tenets: that asbestos diseases were a legacy of the past, that such diseases—even mesothelioma—were the result of breathing 'excessive' dust, and that present regulations were adequate. For a more technical and commercial readership, the ARC (which was intertwined with the AIC) also produced a number of 'Control and Safety Guides', on subjects as diverse as protective equipment and the application of spray, which all underlined the message that asbestos could be used safely.

Another of the asbestos industry's tenets that lodged itself firmly in the public's consciousness in the early 1970s was the belief that crocidolite was the most dangerous type of asbestos. This idea had a long lineage, and even in the inter-war years workers had regarded crocidolite as particularly dangerous (though they regarded amosite as worse).[117] John Waddell had mused to John Knox in 1956, after a spate of suspensions at

---

[116] 'Asbestos—Killer Dust or Miracle Fibre', *Industrial Safety* (Sept. 1976), 11.

[117] In 1946, Cape's physician, Dr Hubert Wyers, highlighted that workers regarded chrysotile as the least dangerous, while 'blue asbestos is regarded . . . to be more dangerous'. As regards amosite, 'its reputation as regards health [is] utterly pernicious; it is seldom now used'. See Wyers, 'That Legislative Measures Have Proved Generally Effective in the Control of Asbestosis' (Glasgow University MD, 1946), 48. Interestingly, TBA director Wilfred Ellison recalled in 1968: 'In spite of the virtues of amosite as an insulator I steadfastly refused to process it at Rochdale. I was convinced that it was lethal when released to the atmosphere. (There were many reasons for this and I will enumerate them if you wish—John Knox knew my views.) Sir Samuel and I had a battle royal and to his great credit he eventually issued an edict—'no dry processing of amosite'. See 301/336–7. Ellison to J. W. [Waddell?], 10 Jan. 1968.

Roberts: 'I cannot help wondering if crocidolite asbestos is more lethal than chrysotile.'[118] The pathbreaking South African mesothelioma research in the late 1950s added scientific weight to this idea: it had implicated crocidolite as the key causative agent. The government's *Memorandum on the Use of Asbestos* in 1967 had accepted this link and recommended the strict control of crocidolite, though it also noted that the evidence was not clear cut. Most asbestos factories (even predominantly chrysotile users, such as TBA) used a mixture of fibres, so that blaming a particular type was difficult. Asbestos diseases, especially mesothelioma, seemed to be especially prevalent at 'blue' factories such as Roberts and among sprayers—but, equally, these tended to be the dustiest locations and jobs. It was also known that mesotheliomas occurred at factories where only chrysotile had been used (such as at TAC in Erith). Critics pointed out that since chrysotile was in such widespread use (it accounted for about 95 per cent of the total asbestos used worldwide), it was hardly likely that all the country's mesotheliomas could be caused by the small tonnage of crocidolite.[119] The suspicion remained that the government and industry had phased out crocidolite so rapidly for economic rather than health reasons: it was a small percentage of production and could be easily substituted. Certainly the so-called 'amphibole hypothesis' was useful to the asbestos industry in the 1970s. The AIC made much of the voluntary crocidolite ban, agreed that the risk of mesothelioma was greatest with blue asbestos from South Africa, and—in turn—suggested that using white asbestos was safe within the government threshold.[120]

These debates took place against some alarming mortality trends. UK mesothelioma deaths (as recorded on death certificates) were increasing each year and were well over 200 annually by 1973. The mesothelioma death that year of Margaret Chrimes, the TBA switchboard operator (mentioned above), should have been a warning to the company. So, too, should the death of 40-year-old Washington worker Margaret Carruthers in 1974. Her mesothelioma and asbestosis had resulted from only two weeks' work in 1952 in the Washington factory's insulation division (though the exposure was probably compounded by living with her sister, who also worked there and died of asbestosis).[121] This was soon followed by the death of 46-year-old Ronald Lightfoot in 1975. He had spent a mere

---

[118] 5/462. Waddell to Knox, 24 Apr. 1957.

[119] See L. T. Stayner *et al.*, 'Occupational Exposure to Chrysotile Asbestos and Cancer Risk: A Review of the Amphibole Hypothesis', *American Journal of Public Health* 86 (Feb. 1996), 179–86; A. H. Smith and C. C. Wright, 'Chrysotile Asbestos is the Main Cause of Pleural Mesothelioma', *American Journal of Industrial Medicine* 30 (1996), 252–66.

[120] 7/1032. AIC, *Mesothelioma* (June 1976). Initially, TBA had been reluctant to admit that it had processed crocidolite at Rochdale since the 1920s. However, after 1970 the company was keen to link its mesotheliomas to a product that it had discontinued.

[121] 600/1115. *Sunderland Echo*, 31 July 1974.

ten weeks in 1954 as a Newalls' lagger, doing labouring jobs in the Barrow shipyards—enough exposure to cause pleural mesothelioma.[122] Another Newalls' labourer in Warrington died from peritoneal mesothelioma in 1973 after six months' work.[123] Such cases were mirrored nationally in the government's Mesothelioma Register, which had been launched in 1967. It showed, for example, a victim who had spent a day sawing up asbestos-cement sheets for a shed and another whose hobby was repairing brakes.[124]

For a while, the asbestos industry's propaganda went unchallenged, though not everyone was convinced. In 1974, a TAC environmental manager gave an interview to a house journal in which he played down the dangers of asbestos and gave TAC a 'clean bill of health'. The article brought a response from the wife of TAC worker, Edward Carnes, who was dying of mesothelioma:

My husband has read the truth about asbestos in your last issue . . . I wish I had the ability to really let you know the misery of suffering of my husband who is a victim of pleural asbestosis this past eight months. You can guess just how he felt after reading your article and so I write on his behalf. He's in terrible pain periodically in his chest, which nearly drives him mad. It's as much as he can do to walk from bed to chair without gasping for breath. He's had radiotherapy treatment which did no good. He's also had a new drug injected in his back. It still is no better and with all that he also has to be aspirated, which means he has fluid withdrawn from his lung every week, which has been repeated up to 27 times up to last Monday. There doesn't seem anything else they can do at the hospital as they do not confess to know a lot about asbestosis. The despondency and frustration he suffers no one knows but myself. He has worked nearly forty years at Rhoose . . . [but] . . . now no one cares or even gives him a second thought. So no more please that asbestos isn't a hazard to health.[125]

Such letters counted for little against the influence that Turner & Newall wielded through the ARC and AIC. These bodies greatly increased their activity in the early 1970s. ARC member-companies were subscribing over £70,000 a year by 1976, which was directed into research at various universities and health groups at Reading, Cambridge, Leeds, Manchester, Bradford, and Pittsburgh. In 1971, an ARC Foundation was established within the Institute of Occupational Medicine in Edinburgh. Meanwhile, the ARC fostered links with the Health & Safety Executive, the MRC, and the International Agency for Research on Cancer. Soon the ARC could claim that over sixty research papers had been published with its support.

---

[122] 600/1284–1354: R. Lightfoot (1929–75). Possibly some exposure had occurred in the six years Lightfoot had previously spent as a stoker.

[123] 600/1116–22. George Murphy (1922–73) file.

[124] M. Greenberg and T. A. Lloyd Davies, 'Mesothelioma Register 1967–68', *British Journal of Industrial Medicine* 31 (1974), 91–104, 96.

[125] 114/1512–13. Mrs P. Carnes to TAC, Rhoose, 8 Aug. 1974.

Turner & Newall also pushed funding towards the TUC Centenary Institute of Occupational Health (at the London School of Hygiene & Tropical Medicine), partly because one of its researchers, Dr Muriel Newhouse, was said to have championed a dose-response relationship for mesothelioma—a theory that was 'important to the industry'.[126]

By 1976, the AIC budget had reached £115,000 a year (with Turner & Newall providing £65,400). One of the AIC's roles was to foster co-operation among asbestos information bodies and lobby groups. In 1971, the AIC organized in London the first International Conference on Asbestos Information Bodies. (A fully fledged Asbestos International Association was to be formed in 1974.) The deputy chairman of the AIC, M. F. Howe, noted with satisfaction that there were now eleven asbestos information groups worldwide. The AIC hoped that the conference would galvanize its European and American friends. Strategies were discussed in warlike terms and at the end of the conference Howe made a clarion call to the industry:

The maxim 'let sleeping dogs lie' has a good deal in its favour when the tempo is slow and public and press interest is light. But sleeping dogs wake up suddenly and use their voices and their teeth. And when they are awake they will not sleep again! That is a lesson which we have learned in Britain and I am sure the AIA/NA has learned in the USA. We have learned the painful way and perhaps we can save you some pain. *You must prepare in advance.*[127]

In Britain, the sleeping dogs were awakening. On 28 June 1971, Granada TV's 'World in Action' devoted a programme to Cape's Acre Mill factory. This plant, which was situated in the textile town of Hebden Bridge near Halifax, had processed white and blue asbestos from 1939 until its closure in 1970. The company was facing scores of claims for asbestos-related diseases, which the TV documentary alleged were due to persistent failures by an incompetent Factory Inspectorate to apply the 1931 Regulations. Turner & Newall regarded it as 'the most damaging attack yet made on asbestos in Britain' and noted that it had caused a hardening of attitude on the part of the Factory Inspectorate.[128]

In the following year, the asbestos industry and the Factory Inspectors were under attack again. In April 1972, the *Sunday Times Colour Supplement* ran an article on 'The Dangerous Dust'.[129] It was an example of the hard-hitting investigative journalism for which that newspaper was then renowned. This time the target was Central Asbestos, one of the members of the AIC, which had operated a factory in south-east London. The authors of the article, journalist Peter Gillman and solicitor Anthony

---

[126] G2179. W. P Howard to C. W. Newton, 21 Oct. 1975.

[127] 117/1367. 'International Conference of Asbestos Information Bodies', London, 24–5 Nov. 1971, 67.

[128] 70/222–5. T & N board meeting, 30 June 1971.

[129] P. Gillman and A. Woolf, 'The Dangerous Dust', *Sunday Times*, 2 Apr. 1972.

Woolf, highlighted the plight of Bob Smith, a 46-year-old who had worked for Central Asbestos between 1958 and 1966: 50 per cent disabled with asbestosis, Smith was breathless with the slightest exertion and his weight had fallen from $11\frac{1}{2}$ to 8 stone. A photograph showed him with his 69-year-old father; yet Bob Smith, with his haggard face and clubbed fingers, looked older. Again, the article was especially critical of the Factory Inspectorate. The latter had eventually sued Central Asbestos in 1964 for breaches of the Asbestos Regulations, but the company had only been fined £170 plus 10*s* [50p] costs.[130] Yet, when Smith and six of his fellow workers eventually took Central Asbestos to court, they won £86,469 damages. Smith was awarded £16,388, but he died only a year after the *Sunday Times* article was published. Turner & Newall thought that the article had given a 'wholly unrepresentative impression of work with asbestos'.[131]

Media reporting increased the political pressure on the Factory Inspectorate, which was now being reorganized. The Employment Medical Advisory Service Act was passed in 1972. The former Medical Factory Inspectorate was replaced by the Employment Medical Advisory Service, whose duties were widened to include the identification of health hazards by clinical and epidemiological studies and evaluation of control measures. A survey of asbestos workers was started in 1971, which included a special schedule of air sampling, separate from the factory management and Factory Inspectors. EMAS had the authority to enter premises and examine workers whenever necessary.

In 1974, the government passed the Health & Safety at Work Act, which extended protective legislation to the 8 million or so workers who were still outside any legislation. The Act aimed to secure the health and safety of *all* persons at work, and it imposed on the employer several general duties, such as the maintenance of safe working conditions and the environmental control of noxious substances. Manufacturers were obliged to ensure that their products were safe in use and that customers were given sufficient warnings. The Act also merged several of the Inspectorates (including that for the factories) into a Health & Safety Executive. The general aim was to increase centralization, boost specialization, and also double the number of Inspectors.[132]

The Health & Safety at Work Act was particularly significant for the asbestos manufacturers. Soon Turner & Newall were being asked by customers to sign undertakings that their products were safe. The company's own managers became concerned that they could be fined or imprisoned. It was clear that some kind of labelling would be required. The Act launched a new phase of adverse media reporting. The whole validity of

---

[130] The conviction is not listed in the Inspectorate's annual reports.
[131] 700/604. T & N board meeting, 31 Mar. 1972.
[132] There were 700 Inspectors at this time, covering 400,000 factories.

the 2-fibre standard was being questioned on the television; while in America, journalist Paul Brodeur was attacking the asbestos industry in articles in the *New Yorker*.[133] Even some Turner & Newall workers were publicizing the dangers of asbestos. In 1974, John Todd, an ex-Newalls worker in Scotland, began campaigning vigorously against the industry. As one TBA director remarked: 'Publicity associated with the Act effectively primed "the bomb", which was [about] to explode . . . over the Acre Mill affair at Hebden Bridge.'[134]

Criticism of Cape's activities in Hebden Bridge had not abated. Northern newspaper articles on the unfolding health disaster demonstrated that although chronic occupational diseases have a low profile, once they develop on a large enough scale they do not quickly disappear. There were demands for a public enquiry from Max Madden, the Labour MP for Sowerby, and from BBC TV's 'Horizon' team, whose documentary on the 'Killer Dust' had dealt mainly with Hebden Bridge.[135] These demands were rejected. However, Madden was more successful with an indirect approach to the Ombudsman, Sir Alan Marre, through asbestosis sufferer and former Acre Mill worker Tom Buick. The latter's 'complaint' to the Ombudsman was that the Factory Inspectors had failed to apply the 1931 Regulations. The Ombudsman's report in March 1976 confirmed the complaint and depicted an appalling catalogue of shortcomings by the Factory Inspectorate that had extended over decades.[136] Marre's conclusion was nothing if not understated: 'I have . . . concluded from my investigation that the attention given to Acre Mill [by the Inspectors] was not as high as it could and should have been.'

The Acre Mill débâcle led directly to the formation of an Asbestos Action Group in Hebden Bridge, which first met in 1975. Besides former Cape employees and those afflicted by asbestos diseases, the Group brought together politicians (such as Max Madden), lawyers, and doctors. These included John Pickering, an outspoken local solicitor, who had begun specializing in personal injury work on behalf of Acre Mill workers. Another prominent supporter of the Group was Dr Bertram Mann, a Halifax chest physician, who was involved with nearly all the asbestosis cases at Hebden Bridge.[137]

---

[133] Brodeur's articles formed the basis for a book, *Outrageous Misconduct* (1985).

[134] 20/203–4. N. Rhodes, 'The Impact of Adverse Publicity', 1976.

[135] BBC2 'Horizon', 'Killer Dust', 20 Jan. 1975.

[136] A. Marre, 'Report . . . to Max Madden MP . . . into a Complaint made by J. P. Buick', 3rd Report of Parl. Commissioner for Administration: HC 259, Session 1975–6, 25 March 1976: Case C. 353/Y, 189–211.

[137] 127/1409–12. R. Picot, 'Notes on First Public Meeting of Asbestos Action Group', 2 May 1975. Later Mann reported that of the 2,200 employed at Hebden Bridge between 1939 and 1970, 262 had asbestosis (12 per cent) and there had been 77 deaths (some with mesothelioma). See Mann, 'Pulmonary Asbestosis with Special Reference to an Epidemic at Hebden Bridge', *Journal of the Royal College of Physicians* 12 (July 1978), 297–307.

Another important victims' pressure-group had emerged in London—and from an unlikely source. Nancy Tait was a civil servant, whose husband, Bill, was a telephone engineer. He died in 1968 from mesothelioma. However, it was not until 1972 that the DHSS were persuaded that Bill Tait's illness was the result of occupational exposure to asbestos. Angered by the struggle for compensation and the apparent ignorance and secrecy of the authorities and the asbestos industry, Nancy Tait began her own research into asbestos diseases and also began campaigning on behalf of sick workers and their relatives. In 1976, she was awarded a Churchill Fellowship to travel to Europe and North America to visit factories, mines, scientists, and government representatives. In the same year she wrote a paperback booklet, *Asbestos Kills*, to promote an awareness of asbestos diseases. Tait's attack on asbestos was wide-ranging, but the thrust of her arguments covered some specific areas of concern. One was that chrysotile was *not* harmless and could also cause mesothelioma; another was that the PMP and other government departments were failing to record or accept many legitimate cases of asbestos disease. Inadequate compensation was another evil that Tait highlighted.

Tait's booklet received wide publicity. The 'killer dust' was now firmly in the headlines, especially after further news stories about sprayed-asbestos in a block of council flats in Deptford, London. This sparked a nationwide search for crocidolite in schools and hospitals, with premises being closed if the asbestos had to be removed. The industry's response was to agree rapidly to a voluntary warning scheme with the government, in which certain asbestos products would carry a label.[138] This had been recommended by a DHSS Report in 1968, which had only been made public in 1975 due to Tait's activities. A logo was devised with a lower-case letter 'a' above the vague words: 'Take Care with Asbestos'. Below in smaller letters were the words: 'Breathing asbestos dust can damage health. Observe the safety rules.' However, there was as yet no labelling of exports, mainly due to the influence of the industry's International Asbestos Information Conference.

The AIC printed a rejoinder to Tait's booklet, entitled *'Asbestos Kills'? A Commentary on Mrs Nancy Tait's Thesis*, but it did little to counter her influence. Although lacking in resources, she was strong-minded, indefatigable, infuriatingly apolitical, and with a personal history that guaranteed sympathy. Attacking her would not prove a fruitful exercise. On the other hand, firms like Turner & Newall, with their antediluvian compensation policies and *ex gratias*, were an easy target for Tait. The company felt her impact after 1973, following the death from asbestosis and lung cancer of Samuel Fisher, a 66-year-old worker from Hindley Green. Fisher's widow

---

[138] Asbestos products in which the fibre was modified by bonding agents or coatings were not included in the labelling scheme.

had written to Turner & Newall complaining about her financial circumstances. After describing how her husband had died and suffered, she said that his death had left her with nothing, apart from a small widow's pension. Aged 63, she still had to work:

Anyway when your firm sent me [a] cheque for £600 my family thought it was [an] insult. I had to sign that I had no further claim on you before I received it. How mean can [a] big firm like Turner & Newall get . . . it is [a] very great insult to a good man and to ease my mind I am thinking to write to one of the papers telling them to see what they think.[139]

The personnel manager was promptly dispatched to mollify her over a cup of tea, but her case was taken up by Tait. In 1976, Tait contacted the Turner & Newall pensions officer on the subject of Mrs Fisher's *ex gratia*:

the payments made to Mrs Fisher (one only of £600 and the small pension of £4.50 a month in 1971, rising to £5.97 a month in 1976), make nonsense of the claim published by the Asbestos Information Committee, that the asbestos industry has willingly undertaken its responsibility to sufferers from asbestos disease and their dependants and has paid many millions of pounds in direct compensation . . . [When] the industry [has] embarked on a £500,000 advertising campaign and when Turner & Newall [has] announced record pre-tax profits of £15.8 million for six months, I feel sure there has been some mistake.[140]

Turner & Newall regarded Tait as a self-appointed meddler, but she forced them to mount a review. It revealed a scandalous situation. The *ex-gratia* widow's pension in asbestosis cases had remained static since the 1930s at £1 a week for hourly paid employees and £2.50 a week for widows of supervisors. In 1976 the total cost to Turner & Newall of all its widows' pensions was a mere £4,576. For reasons of 'equity, company image and expediency', the rate was lifted at a stroke in December 1976 to £6 per week for the hourly paid, £9 for widows of supervisors, and £12 for managers' widows.[141] Even though this rise did not remove the provisional nature of *ex gratias*, it was a striking indication of how pressure groups could influence the policy of even the most powerful companies, albeit in a modest way.

The growth of this opposition had not been without its impact on the asbestos industry. The £½ million public relations campaign that Tait had mentioned was to counter the publicity 'kept alive by groups with powerful motivations', which Turner & Newall described as follows:

• Members of Parliament, with slender majorities, who have built up local reputations as champions of asbestotic constituents;

[139] 65/1613. Mrs M. Fisher to T & N, 1 Dec. 1974.
[140] 65/1540. Tait to O. G. Oliver, 29 Oct. 1976.
[141] 67/2201–2. Board meeting, 13 Dec. 1976.

- physicians and solicitors whose professional reputations now depend on acceptance of an extreme view of the risk;
- Mrs Nancy Tait, whose personal motivation as a widow is understandable; and
- several journalists who have consistently followed the Tait line, appear to believe it, and write for *The Times*, the *Sunday Times*, the *Guardian*, the *Yorkshire Post*, and the *New Scientist*.[142]

However, the industry had another problem on the horizon. In the aftermath of Hebden Bridge, the Labour government had accepted the Ombudsman's criticisms and ordered a national enquiry into asbestos disease by the Health & Safety Commission. It seemed that Turner & Newall and other asbestos firms were at last to be submitted to public scrutiny.

[142] 127/957. Asbestos & Health Progress Report, 30 June 1976.

10

Turner & Newall on Trial

'You murderer.'

50/2443–4. Message to Turner & Newall from P. J. Matthews,
June 1982.

THE SIMPSON COMMITTEE

The government Advisory Committee on Asbestos (ACA) was headed by
the chairman of the Health & Safety Commission, (Sir) Bill Simpson, an
ex-trades unionist with impeccable Labour Party credentials. The ACA
held its first meeting in June 1976 with a straightforward remit: to review
the health risks arising from asbestos exposure among workers and the
public and then make any necessary safety recommendations.

It was not a full public enquiry. A three-day session 'in public' was
planned in June 1977, but there was to be no cross-examination of witnesses. Instead the Committee would examine submissions. On the
other hand, a key feature of the enquiry was that it would consider evidence from all sides. The days when industrial health standards were
simply agreed behind the scenes by meetings between manufacturers and
the government had gone (or so it appeared). After the mid-1970s, the
development of pressure groups and increasing trade union involvement ensured that discussions would not be entirely monopolized by
the industry.

The Hebden Bridge activists were represented through Max Madden
MP. On behalf of Asbestos Action, he called for, *inter alia*, a reduction in
the safety limit to 0.5 f/cc, better compensation payments, and greatly
improved medical monitoring, especially among insulation workers.
Nancy Tait reiterated many of the criticisms from *Asbestos Kills*, making
her submission as a private individual (though she was supported by a
wide range of interested people, such as Madden, June Robinson, Lord
Plant, Bob Cryer, and Lord Avebury). The trade unions, after many
decades of inaction, had now found a voice. In fact, the fifteen-member
committee included three trade unionists, representing the TGWU,
UCATT, and the National Union of Dyers. Most unions made their comments under the blanket of the TUC, which submitted a wide-ranging

review. The TUC's major recommendation was for the threshold to be lowered to 0.2 f/cc for all types of asbestos (with crocidolite banned). The limit was only an *interim* measure (not a recommended safe level), until asbestos could be substituted and its use ended. *Socialist Worker*, which had consistently campaigned against asbestos hazards through its exposés of Cape and Central Asbestos, told the Committee that Britain should follow Sweden and relinquish asbestos as fast as possible. A zero limit was essential. It wanted a *public* enquiry to discover how the industry had escaped with minimal regulation for so long, both at home and overseas. Equally uncompromising was the brief of the British Society for Social Responsibility in Science, a socialist organization founded in 1968. Leading the BSSRS's campaign against asbestos was Alan Dalton, a pharmaceutical chemist and adviser on environmental hazards. The BSSRS attacked the 2-fibre standard, argued that there was no safe level, and wanted trade union safety representatives to be given more power.

Ranged against these organizations were the leading asbestos companies—the Asbestos Cement Manufacturers' Association, BBA, Cape, Eternit, and of course Turner & Newall. The latter produced the most detailed submission of all, which aimed to quash any fears about the continued use of asbestos by arguing that the 2-fibre standard was safe and that further regulation was needless. The main thrust of Turner & Newall's argument was that:

- in its post-1951 cohort of TBA workers, there had been no excess mortality among workers exposed for more than ten years;
- in the TBA weaving shed (where dust levels had been at 2 f/cc for at least twenty-five years), there had been no asbestos-related disease among those who had started work after 1951;
- no cases of mesothelioma had occurred at Turner & Newall after 'slight' exposure;
- there was no record of disease for TBA non-textile processes;
- asbestos was unique and there was no single substitute.

Turner & Newall relied upon the evidence of the Knox–Doll cohort of TBA workers and trumpeted the work of the Asbestosis Research Council, which was covered in a separate submission. In its own evidence, the company included copies of 'killer dust' newspaper articles to show the 'hysterical' opposition that was threatening jobs.[1]

The 'public' three-day session among the various parties in the summer of 1977 was predictably often heated. The ACA published the submissions in the same year;[2] and Simpson and his team then considered the

---

[1] 47/2002. T & N printed submission to ACA, Sept. 1976.
[2] HSE, *Selected Written Evidence Submitted to the Advisory Committee on Asbestos, 1976–77* (1977).

evidence. The ACA published its final report in 1979 in two volumes: the first contained the main text, setting out the principal facts and major recommendations; the second contained specially commissioned scientific reports.[3]

The ACA reports present a mass of useful information for the historian, but its immediate impact was negligible. The government had followed a tried and trusted formula: announce an inquiry to satisfy public opinion, allow various distinguished experts to cogitate for several years; deliberate over the recommendations—by which time, with a bit of luck, the original problem will have been solved or completely forgotten.

The Committee's conclusions were hardly the stuff of which headlines were made. A ban was recommended on the import of crocidolite (already voluntarily withdrawn by the industry); and it was also thought best that spraying should be banned (another defunct process). The stripping of old lagging should be done by licensed contractors, but the ACA did not suggest that it should be an offence for a client to use a non-licensed removal firm. Dust was still to be monitored by the membrane filter method (despite the fact that the ACA had confirmed its gross inaccuracy) and not the electron microscope. The key proposal as regards dust in the workplace was that the control limit for exposure to chrysotile should become 1 f/cc by the end of 1980, with 0.5 f/cc the target for amosite (thus introducing a controversial differential between fibres). This tighter threshold reflected the influence of Julian Peto, an Oxford cancer epidemiologist, whose presentations to the Committee were strongly critical of the BOHS 2-fibre limit.

These, of course, were only recommendations and there was no timetable for their actual implementation. The asbestos industry would first be consulted about the ACA's targets and Turner & Newall director Harry Hardie, who had been on the Simpson Committee, made it clear to the government that there was no chance anything would happen by the end of 1980.[4] It would be some time, too, before the reaction of trade unions and the public would be known.

Turner & Newall immediately began a confidential assessment of the implications of tighter controls.[5] The situation, as Turner & Newall saw it, was different from 1969. The Regulations then had set a 2 f/cc target, but the industry had not legally been required to meet that threshold until

---

[3] HSE, *Asbestos. Vol. 1: Final Report of the Advisory Committee. Asbestos: Vol. 2: Papers Commissioned by the Committee* (1979). The ACA had already published an interim statement: *Asbestos—Health Hazards and Precautions (An Interim Statement by the ACA)* (1977); and two other reports: *Work on Thermal Acoustic Insulation and Sprayed Coatings* (1978); *Asbestos: Measurement and Monitoring of Asbestos in Air* (1978).

[4] 151/150–1. Hardie to S. Newton, HSE, 16 Jan. 1979.

[5] 150/1181–1209. 'The Economic Implications of a Tighter Hygiene Standard for Asbestos in the UK', June 1978.

it was ready. Turner & Newall had not needed to revise radically its basic strategy of steady improvement, with the result that the 2 f/cc threshold had not been reached until 1977. The problem now, however, was that existing textile equipment (notably carding, spinning, and doubling) could not be controlled to a tighter standard than 2 fibres.[6] A major investment would be needed to re-equip, but this would necessarily be complicated by market factors. What, for example, would be the reaction of asbestos users to the ACA report? Would overseas competitors, working under less stringent regulations, be able to dump goods in the British market?

Hanging over all these deliberations were asbestos substitutes, which had never been wholeheartedly embraced by Turner & Newall while it could make money on asbestos. Now, however, it was clear (to everyone but the company) that their time had come. As we have seen, asbestos was not unique. Its heat resistance and insulating properties were not outstanding enough in some areas, such as spraying, to prevent successful competition from mineral wools. Other materials that were replacing asbestos included nylon fibre for fireclothes, vermiculite for filters, and ceramic fibres for insulators. Nearly *half* the asbestos fibre imported into the UK in the early 1970s was used for asbestos-cement building materials and products such as floor tiles. The primary function of the asbestos in these applications was to provide mechanical strength—providing that condition was met, then asbestos could be substituted in this field too. Glass fibre looked like the best candidate, though this was one area (like friction materials) where substitution was more difficult and would need more research. Nevertheless, a study published in 1979 concluded: 'For most applications of asbestos, it is possible to find an alternative, often in glass or ceramic fibre.'[7] There was often a cost penalty and also the possibility that the substitutes themselves could cause disease. On the other hand, asbestos was a finite resource, the price of which would inevitably rise—especially in view of political uncertainty in Africa and the fact that asbestos could not be mined at low wages indefinitely. As regards the health hazard: experience with some substitutes was limited, but already it was obvious that they were far less dangerous than asbestos.

The ACA itself had recommended substitutes where possible. However, Turner & Newall maintained its old position: that asbestos was unique for safety requirements, that asbestos could not be beaten on cost, and that there was no guarantee that substitutes were safe. Such attitudes dictated a traditional response to the ACA: superficial compliance with a 1 f/cc standard, combined with a policy of delay until at least the end of

---

[6] 153/1412–13. K. H. Dixon to W. P. Howard, 18 Aug. 1978.
[7] A. M. Pye, 'Alternatives to Asbestos in Industrial Applications', in L. Michaels and S. S. Chissick (eds.), *Asbestos* (1979), i, 339–73, 372.

1982.[8] By then, TBA chief executive Brian Heron believed that the asbestos market would decline by about 30 per cent. He told a fellow director:

I would like to underline that the main reason for delaying the timescale is not the engineering work itself which could probably be completed in about 18 months, but the vital need to gauge the effect of the report on the overall asbestos market . . . I think we are all agreed that the reaction to the ACA report should be played in a low key and that essentially we should focus on a sensible extension of the implementation time-scale recognising, however, that there will be many external forces including the trade unions (although not the union members in our own factories) who will be anxious to see the timescale reduced.[9]

While TBA warned Rochdale folk about lost jobs and in the newspapers inflated the modernization costs from £$\frac{1}{2}$ million to £$1\frac{1}{2}$ million, the company kept up more discreet pressure. At private lunches with government ministers, Turner & Newall raised the spectre of business lost to foreign countries. According to Turner & Newall, harmonization with the EEC (whose asbestos directive would not be due until 1985) was of prime importance. By early 1981, the company's strategy was rewarded: the government informed them that the implementation date for the regulations would be the same as that proposed by the EEC—1 January 1985. Hardie, who obtained a leaked copy of the decision told his fellow directors: 'I do not think we could have expected more.'[10]

Initially, the reaction of Heron's 'external forces' to the ACA report was surprisingly muted. In some respects, this was understandable. The industry was still powerful and its opponents weak. Some of the severest criticism was soon silenced. The BSSRS had continued its campaign against the industry after the ACA hearings with the publication of *Asbestos Killer Dust*.[11] This book, authored by Alan Dalton, was described as a worker/community guide in the fight against asbestos. Dalton's attack on the industry targeted, *inter alia*, Dr Robert Murray, the TUC's former medical adviser. Murray was criticized for his pro-industry views and for his failure to police effectively Cape's activities at Hebden Bridge (when Murray had been a Factory Inspector). Murray sued Dalton, who under English libel law had to satisfy a jury that his statements were true. He failed and Murray was awarded £500. Dalton's supporters would later point to Murray's subsequent activities—as an expert witness for Turner & Newall and as a defender of the use of asbestos—as proof of the truth of the contentious statements. However, this did not help Dalton at the

---

[8] See 150/1086–1101. T & N board meeting to discuss Final Report of ACA, 21 Sept. 1979; 49/1694–1703. TBA, 'Views on the Third Report of the ACA', Oct. 1979.
[9] 49/1826–7. J. Heron to W. P. Howard, 15 Aug. 1979.
[10] 151/69. Hardie memo, 25 Mar. 1981.   [11] A. Dalton, *Asbestos Killer Dust* (1979).

time: he was ordered to pay Murray's legal costs and the £30,000 bill crippled the BSSRS.

Pressure-groups lacked the resources to mount a coherent response to the industry. Without funding, they also lacked the substantial scientific evidence needed to counter the industry's claims. The asbestos firms were still pumping money into the AIC (renamed the Asbestos Information Centre in 1979) and the ARC. By 1982 the ARC budget reached £230,000. After his libel trial, Murray himself approached the head of the Asbestos International Association with a proposal (later rejected), which was intended to show that dockers had not suffered from much asbestos disease and that tearing out asbestos from schools and offices was a waste of the taxpayers' money.[12] Hardly surprisingly, the industry's views were still treated sympathetically by scientists and academics, while the opposition groups (the 'forces of darkness', according to Murray) were regarded with disdain. In a two-volume edited collection of scholarly articles on asbestos and health, published in 1979, one writer expressed dismay at the rise of the self-appointed anti-asbestos lobby and the way in which it (so he contended) manipulated information. Asbestos Action was singled out for comment as an independent group of individuals and representatives. Representatives 'of what?', sneered the editor in the middle of the sentence.[13] *Socialist Worker* was criticized for its description of Hebden Bridge as a 'terrible scandal'.

To be sure, the labour movement lacked the industry's expertise. Trade unions had never funded a major medical study. (It was significant that many of the non-industry ACA witnesses had drawn upon Selikoff's work, because the unions had never sponsored any similar research in the UK.) The unions were now belatedly attempting to catch up by visiting asbestos factories, such as TBA. Overall, their response to the ACA report was hesitant and divided. Some of the unions involved were antagonistic to asbestos. These included the GMWU, which was influenced by its experience with the laggers and also by its health and safety adviser, David Gee. But even the major unions only pushed their opposition so far. The reason was simple: jobs were at stake. As Gee remarked: 'Asbestos workers could choose to settle for a 1 in 1,000 risk [instead of 1 in 100], but that would mean closing down the asbestos industry tomorrow.'[14] The local response to increased regulation was sometimes decidedly guarded. Here there was much convergence between labour and capital, with the health issue very much secondary to jobs. At Rochdale, the staff union APEX had little time for Max Madden, Nancy Tait, and 'rabble rousers'

---

[12] 158/492. Murray to Sir Neville Stack, 29 Nov. 1984.
[13] S. Chissick, 'The Literature Relating to Asbestos', in L. Michaels and S. S. Chissick (eds.), *Asbestos* (1979), i, 114–69, 150.
[14] 162/270–81. 'Asbestos: The Trade Union Response', 1982.

such as Dalton. It also did not fully support the TUC. At the ACA hearings, the APEX representative reported that Turner & Newall's presentation reflected 'great credit on the company in all areas', while 'if the recommendations of the TUC, Max Madden MP, etc., were accepted, the asbestos industry would cease to produce and mass unemployment would result, and, in my opinion, the asbestos textile section would be the first to be affected'.[15]

Nancy Tait, meanwhile, was spurred to greater activity by the ACA experience. In 1977, she was descending an escalator in Euston Station and saw a Turner & Newall advertisement that proclaimed: 'You know asbestos protects—Why not say so!' Outraged at this slogan, in 1978 she decided to formalize her efforts by launching the Society for the Prevention of Asbestosis & Industrial Diseases (SPAID) in her house in Enfield.[16] From there, she continued to publicize injustices in the benefits system and Turner & Newall's niggardly compensation.

The company was now beginning to face bad publicity on this score from other quarters. In 1977, a group of protesters—relatives of sick workers—interrupted a Turner & Newall annual meeting and poured 'blue asbestos' (it was actually washing powder) over chairman, Dennis Burling. The number of common law actions began to rise. In 1982 there were said to be seventeen cases pending, with a provision in the accounts for £240,000.[17] Ferodo workers, for example, began issuing writs for damages in the 1970s and pursued Turner & Newall for relatively large sums. They were not always successful, though by 1980 some claimants were receiving about £10,000.[18] Generally, most of the compensation cases for which we have details were settled for less than £10,000 in the 1970s, though by the end of the decade the £50,000 barrier had been broken.

Even so, many older workers were apathetic. In Leeds, a Turner & Newall manager visited several disabled Roberts' workers in 1977, partly with the purpose of 'uncovering any plots' against the company for better compensation payments. He painted a rosy picture: 'Everyone was pleased to see me and we "raked over" the past and enjoyed our conversations. Mostly the talk was of anything but asbestosis and illness.'[19] He continued: 'John Cromack is not too fit . . . [but] . . . his main topic of conversation is that he has more money than he can spend (!) and has to put all his old age pension in the bank! Albert Rothera is quite ill and feeble . . . I have known him and his family for 30 years . . . and there is no bit-

---

[15] 154/419–30. John R. Brown, Report on ACA Hearings, 18 July 1977.
[16] In 1996 SPAID became OEDA—Occupational & Environmental Diseases Association.
[17] See 128/3874. 'Asbestos and Health' (1982), 13.
[18] For example, Ferodo worker Nathaniel Whyte won £11,000 plus costs for asbestosis in about 1975, apparently while he was still alive (33/358).
[19] 230/332–3. A. R. Milnes to J. D. Pennington, 8 June 1977.

terness or complaint from them. They remember old times with great pleasure and are financially comfortable and secure.' He considered that organized action from former Armley workers was unlikely. That was certainly true of Cromack and Rothera: they were dead within a year from asbestosis. However, there would be other critics of the industry ready to take their place and they had a much less resigned attitude.

ALICE: TRIAL BY TELEVISION

Despite (or perhaps because of) the Simpson Committee, asbestos dropped out of the headlines and Turner & Newall believed that much of the steam from the anti-asbestos lobby had been dissipated. However, it proved to be a lull before the storm. In 1980, a team from Yorkshire TV had begun work on a documentary about the asbestos industry.

'Alice—A Fight for Life' was a two-hour documentary screened on 20 July 1982 at prime viewing time. It featured the agonizing battle against mesothelioma of Alice Jefferson, a 47-year-old Yorkshire mother, who in her youth had worked for a few months at Cape's notorious factory in Hebden Bridge. The documentary makers—producer John Willis and researchers James Cutler and Peter Moore—used Jefferson's fight as a launching pad for a full-scale attack on the asbestos industry. Their agenda was to highlight the slow implementation of the ACA recommendations, which were still in abeyance. They also tried to heighten public awareness of the mesothelioma risk and attempted to show that asbestos-related diseases were more prevalent than industry and government statistics suggested.

'To watch the programme', remarked one reviewer, 'was like being dragged naked over a bed of nails';[20] and even after nearly thirty years the documentary has not lost its power to shock. Its main subject was death: unpleasant enough in any circumstances, but particularly so when it involved the dreadful physical misery of asbestos cancer victims. Besides Alice's final days, which were followed to their inevitable end in the cemetery, viewers were confronted by the sight of children and young adults cut down by mesothelioma; they saw the Cape manager (himself an asbestosis sufferer), who always kept a black tie in his desk for funerals; they saw the white asbestos tips in Canada; and they witnessed the dissembling of doctors, the tight-fistedness of the government, and the denials of the asbestos companies.

Turner & Newall were heavily criticized for misleading the government, the unions, and its workers. In particular, the programme-makers

---

[20] J. Naughton, 'New Campaigners', *Listener*, 29 July 1982.

focused on the company's statements to the Simpson Committee. Turner & Newall had, for example, denied that asbestosis existed in TBA's weaving shed among those employed after 1951; and had stated that none of its mesothelioma cases could be described as due to 'slight exposure'. As 'Alice' highlighted, the first claim—which was a central plank in the company's argument that a 2-fibre limit was safe—was certainly misleading: several weavers employed after 1951 had developed asbestosis.[21] Others had been stricken by mesothelioma, even though they were not scheduled workers. One was Margaret Chrimes, the switchboard operator who had died from mesothelioma in 1973, aged 61; another was Emma Marshall, who had died from the disease in 1972 after ten years as a TBA cleaner. For good measure, 'Alice' highlighted the death of Wallace Childs from mesothelioma in 1979. He had contracted the disease from dust brought home on the overalls of his father, Harry Childs, a Roberts' spinner who had been suspended with asbestosis in 1956.[22] The documentary-makers argued that lung cancer was a greater risk for Rochdale workers than the company suggested. They also accused the company of not paying enough compensation—an allegation that they had little difficulty in substantiating.[23] Turner & Newall's miserly *ex gratias* were contrasted with the situation in America. Here a high-school teacher in Missouri, Richard Bond, had contracted mesothelioma after three weeks' summer work with his father spraying Limpet on the steel girders of high-rise buildings. He died aged 33, and in a court case in 1981—*Dana Bond v. Atlas Asbestos Company and Turner & Newall*—his widow was awarded a record $1.4 million (£823,000), of which $650,000 was paid by Turner & Newall.

The programme-makers used a scatter-gun approach. Not all of the targets were hit: some of the presentation was selective and the documentary was vulnerable to the charge of being unscientific and emotive. On the other hand, this was perhaps to be expected in view of the industry's secrecy. Generally, Willis and Cutler had done their homework well. For the first time, they had exposed the inaccuracies relied upon by Turner & Newall, and had publicized the methods of minimizing asbestos disease that the company had been practising since the 1930s. When the programme's evidence was reviewed before a House of Commons

[21] HC Employment Committee, *The Work of the Health and Safety Commission and Executive: Asbestos—Minutes of Evidence* (1983), 182–3. Fourteen such weavers were identified in a study by TBA's Dr Morris, some of whom (Tataryn and Coop) can be identified from the T & N compensation files. It appears that the removal of workers from the scheduled areas with early signs of asbestosis allowed the company to ignore them in its head count, as they had not been suspended by the PMP.

[22] 114/764–8: W. C. Childs file; and 111/718–44: H. Childs file.

[23] Alice herself was awarded £36,000 from Cape (after an original offer of £13,000). However, this was only after the dying woman had been made to attend court.

Employment Committee in 1983, the documentary makers stood by their accusations.[24]

'Alice' was a sensation, hitting Turner & Newall's share price and sending shock waves through the Rochdale community. The company was not without some local support, including former workers and local politicians. Older employees remembered a firm 'who look after you', where every health precaution was taken and where you could always get a well-paid job.[25] When one of the television researchers visited the widow of a mesothelioma victim and criticized Turner & Newall's *ex-gratia* policy, he was shown the door. She then informed the company of his visit.[26] It is noteworthy that attempts to form a Rochdale Action Group in 1982, similar to the one in Hebden Bridge, met with apathy. Local Liberal MP, Cyril Smith, who ironically had once applied unsuccessfully for a job at TBA, proved a staunch defender of the company. He was already active on TBA's behalf and was one of the channels by which the company made its views known over EEC asbestos regulations.[27] Clearly worried about jobs in his constituency, Smith's stance as reported in the local press was one of solid backing for the company.[28]

Turner & Newall also looked to Sir Richard Doll. The latter had continued his studies on TBA workers and he was now assisted by the statistician, Julian Peto. Together they pushed forward the analysis of the Rochdale cohort, but the publicity over asbestos was inevitably making the work more difficult and controversial. This was especially so as further research showed that in the 1970s the excess lung cancer (and mesothelioma) deaths had not disappeared.[29] Peto, with his complex mathematical models and statistics, at last began undermining the 2-fibre threshold, which he believed privately was 'wildly wrong'—a fact which he thought should be made public. Basing his research on the same TBA workers used in setting the BOHS standard, Peto calculated that 10 per cent of asbestos workers exposed to $2\,f/cc$ years for fifty years would die from asbestos diseases.[30] When Peto's findings began hitting the newspaper headlines after he had presented them at an overseas conference

---

[24] HC Employment Committee, *Minutes of Evidence*, 187.

[25] 601/958–9. Radio Manchester typescript, n.d.

[26] 126/1537–8. H. L. Pearson to Mr Oliver, 1 June 1982. Mrs Pearson's late husband was James Pearson, who died in 1979. She was receiving £574 per annum *ex gratia*.

[27] 50/1329. Smith asked TBA on 5 Aug. 1981: 'Could you please, within the next eight weeks, let me have the speech you would like to make (were you able to!), in that [EEC] debate?' See also 50/1330–3. 'Suggested Speech by Cyril Smith in Forthcoming Debate . . . on EEC Directives'.

[28] Under the headline 'Sue 'em, Cyril tells TBA', *Rochdale Observer*, 14 Aug. 1982, reported that the MP had urged T & N to take legal action and also that he was instructing his bankers to buy some of the company shares for himself.

[29] J. Peto *et al.*, 'A Mortality Study among Workers in an English Asbestos Factory', *British Journal of Industrial Medicine* 34 (Aug. 1977), 169–73.

[30] J. Peto, 'The Hygiene Standard for Chrysotile Asbestos', *Lancet* (4 Mar. 1978), i, 484–9.

in 1977, TBA directors complained that they had not given their approval. In retaliation, they threatened to withdraw their collaboration. Doll denied publicly that his department's work cast serious doubt on safety standards.[31] He also told TBA: 'All my colleagues now understand that the material that we can get from the firm is confidential to us until approval has been given for its publication.'[32] The work resumed. Doll wanted to continue the mortality studies of Rochdale workers and so did Turner & Newall. Already beset by litigation in America, the company occasionally consulted Doll on the extent of past knowledge about the cancer problem and asbestos.[33] When 'Alice' hit the headlines, Doll (and his wife) accepted an invitation to journey to Rochdale to provide a scientific view of the asbestos hazard at TBA.

This was a considerable coup for the company. Now approaching 70, Doll was no longer the young and unknown researcher that the company had tried to browbeat in 1955.[34] He was a national figure in his own right—a man regarded as one of the world's foremost cancer epidemiologists. Doll thought 'Alice' was 'far and away more harmful than anything it could be claimed to counter', while his wife was unsympathetic too.[35] Together they sat through another showing of the film, before Doll addressed his audience of managers and trades unionists. After stressing his independence, Doll began a wide-ranging discussion of the asbestos hazard and his research on TBA workers. His presentation was mainly an assessment of the health risk for current TBA staff. He told his audience that for long-serving workers in the scheduled areas, the chance of developing an asbestos-related disease was about one in forty. He described this as a 'pretty outside chance'.[36] It was no more than the risk of working in the nuclear industry; in fact, much less than the difference in risk between living in London and Liverpool, and amounted to no more than a reduction in life span for a 70-year-old of three months. The message was clear: the risk of working with asbestos at TBA was acceptable.

However, not everyone, even in Rochdale, was convinced. A son of Albert Copestick—a TBA worker who had died from asbestosis in 1948— reminded readers of the *Rochdale Observer* that the compensation the family had received 'would not even pay the cost of a headstone', and that he would never swallow any of the 'false propaganda' of the

[31] 229/2002. 'Don Denies Asbestosis Allegations', *Oxford Mail*, 31 Jan. 1977.
[32] 301/1953. Doll to S. Holmes, 25 May 1977.
[33] 506/2163–5. Letters re. Doll's meeting with T & N's New York attorneys, 10, 11 Nov. 1980, 30 Dec. 1980.
[34] 'Alice' had not mentioned Doll. The company's attempt to suppress his work in 1955 did not become widely known until T & N was sued in America in the early 1990s.
[35] 350/1688–9. Doll to S. Marks, 15 Oct. 1982. After the lecture, Lady Doll wrote to TBA chief executive, Brian Heron: 'We not only live in wretched times, but they are so often made 100% worse by the media!' 50/2247. Lady Doll to J. B. Heron, 19 Aug. 1982.
[36] 350/1636. Transcript of Doll's talk to TBA workers, 17 Aug. 1982.

company.[37] For every worker defending the firm, there was another with similarly bitter memories. Nationally, the reaction to Turner & Newall was even more hostile. In vain did the company claim that the programme was inaccurate and that it was the work of 'subversive organisations'.[38] Put firmly on the defensive, they were unable to do more than issue complaints that they had not been fairly represented or given sufficient right of reply. With little ammunition to counter the allegations, the company once more trotted out its familiar line that any asbestos disease was a result of exposure many years ago.

The government evidently found these reassurances less persuasive than the gale of public outrage. Within days of the 'Alice' programme, the government implemented the Simpson recommendations, which were to become effective at the end of 1982: 1 fibre f/cc for chrysotile; 0.5 f/cc for amosite; and 0.2 f/cc for crocidolite (unchanged). The HSE denied that this was the result of pressure from trial by television, but others not surprisingly found the timing of this 'significant policy change more than coincidental'.[39]

Almost immediately more bad news arrived from Turner & Newall's overseas subsidiaries. The study of asbestos disease at the Havelock Mines had been completed by the end of 1979, with the help of the MRC. The findings could hardly have been worse. The company's medical adviser, Dr James Allardice, informed the company that 2,200 employees had been investigated: of these 183 had asbestosis and there were 154 possible cases, up to half of which would become definite after a few years. The dust situation was being improved rapidly, but counts were still above 2 f/cc. Allardice watched maintenance men showering the lower levels with asbestos dust as they cleaned stairways with brushes.[40] A subsequent survey of 178 wives of workers with more than fifteen years at Havelock, showed that twelve had asbestosis and there were also ten possible cases.[41] The publication of the results of the MRC survey in the same year as the 'Alice' documentary brought Turner & Newall yet more bad publicity.[42] Cape, which apparently had an even worse health record than

[37] James Copestick, letters to *Rochdale Observer*, 4, 18 Aug. 1982. James Copestick and his brother had not been classed as dependent by the company, as they were over 16, despite the fact that their mother was dead. They received £15 funeral costs. See Albert Copestick file: 8/1798; 111/485.

[38] The company compiled a dossier on the anti-asbestos ringleaders. According to T & N, 'Alice' showed to 'what length these groups can go in their efforts in attempting to bring about the demise of a company'. See 126/1550–3.

[39] Angela Singer, 'More Time to Do Nothing', *Guardian*, 6 Aug. 1982.

[40] 68/430–1. Allardice to K. Dixon, 17 Dec. 1979.

[41] 68/428–9. Allardice to Dixon, 28 Apr. 1980. Only one case of primary lung cancer was said to have been found.

[42] M. McDermott *et al.*, 'Lung Function and Radiographic Change in Chrysotile Workers in Swaziland', *British Journal of Industrial Medicine* 39 (1982), 338–43. See also, 'Shock Report on UK Asbestos Firm', *Observer*, 15 Aug. 1982.

Turner & Newall, in 1981 had its mesothelioma problems in its South African factories highlighted in the World in Action documentary 'Dust to Dust'.[43]

Responding to increasing public and political pressure, the government tightened the regulations further. A review, requested by the HSC, on the control limit for asbestos, was issued in July 1983.[44] In the same month, the Under-Secretary of State, John Gummer, stated that there was no safe level, and that 'a single fibre could do real damage which may not be seen for 20 years or more'.[45] The Asbestos (Licensing) Regulations came into force in August 1984, alongside more stringent thresholds: 0.5 f/cc for chrysotile; 0.2 f/cc for amosite; 0.2 f/cc for crocidolite (no change). Importation and manufacturing of amosite and crocidolite were banned, but exposures would continue due to asbestos already in place.

THE WORST STORM IN TURNER & NEWALL'S HISTORY

'Alice' badly tarnished Turner & Newall's image; however, it was merely a symptom of other wide-ranging problems for the group in 1982. The asbestos hazard was beginning to sap the company's vitality, but deeper, structural problems (not all of them linked to health) were at work. Some of these were related to long-term trends in the British economy.

The 1970s and early 1980s had seen a marked slowing down of UK industrial growth and a fall (at first slow and then steep) in manufacturing employment. Other features of this period were an increasing divergence between old and 'new' industries, a marked shift in output and employment towards the service sector, and rising import penetration (combined with a poor British export performance). In short, this was an era when Britain (at least in the popular view) became 'de-industrialized', as its old smokestack industries were replaced by a computerized and service-driven economy.

This had important implications for Turner & Newall. In the early 1970s, imports of asbestos fibre into the UK hit a peak of over 190,000 tonnes and then began to decline rapidly—a fall not entirely due to the health hazard. With the decline of Britain's major industries went the full order books for insulation and other asbestos products. No one needed asbestos insulation for transatlantic liners, mattresses for locomotives, jointings for steam engines, and acoustic spray for large cinemas. The magic of asbestos was fading and by the 1970s it was plain that future

---

[43] 30/1712. 'Dust to Dust' transcript, 16 Nov. 1981.
[44] E. D. Acheson and M. J. Gardner, *Asbestos: The Control Limit for Asbestos* (1983).
[45] 'Asbestos (Power Stations)', *Hansard* 46 (1983–4), 1412.

needs for fireproofing and insulation would be met by more modern materials. Like most older British industries in the 1970s, therefore, asbestos would have to adapt to survive.

Far-sighted directors plan for change in advance. More usually, companies have change forced upon them and often when they are least able to adapt. This was so with Turner & Newall. What had once been a highly profitable and technologically advanced concern, now resembled a ragbag of unappealing textile and cement companies engaged in low-growth areas. In Rochdale, TBA was still making a nineteenth-century product on equipment that had been designed in the Industrial Revolution. The company had more modern technologies, such as plastics, but these too were tied into asbestos. Above all, the company depended on consumer demand, which had been hit by a recession. The result was that after the sellers' market of the 1950s had evaporated, the company's profits (which had once been the envy of other firms) flattened out and were no better than the average. Complicating the picture were the overseas mining and cement subsidiaries. Many of these were in former colonies, which brought political problems of disinvestment or, worse, the freezing of assets. Rhodesia's Unilateral Declaration of Independence in 1965, which affected Turner & Newall's mining interests there, was a prime example of the latter. The company's whole method of organizing its business was proving inadequate. By the 1970s, it was no longer possible to run British industry with the help of cartels and secret and restrictive deals with competitors. These were now unlawful. The company's strategy for decentralization also seemed to have gone too far. By the 1970s, it was evident that more effective co-ordination and central supervision were needed, though whether Turner & Newall's management was up to the job seemed doubtful. A government report in 1973 noted: 'until recently, the [Turner & Newall] management have been unwilling to contemplate changes in long-established habits, even when changing circumstances have made them obsolete.'[46]

Like most giants, Turner & Newall was not very nimble-footed. Diversification had begun in the 1960s, but, as we have seen, this did not accelerate until the 1970s. In the beginning, the company had invested in plastics by acquiring BIP in 1961. This subsidiary performed unspectacularly until 1977, when Turner & Newall tried to improve matters by spending £23 million on Storey Brothers, a north-west manufacturer of plastic sheeting. The intention was to break into the PVC market. But the expected plastics boom never materialized in a market with too many PVC producers and with the price of oil rising. By 1982, Turner & Newall had decided to abandon the business and invest in America. It sold its

---

[46] Monopolies Commission, *Asbestos and Certain Asbestos Products* (1973), 114.

interest in the asbestos-cement company Certain-teed in 1976 and in the following year bought a half share in the Philip Hunt Chemical Corporation for £34 million (a stake increased to 63 per cent in 1979). This firm, which made chemicals for the semi-conductor industry, looked a winner with the growth of electronics, but again the performance was unexceptional. Meanwhile, Turner & Newall tried to cut its asbestos usage—a strategy encouraged in 1980 by the sale of the strike-prone Bell Mine and the Atlas and Cassiar interests in Canada. Rhodesian UDI had, ironically, fostered this policy. However, when the Zimbabwe interests were re-absorbed in 1979 the company's dilution strategy for asbestos received a setback. By 1979, about 60 per cent of the firm's operations were still dependent on the mineral. Great uncertainty surrounded the firm's African operations and the mines added to the losses that were being incurred elsewhere.

By 1980, Turner & Newall was in the red (see Table 10.1). In the following year, chairman Stephen Gibbs told shareholders that the company was at 'the centre of the worst storm in our history'. The 'Alice' year, 1982, was the nadir. Losses were approaching £30 million. Even more serious, the company had debts approaching £100 million—a product of its closure or re-organization of unprofitable businesses. On the verge of bankruptcy (with the added spectre of unknown asbestos disease liabilities), the banks became unwilling to extend their lending. In 1982, the Bank of England organized a rescue and Sir Francis Tombs was appointed as the new chairman. Tombs, who had a reputation as a company trouble-shooter, began an immediate reorganization. He sold Hunt Chemical for £59 million, shed Storey Brothers and BIP, and also ordered closures and redundancies. This was partly to reduce debt, but the cash was also used to rejuvenate the group with new purchases. In 1985, Tombs recruited Colin Hope from Dunlop as his managing-director and together the two men evolved a plan. While the old asbestos-cement plants and mines (such as the Havelock) were sold to pay off debts, the company's friction materials and gasket businesses were retained to form the core of a new group linked to the automotive industry.

Occupational health was also part of the shake-up. Dr Peter Elmes, the newly retired head of the MRC Pneumoconiosis Unit, was recruited as a consultant to review the health situation at its factories, both at home and overseas. At the beginning of 1983, Elmes presented a preliminary assessment of health and safety at Turner & Newall. Describing TLV's as informed guesswork rather than scientific fact, he told the company that workers who had been or still were exposed to asbestos would remain at risk, whether they remained at Turner & Newall, left, or retired. He also felt that asbestos had led to the neglect of other occupational respiratory problems, such as asthma. Fortex production, he believed, created an

Table 10.1. *T & N profits and asbestos-related disease and litigation costs, 1980–97*

Year	Profit [loss] after tax £m	Asbestos disease /litigation costs £m
1980	[7.5]	2.1
1981	[3.5]	3.9
1982	[29.5]	6.4
1983	6.2	7.6
1984	13.4	10.7
1985	29.4	6.0
1986	34.1	1.8
1987	62.0	5.1
1988	71.3	10.7
1989	65.6	20.1
1990	49.7	11.4
1991	21.9	15.7
1992	28.7	16.6
1993	45.1	21.1
1994	[11.3]	140.0
1995	78.7	51.3
1996	[396.3]	515.0
1997	127.3	0

Source: T & N, *Reports and Accounts*.

'aerosol' of dangerous small fibres.[47] General housekeeping was poor, with bits of waste and machinery evident.[48] Elmes's depressing picture was supported by Dr Timothy Goffe, who had become the company medical adviser in 1982. Goffe highlighted the decline in resources available for health and safety and felt that both he and the company were slipping behind in their ability to deal with such issues.[49]

Goffe forwarded his memorandum to Sidney Marks, the personnel officer at TBA, with the intention that it should be passed to chairman Harry Hardie. Marks declined to pass on all of Goffe's comments and told him: 'If the BMA had its way, all we would do is operate the NHS and nothing else.'[50] Goffe later commented: 'I thought that the bad old days

[47] Mesothelioma victim Donald Robinson (1942–84), a father of four, was awarded an unprecedented £75,000 damages in 1982. He had been a foreman in the Fortex department.
[48] 301/1670–5. P. C. Elmes, 'A Short Report on the Health & Safety Requirements for T & N UK Factories', 26 Jan. 1983.
[49] 301/1659–60. Goffe to S. Marks, 6 May 1983.
[50] 301/1657. Handwritten note, Marks to Goffe, n.d.

of suppression of reports, secrecy on health and safety matters, non-investigation of sensitive problems were long since over and I thought that new directive from the top was a more open attitude to health hazards, and a willingness to investigate and control them.'[51]

Elmes resumed his survey in 1986, beginning with a close look at TBA. The headquarters of the Asbestos Giant was now showing its age. The workforce was much reduced, with remaining employees unable to achieve satisfactory health standards. Elmes attributed this to 'poor morale resulting from the climate in which these workers live, the shabby, dingy buildings where they work and eat . . . I did not get the impression that many of the men on the shop floor are proud of the work they are doing or of working for the company; it is just a job.'[52] Elmes's comments echo similar reports going back to the 1930s. Bag opening and blending were still hazardous, with frequent fibre spillages; while under the spinning and doubling machines, fly piled up on the floor. Antiquated technology, such as dry asbestos spinning, needed many improvements to control the dust. Elmes also went to South Africa to see the company's asbestos mines at Shabani and Mashaba. At Shabanie Mine, dust control was much improved, but the narrow margins in selling asbestos meant that the plant was worked at full capacity. Breakdowns and blockages were frequent, resulting in increased risk. A similar situation was apparent at the Gath and King mills.[53]

The company's reluctance to commit more resources to these areas was partly due to its rapidly evolving strategy to abandon asbestos as soon as possible. In 1986, Tombs and Hope made an offer for Associated Engineering, one of the leaders in the British car industry. After a take-over fight, the deal was closed for £279 million. This laid the foundations for a modern business in pistons, sealing systems, and bearings. In 1987, the company's name was changed to T & N. Within two years, Hope became chairman and chief executive. Aided by a number of rights issues, he continued the strategy of aggressive expansion, especially in the UK, Europe, and North America. Meanwhile, between 1989 and 1995, the company's asbestos cement and mining interests in India and Africa were relinquished and organizations such as the Asbestosis Research Council were dissolved. The company's rescue plan was now almost complete and by the 1990s T & N was once again a technically advanced and prosperous company. This was a considerable achievement for Hope and his team. It needed to be: the bill for asbestos liabilities had been continuously increasing and the main question for interested observers was whether Hope would be able to keep the company ahead of the rising tide of litigation.

[51] 301/1658. Goffe to Hardie, 11 May 1983.
[52] 301/1572–9. 'Audit of Health & Safety at . . . TBA, 17 July 1986'.
[53] 419/965–6; 419/939–42. Visit to Shabanie and Gath Mines, Aug. 1985, Mar. 1987.

TURNER & NEWALL IN THE DOCK

The problem that John Collins had once complacently described as purely an 'internal' one for the company was now threatening to engulf it. In the early 1980s, the number of writs served on T & N began to mushroom. At least 700 claims files survive in the company archive for the post-1982 period, each one usually filled with solicitors' letters, writs, depositions, doctors' examinations, life histories, post-mortem reports, and inquest proceedings. The files make unbearable reading, with a level of human suffering that is impossible to convey in mere words. What the documents demonstrate beyond any doubt are the poor working conditions between the 1940s and 1970s—especially in the lagging trades, but also in the factories—and the company's failure to enforce basic safety rules. By the mid-1980s, the consequences could be seen in the following cases (which are only examples from hundreds of files):[54]

- Asbestosis in a Newalls' worker after less than six months' work in 1940–1, lagging steam pipes and cutting up sheets, mostly in the open air.
- TAC pipe-maker, with asbestosis and pleural plaques, after six months' work in 1973.
- Roberts' textile worker, employed for less than a year in 1954. Dead from asbestosis in 1983.
- Newalls' lagger with six months' exposure in the 1950s and 1960s. Dead from mesothelioma in 1984.
- Birmingham Carriage & Wagon Company coach finisher, who had worked near Limpet sprayers. Dead from lung cancer/asbestosis in 1984.
- Washington Chemical Company labourer, whose six-month stint between 1941 and 1942 involved sweeping out a dust chamber. Dead from peritoneal mesothelioma in 1986.

By the 1990s, such claims—once paid *ex gratia* from loose change at head office—were racking up millions in compensation and legal costs. Expenditure for asbestos-related disease claims was first mentioned in the company's annual report in 1981, with a figure of £2.1 million for 1980 and £3.9 million for 1981 (see Table 10.1). By 1996, total costs had spiralled to over £380 million—a serious drain on the company's profits.

It was an experience shared by all the asbestos companies still in existence, especially in America. By 1982, US asbestos firms and their

---

[54] W. E. Ratcliffe (b.1921–). 603/161; J. P. Dunn (b.1926–). 602/1744; G. Jackson (1932–83). 602/1216; F. W. Moore (1929–84). 602/1890; A. Webb (*c*.1919–84). 603/966; George Willcock (1922–86). 603/2004.

insurers had already incurred costs totalling $1 billion. In that eventful year, three defendant manufacturers—the most notable of which was Johns–Manville—hit the headlines by taking refuge in a federal bank-ruptcy law known as Chapter 11. This tactic allowed them voluntarily to declare themselves insolvent (even though they were still profitable), so that litigation costs could halted and then controlled. Other manufactur-ers and insurers banded together to form an Asbestos Claims Facility in 1984, which was replaced after 1988 by a Center for Claims Resolution (CCR)—both of which aimed to pay a fixed proportion of personal injury claims, thereby decreasing costly litigation.[55] Thus began a seemingly never-ending and tortuous legal process, which has raised problems that are as much political and social as economic: who should pay for the costs of using hazardous materials and how much? Should companies be li-quidated and the present management and workers punished for past misdeeds? Or should firms be protected and kept alive, so that cash cows can continue to be milked?[56]

Chapter 11 was not an option for T & N in Britain, so it had little choice other than to continue paying compensation—hence the massive provi-sions and litigation costs. Some might see this as the enactment of a simple morality tale, in which T & N finally got its just deserts. However, the lit-igation story at T & N—in so far as it can be told presently—is more complex than that. Ironically, only a relatively small amount of the £380 million costs mentioned above has been paid by T & N to British plain-tiffs. More than half the total has paid legal bills and much of the rest, as we shall see, has been spent on American costs. Meanwhile, although T & N became vulnerable to take-over, it avoided bankruptcy and survived. This was a remarkable achievement in itself considering the fact that, whatever yardsticks are applied, the social costs of its actions exceeded all that T & N was worth or insured for.

In the UK, as we have seen, Turner & Newall carried its own risk and successfully kept the lid on costs for many years by, in effect, shift-ing the burden to the sick and society at large. The Midland Assurance Company continued to cover the firm's employers' liability insurance, but this excluded asbestos-related diseases. In 1950, the Midland offered, on the basis of information supplied by Turner & Newall, to insure future asbestosis cases for an additional £1,000 a year. However, the company thought this premium 'excessive' and, in a decision that would later prove embarrassing, not to say expensive, declined the offer.

---

[55] B. I. Castleman, *Asbestos: Medical and Legal Aspects* (1996), 797–810.

[56] C. Calhoun and H. Hiller, 'Coping with Insidious Injuries: The Case of Johns-Manville Corporation and Asbestos Exposure', *Social Problems* 35 (Apr. 1988), 162–81; R. Warren, 'The Enforcement of Social Accountability—Turner & Newall and the Asbestos Crisis', *Corporate Governance* 5 (Apr. 1997), 52–9.

Later, its employers' liability insurance was transferred to the Royal Insurance Group in 1969, and then to a Lloyd's syndicate in 1977. On each occasion, Turner & Newall made it clear that they wished to continue covering their own asbestos-disease liabilities, despite the emerging cancer problem.[57]

What bred this remarkable complacency? It was mostly a reflection of the extraordinarily favourable legal situation in Britain for the industry. For example, between 1972 and 1984 only fifty common law claims were made against TBA for asbestosis with a few for mesothelioma. To be sure, by 1994 T & N was a defendant in 433 asbestos personal injury cases— but this sudden rise was a relatively late phenomenon. The problems for British workers suing for compensation have remained formidable. In the 1990s, litigation could still take years and legal costs were enormous; claimants needed to prove actual exposure to asbestos; and, above all, they had to prove that the company was negligent. Sometimes they also needed to trace insurers. For those who had worked in the insulation trade, the picture was complicated by the fact that they had often worked for different employers. Proving exposure and negligence might seem simple matters, but individual cases could be complex, even against a high-profile company like T & N. Many of its old factories were derelict, legally no more than 'shells', with any incriminating documentation apparently destroyed. Thus T & N could settle most cases out of court. Awards even in successful civil actions that went all the way were not high (rarely surpassing £50,000) and firms were not subject to punitive damages.[58] T & N was further protected by other vagaries in English law. Many exposed workers sued their immediate employers—such as the shipbuilding companies, British Gas, or BT (British Telecommunications)[59]—and not T & N. Only after the 1960s has T & N been pulled into court in third party proceedings. Even better for the company, there has been no asbestos product liability litigation in Britain; while property-damage litigation has been unknown.

In some overseas countries, the situation also favoured T & N. In South Africa, the company's devolved structure, the lack of compensation law, a poor and uneducated workforce, and the sale of companies gave T & N and Cape complete protection from costly litigation. Claims against them

---

[57] B. N. Barker, 'The History of Turner & Newall . . . [and] . . . its Dealings with Asbestos-Related Diseases and Its Employers' Liability Coverage with the Midland Assurance Ltd' (Feb. 1989).

[58] However, W. L. F. Felstiner and R. Dingwall, *Asbestos Litigation in the United Kingdom: An Interim Report* (1988), argue that many claimants are reasonably well compensated and that the system is quicker and more equitable than in the US—though they admit that many plaintiffs with legitimate cases do not claim.

[59] Channel 4 News, 18 Mar. 1998, criticized these companies for employing the same delaying tactics as the asbestos industry in settling legitimate claims.

were unknown. Not until 1998 was the principle established that South
African plaintiffs could sue a UK asbestos firm (Cape) in the English
courts, but the decision was almost immediately overturned.[60]

However, this was counterbalanced by problems in America, where T
& N still had substantial interests.[61] Ironically, the country that Walker
Shepherd had once envisioned as a land of unlimited possibilities for his
company now enmeshed it in a web of seemingly unending litigation. The
situation in this, the world's most litigious society, was almost the
exact opposite of Britain. Although the UK's death rate from asbestos
disease in per capita terms is four times that of America, asbestos victims
in the US are four times more likely to sue for damages.[62] American
doctors, lawyers, and trade unions are more active in helping victims fight
for their rights. The contingency fee system (which allows lawyers to take
on a case without fee for a share of the damages), and punitive awards in
millions of dollars, helped produce the biggest wave of litigation in
history. Some personal-injury lawyers became very wealthy, with reputations as the kind of men who once they got their teeth into an asbestos
company never let go. As an employer of American labour, a maker of
asbestos products, and an importer of fibre, T & N was vulnerable to
claims from such lawyers across the whole spectrum from personal injury
to property damage, and from product liability to multiple-defendant
claims.

By 1982, the number of T & N's American claims was approaching a
thousand a year (compared to only seventy-seven in the UK) and the
potential costs looked phenomenal enough to bankrupt the company. In
the US, however, T & N was covered by insurance, though this led to its
own complications. Like other asbestos manufacturers, T & N was soon
in dispute with insurance companies as it tried to claim under old policies, while the insurers counter-claimed that they had not been alerted to
the extent of asbestos health hazards. The history of T & N's insurance
coverage has been described as 'an unfolding, multi-layered story involving British insurance companies, re-insurers, co-insurers, excess layer
insurers, numerous syndicates of Lloyd's of London, employers' liability
policies, workmens' compensation policies, umbrella policies, product liability policies, and the Asbestosis Fund'.[63] The whole process generated
waves that rocked City institutions such as Lloyd's, where syndicates

---

[60] *British Asbestos Newsletter* (Autumn, 1999).

[61] In contrast, Cape had shed its interests in the US and its asbestos health liabilities. For
example, Cape's US subsidiary—the North American Asbestos Corp., Chicago, Illinois—left
a communal legacy of asbestos diseases and unpaid court awards. See 69/1719–32. World
in Action (ITV), 'A Small Town Tragedy', 5 July 1982.

[62] 'Don't Inhale', *The Economist* (25 Mar. 1995), 42.

[63] Laurie Kazan-Allen, 'T & N plc: Insurance Coverage', unpublished typescript (1996).
Courtesy of the author.

exposed Names to personal bankruptcy through unlimited American asbestos liabilities.[64]

By 1991, the insurance industry had paid out $2 billion in American asbestos cases, with Lloyd's syndicates paying half that total. Lloyd's would complain that the American courts had made insurers the scapegoats for the asbestos health disaster, a calamity which the London firm would argue was 'impossible to foresee'. However, insurers had not helped themselves by taking on excessive amounts of risky insurance coverage between the 1940s and 1970s, when claims were few and profits good. Like the asbestos industry itself, they had greatly underestimated the risk. The consequences hit home in the 1980s, when the claims began arriving, and when Names found it 'quite incredible' that they should have to pay something towards somebody who had developed asbestos disease fifty years ago.[65] Others might see a belated element of justice in the way in which the ghosts of Nellie Kershaw and other Turner & Newall workers had reached out and shaken the comfortable lives of the English Establishment.

The deep pockets of insurers such as Lloyd's, the Midland (Eagle Star), Royal Insurance, American Mutual, and the Insurance Company of North America saved T & N from bankruptcy. Insurers of T & N's American liabilities honoured policies for asbestosis claims; and T & N was able to protect its market value by resolving privately any disputes with insurers. In a further attempt to limit costs, the company became a member of the CCR and later joined other defendants in the so-called Georgine Settlement.[66] All told, the Fates had proved extremely kind to the company.

American litigation, though, did have one negative consequence. As a result of the first US personal injury case lodged against the company in 1977, a 'non-destruction directive' was issued to Turner & Newall, so that any relevant documents would not be destroyed. In the mid-1980s, further stipulations and orders prompted Turner & Newall to index and gather the documents from their headquarters and subsidiaries and place them in a central repository at 21 St Mary's Parsonage, Manchester (an archive later transferred to Trafford Park).

This large repository was not publicized in Britain or disclosed to plaintiffs, though its existence and contents slowly began seeping into the public domain. This was largely due the rising tide of US property

---

[64] The Names were individual investors at Lloyd's. The social cachet of being a Lloyd's member (which was by introduction only) and the promise of guaranteed returns led many Names to overlook their unlimited liability.

[65] A. Raphael, *Ultimate Risk* (1994), 99–126.

[66] The Georgine Settlement stemmed in 1993 from a class action arrangement in *Georgine et al. v. Amchem et al.*, in which CCR members agreed to an administrative system to control costs. The Settlement was overturned by the Supreme Court in 1997.

litigation after the mid-1980s when T & N were sued by various companies which had purchased Limpet or other asbestos products. By 1987, seventy-four property-damage suits had been brought in the US courts against T & N. Initially, some of these actions were successfully defended; others were settled for relatively small amounts. But some of the plaintiffs were multinational banks and insurance companies—groups well able to spend enormous sums on legal fees and document searches. They could take on T & N on equal terms. The first significant suit was brought in 1985 by the Prudential Company of America for $175 million in compensatory and punitive damages against Turner & Newall (and other defendants) for the removal of Limpet from the Prudential Centre in Boston, Massachusetts. Patrick Guilfoyle, who acted for the insurance company, began opening up the T & N repository for plaintiffs by using the legal process of 'discovery'.

In the UK, the discovery process has hardly helped plaintiffs against asbestos companies. In Britain, the courts expect businesses to make relevant documents available, but the rules for enforcing this are limited. For example, victims of asbestos disease and their dependants were often told by Turner & Newall that only employment record cards had survived, or that it no longer had control over the records of subsidiary companies. In America, however, discovery rules are far more wide-ranging and the courts enforce them rigorously. In contrast to the UK, plaintiffs and their lawyers have sweeping powers to search for records, and can even roam through factory premises and demand to see documents *in situ*.

Prudential eventually lost its case on a technicality in 1992 and the cache of T & N documents did not receive widespread publicity in Britain. However, by then discovery was being used with even greater force against T & N by one of the biggest banks in the world. The plaintiff was Chase Manhattan Bank, whose sixty-storey Wall Street skyscraper had been built in 1959 with Limpet sprayed onto the steel decking. As the biggest sprayed fireproofing job in history, it was a prestige contract for the British company. But Chase had decided to begin removing the asbestos in 1986 and the following year decided to sue T & N for the cost. In 1991, Chase lawyers, led by vice-president and senior counsel Michael O'Connor, won a major discovery ruling that gave the Bank sweeping access to all documents in the T & N repository. The Chase team packed their bags and headed for Manchester.

When O'Connor and his five-strong team arrived at the repository, they were taken up to the sixth floor and led into a large locked room, filled with dozens of filing cabinets. Not knowing where to begin, they wandered around, randomly opening drawers that were stuffed with papers. Soon they got down to work, methodically examining each drawer in turn, and deciding on the spot what records should be copied. Chase's trawl netted a million pages of documentation from what was the biggest corporate archive in the asbestos industry: but its efforts did not stop there. In its $1 million quest for information, the Bank searched relevant archives around the world and deposed numerous witnesses.

Chase was pursuing its own economic self-interest. The Bank demanded $1 million per floor for clearing 1 Chase Manhattan Plaza of Limpet: $50 million in lost office rental; and also punitive damages that raised the total claim to $185 million (about £117 million)—more than T & N had paid in compensation in its history. On the other hand, as Chase lawyers pored over the records, they were genuinely dismayed at the story they uncovered. Michael O'Connor, an affable Dublin-born litigator, developed a strong commitment to the case and under his direction Chase began publicizing the case worldwide. In New York, no protective court order had been placed on the bulk of the archive, so allowing Chase to disclose records to third parties. O'Connor immediately began sending large bundles of key T & N documents to the media, lawyers, doctors, victims' support groups, and historians. His action—which would have been impossible in Britain, where court records are given absolute protection—ensured that this time the archive hit the headlines. British radio programmes and television documentaries used the material to take a fresh look at T & N's attitude to workers' health.

Chase soon found that the archive was far from complete. Personal or company papers relating to the company chairmen, such as the Turners, Soothill, Bateman, and Shepherd were surprisingly scanty. Information on T & N's American activities was also sparse. Shepherd's detailed US reports had survived and were full of fascinating commercial details: however, they also proved to be devoid of any mention of asbestos disease. The Chase lawyers were also disappointed to find that TBA Health Committee minutes were missing for several crucial years in the 1950s, when Chase contended that the company should have warned customers about the mesothelioma hazard.[67]

Nevertheless, Chase believed that they had a watertight case. When the trial began in October 1995, the Bank paraded T & N's most incriminating documents in front of the jury and rehearsed the blackest episodes from its past: the emergence of asbestosis in the 1920s; the deaths of laggers and sprayers in the 1940s; the stonewalling of the shipyard regulators; the attempted suppression of the Doll cancer article; and the mesothelioma warnings that had been given to the company at about the time Limpet was sprayed on the building. The Chase in-house lawyers were joined by legal heavyweights such as Arthur Liman (of Iran–Contra

---

[67] Author's interview with Michael O'Connor, New York, 10 Mar. 1997.

hearings fame), who at the start of the trial sought to characterize T & N's conduct as 'morally shocking and repugnant and repulsive'.[68]

On the other hand, asbestos property-damage litigation is often fraught with problems for plaintiffs. There is usually no element of personal injury in such cases—in other words, there are no sick workers to sway a jury. The plaintiffs are wealthy institutions who can usually afford the renovations. Since dust counts in office buildings are invariably very low, it is difficult to demonstrate a clear hazard.[69] All these factors worked in T & N's favour when the trial began. The American defence team, led by Paul Hanly and Kenneth Warner, did not even bother contesting the argument that Turner & Newall were well aware of the dangers of asbestos and that it had failed to warn Chase. Instead, Hanly and Warner turned the spotlight on Chase. Using discovery processes themselves, they unearthed Chase letters that suggested that the Bank itself regarded asbestos levels in the skyscraper as safe and that Limpet posed no threat under most conditions. The fireproofing had done its job—indeed, it had once prevented a fire—and Chase's removal of it, argued Warner, was purely a business decision. Chase's huge claim was ridiculed: 'We're here', the jury were told, 'because Chase wants money. Big, big money. And they want money for themselves. They don't want money for factory workers or maintenance workers. They don't want money for employees. They want money for themselves.' The argument played well with a New York jury, which had, it seems, a traditional American dislike of big banks. They dismissed all the charges against T & N in December 1995. 'In hindsight, it appears', wrote one observer, 'that the Chase lawyers had overestimated the sympathy among working-class jurors for a $305 billion bank.'[70]

T & N had apparently emerged from the bitter fight unscathed. Colin Hope gloated to reporters: 'I don't think Chase can believe it'.[71] The saving of money was considerable and it drew a line under future actions, which could now be settled for minor sums. On the other hand, T & N had been badly mauled, too, and its reputation hit a new low point. Chase material had primed several documentaries and television exposés, which once more vilified T & N. BBC TV's 'An Acceptable Level of Death', screened in 1994, was particularly effective at highlighting T & N's uncompromising attitude to asbestos claims. The documentary was notable for a hotel confrontation between reporter John Ware and Colin Hope. Responding to a polite, if impromptu, question, Hope lost his

---

[68] *Chase* v. *T & N* (1995). Trial transcript, 45.

[69] Doll prepared an affidavit for T & N's attorneys in which he estimated that the asbestos health risks in buildings such as Chase Manhattan Bank were negligible. See 505/1902–28. Affidavit of Sir Richard Doll, 14 Jan. 1988.

[70] V. Titunik, 'Chase's Case Turns to Dust', *The American Lawyer* (May 1996), 73–80, 79.

[71] *Financial Times*, 8 Dec. 1995.

temper and then retreated into the gents' lavatory.[72] Meanwhile, British working-class people had formed an entirely different opinion of Chase's lawyers than their counterparts in America. Michael O'Connor emerged as a champion of the underdog. In 1996, he was fêted with an award from the Campaign for Freedom of Information for his 'remarkable efforts to supply British asbestos victims with documents'. These victims included John and Alice Standen and their three sons, Dick, George, and David. John and his sons were all Newalls' laggers. The father died from a heart attack and asbestosis and in the 1970s all three brothers succumbed to mesothelioma.[73] George and David Standen died within hours of each other in May 1979. When the widow of George made a claim for damages, she had been told by T & N's lawyers that the company had no records. Chase's release of vital company papers undermined this contention and she was awarded £85,000 damages in 1994.

Chase had also turned the spotlight on the gruesome tragedy that was still being played out in the streets around Armley. In the early 1970s, a Turner & Newall public relations officer had reviewed the files on the Roberts' factory and wrote: 'I hope very much indeed that we are never called upon to discuss Armley in the public arena.'[74] At that time, it must have seemed likely that the factory's past would be forgotten. The old Midland Works was soon occupied by other tenants and the only other reminder of Armley's past was a few remaining asbestosis cases. But asbestos is virtually indestructible. In 1978, Leeds City Council alerted Turner & Newall to the fact that the old factory was badly contaminated with blue asbestos. The company began a £13,000 clean-up, accepting a moral though not a legal responsibility. Mesothelioma deaths among former workers began increasing in the 1970s, by which time another ominous trend was appearing—mesothelioma cases among people who had never worked at Roberts, but had been exposed through living close to the factory or through relatives who had worked there.[75] So-called 'bystander' or environmental cases were also experienced by families

---

[72] BBC2, 'An Acceptable Level of Death', 14 Apr. 1994. Two radio programmes discussed the Chase material: BBC Radio 4 Face the Facts: 'The Shocking Story of Asbestos', 6 Oct. 1993; and BBC Radio 4 Face the Facts :'Asbestos and the Third World', 13 Oct. 1993.

[73] See B. McKessock, *Mesothelioma: The Story of an Illness* (1995), 91–8; and 601/68: David Standen (1924–79) file. Family tragedies like the Standen cases were not unique. For example, Newalls' lagger Allan Brown (b.1924) was suspended with asbestosis in 1985: his twin brother had died from the disease in 1972; and his sister had died from pleural mesothelioma. See 603/1589.

[74] 82/132. W. P. Howard to J. K. Roberts, 14 Nov. 1974.

[75] The first non-occupational death in Leeds may have been Nellie Kirby in 1970. BBA reported the case to W. P. Howard, of the AIC, on the understanding that it was kept secret. See 125/745. Howard memo, 29 Oct. 1970. See also L. Arblaster *et al.*, 'Occupational and Environmental Links to Mesothelioma Deaths Occurring in Leeds during 1971 and 1987', *Journal of Public Health Medicine* 17 (1995), 297–304.

around other T & N factories in the 1980s—notably Washington Chemical Company—or by relatives of contract workers. A few examples can be seen in Table 10.2. However, the Midland Works' unusual proximity to local houses and a school sowed the seeds for a social disaster that was to kill at least 200 workers and residents by the 1990s.[76]

In 1988, the Leeds coroner expressed concern at the number of mesothelioma deaths—twenty-two between 1977 and 1988—referred for inquest. A reporter for the *Yorkshire Evening Post*, traced the deaths to Roberts' factory. In November 1988, local MP John Battle called for a government inquiry into the deaths—a call supported by Leeds City Council. This was rejected by a Conservative government, which argued that an enquiry would cause needless concern, that it was impossible to discover what had happened at Roberts, and that no one could then have imagined that the dust would have harmed residents. Within a month, however, Yorkshire Television had transmitted a documentary on the factory entitled 'Too Close to Home', which cast serious doubt on these statements.[77]

Yet T & N directors gave the impression that Roberts had ceased to exist. Colin Hope wrote to a medical researcher in 1989 that Roberts had long ago been sold to a third party, that it had neither premises nor employees, and no archive. He described the records relating to the Armley period as 'extremely scanty' and 'largely confined to basic employee record cards'.[78] Chase soon demonstrated that this was inaccurate. O'Connor, besides briefing another television programme on the Armley tragedy,[79] also had enough archive material to provide important ammunition for dependants and victims mounting further challenges against T & N. One of them was Evelyn Margerson, whose husband Arthur had died of mesothelioma; another was June Hancock, also ill with mesothelioma, whose mother had died from the disease. The claims seemed straightforward, as both Arthur Margereson and June Hancock had clearly been exposed to asbestos as children when playing in the contaminated streets around the Roberts' factory. However, this was 'environmental' exposure. No one had ever won such a case and T & N decided to contest it.

The trial took place in Leeds in 1995, with Hancock, a softly-spoken 59-year-old housewife, as very much the focus of the case. Although she was

---

[76] This is my estimate based on the T & N records and the Arblaster survey. However, the death toll could be considerably higher. Oldham solicitor John Pickering has told me that deaths from Hebden Bridge (where there were also several bystander cases) had reached about 400 by 1998. This almost ranks with Britain's worst industrial disaster—the Universal Colliery mining explosion in Senghenydd, South Wales, in 1913, when the death toll was 439.

[77] Yorkshire TV, 'Too Close to Home', 6 Dec. 1988.

[78] 230/7–10. C. F. N. Hope to L. Arblaster, 25 Oct. 1989.

[79] BBC TV, 'Deadly Legacy', 14 Apr. 1993.

Table 10.2. *Examples of 'bystander' and environmental asbestos-related disease cases at Turner & Newall*

Name	Location	Disease	Comments
Wallace C. Childs (d.1979)	Leeds	Mesothelioma	Childhood exposure from father, an asbestotic JWR worker. 114/764–8.
Norah Cook (1929–85)	Washington	Mesothelioma	Played on factory tip as a child and exposed by husband's overalls, 1944–9 (he had asbestosis). 602/1304.
Dolores Gonzales (1925–86)	Washington	Mesothelioma	Lived near factory until 14 and also exposed to father's dusty overalls. Father died from same disease in 1973. 603/1428.
June Hancock (1936–97)	Leeds	Mesothelioma	Lived near JWR. Mother died from same disease.
Nellie Kirby (1928–70)	Leeds	Mesothelioma	Childhood exposure from father who worked at JWR.
Arthur Margereson (1925–91)	Leeds	Mesothelioma	Lived close to JWR.
Elsie V. Smith (1938–85)	South Wales	Mesothelioma	Husband a Newalls' lagger. Washed his overalls. 603/336.
George Watson (c.1905–84)	Washington	Mesothelioma	79-year-old coal miner, lived near Washington works during the last twelve years of his life. 602/1102. *Washington Echo*, 5 July 1984.
Beatrice Welsh (b.1921)	Belfast	Asbestosis	Husband a Newalls' lagger. Washed his overalls. 603/748.
David Young	Leeds	Asbestosis	Son of JWR worker, John Young, who died from asbestosis in 1943.
Doris Young (d.1969)	Leeds	Mesothelioma	Married to John Young.
Hubert Young	Leeds	Asbestosis	Son of Doris and Robert Young.

Source: T & N compensation claims files.

slowly being worn down by mesothelioma, she nevertheless appeared in court every day to plead her case. She was determined to win the David and Goliath contest, not so much for herself—she did not have long to live—as for claimants who would come after her. T & N and its lawyers were equally determined to oppose her claim. At first, the company refused to admit that its activities and liabilities were coterminous with those of its old unit company. It also declined to release relevant documents, contending that these could not be found or did not exist. This was inaccurate. Not only had Roberts been totally owned by Turner & Newall, it also still held onto it as a shell. Roberts had no assets, but T & N retained 'power' over its records, which, as Chase so gleefully demonstrated, were hardly 'scanty'. Reluctantly, after four years of court orders and appeals from the plaintiffs' solicitors, T & N released 27,000 documents—but this was done only a few weeks before the trial, hardly allowing the plaintiffs' solicitors time to read them. As in the Standen case, no action was taken against the company for these tactics, though the trial judge, Mr Justice Holland, took the unusual step of criticizing the company for using 'any means possible, legitimate or otherwise . . . to wear [the plaintiffs] down by attrition'.[80] Further, he awarded Margereson and Hancock £115,000 in damages against T & N (with Hancock's share £65,000). Mr Justice Holland ruled that, although mesothelioma could not have been foreseen as a consequence of the asbestos dust that was expelled from the factory before the 1960s, some form of pulmonary injury should have been anticipated by the company—and therefore it was liable.[81]

T & N immediately appealed against the judgement as 'unsound'. Their arguments were subtle. According to T & N's counsel, inhaling asbestos was like a 'lottery'—no one knew which fibre could kill and so inhaling dust was like drawing prize tickets. Since the plaintiffs could theoretically have been exposed anywhere, then there was no proof that T & N's asbestos was responsible for their injury. This grotesque reasoning—of which John Collins and his fellow directors would have been proud—was rejected,[82] though not before more legal costs had been incurred (eventu-

---

[80] *Margereson and Hancock v. Roberts and T & N*, High Court Leeds, before Mr Justice Holland, 1995. Trial transcript, Judgement, 5.

[81] J. Steele and N. Wikeley, 'Liability in Tort for Environmental Mesothelioma: A UK Perspective', in G. A. Peters and B. J. Peters (eds.), *Asbestos Pathogenesis and Litigation. Vol. 13: Sourcebook on Asbestos Diseases* (Charlottesville: VA, 1996), 297–32; Steele and Wikeley, 'Dust on the Streets and Liability for Environmental Cancers', *Modern Law Review* 60 (1997), 265–76.

[82] T & N's argument about 'guilty' and 'not guilty dust' was reminiscent of another common law action brought against Roberts in 1951. John Waddell thought it might be useful to distinguish between statutory and non-statutory dust. By arguing that the dust that had killed the worker came from his work in non-scheduled areas, rather than from machinery covered by the Regulations, then the company might reach a 'settlement by admitting some measure of general common law liability without admitting that there was any breach of statutory duty, or that, if there was such a breach, it contributed in any way to the asbestosis'. See 9/1547. J. Waddell to N. Morling, 22 Oct. 1951.

ally they totalled over £1 million) and a final hurdle had been placed in the path of Margereson and Hancock. The latter did not have long to savour her victory—she died in 1997.

Why did T & N act this way? The only rationale, as ever, was economic: to delay and hold back future claims (in this case for environmental exposure) and try and deny victims the chance to claim a precedent. T & N had served a warning to future claimants (estimated at forty cases in Armley and up to 500 nationally) as to what they could expect if they demanded compensation; this also made sense in the boardroom, where Hope and his team were still grappling with the survival of the company.

11

An Acceptable Level of Death

Every day in a thousand situations and with a thousand substances managers, doctors, public representatives and officials have to decide what are acceptable levels of risk for the things which make our lives more safe, more pleasant, more rewarding. The drug or vaccination which saves thousands kills the very few who are sensitive to it; the seat belts which protect 999 from death or injury inflict them on the thousandth. The same paradox holds true for asbestos.

'Asbestos: Miracle Fibre? Killer Dust?', Asbestos Information Committee Bulletin, 1976.

Obviously, conditions in the past were worse than they are now but . . . I do not think one can ever be complacent about the risk to workers now . . . If 5 or 10 per cent are going to die, that may be better than 30 or 40 in the past; but is that the level of deaths as a result of employment which society can tolerate, let alone the individuals involved can tolerate?

John Willis, House of Commons Employment Committee, *Asbestos: Minutes of Evidence*, 16 Mar. 1983, 187.

Nearly a hundred years after the Factory Inspectors had first reported the dangers of asbestos, T & N disappeared as an independent business. In 1994, it made a provision of over £100 million for American costs and declared that its insurance cover was almost exhausted. In the following year, it shed its last links with the magic mineral by selling the Zimbabwe mines and also moved to contain its asbestos disease liabilities with a new insurance policy. It made a further £338 million provision for claims, which with interest was intended to give it £690 million to pay out over time. It also purchased a £92 million insurance package to pay the next £500 million in claims. If these topped £1 billion, then it would start paying out again. The expenditure sliced into T & N's balance sheet, which recorded a loss of nearly £400 million in 1996. However, the insurance deal was well trailed in the press as another management masterstroke. Financiers in the City, it was said, 'can now appreciate the quality of [T & N's] engineering business rather than fretting over asbestosis claims.'[1] It proved to be the prelude to the take-over that had been

---

[1] N. Bennett, 'T & N Can Breathe Again', *Sunday Telegraph*, 1 Dec. 1996.

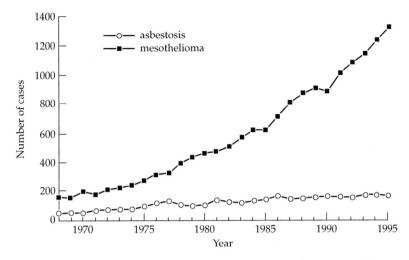

Graph 11.1 Death certificates mentioning asbestosis and
mesothelioma, 1968–95
Source: Health & Safety Commission, *Health & Safety Statistics* (1997).
NB. Figures are provisional for 1990–5.

rumoured for some time. In 1997, Federal Mogul, an American engineering firm, made a successful £1.5 billion bid for T & N, helped ironically
by a loan from Chase Manhattan Bank. While T & N's top directors lined
up for an estimated £3 million in severance and consultancy packages, the
chief executive of Federal played down the asbestos claims. He thought
that they were 'more of a concern to UK investors than US ones, who are
used to remedies for litigation', adding praise for the 'professional efforts
by T & N management to cap this issue'.[2]

Asbestos deaths in the UK will prove less easy to cap. The bleak scenario
is depicted in Graph 11.1. As usual, the figures need to be treated with
caution. Statistics are still collected piecemeal;[3] mesothelioma is still misdiagnosed; and lung cancer is only officially recognized alongside asbestosis.
In fact, the Health & Safety Commission regard the official figures as only
about half the true count. In other words, the current death rate is about
3,000 or more.[4] That said, we can look at the trends more closely. Asbestosis

---

[2] K. Gopal, 'The Local Takeaway', *Insider*, Jan. 1998, quoting Dick Snell.
[3] Several studies have highlighted the continued inaccuracy of official statistics. For
example, see C. R. Gillis *et al.*, 'Incidence of Mesothelioma in Glasgow 1981–1984', *Journal of
Society of Occupational Medicine* 40 (1990), 5–10. This survey found 113 cases (mostly occupational): no single source identified more than 81 per cent of the total.
[4] See HSC, *Health and Safety Statistics 1994–95* (1995), 55, 148–51; HSC, *Annual Report
1994–95* (1995), 107–17; S. Hutchings *et al.*, 'Asbestos-Related Diseases', in HSE, F. Driver
(ed.), *Occupational Health: Decennial Supplement* (1996), 127–52.

deaths have remained relatively stable, though a steady rise is noticeable from about 50 a year in 1968 to over 150 in 1995. This is not a dramatically high figure, but since asbestosis was recognized at least seventy years ago it is nevertheless a stark reminder of a failure of government regulation. Obviously, the most striking feature of the graph is the steeply rising trend in mesothelioma deaths, which shows no sign of slackening.

How much longer will these deaths continue to rise? What will be the final toll? No one really knows for certain. Current predictions in Britain are that mesothelioma deaths for men will peak about the year 2020 with between 2,700 and 3,300 deaths.[5] For the worst affected group—men born in the 1940s—mesothelioma may account for 1 per cent of all deaths. This total does not include women or asbestosis or lung cancer deaths. The government has suggested that when these are included the overall death toll could reach between 5,000 and 10,000 annually. Excess deaths in Britain from asbestos-related diseases could eventually reach 100,000, though some have predicted much higher figures. (In the USA, a figure of over 130,000 excess deaths from asbestos cancers alone has been projected.) In 1999, one study projected that in Western Europe 250,000 men would die of mesothelioma between 1995 and 2029; with half a million as the corresponding figure for the total number of West European deaths from asbestos.[6]

The steadily rising mortality is not only due to the latency of the diseases, it also reflects the fact that individuals are still being exposed. By the late 1990s, increasingly stringent government regulations have driven the British asbestos industry out of existence.[7] Crocidolite, amosite, and chrysotile have been banished, so that workplace exposure in asbestos *manufacture* is now a thing of the past. But most of the asbestos imported into the UK between 1960 and 1980 is still in place in buildings everywhere. Carpenters, plumbers, electricians, and maintenance workers may still suffer exposure (sometimes unsuspectingly) as they renovate or demolish buildings. More disturbingly, such men—like the contract asbestos workers who initially sprayed and installed the mineral—are often unmonitored and unregulated. Asbestos has gone, but it is still with us. It has remained paradoxical to the last.

This book has highlighted the role of the leading British asbestos company in this unprecedented occupational health disaster. It is a story

[5] J. Peto *et al.*, 'Continuing Increase in Mesothelioma Mortality in Britain', *Lancet* 345 (4 Mar. 1995), 535–9.

[6] J. Peto *et al.*, 'The European Mesothelioma Epidemic', *British Journal of Cancer* 79 (Feb. 1999), 666–72.

[7] Current HSC 'action levels' are 0.3 f/ml for chrysotile averaged over four hours (0.9 f/ml over ten minutes), with 0.2 f/ml and 0.6 f/ml as the respective figures for all other forms of asbestos. See *The Control of Asbestos at Work. Regulations 1987* [updated 1999] (Sheffield, 3rd edn. 1999).

which begs a number of key questions: what were the most important factors at the root of the tragedy? Could it have been avoided? Does it hold any important lessons for the future?

Despite the huge amount of evidence, the task of providing an answer to any of these questions is not easy. Occupational health hazards, as this account has shown, involve a complex range of social, political, and economic issues. Moreover, as anyone will find if they examine the post-mortem and inquest files on the Chase microfilms, the story of the magic mineral revolves around the suffering and agonizing death of thousands of individuals. Maintaining impartiality and a proper perspective where such events are concerned presents the historian with a most difficult task. Complicating the picture is asbestos itself. It has always been one of those products that has invited bitter controversy, splitting people into those 'for' and 'against'. Even in the 1990s, asbestos still has its defenders. A fresh account of the asbestos hazard is likely to be dismissed as sensationalist, socialist, or tinged with the benefit of hindsight.

Yet the attempt to provide a perspective on Turner & Newall's experience is worth making for two reasons. First, the industry is still important globally, with obvious implications for workers' health. Over 2 million tonnes of asbestos are still mined each year, with Russia and Canada as the leading producers. India, the Far East, and South America are still important markets, especially for construction materials.[8] Even in Britain, the industry is not quite dead. The Labour Party's decision in 1998 to delay its promised ban on the import of chrysotile showed that vested interests still had some life in them.[9] Second, asbestos is only one of a number of hazardous substances in our lives. The way in which we have dealt with this problem could influence our occupational health attitudes and policies in the future.

The argument that it is only with *hindsight* that we can appreciate asbestos's ill-effects must be considered first. This view is occasionally advanced by a few writers in academic journals, though not, I believe, very convincingly.[10] Fortunately, hindsight is unnecessary in assessing the actions of the asbestos companies, as their conduct can be appraised using contemporary standards. The 1931 Regulations,

[8] M. Huncharek, 'Exporting Asbestos: Disease and Policy in the Developing World', *Journal of Public Health Policy* (Spring 1993), 51–65.

[9] The Labour government's action (like the failure to ban tobacco sponsorship in motor racing) meant reneging on an election promise. It was rumoured to be due to pressure from Canada, which is still a major exporter of chrysotile. The use of white asbestos in the UK was eventually barred in 1999.

[10] P. Bartrip, 'Too Little, Too Late? The Home Office and the Asbestos Industry Regulations, 1931', *Medical History* 42 (Oct. 1998), 421–38; and R. Murray, 'Asbestos: A Chronology of its Origins and Health Effects', *British Journal of Industrial Medicine* 47 (1990), 361–5. See also the argument between R. Murray and Castleman, *British Journal of Industrial Medicine* 48 (1991), 427–32.

whatever their deficiencies, set out a series of legal requirements to prevent 'the escape of asbestos dust into the air of any room in which persons work'. As this book has shown, it was the industry's failure to meet those rules that sowed the seeds of its later problems—not the 'apostles of hindsight', who, it is claimed, have exaggerated the asbestos hazard retrospectively.

This is not to deny that there was an important contemporary context. Indeed, the first key factor in the asbestos tragedy was historical circumstance. Given the development of the industry in the late nineteenth century and the latency of asbestos-related diseases, some workers' mortality was inevitable. This was simply because no one could have fully anticipated the dangers. We now know that most asbestos dust is invisible (even under optical microscopes), that it causes cancer, and that the mineral cannot be manufactured or used without complete enclosure and protection. None of these things was obvious to the Turner family, when they first launched the business. Things had become a little clearer by the 1920s, when asbestosis deaths began to increase markedly, yet by then a large and thriving business had developed. Workers depended on asbestos for their jobs and so too did an increasingly wide range of industries. In other words, the seeds for a future health problem had been sown, even before the government had legislated for asbestosis.

The Rochdale setting must also not be discounted. Turner & Newall was not an unusually hard-nosed and evil company by the standards of the day. Its attitudes and strategies—such as its paternalism, anti-unionism, and *laissez-faire* approach to workers' health—were entirely typical among Lancashire firms in the inter-war period. At that time, the town's dismal industrial history cast a long shadow. Only a generation before (and perhaps within the living memory of a few), Rochdale had experienced appalling levels of mortality. For example, it has been calculated that life expectancy in 1848 in the UK was 27; in Rochdale it was 21. Mortality rates continued to rise until the 1860s and then fell only slowly over the next twenty years.[11] Tuberculosis and other bronchial conditions were still common in the town between the wars; so, too, was widespread unemployment. Rochdale life was tough. When Wilfred Ellison arrived in the town for his job interview at TBA in 1911, one of the first sights that greeted him was a Saturday afternoon pub brawl between two women who were kicking each other with clogs! In this context, what price a relatively small number of asbestosis deaths?

Yet although the occurrence of an asbestos health problem was inevitable in the twentieth century, its future scale owed much to management and regulatory failings.

---

[11] John Cole, *Rochdale Revisited: A Town and Its People* (1988), 15–16.

It is the asbestos companies themselves which have usually been seen as the major culprits. The most persuasive proponents of this view have been Americans—notably journalist Paul Brodeur and environmental health consultant Barry Castleman. In a devastating critique, the latter has accused the asbestos industry of placing profit before health and has argued that the subsequent disaster 'stands as an indictment of our social order'.[12]

Plenty of evidence from the Turner & Newall archive can be found to substantiate a similar view for the British asbestos industry. The company's attitude towards matters of health over so many years may be regarded as strikingly irresponsible. In the last decade or so, T & N has tried to defend itself in court actions by arguing that it has always applied government safety regulations, that it has always adequately warned workers about the risks, that it has paid 'fair' compensation, and that it has supported medical research. Its archive shows such claims owe more to public relations than to fact. Turner & Newall provided significant opposition to the government dust control and medical schemes between the 1930s and 1960s; it neglected to implement such schemes fully both in the UK and especially overseas; it failed to warn customers; refused frequently to admit financial and moral liability for the consequences of its actions; often paid only token amounts of money for industrial injuries and deaths; tried to browbeat doctors, coroners, and the Medical Board; sought to suppress research linking asbestos and cancer; gave the government inaccurate data about disease among its shipyard workers; and disseminated imprecise information about the 'safety' of asbestos. Most of this had been suspected for some time: indeed, thanks to the courageous efforts of a few journalists and activists, some of the evidence had already appeared in the 1970s and 1980s. Now, due to Chase Manhattan Bank and the greater freedom of information enjoyed by Americans, a more complete and detailed picture can be drawn.

Certainly the company made a partial effort to control the dust (at least in some areas) and its technologists and physicians did help improve workers' safety. On the other hand, the knowledge was available to do much more, as there can be no doubt that Turner & Newall had vast amounts of information at its disposal. The continuing asbestosis problem in the 1940s, closely followed by the appearance of cancer, should have resulted in much tighter regulations in the workplace, either on the company's initiative or in conjunction with the government. Ventilation should have been improved and extended; good housekeeping rigidly enforced; and the workers and unions educated in what Merewether had thought so important—a 'sane appreciation' of the risk.[13] In particular,

---

[12] Castleman, *Asbestos*, 827.

[13] E. R. A. Merewether and C. W. Price, *Report on Effects of Asbestos Dust on the Lungs and Dust Suppression in the Asbestos Industry* (1930), 17.

medical surveillance and dust protection should have been extended to the lagging trades. In the long term, the company should have sponsored well-funded and wide-ranging epidemiological studies and then acted upon the findings. Ultimately, it should have moved as soon as possible to replace asbestos with safer materials. All these measures would not have obliterated asbestos disease entirely, but the future scale of the problem would have been greatly reduced.[14]

As we have seen, this never happened. Forty years passed before the government regulations were revised, a delay partly caused by the industry. Firms such as Turner & Newall made piecemeal improvements, while they massively increased output, especially in the unscheduled areas of the industry. Inconvenient research findings were ignored; and a switch to substitutes was delayed until the company was pushed into it by external forces. We need not look very far for the reasons. As one lawyer has remarked, there was just so much money being made by this huge multinational business, that 'they were not persuaded that enough people were dying or suffering an asbestos-related disease to find substitute materials or shut down and walk away. There was always an acceptable level of death.'[15]

Yet Turner & Newall were not the only actors in the asbestos drama who found the level of death acceptable. So did the Factory Inspectorate. The sheer lack of government constraint on the asbestos industry in matters of health and safety is troubling. The 1931 Regulations were intended to be 'provisional', and yet clearly between the 1930s and 1950s there was little chance that the asbestos legislation would be tightened. In fact, in this period the regulations were mostly never properly enforced. Factories such as Roberts were allowed to produce asbestos almost as though government regulations did not exist.

Why was the government's regulatory hand so weak? Many reasons can be advanced: in the Depression of the 1930s, workers needed jobs; during the Second World War, strategic concerns pushed health issues into the background; and during the 1950s, expanding markets made production paramount. The Factory Inspectorate was understaffed and often overworked. Another factor may have influenced both the Inspectors and the asbestos firms. The number of UK asbestosis deaths listed by the Factory Inspectorate was numerically small (see Graph 11.2). Between the 1930s and late 1950s, deaths from asbestosis averaged about twenty each year. Of

---

[14] A former Johns–Manville executive has argued that medical research, assiduous communication, insistent warnings, and a rigorous dust-reduction programme 'could have saved lives and would probably have saved the stockholders, the industry, and, for that matter, the product'. See B. Sells, 'What Asbestos Taught Me About Managing Risk', *Harvard Business Review* (Mar.–Apr. 1994), 76–89, 76.

[15] Kieran May interview, BBC2 TV, 'An Acceptable Level of Death', 14 Apr. 1994.

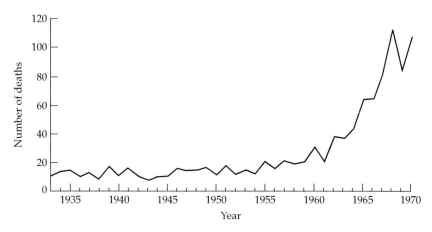

Graph 11.2 Deaths from asbestosis, 1933–70
Note: Before 1933, 42 asbestosis deaths had been notified.
Source: Chief Medical Inspector of Factories, *Annual Reports* (1932–).

course, this does not reflect the true incidence of the disease, as the Factory Inspectorate made no special effort to tally asbestosis deaths and only listed those cases where there was 'no doubt as to the cause of death'—in other words, usually only if there had been a post-mortem and inquest. As we know, many cases were missed by the authorities or ignored by the industry. None the less, we can see why it was tempting to disregard asbestos mortality for so long. It was simply not seen as a very big problem. It certainly does not appear to have greatly troubled the Factory Inspectorate, and it did not greatly worry an industry that was always inclined to blame present troubles on the latency of asbestosis and pre-1931 conditions.

Asbestosis was only one dusty disease and it was overshadowed by silicosis in the mining and grinding trades. As Table 11.1 shows, by 1940 annual registered deaths from silicosis had topped 500. By 1960, annual deaths from coal miners' pneumoconiosis alone were over 1,500 (a year when there were 31 certificated asbestosis deaths). In 1954, John Collins argued that 'we should not lose our sense of proportion as to the extent of the asbestosis risk. Throughout the country the number of asbestosis cases is insignificant in relation to the number of silicosis and other types of pneumoconiosis cases. As compared with other industrial disease, the risk of contracting asbestosis in the asbestos industry is relatively slight.'[16] Collins, however, forgot to mention one small matter: the relative size of these industries. Employment in the asbestos industry was nowhere near

[16] 9/1133–5. 'Miscellaneous Points', Dec. 1954.

Table 11.1. *Deaths from asbestosis and silicosis, 1935–70*

	1935	1940	1945	1950	1955	1960	1965	1970
Silicosis	281	290	185	218	385	469	407	351
Coal miners' silicosis/ Pneumoconiosis	111	232	387	846	1,624	1,596	1,668	1,267
Asbestosis	15	11	11	12	21	31	64	107

Source: Chief Medical Inspector of Factories, *Annual Reports* (London, 1932–).

the size of that in coal and other dusty trades.[17] When that is taken into account, asbestos moves closer to centre-stage as a hazardous industry. Nevertheless, the low absolute head count clearly weighed heavily in influencing contemporary attitudes.

Even when mesothelioma was recognized in the 1960s, economic considerations and not health counted most with the Factory Inspectorate. The asbestos industry was virtually allowed to make its own regulations, using its own data, and setting its own pace in meeting new standards. The Inspectorate's priorities were stated quite frankly. In 1967, a BBC reporter asked the Chief Inspector of Factories, Ronald Christy: 'When men's and women's lives are at risk, or maybe at risk, isn't there a case of banning [asbestos] until it's proved safe?' Christy replied: 'No, I don't think there is, because if we were to ban it there would be considerable upheaval in industry among the people that so far feel they have got to go on using it.'[18]

Similar views can be found among the medical community—a fact which, at first sight, might seem surprising. After all, their oath enjoins doctors to follow a clear precept—to use their power to help the sick and abstain from harming any man. However, as this book amply demonstrates, the medical community did not always find it easy to obey this rule when dealing with asbestos. This was partly because, as with any occupational health problem, doctors were sometimes brought into close proximity with industry. A few worked within it or followed research agendas set by business, and others had their investigations funded by companies. Even when they did not, they were still subject to powerful social and political pressures that, as Fred Hasson has observed, often 'politicized' the medical profession.[19]

---

[17] Coal mining employed well over 800,000 in the early 1930s (and about 700,000 in the late 1940s). The figures for asbestos were about 7,000 and 15,000 respectively.

[18] Leonard Parkin, BBC TV, 24 Hours, 'Blue Asbestos and Mesothelioma', 19 Jan. 1967.

[19] F. Hasson, 'Asbestos—The Political Disease', *The Health Services* (20 Aug. 1982), 12–13.

Before the 1950s, the asbestos industry was largely unfettered by medical fact and opinion and companies readily sequestered doctors whenever they were needed. Turner & Newall's own physicians, Bateman and Knox, were thus primarily company men, whose attitudes support the view of one critic that: 'The history of physicians in industry, certainly in the asbestos industry, indicates that they were a self-select, management-oriented group. They served at the pleasure of higher management for the purpose of controlling employers' costs for illness and injuries at work.'[20] Certainly that was how Turner & Newall viewed leading pathologist Matthew Stewart, who was retained not to advise the company on how to reduce asbestosis deaths, but to help rebut compensation claims. In this period, the UK experience paralleled that in the USA, where the slow development of industrial medicine as a discipline, the industry's control of the research agenda, and its restrictions on the dissemination of information, always ensured that economic imperatives predominated.[21]

In the 1950s and 1960s, this slowly began to change. Doll and Schilling made a stand for academic freedom when they declined to withdraw the TBA lung cancer article in 1955. Kerns resigned from Turner & Newall on a point of principle in 1965; and thereafter Lewinsohn demonstrated a commitment to his worker-patients that would ultimately make it impossible for him to continue at the company. But these were little-publicized events. What is equally striking is the fact that no British doctor ever seems to have taken a prominent public stand against asbestos, even when its lethal nature was revealed, and even though medical science has never been able to treat any asbestos disease. Thus the British asbestos scene contained no public-spirited figure of the stature of Irving Selikoff in America. Certainly, hardly anyone called for the product to be banned. In the innumerable books, articles, and documents that I have read in compiling this book, the only doctor who seems to have come close to suggesting such a course was Dr Leonard Williams, the officer of health in Barking, who witnessed the fall-out from Cape's London factory. In 1945, he wrote:

I am firmly of the opinion that [asbestos] is a deadly and dangerous commodity and unless those who are charged with the responsibility of safeguarding the health of the people in the industry can give positive assurances that they have now after all these years removed every possible danger, the processing of

[20] Castleman, *Asbestos*, 272–3.
[21] See D. Ozonoff, 'Failed Warnings: Asbestos-Related Disease and Industrial Medicine', in R. Bayer (ed.), *The Health and Safety of Workers* (1988), 139–218; and also T. H. Murray, 'Regulating Asbestos: Ethics, Politics and the Values of Science', in the same vol., 271–92. A more general American study, C. C. Sellers, *Hazards of the Job* (1997), also highlights the dilemmas involved in industrial medicine.

asbestos, except in so far as it is essential to our national economy, should be barred.[22]

Why did doctors not adopt this strong line? Two reasons will be advanced here. The first is that in Britain, with government and the trade unions taking so little interest in the problem, doctors found themselves working *with* industry rather than against it.[23] Some physicians, such as Knox, owed their livelihood directly to the industry. Doctors and medical researchers also worked with Turner & Newall and other firms through their links with the Asbestosis Research Council. The Rochdale cohort studies were another point at which industry and medicine intersected. The TBA studies allowed, on the one hand, physicians access to otherwise confidential data; while on the other, the industry retained some control over the scope of the research. This joint approach proved both prolific and enduring and was unruffled by the 'Alice' furore and Turner & Newall's increasingly controversial image. By the time Doll organized a seminar on asbestos and health (and litigation) for T & N directors at his Oxford college in 1984, the TBA health studies had been in progress for about thirty years.[24] Besides Doll, speakers at the conference included Newhouse, Elmes, and Julian Peto—all of whom had been involved in analysing medical data at T & N.[25] Another article on disease at a 'Rochdale asbestos factory' appeared in the following year.[26] However, T & N's retreat from asbestos and the fact that most new cases of disease were outside the asbestos plants signalled the end for this type of study. Later Peto lamented that focusing so exclusively on the asbestos factories had been a 'stupid mistake'.[27]

The second reason that doctors never campaigned against asbestos usage revolves, as with the Factory Inspectors, around the concept of acceptable risk. Here there was considerable convergence between the industry, government, and the medical community. Most shared a basic philosophy: despite the dangers, asbestos production should not be curtailed for economic and (ironically) safety reasons. This led doctors, occasionally, to pass opinions on matters that, strictly speaking, were non-medical.

[22] *The Annual Report of the [Barking] Medical Officer of Health* (1945), 23.
[23] For interactions between business and doctors in France, see F. Malye, *Amiante: Le Dossier de l'Air Contamine* (1996).
[24] 150/350–1. Workshop on Asbestos & Health at Green College, 20–1 July 1984.
[25] Newhouse had by now conducted an analysis at Ferodo. See G. Berry and M. L. Newhouse, 'Mortality of Workers Manufacturing Friction Materials Using Asbestos', *British Journal of Industrial Medicine* 40 (1983), 1–7.
[26] J. Peto *et al.*, 'Relationship of Mortality to Measures of Environmental Pollution in an Asbestos Textile Factory', *Annals of Occupational Hygiene* 29 (1985), 305–55. See also R. Doll and J. Peto, *Asbestos: Effects on Health of Exposure to Asbestos* (1985).
[27] Peto interview with John Waite, BBC Radio 4, 'Too Little, Too Late', 15 Oct. 1998.

The views of Cape Asbestos physician Dr Hubert Wyers were typical. He realized that government regulation would not prevent asbestos killing workers. However, he thought that further legislation would be 'unwise and unnecessary', and that to ban the product 'would put back [the] nation's industrial capacity for half a century, a blow which this country, at any rate, would not survive'.[28] Wyers was writing at the end of the Second World War. However, even after 1960, when mesothelioma had shown its hand, doctors were reluctant to recommend the complete withdrawal of asbestos. Indeed, quite the reverse was the case. In 1967, the *Lancet* cautioned trade unions not to overrate the dangers of asbestos, as it would be:

ludicrous to outlaw this valuable and often irreplaceable material in all circumstances [as] asbestos can save more lives than it can possibly endanger. Perhaps a reasonable perspective can be generated by a free and frank discussion of risks between management and labour, replacing some of the evasions of the past. Workers in general are willing to take a calculated risk for the benefit of the community if they feel they have it frankly explained to them and if they have confidence that all reasonable practical measures are being taken to protect them.[29]

Perhaps it took time for the idea to be accepted that the cancer risk from asbestos was likely to be proportional down to trivial levels (as such a relationship was only then beginning to be accepted in relation to ionizing radiation).[30] However, it is also clear that doctors were persuaded that the economic and social benefits of asbestos should not be abandoned lightly. In the 1970s, leading pathologists warned against safety measures which would lead to '*unnecessary* dislocating decisions with severe economic repercussions', and argued that the 'tremendous potentiality and value to modern society of asbestos are too great to stop its use without very sound reasons'.[31] In 1987, Doll still remained optimistic that the dangers of asbestos usage could be satisfactorily controlled to allow for its continued use, especially in view of the 'tremendous contribution ... to human welfare' made by the mineral's 'insulating power and indestructibility by fire and friction'.[32] Even in the 1990s, some doctors were advancing a cost-benefit type of analysis to justify the continued use of asbestos. Dr Robert Murray (who appeared as a T & N defence expert witness in the early 1990s) argued that the number of lives saved by using

[28] H. Wyers, 'That Legislative Measures Have Proved Generally Effective in the Control of Asbestosis' (Glasgow University MD, 1946), 6, 137.

[29] *Lancet*, 17 June 1967, i, 1311–12.

[30] This is the view of Sir Richard Doll, communicated to author, letter 10 Dec. 1998.

[31] J. C. Wagner *et al.*, 'The Role of International Research in Occupational Cancer', *La Medicina del Lavoro* 63 (1972), 213–20, 213, 219.

[32] 228/1251–62. Doll's closing address to International Agency for Research on Cancer Symposium, 'Mineral Fibres in the Non-Occupational Environment', Lyon, France, 10 Sept. 1987.

asbestos-cement pipes for supplying water in the developing world more than outweighed the 'minimal risk' incurred in making them. Thus 'the advantages of asbestos or any other fibre reinforcement may be accepted by the people of the world without fear'.[33]

The asbestos industry's critics have, however, argued that many of the 'benefits' of asbestos are illusory and are largely based on industry-generated propaganda (a view apparently supported by the speed with which the 'indispensable' mineral has been rapidly substituted across the board). They have refused to accept that the risks of making any asbestos product abroad are minimal. Indeed, they have argued that no risk is acceptable and have pointed to the repeated failure to set an enduring safe threshold (a rule-of-thumb exercise anyway).[34] They have also highlighted the fact that since the 1930s doctors have sometimes been as fallible as anyone else in predicting mortality from asbestos.[35]

The debate has often taken on overtones of class warfare. This is hardly surprising as, above all, asbestos-related diseases were linked to social class. The majority of sufferers were working-class people—usually manual workers—and their 'masters' rarely developed asbestos disease. While hundreds of its workforce perished, Turner & Newall's higher echelons remained immune. Whatever their fate in the next world, the likes of John Collins suffered little in this one, at least not from asbestos. Collins himself died suddenly, aged 70, of a heart attack. So did Walker Shepherd (on a sleeper-train in Canada); John Knox (on a golf course); and Steve Holmes (on his way to make an asbestos court deposition). None of the Turner family appears to have suffered from asbestos disease. Sir Samuel Turner III was long lived, like his father, dying at 77 from an ulcer and stroke. Bussy died from 'cardiac asthma' and influenza, aged 71. The Ellison brothers, William and Wilfred, lived into their 'eighties and 'nineties, respectively, and died from diseases of old age unconnected with asbestos. Only at the small Roberts' factory is there any suggestion that asbestos might have harmed the directors: Dolbey died in 1965, aged 67, from carcinomatosis and prostate cancer; and Wilfred Roberts in 1941 from cancer of the rectum. Only one asbestos company director is thought to have died from mesothelioma—Richard

---

[33] Murray, 'Asbestos', 364–5.

[34] Julian Peto once described the concept of acceptable risk as a 'can of worms' and noted how scientists failed to agree upon it. He concluded that it was 'all a matter of personal judgement'. 412/1456–7. Peto to R. Sykes, 10 Oct. 1979.

[35] Robert Murray wrote to T & N director Harry Hardie, 5 Feb. 1985, that he had met a man on a train who made a lot of money out of covering up asbestos: 'He was an "expert" on asbestos as well, so I had some pleasure in informing him that the downturn in mesothelioma would occur about 1990 and would have nothing to do with the campaign which is being conducted by the media over the last ten years. He seemed surprised!' 84/1873–4.

Gaze at Cape Asbestos[36]—and there appear to be no recorded cases among health physicians in the industry. Except for actor Steve McQueen,[37] no celebrities have died from asbestos, and asbestosis and mesothelioma remain very much diseases associated with Britain's dreary and declining industrial heartlands.

It is the class dimension that explains a striking feature of the Turner & Newall archive. Until Kerns and Lewinsohn arrived on the scene, the company files demonstrate a marked indifference to workers' sufferings. Hardly ever do they express, except in the most formal way, emotions such as sympathy for physical suffering, regret over a death, or anxiety over conditions within the factory. Frank Bussy once described asbestotics as those 'unfortunate men',[38] but that is virtually the only sympathetic note in the entire Turner & Newall archive before the 1970s, at which point the company began making more conciliatory noises about treating victims sympathetically. Dealing with asbestos-related disease became routine at Turner & Newall—merely a kind of administrative problem. Attitudes from the 1930s seem to have survived thirty years or more later. In 1961, when Sarah Holt died aged 75 from asbestosis, the company's assistant secretary wrote that the case was nothing special: 'Mrs Holt, despite working in the scheduled [carding and spinning] areas for almost 36 years, had never been suspended on account of asbestosis and lived to a good old age . . . In any event asbestosis was only an indirect cause of death.'[39]

This insensitivity should not surprise. Since its formation, Turner & Newall has mingled conservative political beliefs with a suspicion of the rights of labour. Walker Shepherd feared that in the aftermath of the Second World War workers' organizations would take over the country. In 1944, he described trade unions as the most powerful vested interest in Britain. 'Compared with the restrictionist practices of trade unions', he wrote, 'even the worst cartels are as cooing doves.'[40] In the 1970s, when the company contributed to various right-wing think tanks and political organizations, its chairmen argued that trade unions had an 'outdated and privileged position above the law [that] must be altered and balanced with that of management'.[41]

It is no coincidence that the people who emerge with the most nobility from this story are the ordinary working-class people who have suffered most. Their gritty determination and fortitude stand

---

[36] Gaze's death certificate records 'metastatic peritoneal carcinoma'. There was no inquest.
[37] McQueen died from mesothelioma in 1980, having been exposed to asbestos when he was a marine in the US Navy.
[38] 351/928. Bussy to Collins, 15 Feb. 1936.
[39] 66/0328. Assistant Secretary to G. Chadwick, 7 Dec. 1961.
[40] Board Papers, Shepherd to Lord McGowan, 27 Oct. 1944.
[41] T & N, *Reports and Accounts* (1978).

in sharp contrast to the indifference and evasions of those running the industry. Many of them have been women. Indeed, it is notable how often crucial events have revolved around individuals such as Alice Jefferson, June Hancock, Nellie Kershaw, Nora Dockerty, and Nancy Tait.[42]

When the destructive potential of asbestos was revealed, the sense of betrayal felt by the workers towards those in authority was consequently very acute. As one Scottish shipyard worker complained bitterly: 'We were never told about it, there were never any warnings about it, and when I think of the number of doctors who have told us to stop drinking and stop smoking, no one has ever told us to stop working with asbestos.'[43] Asbestos workers became victims 'twice over': their health ruined by their job, they were then cheated by an inequitable social and political system.[44] However, the workers could also turn a blind eye to the dangers. It was evident that there was some element of 'bargaining' in the asbestos industry and that some workers seem to have accepted an element of risk for extra money. This allowed companies such as TBA and Roberts to spend modestly on dust control and reserve any extra expend-iture for the higher than average wages needed to attract workers given the dusty conditions, and for the payment of *ex gratias*. Many workers and dependants (though certainly not all) accepted their *ex gratias* and reduced lump sums without protest: indeed in some cases, they accepted the company's hand-outs with profuse thanks. It was not until after the 1970s that the organization of asbestos victims' action-groups and media pres-sure signalled a change of attitude in society, when sick workers began fighting for their rights.

Ironically, when that action did come in the 1990s, it was organized more by external parties—by the media, bankers, and lawyers—than by trade unions. As we have seen, labour organizations played only a limited role in health and safety matters during the asbestos industry's heyday. Admittedly, they were in a difficult position. They were effectively excluded from decision-making by Turner & Newall; they did not have access to the company's medical files or research; and they also lacked funding. Asbestos diseases were entrenched in precisely those areas of the industry—such as contract insulation work—that were only weakly unionized. Legal actions for trade union members were blocked until the 1960s by costs and by the legal limitation period for claims. On the other

---

[42] For a graphic story of a Glasgow housewife Ellen McKessock's dogged battle against mesothelioma, see B. McKessock, *Mesothelioma: The Story of an Illness* (1995).

[43] 500/1780. Mesothelioma victim Pat McCrystal interviewed, BBC TV2, Newsnight, 8 Sept. 1992.

[44] J. Leneghan, *Victims Twice Over* (1994). See also Clydeside Action on Asbestos video, 'A Struggle for Breath: An Overview of the Asbestos Problem' (1996).

hand, even after that date the labour response to the asbestos health problem was muted. As early as 1906, a government committee had requested information on the prevalence of asbestosis after the death of Montague Murray's patient: but the TUC was unable to provide it. As Alan Dalton has remarked, the situation was unchanged at the end of the 1970s.[45] He highlighted that, in contrast to Selikoff's work on union records in the USA, British trade unions had never conducted health surveys of their members. He concluded: 'Trade unions have done little for their members as regards compensation, but even less as regards prevention, the primary trade union demand. They were consulted with regard to the 1969 Asbestos Regulations, but it is difficult to see what, if any, changes they suggested.' This book supports these statements. It also indicates why trades union officials were so indifferent. They too were inclined to place jobs above health. Only rank and file trade unionists, such as Newalls' lagger John Todd, who fought a lone campaign for better safety measures and compensation in the 1960s, were uncompromising in their demands. They were sidelined for their trouble by their unions, for whom—like the employers—there was sometimes an acceptable level of death.

Asbestos was not the only industry in which workers' mortality was part of the natural order. One of the biggest occupational health scandals in British history is the story of the miners. Thousands of them have been killed by pneumoconiosis (black lung), besides other industrial accidents. In 1998, the High Court—after the longest-running personal-injury trial in British legal history—ruled in favour of a major compensation payout for the remaining sick miners. The judge damned the former National Coal Board for failing to protect miners from coal dust. But prevarication had saved the government and the taxpayer £1 billion. The news made front-page headlines for a day and was swiftly forgotten. Nine months after the case, no one—apart from the six test cases—has had full compensation.[46] Many other occupational diseases do not even achieve that level of prominence. Although it never became as notorious as asbestosis, byssinosis from cotton dust was another cause of respiratory disease deaths. In the 1960s, the Labour government ignored pleas from physicians for medical examinations and dust monitoring in the textile industry.[47] Coronary heart disease was identified as a health hazard for viscose rayon workers in the 1960s, but never became a prescribed disease.

[45] A. Dalton, *Asbestos Killer Dust* (1979), 80.
[46] 'Miners Died Without Justice', *Guardian*, 24 Jan. 1998; BBC Radio 4, 'Too Little, Too Late', 15 Oct. 1998.
[47] R. F. Schilling, *A Challenging Life* (1998), 81–116. This posthumous autobiography has a useful discussion on many other 'forgotten' industrial diseases.

However, asbestos achieved a notoriety denied these other occupational diseases. Why? It can hardly be because the death toll is so high.
After all, smoking-related lung cancer kills at least 30,000 people a year
in the UK (without including the mortality from other smoking-related
disorders). A greater number of alcohol-related disease deaths are
recorded each year. Automobile accidents kill over 3,500 each year in
Britain. Yet no one has suggested banning cigarettes, drink, or cars—
indeed, society happily sees them glamorized daily in advertising. The
answer lies in mesothelioma: no other cancer has such a horrific combination of extended latency, pain, certain death and, often, transient exposure. It was mesothelioma that earned asbestos its 'Killer Dust' label. By
1983, for example, the *Daily Star*, on 24 August 1983, was asking for
'Tough Curbs on Killer Asbestos', pointing out that: 'thousands of homes,
a third of our schools and a third of our water supplies were riddled with
it.' The language is instructive: the *relative* risk of developing mesothelioma from domestic exposure has always been very small (some medical
authorities have described it as negligible). However, as the publicity
accorded to the current Creutzfeld–Jacob Disease outbreak has shown, it
is not the actual risk that matters, but the public's perception of it. The
invisible hidden 'killer' that is all around us and can kill without warning
after fifty years, evokes particular fears, even panic. Newspaper articles
and television documentaries fastened particularly on the mesothelioma
victims of non-occupational exposure—the handyman who had died after
sawing up asbestos sheets for a day; the housewife who had shaken out
her husband's dusty overalls; the mother who as a child had inhaled blue
asbestos from the nearby factory.

By the 1980s and 1990s, mesothelioma compelled the public to adopt
Willis's view that the risk was no longer acceptable. People who had been
so indifferent to the asbestos hazard as long as it was confined inside the
factories, now demanded that the product be strictly controlled. The
media played a key role in this development. The asbestos industry had
long feared it, ever since the 1930s when worker's inquests were so incon-
veniently reported in the local press. Now television documentaries and
newspapers dragged at least one occupational disease into the open.
People, often for the first time, saw the effect of crippling industrial diseases. They also saw the secrecy of the asbestos industry and the parsimony of government. Suddenly, society discovered that it owed a debt.
As one television reporter put it, when discussing a Turner & Newall
asbestos widow:

We've never had a chance to assess for ourselves the true costs of using asbestos
[or] decide whether or not the price was too high to pay. It may be that the cancer
risk from asbestos is on the wane as controls become tighter, but for years,
unknown to most, the private tragedies of a few people . . . have been the real

price we've had to pay for the use of asbestos and not knowing the debts we owed we've not repaid them.[48]

Can such a situation be avoided in the future? In theory, the answer must be yes. Asbestos is harmless until it is released from the ground, which means that the asbestos disease epidemic—like all occupational health problems—is entirely man-made. Controlling hazards like asbestos could therefore be accomplished, if the problems can be analysed rationally. In this respect, Turner & Newall's experience is useful: it highlights the factors that allowed asbestos-related diseases to mushroom and also points the way towards possible solutions.

This book has shown that countervailing forces were simply too weak for most of the twentieth century to enforce adequate safety standards on an industry that was always inclined to put profit above health. Particularly damaging was the ineffectiveness of the Factory Inspectorate and the inability of the government medical officers to protect workers properly. Fines for misdemeanours were absurd, even on the rare occasions when they were imposed. The medical community was sometimes swayed by economic and political pressures. Trade unions were denied significant powers. Compensation payments were ridiculously low, providing neither a significant cost (and penalty) on the industry nor an adequate safety net for sick workers. As a system of final restitution, tort law merely compounded these problems. The courts neither punished the conduct of asbestos companies, nor dealt fairly with workers' injuries, while the adversarial atmosphere of litigation encouraged firms to deny liability and suppress information. Above all, the government demonstrated a disquieting tendency to allow industry a free hand.

All these trends and practices need to be reversed. The government's health and safety departments obviously need strengthening, with better funding, increased manpower, and wider powers. The former policy of persuasion should be replaced by one that rigorously enforces safety regulations and fines heavily, and perhaps even imprisons, offenders. Medical facilities within industry should be improved and occupational diseases more closely monitored by a truly independent body. Trade unions need to pay far more attention to the health and safety of their members. Effective data collection, analysis, and the widest dissemination of information should be given a high priority. Above all, the grotesque inequalities in the compensation system should be corrected, so that victims of industrial disease do not shoulder financial burdens that should be borne by management, shareholders, and society.

However, it would be naive to believe that such actions would

---

[48] 129/1820–7. Richard Stilgoe, BBC TV Nationwide, 17 Mar. 1976, discussing the case of the widow of Samuel Fisher.

immediately banish industrial health disasters. The implementation of
any one of these measures is complex and has already been much debated.
For example, criminalizing corporate behaviour has recently received
much attention in the aftermath of several high-profile cases such as
Union Carbide's chemical poisoning of the Indian community in Bhopal.
However, most of the debate about corporate crime has centred on financial misdeeds and isolated catastrophes.[49] Occupational health has rarely
featured in the discussions. Even so, it is clear that fines and imprison-
ment are a poor instrument for corporate accountability in the case of
asbestos-related diseases, since their latency inevitably means that the
principal offenders are dead or retired. Hitting a company may provide
a vicarious sense of justice, but little long-term satisfaction, and will probably only hurt the interests of present and future claimants. Predictably,
the only individuals who have been penalized for asbestos misdemeanours have been those on the lowest rung of the business ladder: such
as the Birmingham asbestos stripper, who in 1998 was jailed for nine
months for dumping 300 bags of asbestos around the city.

The asbestos experience demonstrates starkly the political and social
problems involved in any revamping of health and safety laws, compensation payments, and medical surveillance. Occupational diseases are
deeply social and political.[50] Industry inevitably influences both politicians and the formulation of industrial laws. The events surrounding the
introduction of the Asbestos Regulations in 1969 should banish any naive
ideas that government and industry will logically follow the healthiest
and safest option. Even if they did, decisions still have to be sold to the
electorate, which traditionally abhors higher taxes, more expensive products, and lost jobs. Put simply, nothing will change until society at large
agrees to forsake the technologies and social organization that have led
to the present health situation with asbestos. What is needed is a completely new mentality regarding occupational health in all sectors of
society, from management down to the shop floor, and a recognition that
the subject is vitally important.[51]

However, despite the fact that work-related illnesses and injuries
are estimated to cost the UK economy between £11 billion and £16 billion
a year—about 2–3 per cent of the gross domestic product—there is
little sign of that happening yet. In fact, while Britain's new enterprise
culture has been much trumpeted, the country's commitment to occupational health—as the late Richard Schilling has highlighted—has

[49] M. Punch, *Dirty Business* (1996) provides a useful overview of the large and growing literature on corporate misconduct.
[50] See D. Rosner and G. Markowitz, *Deadly Dust* (1987).
[51] This is not a novel conclusion. Jock McCulloch has argued, in *Asbestos: Its Human Cost* (St Lucia, 1986), that the best defence against industrial hazards is a vigilant workforce and a sceptical public. See also Alan Dalton's socialist views in *Killer Dust*, 259.

weakened.[52] The war saw a rapid expansion in industrial health care, which continued into the 1950s. But the chance to include a comprehensive occupational health service within the NHS was not taken. By the 1960s, Britain was failing to keep pace with occupational health developments in the European Community. In 1985 it was one of the few countries that failed to implement the International Labour Office's recommendation for comprehensive and compulsory health services in workplaces. Thus less than half of the British workforce now has access to occupational health services; while disablement benefits are a regular target for trimming, with only very modest extensions in coverage.

Moreover, the type of business organization that nurtured asbestos disease—the large-scale, multidivisional, global enterprise—is still with us. Indeed, despite the evidence that decentralized structures allow poor health conditions to flourish unchecked and also hinder workers gaining compensation, it seems that they will become increasingly dominant. The old British diseases that helped prime the asbestos bomb—secrecy and restrictions on freedom of information—have not changed either. The same political ideologies are around too, whether Labour or Conservative. They involve increasing social inequality, 'downsizing', privatization, short-term job contracts, and tighter controls on trade unions and individual liberty—all bad news for occupational health.

These developments should concern us all. As this book is being written, the country is once more worried about a health epidemic in which the final toll of casualties is unknown—this time caused by beef infected with human-variant CJD. This disease, too, is caused by an invisible agent, which has a long latency (though how long no one knows) and causes appalling mental and physical symptoms. Big business, government, and medical science are once again under the media spotlight. A major inquiry has been held. It all has disturbing echoes of asbestos.

---

[52] Schilling, *Life*, 175–7. Schilling was director of the Occupational Health Institute at the London School of Hygiene and Tropical Medicine—a foundation endowed by the TUC. It was closed in 1990.

BIBLIOGRAPHY

Primary Sources

The major archive source for this book was the Turner & Newall records, as copied by Chase Manhattan Bank during their 'discovery' process against T & N. The collection is split into two parts: one on microfilm; the other on microfiche.

The microfiche collection contains over 2,400 sheets, the bulk of which covers Turner & Newall board meetings between 1944 and 1970. The information contained on the fiche is mostly commercial in nature. The microfilms number 225, with each reel containing about 2,000 frames. These films provided the bulk of the information on the asbestos health problem at the company.

The T & N archive has been described, aptly, as a giant haystack—a huge mountain of unsorted records that is difficult to navigate and even more difficult to describe in short compass. The archive contains not only an enormous variety of company records, but also trade union documents, government reports, court proceedings, newspaper cuttings, published articles, radio and TV transcripts, and overseas literature.

A journal article describing this unique collection is currently being prepared by the author.

Television and Video Sources

BBC RADIO 4 Face the Facts, 'The Shocking Story of Asbestos', 6 Oct. 1993.
——Face the Facts, 'Asbestos and the Third World', 13 Oct. 1993.
——'Too Little, Too Late', 1, 8, 15 Oct. 1998.
BBC1, 'Deadly Legacy', 14 Apr. 1993.
——24 Hours, 'Blue Asbestos and Mesothelioma', 19 Jan. 1967.
BBC2 Horizon, 'Killer Dust', 20 Jan. 1975.
——'An Acceptable Level of Death', 14 Apr. 1994.
CLYDESIDE ACTION ON ASBESTOS, 'A Struggle for Breath: An Overview of the Asbestos Problem' (1996).
ITV GRENADA World in Action, Acre Mill documentary, 28 June 1971.
——World in Action, 'Killer Dust—A Standard Mistake', 14 Oct. 1974.
YORKSHIRE TV, 'Alice—A Fight for Life', 20 July 1982
——'Too Close to Home', 6 Dec. 1988.

Unpublished Printed Sources

BARKER, B. N., 'The History of Turner & Newall . . . [and] . . . its Dealings with Asbestos-Related Diseases and Its Employers' Liability Coverage with the Midland Assurance Ltd' (Feb. 1989).

FLYNN, L., *Studded with Diamonds and Paved with Gold: Mines, Mining Companies, and Human Rights in South Africa* (London: Bloomsbury, 1992).

GLANTZ, S., SLADE, J., BERO, L. A., HANAUER, P., and BARNES, D. E. (eds.), *The Cigarette Papers* (Berkeley: University of California Press, 1996).

JONES, R. H., *Asbestos and Asbestic* (London: Crosby, Lockwood & Son, 1897).

LEGGE, T., *Industrial Maladies* (Oxford: OUP, 1934).

LENEGHAN, J., *Victims Twice Over: A Report into How Members of Clydeside Action on Asbestos are Disabled by Lung Disease and Further Handicapped by Medical and Social Services* (Glasgow: Clydeside Action on Asbestos, 1994).

McCULLOCH, J., *Asbestos: Its Human Cost* (St Lucia: University of Queensland Press, 1986).

McKESSOCK, B., *Mesothelioma: The Story of an Illness* (Argyll: Argyll Publishing, 1995).

MALYE, François, *Amiante: Le Dossier de l'Air Contamine* (Paris: Sciences Avenir, Les Editions Le Pre aux Clercs, 1996).

MARKOWITZ, G., and ROSNER, D., *'Slaves of the Depression': Workers' Letters about Life on the Job* (New York: Cornell University Press, 1987).

PROCTOR, Robert, *The Nazi War on Cancer* (Princeton: Princeton University Press, 1999).

PUNCH, M., *Dirty Business: Exploring Corporate Misconduct* (London: Sage, 1996).

RAPHAEL, Adam, *Ultimate Risk* (London: Banham, 1994).

ROSNER, D., and MARKOWITZ, G., *Deadly Dust: Silicosis and the Politics of Occupational Disease in Twentieth-Century America* (Princeton: Princeton University Press, 1987).

SCHILLING, R .F., *A Challenging Life* (London: Canning Press, 1998).

SELIKOFF, I. J., and LEE, D. H. K., *Asbestos and Disease* (New York: Academic Press, 1978).

SELLERS, C. C., *Hazards of the Job* (Chapel Hill: University of North Carolina Press, 1997).

SKINNER, H. C. W., Ross, M., and FRONDEL, C., *Asbestos and Other Fibrous Materials* (New York: Oxford University Press, 1988).

SUMMERS, A. L., *Asbestos and the Asbestos Industry: The World's Most Wonderful Mineral and Other Fireproof Materials* (London: Pitman, 1919).

TAIT, Nancy, *Asbestos Kills* (London: priv. pub., 1976).

TURNER & NEWALL LTD, *Turner & Newall Ltd: The First Fifty Years 1920–1970* (Manchester: T & N, 1970).

——*Reports* and Accounts (1925+).

TURNER, S., *What is Wrong with Britain and Why?* (London: Nisbet & Co, 1930).

WEINDLING, P. (ed.), *The Social History of Occupational Health* (London: Croom Helm, 1985).

WIKELEY, N. J., *Compensation for Industrial Disease* (Aldershot: Dartmouth Publishing, 1993).

WILSON, A., and LEVY, H., *Workmen's Compensation* (Oxford: Oxford University Press, 1939).

Articles

ADDINGLEY, C. G., 'Asbestos Dust and its Measurement', *Annals of Occupational Hygiene* 9 (1966), 73–82.

ALLMAN, J. E., and MOSSMAN, B. T., 'Asbestos Revisited', *Scientific American* (July 1997), 54–7.

ARBLASTER, L., HATTON, P., HOWEL, D., RENVOIZE, E., SCHWEIGER, M., and SWINBURNE, L. M., 'Occupational and Environmental Links to Mesothelioma Deaths Occurring in Leeds during 1971 and 1987', *Journal of Public Health Medicine* 17 (1995), 297–304.

AURIBAULT, M., 'Note sur l'Hygiene et la Securité des Ouvriers dans les Filatures et Tissages d'Amiante', *Bulletin de l'Inspection du Travail* (Paris, 1906), 120–32.

BAMBLIN, W. P., 'Dust Control in the Asbestos Textile Industry', *Annals of Occupational Hygiene* 2 (1959), 54–74.

BARTRIP, P., 'Too Little, Too Late? The Home Office and the Asbestos Industry Regulations, 1931', *Medical History* 42 (Oct. 1998), 421–38.

BECKETT, S. T. B., 'Monitoring and Identification of Airborne Asbestos', in L. Michaels and S. S. Chissick, *Asbestos* (Belfast/Bath: J. Wiley & Sons, 1979), i, 207–45.

BELT, T. H., FRIEDMANN, I., and KING, E. J., 'The Effect of Asbestos on Tissue Cultures: A Comparative Study of Quartz and Coal Dust', *Journal of Pathology and Bacteriology* 59 (Jan.–Apr. 1947), 159–64.

BERRY, G., and NEWHOUSE, M. L., 'Mortality of Workers Manufacturing Friction Materials Using Asbestos', *British Journal of Industrial Medicine* 40 (1983), 1–7.

BONSER, G., and STEWART, M. J., 'Occupational Cancer of the Urinary Bladder in Dyestuffs Operatives and of the Lung in Asbestos Textile Workers and Iron-ore Miners', *American Journal of Clinical Pathology* 25 (Feb. 1955), 126–34.

BRITISH OCCUPATIONAL HYGIENE SOCIETY, 'Hygiene Standards for Chrysotile Asbestos Dust', *Annals of Occupational Hygiene* 11 (1968), 47–69.

——'Review of the Hygiene Standard for Chrysotile Asbestos Dust', *Annals of Occupational Hygiene* 16 (1973), 7.

BUCHANAN, W. D., 'Asbestosis and Primary Intrathoracic Neoplasms', in H. E. Whipple (ed.), 'Biological Effects of Asbestos', *Annals of New York Academy of Sciences* 132 (31 Dec. 1965), i, 507–18.

BURDETT, G., 'A Comparison of Historic Asbestos Measurements Using a Thermal Precipitator with a Membrane Filter-Phase Contrast Microscopy Method', *Annals of Occupational Hygiene* 42 (1998), 21–31.

BYROM, J. C., HODGSON, A. A., and HOLMES, S., 'A Dust Survey Carried Out in Buildings Incorporating Asbestos-Board Materials in their Construction', *Annals of Occupational Hygiene* 12 (1969), 141–5.

CALHOUN, C., and HILLER, H., 'Coping with Insidious Injuries: The Case of Johns–Manville Corporation and Asbestos Exposure', *Social Problems* 35 (Apr. 1988), 162–81.

CHISSICK, S., 'The Literature Relating to Asbestos', in L. Michaels and S. S. Chissick (eds.), *Asbestos* (Belfast/Bath: J. Wiley & Sons, 1979), i, 114–69.

COLLINS, T. F. B., 'Asbestos—The Lethal Dust', *South African Medical Journal* 41 (15 July 1967), 639–46.

COOKE, W. E., 'Fibrosis of the Lungs Due to the Inhalation of Asbestos Dust', *BMJ* (26 July 1924), ii, 147.

——'Pulmonary Asbestosis', *BMJ* (3 Dec. 1927), ii, 1024–5.

CORN, J. K., 'Historical Perspectives on Asbestos: Policies and Protective Measures in World War II Shipbuilding', *American Journal of Industrial Medicine* 11 (1987), 359–73.

CROSS, A. A., 'Practical Methods for Protection of Men Working with Asbestos Materials in Shipyards', in International Labor Office, *Safety and Health in Shipbuilding and Ship Repairing* (Geneva, 1972), 93–101.

DOIG, A. T., 'Asbestos Disease', *Health Bulletin* 26 (1 Jan. 1968), 24–9.

DOLL, R., 'Mortality from Lung Cancer in Asbestos Workers', *British Journal of Industrial Medicine* 12 (1955), 81–6.

EGILMAN, D. S., and REINHART, A. A., 'The Origin and Development of the Asbestos Threshold Limit Value: Scientific Indifference and Corporate Influence', *International Journal of Health Services* 25 (1995), 667–96.

ELLISON, W. J., 'Early Years in the Life of Turner Brothers Asbestos Co Ltd', *Firefly* (Winter Supp., 1966).

ELLMAN, P., 'Pulmonary Asbestosis: Its Clinical, Radiological and Pathological Features, and Associated Risk of Tuberculous Infection', *Journal of Industrial Medicine* 15 (July 1933), 165–83.

——'Pulmonary Asbestosis', *British Journal of Radiology* 7 (1934), 281–95.

ELMES, P. C., 'Cancer Due to Inhaled Dusts', repr. of paper read before Health Congress of the Royal Society of Health (25–9 Apr. 1966), 6.

ELMES, P. C., McCAUGHEY, W. T. E., and WADE, O. L., 'Diffuse Mesotheliomas of the Pleura and Asbestos', *BMJ* (6 Feb. 1965), i, 350–3.

GILLIS, C. R., HOLE, D. J., and LAMONT, D. W., 'Incidence of Mesothelioma in Glasgow 1981–1984', *Journal of Society of Occupational Medicine* 40 (1990), 5–10.

GILLMAN, P., and WOOLF, A., 'The Dangerous Dust', *Sunday Times Colour Supp.*, 2 Apr. 1972.

GILSON, J. C. , 'Health Hazards of Asbestos: Recent Studies on its Biological Effects', Wyers Memorial Lecture 1965, *Transactions of the Society for Occupational Medicine* 16 (1966), 62–74.

GLOYNE, S. R., 'Pneumoconiosis: A Histological Survey of Necropsy Material in 1205 Cases', *Lancet* 260 (14 Apr. 1951), i, 810–14.

GREENBERG, M., 'Classical Syndromes in Occupational Medicine: The Montague Murray Case', *American Journal of Industrial Medicine* 3 (1982), 351–6.

——'Reginald Tage: A UK Asbestos Prophet—A Postscript', *American Journal of Industrial Medicine* 24 (1993), 521–4.

——'Knowledge of the Health Hazard of Asbestos Prior to the Merewether and Price Report of 1930', *Social History of Medicine* 7 (Dec. 1994), 493–516.

——'Professor Matthew Stewart: Asbestosis Research 1929–1934', *American Journal of Industrial Medicine* 32 (1997), 562–9.

——'The 1968 British Occupational Hygiene Society Chrysotile Asbestos Hygiene Standard', in G. A. & B. J. Peters, *Asbestos Disease and Asbestos Control. Vol. 14: Sourcebook on Asbestos Diseases* (Charlottesville, VA: Michie, 1997), 219–55.

GREENBERG, M., and LLOYD DAVIES, T. A., 'Mesothelioma Register 1967–68', *British Journal of Industrial Medicine* 31 (1974), 91–104.

HADDOW, A. C., 'Clinical Aspects of Pulmonary Fibrosis', *BMJ* (28 Sept. 1929), ii, 580–1.

HARRIES, P. G., 'Asbestos Hazards in Naval Dockyards', *Annals of Occupational Hygiene* 11 (1968), 135–42.

HARRIES, P. G., 'Asbestos Dust Concentrations in Ship Repairing: A Practical Approach to Improving Asbestos Hygiene in Naval Dockyards', *Annals of Occupational Hygiene* 14 (1971), 241–54.

HASSON, F., 'Asbestos—The Political Disease', *The Health Services* (20 Aug. 1982), 12–13.

HILLS, D. W., 'Economics of Dust Control', *Annals of the New York Academy of Sciences* 132 (1965), 322–34.

HOLMES, S., 'Developments in Dust Sampling and Counting Techniques in the Asbestos Industry', *Annals of the New York Academy of Sciences* 132 (1965), 288–97.

HUNCHAREK, M., 'Exporting Asbestos: Disease and Policy in the Developing World', *Journal of Public Health Policy* (Spring 1993), 51–65.

JEREMY, D. J., 'Corporate Responses to the Emergent Recognition of a Health Hazard in the UK Asbestos Industry: The Case of Turner & Newall, 1920–1960', *Business and Economic History* 24 (Fall 1995), 254–65.

JONES, Helen, 'An Inspector Calls: Health and Safety at Work in Inter-war Britain', in P. Weindling (ed.), *The Social History of Occupational Health* (London: Croom Helm, 1985), 223–39.

KING, E. J. KING, CLEGG, J. W., and RAE, V. M., 'The Effects of Asbestos, and of Asbestos and Aluminium, on the Lungs of Rabbits', *Thorax* 1 (Sept. 1946), 188–97.

KNOX, J. F., DOLL, R. S., and HILL, I. D., 'Cohort Analysis of Changes in Incidence of Bronchial Carcinoma in a Textile Asbestos Factory', *Annals of the New York Academy of Sciences* 132 (Dec. 1965), i, 527–35.

KNOX, J. F., HOLMES, S., DOLL, R. S., and HILL, I. D., 'Mortality from Lung Cancer and Other Causes Among Workers in an Asbestos Textile Factory', *British Journal of Industrial Medicine* 25 (1968), 293–303.

KOTELCHUCK, D., 'Asbestos: "The Funeral Dress of Kings"—and Others', in D. Rosner and G. Markovitz (eds.), *Dying for Work: Workers' Safety and Health in Twentieth Century America* (Bloomington: Indiana University Press, 1987), 192–207.

LANE, R. E., 'My Fifty Years in Industrial Medicine', *Journal of the Society of Occupational Medicine* 28 (1978), 115–24.

LEATHART, G. L., 'Asbestos: A Medical Hazard of the 20th Century', *Journal for Industrial Nurses* (1964), 119–31.

——and SANDERSON, J. T., 'Some Observations on Asbestosis', *Annals of Occupational Hygiene* 6 (1963), 65–74.

LEWINSOHN, H. C., 'The Medical Surveillance of Asbestos Workers', *Royal Society of Health Journal* 92 (1972), 69–77.

LILIENFELD, D. E., 'The Silence: The Asbestos Industry and Early Occupational Cancer Research—A Case Study', *American Journal of Public Health* 81 (June 1991), 791–800

McCaughey, W. T. E., 'Primary Tumours of the Pleura', *Journal of Pathology and Bacteriology* 76 (1958), 517–29.

McCaughey, W. T. E., Wade, O. L., and Elmes, P. C., 'Exposure to Asbestos Dust and Diffuse Pleural Mesothelioma', *BMJ* (24 Nov. 1962), iv, 1397.

McDermott, M., Bevan, M. B., Elmes, P. C., Allardice, J. T., and Bradley, A. C., 'Lung Function and Radiographic Change in Chrysotile Workers in Swaziland', *British Journal of Industrial Medicine* 39 (1982), 338–43.

McIvor, A., 'Health and Safety in the Cotton Industry: A Literature Review', *Manchester Region History Review* 9 (1995), 50–7.

McVittie, J. C., 'Asbestosis in Great Britain', *Annals of the New York Academy of Sciences* 132 (1965), i, 128–38, 137–8.

Mann, B., 'Pulmonary Asbestosis with Special Reference to an Epidemic at Hebden Bridge', *Journal of the Royal College of Physicians* 12 (July 1978), 297–307.

Marchand, P. E., 'The Discovery of Mesothelioma in the Northwestern Cape Province in the Republic of South Africa', *American Journal of Industrial Medicine* 19 (1991), 241–6.

Meiklejohn, A., 'The Development of Compensation for Occupational Diseases of the Lungs in Great Britain', *British Journal of Industrial Medicine* 11 (July 1954), 198–212.

Merewether, E. R. A., 'The Occurrence of Pulmonary Fibrosis and Other Pulmonary Affections in Asbestos Workers', *Journal of Industrial Hygiene* 12 (May/June 1930), 198–222, 239–56.

——'A Memorandum on Asbestosis', *Tubercle* 15 (1933–4), 69–81, 109–18, 152–9.

Murray, R., 'Asbestos: A Chronology of its Origins and Health Effects', *British Journal of Industrial Medicine* 47 (1990), 361–5.

Murray, T. H., 'Regulating Asbestos: Ethics, Politics and the Values of Science', in R. Bayer (ed.), *The Health and Safety of Workers* (New York, 1988), 271–92.

Newhouse, M. L., and Thompson, H., 'Mesothelioma of Pleura and Peritoneum Following Exposure to Asbestos in the London Area', *British Journal of Industrial Medicine* 22 (1965), 261–9.

Oliver, C., 'Asbestos in Buildings: Management and Related Health Effects', in M. A. Mehlman and A. Upton (eds)., *Advances in Modern Environmental Toxicology. Vol 22: The Identification and Control of Environmental and Occupational Diseases: Asbestos and Cancers* (Princeton: Princeton Scientific Publishing Co., 1994), 175–88.

Oliver, T., 'Pulmonary Asbestosis in Clinical Aspects', *Journal of Industrial Hygiene* 9 (1927), 483–5.

Owen, W. Glyn, 'Diffuse Mesothelioma and Exposure to Asbestos Dust in the Merseyside Area', *BMJ* (25 July 1964), ii, 214–21.

Ozonoff, D., 'Failed Warnings: Asbestos-Related Disease and Industrial Medicine', in R. Bayer (ed.), *The Health and Safety of Workers* (New York: Oxford University Press, 1988), 139–218.

Parsons, J. M., 'Asbestos-Related Disease Claims—A Continuing Cause for Concern in the 1990s and Beyond', *Journal of Personal Injury Litigation* Issue 1 (1997), 5–35.

Peto, J., Doll, R. S., Howard, S. V., Kinlen, L. J., and Lewinsohn, H. C., 'A Mortality Study among Workers in an English Asbestos Factory', *British Journal of Industrial Medicine* 34 (Aug. 1977), 169–73.

PETO, J., 'The Hygiene Standard for Chrysotile Asbestos', *Lancet* (4 Mar. 1978), i, 484–9.

PETO, J., 'Dose-Response Relationships for Asbestos-Related Disease: Implications for Hygiene Standards. Part II: Mortality', *Annals of the New York Academy of Sciences* 330 (1979), 195–203.

PETO, J., DOLL, R., HERMAN, C., BINNS, W., CLAYTON, R., and GOFFE, T., 'Relationship of Mortality to Measures of Environmental Pollution in an Asbestos Textile Factory', *Annals of Occupational Hygiene* 29 (1985), 305–55.

PETO, J., HODGSON, J. T, MATTHEWS, F. E., and JONES, J. R., 'Continuing Increase in Mesothelioma Mortality in Britain', *Lancet* 345 (4 Mar. 1995), 535–9.

PETO, J., LA VECCHIA, C., LEVI, F., and NEGRI, I., 'The European Mesothelioma Epidemic', *British Journal of Cancer* 79 (Feb. 1999), 666–72.

PRICE, C. W., 'Exhaust Ventilation in Asbestos Textile Works', reprint from Institution of Heating & Ventilation Engineers, 6 Oct. 1931.

PYE, A. M., 'Alternatives to Asbestos in Industrial Applications', in L. Michaels and S. S. Chissick (eds.), *Asbestos* (Belfast/Bath: J. Wiley & Sons, 1979), i, 339–73.

SCHEPERS, G. W. H., 'Changing Attitudes and Opinions: Asbestos and Cancer 1934–1965', *American Journal of Industrial Medicine* 22 (1992), 461–6.

SCHEPERS, G. W. H., 'Chronology of Asbestos Cancer Discoveries: Experimental Studies of the Saranac Laboratory', *American Journal of Industrial Medicine* 27 (1995), 593–606.

SELIKOFF, I. J., HAMMOND, E. C., and CHURG, J., 'Asbestos Exposure and Neoplasia', *Journal of the American Medical Association* 188 (1964), 22–6.

SELIKOFF, I. J., and GREENBERG, M., 'A Landmark Case in Asbestosis', *Journal of the American Medical Association* 265 (20 Feb. 1991), 898–901.

SELLS, Bill, 'What Asbestos Taught Me About Managing Risk', *Harvard Business Review* (Mar.-Apr. 1994), 76–89.

SHEERS, G., and TEMPLETON, A. R., 'Effects of Asbestos in Dockyard Workers', *BMJ* (7 Sept. 1968), 574.

SIMSON, F. W., 'Pulmonary Asbestosis in South Africa', *BMJ* (26 May 1928), i, 885–7.

SMITH, A. H., WRIGHT, C. C., 'Chrysotile Asbestos is the Main Cause of Pleural Mesothelioma', *American Journal of Industrial Medicine* 30 (1996), 252–66.

STAYNER, L. T, DANKOVIC, D., and LEMEN, R. A., 'Occupational Exposure to Chrysotile Asbestos and Cancer Risk: A Review of the Amphibole Hypothesis', *American Journal of Public Health* 86 (Feb. 1996), 179–86.

STEELE, J., and WIKELEY, N. J., 'Liability in Tort for Environmental Mesothelioma: A UK Perspective', in G. A. Peters and B. J. Peters (eds.), *Asbestos Pathogenesis and Litigation. Vol. 13: Sourcebook on Asbestos Diseases* (Charlottesville, VA: Michie, 1996), 297–32.

——'Dust on the Streets and Liability for Environmental Cancers', *Modern Law Review* 60 (1997), 265–76.

STEWART, M. J., 'Asbestosis Bodies in the Lungs of Guinea Pigs after Three to Five Months' Exposure in the Asbestos Factory', *Journal of Pathology and Bacteriology* 33 (1930), 848.

—— 'The 1968 British Occupational Hygiene Society Chrysotile Asbestos Hygiene Standard', in G. A. & B. J. Peters, *Asbestos Disease and Asbestos Control. Vol. 14: Sourcebook on Asbestos Diseases* (Charlottesville, VA: Michie, 1997), 219–55.

——and LLOYD DAVIES, T. A., 'Mesothelioma Register 1967–68', *British Journal of Industrial Medicine* 31 (1974), 91–104.

HADDOW, A. C., 'Clinical Aspects of Pulmonary Fibrosis', *BMJ* (28 Sept. 1929), ii, 580–1.

HARRIES, P. G., 'Asbestos Hazards in Naval Dockyards', *Annals of Occupational Hygiene* 11 (1968), 135–42.

HARRIES, P. G., 'Asbestos Dust Concentrations in Ship Repairing: A Practical Approach to Improving Asbestos Hygiene in Naval Dockyards', *Annals of Occupational Hygiene* 14 (1971), 241–54.

HASSON, F., 'Asbestos—The Political Disease', *The Health Services* (20 Aug. 1982), 12–13.

HILLS, D. W., 'Economics of Dust Control', *Annals of the New York Academy of Sciences* 132 (1965), 322–34.

HOLMES, S., 'Developments in Dust Sampling and Counting Techniques in the Asbestos Industry', *Annals of the New York Academy of Sciences* 132 (1965), 288–97.

HUNCHAREK, M., 'Exporting Asbestos: Disease and Policy in the Developing World', *Journal of Public Health Policy* (Spring 1993), 51–65.

JEREMY, D. J., 'Corporate Responses to the Emergent Recognition of a Health Hazard in the UK Asbestos Industry: The Case of Turner & Newall, 1920–1960', *Business and Economic History* 24 (Fall 1995), 254–65.

JONES, Helen, 'An Inspector Calls: Health and Safety at Work in Inter-war Britain', in P. Weindling (ed.), *The Social History of Occupational Health* (London: Croom Helm, 1985), 223–39.

KING, E. J. KING, CLEGG, J. W., and RAE, V. M., 'The Effects of Asbestos, and of Asbestos and Aluminium, on the Lungs of Rabbits', *Thorax* 1 (Sept. 1946), 188–97.

KNOX, J. F., DOLL, R. S., and HILL, I. D., 'Cohort Analysis of Changes in Incidence of Bronchial Carcinoma in a Textile Asbestos Factory', *Annals of the New York Academy of Sciences* 132 (Dec. 1965), i, 527–35.

KNOX, J. F., HOLMES, S., DOLL, R. S., and HILL, I. D., 'Mortality from Lung Cancer and Other Causes Among Workers in an Asbestos Textile Factory', *British Journal of Industrial Medicine* 25 (1968), 293–303.

KOTELCHUCK, D., 'Asbestos: "The Funeral Dress of Kings"—and Others', in D. Rosner and G. Markovitz (eds.), *Dying for Work: Workers' Safety and Health in Twentieth Century America* (Bloomington: Indiana University Press, 1987), 192–207.

LANE, R. E., 'My Fifty Years in Industrial Medicine', *Journal of the Society of Occupational Medicine* 28 (1978), 115–24.

LEATHART, G. L., 'Asbestos: A Medical Hazard of the 20th Century', *Journal for Industrial Nurses* (1964), 119–31.

——and SANDERSON, J. T., 'Some Observations on Asbestosis', *Annals of Occupational Hygiene* 6 (1963), 65–74.

LEWINSOHN, H. C., 'The Medical Surveillance of Asbestos Workers', *Royal Society of Health Journal* 92 (1972), 69–77.

CHASE MANHATTAN BANK v. T & N (87 Civ. 4436, Judge J. G. Koeltl), US District Court, Southern District of New York, 27 Oct.–6 Dec. 1995. Trial transcript.

DEPARTMENT OF HEALTH AND SOCIAL SECURITY, Standing Medical Advisory Committee: Sub-Committee on Cancer. SAC (M) SSC (68,71) 7.

GORMAN, T., 'Hidden Hazard/Forgotten Victims: Some Aspects of Asbestos Abuse in Britain', (Glasgow Caledonian University BA, 1997).

GRIEVE, I. A. D., 'Asbestosis' (Edinburgh University MD thesis, 1927).

KAZAN-ALLEN, L., 'T & N plc: Insurance Coverage' (1996).

MARGERESON, E. and HANCOCK, J. v. J. W. Roberts and T & N, High Court Leeds, before Mr Justice Holland, 1995. Trial transcript.

MAIR, A. *et al.*, 'Report on the Asbestos Dust Survey . . . at the Red Road Building Site, Glasgow, for the Corp. of Glasgow, May 1967'.

WIKELEY, N. J., 'Asbestos in the Shipyards: Dust, Disease and Drafting Regulations', Inaugural Lecture, University of Southampton, 4 Feb. 1997. Typescript.

WYERS, H., 'That Legislative Measures Have Proved Generally Effective in the Control of Asbestosis' (Glasgow University MD thesis, 1946).

Medical Journals/Trade Press/Newspapers

Asbestos
Belfast Telegraph
Bristol Evening Post
British Asbestos Newsletter
BMJ
Daily Herald
Daily Telegraph
Daily Star
Daily Worker
The Economist
Financial Times
Firefly
Guardian
Ilford Recorder
Industrial Safety
Insider
Journal of the American Medical Association
Lancet
Listener
New Scientist
Observer
Rochdale Observer
Rochdale Times
Socialist Worker
Sunday Telegraph
Sunday Times
Sunderland Echo

TBA News
The Times
Wall Street Journal
Washington Echo
Yorkshire Post

Official Publications (London published, HMSO, unless stated)

ACHESON, E. D., and GARDNER, M. J., *Asbestos: The Control Limit for Asbestos* (1983).
BARKING TOWN URBAN DISTRICT COUNCIL, *Reports of the Medical Officer of Health* (1928, 1929, 1930, 1945).
BUSINESS STATISTICS OFFICE, *Historical Records of the Census of Production, 1907–1970* (1978).
DEPT OF EMPLOYMENT: HM FACTORY INSPECTORATE, *Technical Data Note 13: Standards for Asbestos Dust Concentration for Use with the Asbestos Regulations 1969* (1970).
DOLL, R., and PETO, J., *Asbestos: Effects on Health of Exposure to Asbestos* (1985).
HANSARD.
HEALTH & SAFETY COMMISSION, *Asbestos—Health Hazards and Precautions (An Interim Statement by the ACA)* (1977).
——*Manufacturing and Service Industries Annual Report* (1977+).
——*Asbestos: Measurement and Monitoring of Asbestos in Air: Second Report by the Advisory Committee on Asbestos* (1978).
—— *Work on Thermal Acoustic Insulation and Sprayed Coatings* (1978).
——*Health and Safety Statistics 1994–95* (1995).
——*Annual Report 1994–95* (1995).
——*Occupational Health: Decennial Supplement* (1996).
——*The Control of Asbestos at Work. Regulations 1987* [updated 1999] (Sheffield, 3rd edn. 1999).
HEALTH & SAFETY EXECUTIVE, *Selected Written Evidence Submitted to the Advisory Committee on Asbestos, 1976–77* (1977).
——*Asbestos. Vol. 1: Final Report of the Advisory Committee. Asbestos: Vol. 2: Papers Commissioned by the Committee* (1979).
HOME OFFICE, *The Asbestos Industry (Asbestosis) Scheme 1931 (Statutory Rules and Orders, 1931, No. 344)* (1931).
——*The Asbestos Industry Regulations, 1931 (Statutory Rules and Orders, 1931, No. 1140)* (1931).
——*Report on Conferences between Employees and Inspectors concerning Methods for Suppressing Dust in Textile Factories* (1931).
——*The Silicosis and Asbestosis (Medical Arrangements) Scheme, 1931 (Statutory Rules and Orders, No. 341)* (1931).
——*The Silicosis and Asbestosis (Medical Fees) Regulations 1931 (Statutory Rules and Orders 1931, No. 412)* (1931).
——*Workmen's Compensation Statistics* (1933–9). Cmd. 4244, 4484, 4784, 5077, 557, 5722, 5955, 6203.
——*Memorandum on the Industrial Diseases of Silicosis and Asbestosis* (1935).

HOUSE OF COMMONS EMPLOYMENT COMMITTEE, *The Work of the Health and Safety Commission and Executive: Asbestos—Minutes of Evidence* (1983).

HOUSE OF COMMONS EXPENDITURE COMMITTEE (TRADE & INDUSTRY SUB-COMMITTEE), Session 1973–4, *Fifth Report . . . on Wages and Conditions of African Workers Employed by British Firms in South Africa.* HC 116; *Minutes of Evidence and Memoranda.* HC 21 I–IV.

HUTCHINGS, S. *et al.*, 'Asbestos-Related Diseases', in Health & Safety Executive, *Occupational Health: Decennial Supplement* (1996), F. Driver (ed.), 127–52.

MARRE, A., 'Report . . . to Max Madden MP . . . into a Complaint made by J. P. Buick', 3rd Report of Parl. Commissioner for Administration: HC 259, Session 1975–6, 25 March 1976: Case C. 353/Y, 189–211.

MEREWETHER, E. R. A., and PRICE, C. W., *Report on Effects of Asbestos Dust on the Lungs and Dust Suppression in the Asbestos Industry* (1930).

MINISTRY OF LABOUR & HM FACTORY INSPECTORATE, *Annual Reports of the Chief Inspector of Factories* (1898+).

——*Problems Arising from the Use of Asbestos: Memorandum of the Senior Medical Inspector's Advisory Panel* (1967).

MINISTRY OF LABOUR, *The Asbestos Regulations 1968: Draft Statutory Instruments* (1968).

MINISTRY OF LABOUR & NATIONAL SERVICE, *Revision of Regulations for Ship-building and Ship-Repairing: Preliminary Draft of New Code* (1950).

——*Toxic Substances in Factory Atmospheres* (1960).

MINISTRY OF NATIONAL INSURANCE, *Pneumoconiosis (Silicosis, Asbestosis. etc.) and Byssinosis* (1952).

MONOPOLIES COMMISSION, *Asbestos and Certain Asbestos Products: A Report on the Supply of Asbestos and Certain Asbestos Products* (1973).

Books/Pamphlets

ASBESTOS INFORMATION COMMITTEE, *Mesothelioma* (June 1976).

BARTRIP, P., *Workmen's Compensation in Twentieth Century Britain* (Aldershot: Gower, 1987).

BAYER, R. (ed.), *The Health and Safety of Workers: Case Studies in the Politics of Professional Responsibility* (New York: Oxford University Press, 1988).

BRODEUR, P., *Outrageous Misconduct: The Asbestos Industry on Trial* (New York: Pantheon Books, 1985).

CAPE ASBESTOS LTD, *The Story of the Cape Asbestos Company Ltd* (London: Cape Asbestos, 1953).

CASTLEMAN, B. I., *Asbestos: Medical and Legal Aspects* (Englewood Cliffs, NJ: Aspen Law & Business, 4th edn., 1996).

COLE, J., *Rochdale Revisited: A Town and Its People* (Littleborough: Kelsall, 1988).

DALTON, A., *Asbestos Killer Dust* (London: BSSRS, 1979).

ELLISON, W. J., *Some Notes on the Earlier History and Development to 1939 of Turner Brothers Asbestos Company Ltd* (Rochdale: TBA, 1939).

FELSTINER, W. L. F., and DINGWALL, R., *Asbestos Litigation in the United Kingdom: An Interim Report* (Oxford: Centre for Socio-Legal Studies, 1988).

FLYNN, L., *Studded with Diamonds and Paved with Gold: Mines, Mining Companies, and Human Rights in South Africa* (London: Bloomsbury, 1992).

GLANTZ, S., SLADE, J., BERO, L. A., HANAUER, P., and BARNES, D. E. (eds.), *The Cigarette Papers* (Berkeley: University of California Press, 1996).

JONES, R. H., *Asbestos and Asbestic* (London: Crosby, Lockwood & Son, 1897).

LEGGE, T., *Industrial Maladies* (Oxford: OUP, 1934).

LENEGHAN, J., *Victims Twice Over: A Report into How Members of Clydeside Action on Asbestos are Disabled by Lung Disease and Further Handicapped by Medical and Social Services* (Glasgow: Clydeside Action on Asbestos, 1994).

McCULLOCH, J., *Asbestos: Its Human Cost* (St Lucia: University of Queensland Press, 1986).

McKESSOCK, B., *Mesothelioma: The Story of an Illness* (Argyll: Argyll Publishing, 1995).

MALYE, François, *Amiante: Le Dossier de l'Air Contamine* (Paris: Sciences Avenir, Les Editions Le Pre aux Clercs, 1996).

MARKOWITZ, G., and ROSNER, D., *'Slaves of the Depression': Workers' Letters about Life on the Job* (New York: Cornell University Press, 1987).

PROCTOR, Robert, *The Nazi War on Cancer* (Princeton: Princeton University Press, ·1999).

PUNCH, M., *Dirty Business: Exploring Corporate Misconduct* (London: Sage, 1996).

RAPHAEL, Adam, *Ultimate Risk* (London: Banham, 1994).

ROSNER, D., and MARKOWITZ, G., *Deadly Dust: Silicosis and the Politics of Occupational Disease in Twentieth-Century America* (Princeton: Princeton University Press, 1987).

SCHILLING, R .F., *A Challenging Life* (London: Canning Press, 1998).

SELIKOFF, I. J., and LEE, D. H. K., *Asbestos and Disease* (New York: Academic Press, 1978).

SELLERS, C. C., *Hazards of the Job* (Chapel Hill: University of North Carolina Press, 1997).

SKINNER, H. C. W., ROSS, M., and FRONDEL, C., *Asbestos and Other Fibrous Materials* (New York: Oxford University Press, 1988).

SUMMERS, A. L., *Asbestos and the Asbestos Industry: The World's Most Wonderful Mineral and Other Fireproof Materials* (London: Pitman, 1919).

TAIT, Nancy, *Asbestos Kills* (London: priv. pub., 1976).

TURNER & NEWALL LTD, *Turner & Newall Ltd: The First Fifty Years 1920–1970* (Manchester: T & N, 1970).

——*Reports* and Accounts (1925+).

TURNER, S., *What is Wrong with Britain and Why?* (London: Nisbet & Co, 1930).

WEINDLING, P. (ed.), *The Social History of Occupational Health* (London: Croom Helm, 1985).

WIKELEY, N. J., *Compensation for Industrial Disease* (Aldershot: Dartmouth Publishing, 1993).

WILSON, A., and LEVY, H., *Workmen's Compensation* (Oxford: Oxford University Press, 1939).

Articles

ADDINGLEY, C. G., 'Asbestos Dust and its Measurement', *Annals of Occupational Hygiene* 9 (1966), 73–82.

ALLMAN, J. E., and MOSSMAN, B. T., 'Asbestos Revisited', *Scientific American* (July 1997), 54–7.

ARBLASTER, L., HATTON, P., HOWEL, D., RENVOIZE, E., SCHWEIGER, M., and SWINBURNE, L. M., 'Occupational and Environmental Links to Mesothelioma Deaths Occurring in Leeds during 1971 and 1987', *Journal of Public Health Medicine* 17 (1995), 297–304.

AURIBAULT, M., 'Note sur l'Hygiene et la Securité des Ouvriers dans les Filatures et Tissages d'Amiante', *Bulletin de l'Inspection du Travail* (Paris, 1906), 120–32.

BAMBLIN, W. P., 'Dust Control in the Asbestos Textile Industry', *Annals of Occupational Hygiene* 2 (1959), 54–74.

BARTRIP, P., 'Too Little, Too Late? The Home Office and the Asbestos Industry Regulations, 1931', *Medical History* 42 (Oct. 1998), 421–38.

BECKETT, S. T. B., 'Monitoring and Identification of Airborne Asbestos', in L. Michaels and S. S. Chissick, *Asbestos* (Belfast/Bath: J. Wiley & Sons, 1979), i, 207–45.

BELT, T. H., FRIEDMANN, I., and KING, E. J., 'The Effect of Asbestos on Tissue Cultures: A Comparative Study of Quartz and Coal Dust', *Journal of Pathology and Bacteriology* 59 (Jan.–Apr. 1947), 159–64.

BERRY, G., and NEWHOUSE, M. L., 'Mortality of Workers Manufacturing Friction Materials Using Asbestos', *British Journal of Industrial Medicine* 40 (1983), 1–7.

BONSER, G., and STEWART, M. J., 'Occupational Cancer of the Urinary Bladder in Dyestuffs Operatives and of the Lung in Asbestos Textile Workers and Iron-ore Miners', *American Journal of Clinical Pathology* 25 (Feb. 1955), 126–34.

BRITISH OCCUPATIONAL HYGIENE SOCIETY, 'Hygiene Standards for Chrysotile Asbestos Dust', *Annals of Occupational Hygiene* 11 (1968), 47–69.

——'Review of the Hygiene Standard for Chrysotile Asbestos Dust', *Annals of Occupational Hygiene* 16 (1973), 7.

BUCHANAN, W. D., 'Asbestosis and Primary Intrathoracic Neoplasms', in H. E. Whipple (ed.), 'Biological Effects of Asbestos', *Annals of New York Academy of Sciences* 132 (31 Dec. 1965), i, 507–18.

BURDETT, G., 'A Comparison of Historic Asbestos Measurements Using a Thermal Precipitator with a Membrane Filter-Phase Contrast Microscopy Method', *Annals of Occupational Hygiene* 42 (1998), 21–31.

BYROM, J. C., HODGSON, A. A., and HOLMES, S., 'A Dust Survey Carried Out in Buildings Incorporating Asbestos-Board Materials in their Construction', *Annals of Occupational Hygiene* 12 (1969), 141–5.

CALHOUN, C., and HILLER, H., 'Coping with Insidious Injuries: The Case of Johns–Manville Corporation and Asbestos Exposure', *Social Problems* 35 (Apr. 1988), 162–81.

CHISSICK, S., 'The Literature Relating to Asbestos', in L. Michaels and S. S. Chissick (eds.), *Asbestos* (Belfast/Bath: J. Wiley & Sons, 1979), i, 114–69.

COLLINS, T. F. B., 'Asbestos—The Lethal Dust', *South African Medical Journal* 41 (15 July 1967), 639–46.

COOKE, W. E., 'Fibrosis of the Lungs Due to the Inhalation of Asbestos Dust', *BMJ* (26 July 1924), ii, 147.

——'Pulmonary Asbestosis', *BMJ* (3 Dec. 1927), ii, 1024–5.

CORN, J. K., 'Historical Perspectives on Asbestos: Policies and Protective Measures in World War II Shipbuilding', *American Journal of Industrial Medicine* 11 (1987), 359–73.

CROSS, A. A., 'Practical Methods for Protection of Men Working with Asbestos Materials in Shipyards', in International Labor Office, *Safety and Health in Shipbuilding and Ship Repairing* (Geneva, 1972), 93–101.

DOIG, A. T., 'Asbestos Disease', *Health Bulletin* 26 (1 Jan. 1968), 24–9.

DOLL, R., 'Mortality from Lung Cancer in Asbestos Workers', *British Journal of Industrial Medicine* 12 (1955), 81–6.

EGILMAN, D. S., and REINHART, A. A., 'The Origin and Development of the Asbestos Threshold Limit Value: Scientific Indifference and Corporate Influence', *International Journal of Health Services* 25 (1995), 667–96.

ELLISON, W. J., 'Early Years in the Life of Turner Brothers Asbestos Co Ltd', *Firefly* (Winter Supp., 1966).

ELLMAN, P., 'Pulmonary Asbestosis: Its Clinical, Radiological and Pathological Features, and Associated Risk of Tuberculous Infection', *Journal of Industrial Medicine* 15 (July 1933), 165–83.

——'Pulmonary Asbestosis', *British Journal of Radiology* 7 (1934), 281–95.

ELMES, P. C., 'Cancer Due to Inhaled Dusts', repr. of paper read before Health Congress of the Royal Society of Health (25–9 Apr. 1966), 6.

ELMES, P. C., McCAUGHEY, W. T. E., and WADE, O. L., 'Diffuse Mesotheliomas of the Pleura and Asbestos', *BMJ* (6 Feb. 1965), i, 350–3.

GILLIS, C. R., HOLE, D. J., and LAMONT, D. W., 'Incidence of Mesothelioma in Glasgow 1981–1984', *Journal of Society of Occupational Medicine* 40 (1990), 5–10.

GILLMAN, P., and WOOLF, A., 'The Dangerous Dust', *Sunday Times Colour Supp.*, 2 Apr. 1972.

GILSON, J. C. , 'Health Hazards of Asbestos: Recent Studies on its Biological Effects', Wyers Memorial Lecture 1965, *Transactions of the Society for Occupational Medicine* 16 (1966), 62–74.

GLOYNE, S. R., 'Pneumoconiosis: A Histological Survey of Necropsy Material in 1205 Cases', *Lancet* 260 (14 Apr. 1951), i, 810–14.

GREENBERG, M., 'Classical Syndromes in Occupational Medicine: The Montague Murray Case', *American Journal of Industrial Medicine* 3 (1982), 351–6.

——'Reginald Tage: A UK Asbestos Prophet—A Postscript', *American Journal of Industrial Medicine* 24 (1993), 521–4.

——'Knowledge of the Health Hazard of Asbestos Prior to the Merewether and Price Report of 1930', *Social History of Medicine* 7 (Dec. 1994), 493–516.

——'Professor Matthew Stewart: Asbestosis Research 1929–1934', *American Journal of Industrial Medicine* 32 (1997), 562–9.

——'The 1968 British Occupational Hygiene Society Chrysotile Asbestos Hygiene Standard', in G. A. & B. J. Peters, *Asbestos Disease and Asbestos Control. Vol. 14: Sourcebook on Asbestos Diseases* (Charlottesville, VA: Michie, 1997), 219–55.

GREENBERG, M., and LLOYD DAVIES, T. A., 'Mesothelioma Register 1967–68', *British Journal of Industrial Medicine* 31 (1974), 91–104.

HADDOW, A. C., 'Clinical Aspects of Pulmonary Fibrosis', *BMJ* (28 Sept. 1929), ii, 580–1.

HARRIES, P. G., 'Asbestos Hazards in Naval Dockyards', *Annals of Occupational Hygiene* 11 (1968), 135–42.

HARRIES, P. G., 'Asbestos Dust Concentrations in Ship Repairing: A Practical Approach to Improving Asbestos Hygiene in Naval Dockyards', *Annals of Occupational Hygiene* 14 (1971), 241–54.

HASSON, F., 'Asbestos—The Political Disease', *The Health Services* (20 Aug. 1982), 12–13.

HILLS, D. W., 'Economics of Dust Control', *Annals of the New York Academy of Sciences* 132 (1965), 322–34.

HOLMES, S., 'Developments in Dust Sampling and Counting Techniques in the Asbestos Industry', *Annals of the New York Academy of Sciences* 132 (1965), 288–97.

HUNCHAREK, M., 'Exporting Asbestos: Disease and Policy in the Developing World', *Journal of Public Health Policy* (Spring 1993), 51–65.

JEREMY, D. J., 'Corporate Responses to the Emergent Recognition of a Health Hazard in the UK Asbestos Industry: The Case of Turner & Newall, 1920–1960', *Business and Economic History* 24 (Fall 1995), 254–65.

JONES, Helen, 'An Inspector Calls: Health and Safety at Work in Inter-war Britain', in P. Weindling (ed.), *The Social History of Occupational Health* (London: Croom Helm, 1985), 223–39.

KING, E. J. KING, CLEGG, J. W., and RAE, V. M., 'The Effects of Asbestos, and of Asbestos and Aluminium, on the Lungs of Rabbits', *Thorax* 1 (Sept. 1946), 188–97.

KNOX, J. F., DOLL, R. S., and HILL, I. D., 'Cohort Analysis of Changes in Incidence of Bronchial Carcinoma in a Textile Asbestos Factory', *Annals of the New York Academy of Sciences* 132 (Dec. 1965), i, 527–35.

KNOX, J. F., HOLMES, S., DOLL, R. S., and HILL, I. D., 'Mortality from Lung Cancer and Other Causes Among Workers in an Asbestos Textile Factory', *British Journal of Industrial Medicine* 25 (1968), 293–303.

KOTELCHUCK, D., 'Asbestos: "The Funeral Dress of Kings"—and Others', in D. Rosner and G. Markovitz (eds.), *Dying for Work: Workers' Safety and Health in Twentieth Century America* (Bloomington: Indiana University Press, 1987), 192–207.

LANE, R. E., 'My Fifty Years in Industrial Medicine', *Journal of the Society of Occupational Medicine* 28 (1978), 115–24.

LEATHART, G. L., 'Asbestos: A Medical Hazard of the 20th Century', *Journal for Industrial Nurses* (1964), 119–31.

——and SANDERSON, J. T., 'Some Observations on Asbestosis', *Annals of Occupational Hygiene* 6 (1963), 65–74.

LEWINSOHN, H. C., 'The Medical Surveillance of Asbestos Workers', *Royal Society of Health Journal* 92 (1972), 69–77.

LILIENFELD, D. E., 'The Silence: The Asbestos Industry and Early Occupational Cancer Research—A Case Study', *American Journal of Public Health* 81 (June 1991), 791–800

McCAUGHEY, W. T. E., 'Primary Tumours of the Pleura', *Journal of Pathology and Bacteriology* 76 (1958), 517–29.

McCAUGHEY, W. T. E., WADE, O. L., and ELMES, P. C., 'Exposure to Asbestos Dust and Diffuse Pleural Mesothelioma', *BMJ* (24 Nov. 1962), iv, 1397.

McDERMOTT, M., BEVAN, M. B., ELMES, P. C., ALLARDICE, J. T., and BRADLEY, A. C., 'Lung Function and Radiographic Change in Chrysotile Workers in Swaziland', *British Journal of Industrial Medicine* 39 (1982), 338–43.

McIVOR, A., 'Health and Safety in the Cotton Industry: A Literature Review', *Manchester Region History Review* 9 (1995), 50–7.

McVITTIE, J. C., 'Asbestosis in Great Britain', *Annals of the New York Academy of Sciences* 132 (1965), i, 128–38, 137–8.

MANN, B., 'Pulmonary Asbestosis with Special Reference to an Epidemic at Hebden Bridge', *Journal of the Royal College of Physicians* 12 (July 1978), 297–307.

MARCHAND, P. E., 'The Discovery of Mesothelioma in the Northwestern Cape Province in the Republic of South Africa', *American Journal of Industrial Medicine* 19 (1991), 241–6.

MEIKLEJOHN, A., 'The Development of Compensation for Occupational Diseases of the Lungs in Great Britain', *British Journal of Industrial Medicine* 11 (July 1954), 198–212.

MEREWETHER, E. R. A., 'The Occurrence of Pulmonary Fibrosis and Other Pulmonary Affections in Asbestos Workers', *Journal of Industrial Hygiene* 12 (May/June 1930), 198–222, 239–56.

——'A Memorandum on Asbestosis', *Tubercle* 15 (1933–4), 69–81, 109–18, 152–9.

MURRAY, R., 'Asbestos: A Chronology of its Origins and Health Effects', *British Journal of Industrial Medicine* 47 (1990), 361–5.

MURRAY, T. H., 'Regulating Asbestos: Ethics, Politics and the Values of Science', in R. Bayer (ed.), *The Health and Safety of Workers* (New York, 1988), 271–92.

NEWHOUSE, M. L., and THOMPSON, H., 'Mesothelioma of Pleura and Peritoneum Following Exposure to Asbestos in the London Area', *British Journal of Industrial Medicine* 22 (1965), 261–9.

OLIVER, C., 'Asbestos in Buildings: Management and Related Health Effects', in M. A. Mehlman and A. Upton (eds)., *Advances in Modern Environmental Toxicology. Vol 22: The Identification and Control of Environmental and Occupational Diseases: Asbestos and Cancers* (Princeton: Princeton Scientific Publishing Co., 1994), 175–88.

OLIVER, T., 'Pulmonary Asbestosis in Clinical Aspects', *Journal of Industrial Hygiene* 9 (1927), 483–5.

OWEN, W. GLYN, 'Diffuse Mesothelioma and Exposure to Asbestos Dust in the Merseyside Area', *BMJ* (25 July 1964), ii, 214–21.

OZONOFF, D., 'Failed Warnings: Asbestos-Related Disease and Industrial Medicine', in R. Bayer (ed.), *The Health and Safety of Workers* (New York: Oxford University Press, 1988), 139–218.

PARSONS, J. M., 'Asbestos-Related Disease Claims—A Continuing Cause for Concern in the 1990s and Beyond', *Journal of Personal Injury Litigation* Issue 1 (1997), 5–35.

PETO, J., DOLL, R. S., HOWARD, S. V., KINLEN, L. J., and LEWINSOHN, H. C., 'A Mortality Study among Workers in an English Asbestos Factory', *British Journal of Industrial Medicine* 34 (Aug. 1977), 169–73.

PETO, J., 'The Hygiene Standard for Chrysotile Asbestos', *Lancet* (4 Mar. 1978), i, 484–9.

PETO, J., 'Dose-Response Relationships for Asbestos-Related Disease: Implications for Hygiene Standards. Part II: Mortality', *Annals of the New York Academy of Sciences* 330 (1979), 195–203.

PETO, J., DOLL, R., HERMAN, C., BINNS, W., CLAYTON, R., and GOFFE, T., 'Relationship of Mortality to Measures of Environmental Pollution in an Asbestos Textile Factory', *Annals of Occupational Hygiene* 29 (1985), 305–55.

PETO, J., HODGSON, J. T, MATTHEWS, F. E., and JONES, J. R., 'Continuing Increase in Mesothelioma Mortality in Britain', *Lancet* 345 (4 Mar. 1995), 535–9.

PETO, J., LA VECCHIA, C., LEVI, F., and NEGRI, I., 'The European Mesothelioma Epidemic', *British Journal of Cancer* 79 (Feb. 1999), 666–72.

PRICE, C. W., 'Exhaust Ventilation in Asbestos Textile Works', reprint from Institution of Heating & Ventilation Engineers, 6 Oct. 1931.

PYE, A. M., 'Alternatives to Asbestos in Industrial Applications', in L. Michaels and S. S. Chissick (eds.), *Asbestos* (Belfast/Bath: J. Wiley & Sons, 1979), i, 339–73.

SCHEPERS, G. W. H., 'Changing Attitudes and Opinions: Asbestos and Cancer 1934–1965', *American Journal of Industrial Medicine* 22 (1992), 461–6.

SCHEPERS, G. W. H., 'Chronology of Asbestos Cancer Discoveries: Experimental Studies of the Saranac Laboratory', *American Journal of Industrial Medicine* 27 (1995), 593–606.

SELIKOFF, I. J., HAMMOND, E. C., and CHURG, J., 'Asbestos Exposure and Neoplasia', *Journal of the American Medical Association* 188 (1964), 22–6.

SELIKOFF, I. J., and GREENBERG, M., 'A Landmark Case in Asbestosis', *Journal of the American Medical Association* 265 (20 Feb. 1991), 898–901.

SELLS, Bill, 'What Asbestos Taught Me About Managing Risk', *Harvard Business Review* (Mar.-Apr. 1994), 76–89.

SHEERS, G., and TEMPLETON, A. R., 'Effects of Asbestos in Dockyard Workers', *BMJ* (7 Sept. 1968), 574.

SIMSON, F. W., 'Pulmonary Asbestosis in South Africa', *BMJ* (26 May 1928), i, 885–7.

SMITH, A. H., WRIGHT, C. C., 'Chrysotile Asbestos is the Main Cause of Pleural Mesothelioma', *American Journal of Industrial Medicine* 30 (1996), 252–66.

STAYNER, L. T, DANKOVIC, D., and LEMEN, R. A., 'Occupational Exposure to Chrysotile Asbestos and Cancer Risk: A Review of the Amphibole Hypothesis', *American Journal of Public Health* 86 (Feb. 1996), 179–86.

STEELE, J., and WIKELEY, N. J., 'Liability in Tort for Environmental Mesothelioma: A UK Perspective', in G. A. Peters and B. J. Peters (eds.), *Asbestos Pathogenesis and Litigation. Vol. 13: Sourcebook on Asbestos Diseases* (Charlottesville, VA: Michie, 1996), 297–32.

——'Dust on the Streets and Liability for Environmental Cancers', *Modern Law Review* 60 (1997), 265–76.

STEWART, M. J., 'Asbestosis Bodies in the Lungs of Guinea Pigs after Three to Five Months' Exposure in the Asbestos Factory', *Journal of Pathology and Bacteriology* 33 (1930), 848.

STOWER, M., 'Dockworkers Land Asbestos-Related Disease', *Health & Safety at Work* (Apr. 1985), 36–8.

TAIT, N., 'The Role of SPAID . . . in the Prevention of Disease and the Welfare of Sufferers', in S. S. Chissick and R. Derricott, *Asbestos* (Bath: J. Wiley & Sons, 1983), ii, 9–50.

TITUNIK, V., 'Chase's Case Turns to Dust', *The American Lawyer* (May 1996), 73–80.

TWEEDALE, G., 'Management Strategies for Health: J. W. Roberts and the Armley Asbestos Tragedy, 1920–1958', *Journal of Industrial History* 2 (1999), 72–95.

——'Sprayed "Limpet" Asbestos: Technical, Commercial and Regulatory Aspects', in G. A. Peters and B. J. Peters (eds.), *Sourcebook on Asbestos Diseases*, vol. 19 (Charlottesville, VA: Lexis Law Publishing, 1999).

——and HANSEN, P., 'Protecting the Workers: The Medical Board and the Asbestos Industry, 1930s–1960s', *Medical History* 42 (1998), 439–57.

——and JEREMY, D. J., 'Compensating the Workers: Industrial Injury and Compensation in the British Asbestos Industry, 1930s–1960s', *Business History* 41 (April 1999), 102–20.

WAGNER, J. C., SLEGGS, C. A., and MARCHAND, P., 'Diffuse Pleural Mesotheliomas and Asbestos Exposure in the North-Western Cape Province', *British Journal of Industrial Medicine* 17 (1960), 260–71.

WAGNER, J. C., BOGOWSKI, P., and HIGGINSON, J., 'The Role of International Research in Occupational Cancer', *La Medicina del Lavoro* 63 (1972), 213–20.

WAGNER, J. C., 'The Discovery of the Association between Blue Asbestos and Mesotheliomas and the Aftermath', *British Journal of Industrial Medicine* 48 (1991), 399–403.

WARREN, R. C., 'The Enforcement of Social Accountability—Turner & Newall and the Asbestos Crisis', *Corporate Governance* 5 (Apr. 1997), 52–9.

WHIPPLE, H. E. (ed.), 'Biological Effects of Asbestos', *Annals of New York Academy of Sciences* 132 (31 Dec. 1965), i, 1–766.

WIKELEY, N. J., 'Measurement of Asbestos Dust Levels in British Asbestos Factories in the 1930s', *American Journal of Industrial Medicine* 24 (1993), 509–20.

WIKELEY, N. J., 'The Asbestos Regulations 1931: A Licence to Kill?', *Journal of Law and Society* 19 (Autumn 1992), 365–78.

WIKELEY, N. J., 'Asbestos and Cancer: An Early Warning to the British TUC', *American Journal of Industrial Medicine* 22 (1992), 449–54.

WIKELEY, N. J., 'Turner & Newall: Early Organisational Responses to Litigation Risk', *Journal of Law and Society* 24 (1997), 252–74.

WIKELEY, N. J., 'The First Common Law Claim for Asbestosis: *Kelly v. Turner & Newall* (1950)', *Journal of Personal Injury Litigation* Issue 3 (1998), 197–210.

WOOD, W. BURTON, 'Pulmonary Asbestosis', *British Journal of Radiology* 7 (1934), 277–80.

——and GLOYNE, S. R., 'Pulmonary Asbestosis', *Lancet* 227 (22 Dec. 1934), 1383–5.

WRIGHT, D. S., 'Man-Made Mineral Fibres: An Historical Note', *Journal of the Society of Occupational Medicine* 30 (1980), 138–40.

WYERS, H. 'Asbestosis', *Postgraduate Medical Journal* 25 (Dec. 1949), 631–8.

WYKE, T., 'Mule Spinners' Cancer', in A. Fowler and T. Wyke (eds.), *The Barefoot Aristocrats: A History of the Amalgamated Association of Operative Cotton Spinners* (Littleborough: Kelsall, 1987), 184–96.

INDEX

Printed in the United Kingdom
by Lightning Source UK Ltd.
93088